AF270327

Whipped

Communication, Strategy, and Politics

Thierry Giasson and Alex Marland, Series Editors

Whipped

Party Discipline in Canada

ALEX MARLAND

UBCPress · Vancouver · Toronto

© UBC Press 2020

All rights reserved. No part of this publication may be reproduced, stored in a retrieval system, or transmitted, in any form or by any means, without prior written permission of the publisher, or, in Canada, in the case of photocopying or other reprographic copying, a licence from Access Copyright, www.accesscopyright.ca.

29 28 27 26 25 24 23 22 21 20   5 4 3 2 1

Printed in Canada on FSC-certified ancient-forest-free paper (100% post-consumer recycled) that is processed chlorine- and acid-free.

Library and Archives Canada Cataloguing in Publication

Title: Whipped : party discipline in Canada / Alex Marland.
Names: Marland, Alex, author.

Series: Communication, strategy, and politics.
Description: Series statement: Communication, strategy, and politics | Includes bibliographical references.

Identifiers: Canadiana (print) 20200268457 | Canadiana (ebook) 2020026883X | ISBN 9780774864961 (hardcover) | ISBN 9780774864978 (paperback) | ISBN 9780774864985 (PDF) | ISBN 9780774864992 (EPUB) | ISBN 9780774865005 (Kindle)

Subjects: LCSH: Party discipline—Canada. | LCSH: Legislative bodies—Canada—Leadership. | LCSH: Political parties—Canada. | LCSH: Canada—Politics and government—21st century.

Classification: LCC JL195 .M37 2020 | DDC 324.271—dc23

Canadä

UBC Press gratefully acknowledges the financial support for our publishing program of the Government of Canada (through the Canada Book Fund), the Canada Council for the Arts, and the British Columbia Arts Council.

This book has been published with the help of a grant from the Canadian Federation for the Humanities and Social Sciences, through the Awards to Scholarly Publications Program, using funds provided by the Social Sciences and Humanities Research Council of Canada.

Additional financial support was provided by Memorial University of Newfoundland.

Printed and bound in Canada by Friesens
Set in Univers Condensed, Sero, and Minion by Artegraphica Design Co. Ltd.
Copy editor: Dallas Harrison
Proofreader: Alison Strobel
Indexers: Hannah Loder and Alex Marland

UBC Press
The University of British Columbia
2029 West Mall
Vancouver, BC V6T 1Z2
www.ubcpress.ca

A lion used to prowl about a field in which four oxen used to
dwell. Many a time he tried to attack them; but whenever he
came near they turned their tails to one another, so that
whichever way he approached them he was met by the horns of
one of them. At last, however, they fell a-quarrelling among
themselves, and each went off to pasture alone in a separate
corner of the field. Then the lion attacked them one by one and
soon made an end of all four. United we stand, divided we fall.

> – Aesop
> "The Four Oxen and the Lion" (sixth century BC)

A foolish consistency is the hobgoblin of little minds, adored by
little statesmen and philosophers and divines. With consistency
a great soul has simply nothing to do. He may as well concern
himself with his shadow on the wall … I hope in these days we
have heard the last of conformity and consistency. Let the
words be gazetted and ridiculous henceforward.

> – Ralph Waldo Emerson
> "Self-Reliance" (1841)

The first rule in this house is discipline.

> – Captain von Trapp
> *The Sound of Music* (1965)

Contents

Figures and Tables

TABLES

Acknowledgments

Research like this is possible because of the willingness of current and former politicians and political staff to be generous with their time to share their expertise, explanations, and stories. Thank you to everyone interviewed for this book, some of you multiple times. All 131 of you listed in Appendix 1 have my sincere appreciation, as do a number of other practitioners who shared uncredited insights.

For providing interview referrals, thank you to Heather Bastedo, Susan Delacourt, Tom Flanagan, Megan Leslie, Hamish Marshall, David McGrane, Anne McGrath, Jane Philpott, Ross Reid, Donald Savoie, Danielle Smith, David Smith, and an anonymous political staffer. The Canadian Association of Former Parliamentarians kindly forwarded interview recruitment letters to some former Members of Parliament. For offering feedback on draft content, thank you to Cathy Bennett, Don Boudria, Alana Cattapan, Michael Chong, Cris de Clercy, Erin Crandall, Jim Edwards, Anna Esselment, Jay Hill, Mireille Lalancette, Dalton McGuinty, Fenwick McKelvey, Stephen Power, Jared Wesley, and some of those who provided interview referrals.

I am indebted to Nick Whalen for taking time while my Member of Parliament (St. John's East) to explain the details of how things work. We talked at length in his constituency office, in my office, in a café, and on the phone. He wrote suggestions on draft material and asked political staff to locate supplementary information. His reverence for caucus confidentiality did not appear to impede an authentic desire (seemingly shared by everyone who participated in this research) to raise awareness about Canadian parliamentary democracy.

Thank you to the Samara Centre for Democracy and Mike Morden for sharing transcripts of exit interviews with former MPs. The Samara Centre is a Toronto-based charity that conducts non-partisan research and engagement programming on Canadian democracy. Canadian society benefits from its efforts to equip citizens with information about Canadian legislatures, political parties, and citizen participation.

Jean-François Godbout generously provided MP vote data for the 42nd Parliament, and Roberto Rocha kindly provided data about candidate retweeting. For providing the photographs of framed whips in Figure 3.1, thank you to Mark Holland, Michael Penney, and an anonymous Conservative Party staffer. Memorial University students Adrian Castro Carrillo, Jessi Drohan, and Joey Rogers provided capable research assistance. Librarians at Memorial University tracked down *The Noblest of Callings* and Library of Parliament archival interviews. For providing other assistance along the way, thank you to Ken Carty, Thierry Giasson, Sean Holman, Guillaume La Perrière, Sean McGrath, Peter Ryan, Feodor Snagovsky, Graham Steele, Zaren Healey White, Paul Wilson, and many others, ranging from the staff in legislative libraries across Canada to the people who appear on the back cover. In particular, political science student Hannah Loder meticulously conducted research, fact-checked, read a draft of the manuscript, and helped prepare the index.

A book is only as good as the publishing team behind it. I appreciate the support of the fine people at UBC Press, including Megan Brand, Laraine Coates, Kerry Kilmartin, Nadine Pedersen, Melissa Pitts, Randy Schmidt, and Carmen Tiampo. Dallas Harrison copyedited the text, Irma Rodriguez typeset it, and Jessica Sullivan designed the cover. Their collective efforts included putting up with my many requests to refine the text.

I hold in high regard the five anonymous referees recruited by UBC Press who delivered encouraging external reports on a draft manuscript. The insightful suggestions from three expert scholars and two former MPs resulted in many improvements. Thank you.

I wish to acknowledge the financial assistance that has made the production of this book possible. *Whipped* has been published with the help of a grant from the Canadian Federation for the Humanities and Social

Sciences, through the Awards to Scholarly Publications Program. Memorial University of Newfoundland provided financial support through its publications subvention program.

Finally, thank you to the Donner Canadian Foundation and the Atlantic Book Awards Society, whose recognition of *Brand Command* inspired me to conduct further research on the intersection of political communications and Canadian democratic institutions.

A key message in most authors' opening remarks is that any errors and omissions are the author's responsibility alone. A further talking point in this case is that opinions expressed in the book do not necessarily reflect those of all participants.

PS: Long after settling on the title of this book, I stumbled on the documentary *Whipped: The Secret World of Party Discipline* (Public Eye Mediaworks, 2013). Its examination of party discipline in British Columbia is an excellent companion. The film is available online from Vimeo.

Abbreviations

BC	British Columbia
CBC	Canadian Broadcasting Corporation
CEO	chief executive officer
COVID-19	coronavirus disease
CRM	constituent relationship management database (Liberal)
DPA	deferred prosecution agreement
LRB	Liberal Research Bureau
MHA	Member of the House of Assembly (Newfoundland and Labrador)
MLA	Member of the Legislative Assembly (western provinces and Maritimes)
MNA	Member of the National Assembly (Quebec)
MoJAG	minister of justice and attorney general of Canada
MP	Member of Parliament
MPP	Member of Provincial Parliament (Ontario)
NATO	North Atlantic Treaty Organization
OECD	Organisation for Economic Co-operation and Development
PC	Progressive Conservative
PCO	Privy Council Office
PM	prime minister
PMO	Prime Minister's Office
PR	public relations

NDP	New Democratic Party
QP	Question Period
RCMP	Royal Canadian Mounted Police
SO 31	Standing Order 31 members' statements (House of Commons)

Disambiguation

backbencher refers to parliamentarians who are not members of a cabinet and do not hold a senior title in an opposition party. Most private members are considered backbenchers.

communications is used in the generic sense and can refer to either humans exchanging messages (communication) or technological methods for transmitting information (communications).

42nd Parliament refers to the period of December 3, 2015, to September 11, 2019.

parliamentarian refers to an elected member of the federal House of Commons or a provincial legislature in Canada. Senators are excluded.

party names refer to national-level organizations or are used in the generic sense, unless otherwise specified.

political party typically concerns a parliamentary party with members in a legislature. Its leader is normally the leader of the private, extra-parliamentary party that fields election candidates.

Prime Minister Trudeau normally refers to Justin Trudeau, who became Canada's twenty-third prime minister in 2015, rather than his father, Pierre Trudeau, the fifteenth prime minister.

Whipped

1

Party Discipline in Canada

Canadians should be proud. Canada is among the best places to live and boasts one of the world's strongest democracies.[1] High levels of freedom and low levels of government corruption are among the reasons why Canadians are some of the happiest citizens on Earth.[2] Yet, if you look deeper than their pride in universal health care, in the maple leaf flag, or in the Charter of Rights and Freedoms, you will discover frustration with the Gordian knot of party discipline.[3]

Political parties are essential actors with a reputation problem.[4] Worldwide, there is democratic malaise, and trust in public institutions, politicians, and political parties is eroding. Party memberships, once a source of pride, have become a mechanism for party operatives to collect personal information for the database marketing that fuels polarization. In democracies using the Westminster parliamentary system, such as Canada, power is concentrated in executive offices, and partisanship infuses impartial public administration. The corollary of communications technology focusing more attention on party leaders is that most of Canada's elected representatives are increasingly peripheral actors. Canadians are right to believe that many people elected to the House of Commons and provincial legislatures are under the thumb of a political party.

Discipline permeates almost all aspects of politics in Canada, especially communications. In the Westminster system, some parliamentarians are part of the government (the cabinet), whereas the rest (known as private members) are not. In a parliamentary assembly, the functions of private members as legislators include

1   participating in law-making by debating bills and motions, proposing amendments, voting for or against proposals
2   scrutinizing the government, such as by seeking information through Question Period, submitting written questions or requesting documents
3   considering proposals to raise and spend public money.[5]

Status in a parliamentary party influences a parliamentarian's role in the above activities. Hierarchy is reflected in seating arrangements in the legislative chamber, which assign titleholders such as ministers and their official critics to the front benches and relegate rank-and-file private members to the back benches – hence the moniker of backbencher, which denotes a politician with little power.[6] A hidden forum for them to exert influence is a caucus meeting, which convenes all of a party's members of the assembly, where anything said is confidential. That influence is in flux in a digital society that amplifies partisanship.

Political parties are using communications technology to tighten their grip on political life in Canada. Parties are considered "the most important organizations in modern politics."[7] They are gateways for citizens to become involved in parliamentary politics by recruiting election candidates, presenting voters with clear choices in elections, and bringing order to legislatures. The leader of the party that has the confidence of the representatives in a parliamentary assembly heads a government. Political parties are essential for keeping large numbers of politicians organized; however, the systematic integration of politicians is so successful that some believe Canada has the most rigid party discipline of any liberal democracy[8] and that party government has supplanted parliamentary government.[9] The tight binds of partisanship among Canadian politicians are at odds with political parties' loosening grip on the electorate.[10] The "near iron hand of party discipline" that keeps parliamentarians in the fold is arguably "the greatest frustration" that Canadians have with their system of government.[11]

The reluctance of private members to contravene their party engenders a repertoire of complaints that Canada's political system is broken. Discipline saps their ability to represent constituents or vocalize constructive criticism, resulting in a "democratic deficit" whereby power is concentrated in prime ministers, premiers, and a cluster of senior advisers.[12] Historically, party discipline has referred to unity in the legislative chamber and consequences for disobedience. Today, expectations of conformity extend to most public interactions. Preoccupation with coordinating votes on bills and motions has mutated into message discipline.

The calculated strategy of self-control over public communications now pervades Canadian politics. If a political handbook for Canadian parliamentarians existed, then rule number one ought to occupy the entire first page: *Exercise extreme caution about going off-message in public.* Message discipline involves sticking to core phrases and political values in all public information exchanges. It is a form of self-censorship. The anthropomorphism of parrots who learn to repeat phrases and buzzwords is replacing the time-worn comparison of Canadian backbenchers to trained seals who vote according to the party whip's instructions. For many of today's elected officials, the "party line" refers interchangeably to voting and messaging (i.e., message lines).

This book is about the struggle for an equilibrium between the need for discipline in party politics and its suppression of political representation. The research endeavours to expose the communications management practices that intensify party discipline, suffocate policy entrepreneurialism, and stifle individualism. It provides a fresh take on how a leadership circle leverages group psychology, reward systems, team socialization, and lopsided rules to exert influence on backbenchers. The general frame of reference is the 42nd Parliament (December 3, 2015, to September 11, 2019), during which Prime Minister Justin Trudeau presided over a Liberal majority government. Documenting how things work can help readers to think about ways that members of Canadian legislatures can be strong representatives within institutional constraints.

In this opening chapter, I synthesize what is known about party discipline in Canada. I begin by defining the practice and by showing that Canadian parliamentarians tend to vote the party line. I summarize the advantages and disadvantages of discipline in parliamentary politics. I also trace the origins of political parties and the need for order in legislatures, and treat party constitutions and platforms as the anchors of all messages that permeate party politics. Finally, I consider politics without political parties. This tour of the political institutions, practices, and structures that make party discipline such a powerful force in Canada sets up the research objectives and communications-related focus of the book. Readers already familiar with the history of party discipline might consider jumping to the research method on page 25.

POLITICAL PARTIES AND PARTY DISCIPLINE

Tallies of votes in Canadian legislatures that show elected representatives behaving as partisan blocs usually reflect their inherent support for party positions. Yet legislators frequently endorse policies that they know little about. Sometimes they publicly support things that they privately oppose. They dissent by staying quiet and missing a vote. Their acquiescence comes with a quid pro quo understanding: siding with the parliamentary group improves their ability to champion a policy that they care about, to access resources, and to improve their prospects for promotion and re-election. Discipline is far less chafing for Canadian parliamentarians than might appear – and this is part of the problem of representation.

Defining Party Discipline

In all aspects of life, discipline can be a laudable trait or a maligned practice. Discipline refers to actions that encourage, if not enforce, standards of behaviour. Ideally, it involves self-restraint to achieve a shared objective in an efficient manner. In a group hierarchy, leaders implement structure to guide individual actions, and they correct behaviour by applying punishments. In workplaces, discipline refers to problems with an employee's work performance. Oral and written warnings are delivered as well as disciplinary measures up to the point where the employee is suspended or fired. Some organizations have reasonably standardized, transparent processes for exacting discipline, whereas inconsistent or hidden processes are common in others. Its absence cultivates disorganization, confusion, and chaos.

In parliamentary politics, party discipline is a system of norms, rules, and consequences designed to ensure the public alignment of group members, especially in legislative voting. It is a mechanism to hold together a diverse coalition of political interests.[13] Social conditioning, persuasion, coercion, and control mechanisms foster unity and dampen dissonance. Members of a parliamentary party set aside their petty differences as diverse points of view are reconciled, and actions not yet committed are influenced.

Party discipline also refers to the parliamentary party leadership, often through the party whip, doling out rewards to sycophants and punishing troublemakers. In the narrowest sense, party discipline is pressure from the party leadership on members of the caucus to vote the party line, which Canadian parliamentarians usually do. Generally, private members in Ottawa defy the party whip's guidance on votes less than 1 percent of the time.[14] Their recorded disagreement tends to arise on innocuous motions and private members' bills.[15] In a tightly knit formation, voting differently is such an affront to the group that it can sever relationships.

Discipline has negative connotations because it supposes an infringement on free will and, in politics, on appropriate representation. It compels politicians to pick sides. It also pressures them to align with the "leadership" – a term used herein to refer to the party leader as well as the leader's entourage, particularly senior political staff – over other interests. For more than half a century, people have been warning that Canadian party leaders are becoming more powerful over private members, and the number of political staff has been growing.[16] Conversely, legislators are lampooned as robots, puppets, lobby fodder, potted plants, or bobbleheads. The impotence of backbenchers comes through in books about the prime minister and senior retinues.[17]

Politicians are among their own harshest critics. In the 1970s, a backbencher lamented that most of them on the government side of the House were "useless," and another believed that they must "stay in line, lick boots and keep their noses clean."[18] Other self-criticisms include descriptions of "a lackey on a leash,"[19] "jacks-in-the-box" who pop up to vote,[20] and backbenchers who are "invisible."[21] Academics refer to a "mindless flock of sheep" and use laborious epithets such as "legislative eunuchs"[22] and "a tribe whose emblem is servitude."[23] Think tank research suggests that Members of Parliament (MPs) are scripted party clones,[24] an impression widely shared by journalists, who dismiss them as "wind-up dolls pawing at the master's feet"[25] and "cheerleaders for the party line."[26] The following opinion is typical among Canadian political observers: "They disagree in private. They clam up in public. They smile and repeat whatever today's line is. The trade-off, whether explicit or assumed, is that party harmony is a necessary condition of effectively contending for power."[27] Tropes of backbenchers playing Follow the Leader are commonplace in Canada.

In the House of Commons, MPs initially opposed their party in order to advocate for constituency interests, but gradually political parties became ideologically cohesive and party unity on votes has been the norm since the end of the Second World War.[28] The drive for cohesion spread to all public forums, both spurred and facilitated by changes in communications technology. Oppressive message coordination climaxed under Prime Minister Stephen Harper (2006–15) who was criticized for imposing the will of the executive on all facets of the government.[29] During the first two years of the 41st Parliament, when Harper led a Conservative majority government, Conservative MPs voted as a unified bloc on 76 percent of votes, the official opposition New Democratic Party (NDP) voted together 100 percent of the time, and Liberal MPs did so in 90 percent of cases.[30] The forward march of message coordination persisted post-Harper. Calculations of recorded divisions in the entire 42nd Parliament (2015–19) when the Trudeau Liberals had a majority find few dissenting votes. Liberal MPs sided with their caucus on 99.6 percent of votes on all types of bills and motions, the official opposition Conservatives voted the party line 99.5 percent of the time, and NDP MPs were unanimous on 99.8 percent of recorded votes.[31] Of 142,189 individual votes in the House of Commons by Liberals, there were 585 dissenting votes; out of 88,628 votes by Conservatives, 418 were dissenting; and among New Democrats, out of 36,336 votes, only 62 were dissenting. Thirty-nine MPs voted exclusively with their party (14 Conservatives, 11 Liberals, 14 New Democrats), and another forty MPs rebuffed the party line once (14 Conservatives, 12 Liberals, 14 New Democrats). The most prolific dissenter was a Liberal who voted with his party 96.1 percent of the time.[32] Pressure to vote the party line is even more intense when the governing party has a minority of seats. Many MPs would doubtlessly protest that the numbers are inflated by routine procedural votes and fail to account for disagreement expressed by not voting. The fact remains that Canadian MPs rarely, if ever, vote against their party.

Deviation from the party line is rare in Canadian provinces as well.[33] An examination of division votes in the National Assembly of Quebec identified party unity in 99 to 100 percent of votes cast between 1935 and 1989.[34] In British Columbia, Members of the Legislative Assembly (MLAs) voted against their party just .25 percent of the time from 2001 to 2012.[35]

Vote cohesion is thought to be even more prevalent in small provinces where there are fewer formalities.[36] Compared with the House of Commons, provincial legislatures have a higher proportion of members in cabinet, fewer resources, and smaller press galleries (Table 1.1). Large or small, in all settings vote cohesion along party lines is particularly visible on high-stakes issues. There are fewer mavericks than in the past, making today's backbenchers vulnerable to perceptions of being interchangeable bit players in a party salesforce. Occasionally, a private member does defy the party on a whipped vote, and sometimes a group of government-side backbenchers aligns with the opposition benches against the whip's explicit instructions.[37] Leaders must calculate whether a pressure release valve will calm caucus unrest or sow the seeds of mutiny.

Researchers warn that the encroachment of party discipline suppresses legislatures as a marketplace for public debate.[38] In *Mr. Smith Goes to Ottawa: Life in the House of Commons,* political scientist David Docherty cautions that the turnover of so many MPs in a general election contributes to the centralization of power. He finds that, because of the high number of rookies, many of whom lack prior elected experience, Canadian legislatures are characterized by their amateurism.[39] New entrants with fresh perspectives confront a system that takes years to master, but their parliamentary careers can be cut short before they accomplish changes. Those who are re-elected become ensconced in established practices as veterans teach them about parliamentary norms and scold them when they go out of bounds.[40] Docherty builds on the work of parliamentary scholar C.E.S. Franks, who observed in his classic book *The Parliament of Canada* that party discipline is "the most dominant and pervasive force" in parliamentary politics and that curtailing it is "the greatest single challenge" to making the role of an elected representative more meaningful.[41] Franks also believed that communications rank among the most important functions of a legislature.[42] He made this observation before twenty-four-hour news cycles, the World Wide Web, social media, smartphones, viral video, and online disinformation, all of which have contributed to turning party discipline into message discipline.

David E. Smith, one of Canada's foremost parliamentary scholars, counters that party discipline is undemocratic only when it is looked at in isolation, not when it is considered as a component of a larger system.[43]

TABLE 1.1

Profile of Canadian legislative assemblies (2018)

Legislature	Population[1]	Members	Quorum[2]	Members in cabinet (%)[3]	Constituents per member (mean)[1]	Legislative reporters[4]
House of Commons	36,890,000	338	20	9	109,100	320
British Columbia	4,974,700	85	10	27	58,550	18
Alberta	4,283,900	87	20	24	49,250	5–10
Saskatchewan	1,159,500	58	15	31	20,000	1
Manitoba	1,347,500	57	10	25	23,650	6
Ontario	14,241,400	124	12	17	114,850	25
Quebec	8,356,300	125	21	26	66,850	41
New Brunswick	769,000	49	14	31	15,700	9
Nova Scotia	955,400	51	15	33	18,750	5
Prince Edward Island	152,200	27	10	41	5,650	2
Newfoundland and Labrador	526,500	40	14	33	13,150	4

Notes:

1　Population estimates for second quarter of 2018. Rounded figures.

2　Includes the Speaker.

3　April 2018 figures, including first ministers and, in Quebec, the chief government whip and the caucus chair. July figures used for Ontario to reflect seat increase as of the 2018 provincial election.

4　Number of national legislative reporters in 2016, provincial reporters in 2017.

Sources: Britneff (2016); Hannay, Alam, and Keller (2017); Statistics Canada (2020); government websites; legislative standing orders.

Party discipline is a mechanism for compromise to prevail over infighting. It nurtures predictability, routine, consistency, and clarity. Bringing order to chaos stabilizes otherwise volatile political situations. Discipline enables government formation, is necessary for the government to deliver on election promises, and enables collective accountability. Smith believes that party discipline is essential for the operation of the parliamentary system. In his opinion, "democracy is about mediating conflict and refining positions. Discipline in Parliament is defended as a way of levelling up, not down."[44] Holdouts are pressed to choose the peace of consensus over the disruption of dissent. Consensus is more organic than we might think.

There are other benefits of party discipline. Voting with a party is easier than figuring out a position on every issue. Individual politicians can place responsibility on their party when it suits them, which buffers lobbying by stakeholder groups and irate constituents. The party's approved message lines are a security blanket when pressure groups urge citizens to flood their elected representative's office with correspondence. Furthermore, party discipline encourages teamwork. Arguably, the parliamentary system cannot work without it.

A fundamental flaw of conformism is that it stifles creativity. Democratic politics must be open to fresh thinking, but most backbenchers are engaged too far along in the decision-making process to offer much more than a communications disaster check (see Figure 2.2). For members of the governing party, distinctions among the government (i.e., the prime minister or premier, the cabinet, political staff in executive offices), the parliamentary party (i.e., the leader, the caucus, political staff funded by the legislature), and the extraparliamentary party (i.e., the national council, election candidates, electoral district associations, staff working in party headquarters) are slight. There is little opportunity for innovation, constructive criticism, public engagement, and big ideas. The perspectives that arise from diverse styles of representation can be missed. Furthermore, governments can exclude caucus input on drawn-out negotiations on sensitive topics and barrel along when they respond to an emerging situation. Parliamentarians understandably struggle to make a mark within a system that minimizes their contributions and encourages public displays of their allegiance to the party leader. They can feel alienated and unhappy, particularly those who are younger and educated.[45] Resentment builds as they conclude that conformity is the only way to advance their interests.[46] As they come to understand their finite roles in policy decisions, and limited prospects for career advancement, the disenchanted do not seek re-election.[47]

Origins of Political Parties and Party Discipline

Why is party discipline so stringent in Canada? To understand how it permeates politics today, we need to look at the history of the parliamentary system of government and acquire some baseline familiarity with the incursion of party organizations.

Canada's main political parties and parliamentary practices originated in the United Kingdom. The UK House of Commons exercised limited influence on public policy for centuries after the signing of the Magna Carta in 1215, an early charter of rights that limited the divine rights of kings to rule. Many parliamentarians were royal loyalists who supported the monarch's government. Knights and burgesses pledged secrecy and loyalty to one another so that they could speak freely and avoid retaliation from the oppressive power of kings and queens.[48] In 1621, the role of the whip originated when the king's supporters were summoned to Parliament.[49] The monarch's divine rights and absolute powers ended in 1689 with the Bill of Rights, which granted Parliament an array of political powers. The Glorious Revolution, as it came to be called, afforded British parliamentarians freedom of speech in the legislative chamber and committees.

The roots of British political parties date to the years leading up to the Glorious Revolution.[50] People loyal to the monarch and religious traditions were known as Tories, whereas reformists were known as Whigs. The labels referred to individual parliamentarians' political tendencies. Political groupings evolved, with political parties forming in the mid-eighteenth century. Partisan mobilizations were largely confined to the legislature. The etymology of *party whip* originated in this period when parliamentarians were likened to a pack of hounds on a fox hunt.[51] The 1832 Reform Act that restructured the British electoral system led to the formalization of extraparliamentary wings of the parties (i.e., a privately funded external organization of party staff, members, and volunteers).

Whig reformers became Liberals, and Tory traditionalists became Conservatives. Party whips ensured that members were present to vote and kept a watchful eye on those sneaking off.[52]

Colonial settlers in British North America carried over these political formations with minimal concern for preserving Indigenous rights and traditions. As well, settlers agitated for new practices. English and French dualism manifested, and in 1848 Nova Scotia become the first British colony to achieve responsible government.[53] The principle that the executive council (i.e., the cabinet) appointed by the monarch's representative to run the government must have the confidence of the elected assembly became an intrinsic characteristic of the parliamentary system. The connection between the confidence convention and party discipline is formidable.

Political parties congealed along religious, ethnic, regional, and nationalist dimensions before and after the formation of the Dominion of Canada in 1867. The Constitution of Canada identifies the supremacy of executive power, organizes the legislative branch, and outlines the federalist division of powers, but does not mention parties. In the immediate post-Confederation era, political parties were still forming, and representatives were elected to the House of Commons without an official party affiliation. They either pledged support to a party or waited until after the election to decide which one to join. Consequently, affiliations of MPs in early Parliaments included Conservative, Independent, Independent Conservative, Independent Liberal, Liberal, Liberal-Conservative, and Liberal Reformer. The cabinet advanced its legislative agenda without being able to rely on the support of quasi-Independent MPs. Patronage commitments for infrastructure spending and jobs were handed out in exchange for the votes of so-called loose fish, shaky fellows, ministerialists, and waiters on providence.[54] Buying votes with the spoils of office was such a normalized practice that some local shopkeepers believed that the survival of their businesses depended on their MP's ability to access public funds.[55]

Parties fortified in order to maintain stable coalitions. They became vehicles for groups of like-minded politicians to present electors with choices during elections, to mobilize voters, and to form the government.[56] The expansion of the right to vote, the socialization of parliamentarians, patronage appointments, and ideological groupings spurred the trek toward party cohesion.[57] The party system fractured in the 1921 federal election, resulting in an array of MP affiliations during the 14th Parliament, including Conservative, Independent, Labour, Liberal, Progressive, and United Farmers. Some members' dependence on their party to pay for election expenses instilled a compulsion to vote the party line, as this 1926 *Ottawa Citizen* editorial indicates:

> The party member is bound to vote in accordance with the crack of the whip, or face the ordeal of being branded as disloyal, or even dishonest. The majority of members are obligated to central party funds for financial aid in paying election expenses. After accepting such aid, they cannot feel wholly free to express themselves as free men in the House of Commons ... [MPs] learn too late that they have tied themselves, according to conventional standards of morality, to support the party blindly.[58]

Less significant factors in party cohesion included adopting the secret ballot, replacing staggered elections with ones held on the same day, and ending the practice of members simultaneously holding seats in federal and provincial legislatures.[59] The growing rigours of party discipline coincided with intensifying party identification and leadership power even as the extraparliamentary parties remained a network of localized interests.[60] As parliamentary parties gained momentum, some MPs insisted that parties were for elections only, and they expressed loyalty to Parliament and their constituents.[61] Nevertheless, recurring influences and processes – most of them hidden from public view – gradually treated parliamentarians as cogs in a party voting machine, especially those beholden to the governing party.

The rights and privileges of private members eroded as they consented to granting government representatives more control. Party leaders assigned House officers, namely the House leader and whip, to organize parliamentary business around procedural rules known as standing orders set by parliamentarians and enforced by the Speaker. These permanent written rules govern the structure of how each legislature is organized. Standing orders also limit the ability of an individual member to impede the will of the assembly. Beginning in 1906, private members' ability to introduce motions in the House of Commons was restricted. Closure was adopted in 1913, a procedure that suspends the normal rules by dealing with several stages of debate in one day. Private members' speaking time was reduced to forty-five minutes in 1927.[62] In 1962, the time for private members' business became secondary to the time for government business, a reflection of the growing size of government.[63] In the 1970s, the time management tool of parties preparing lists of speakers was introduced for Question Period. In 1982, an annual parliamentary calendar was adopted, evening sittings ceased, ninety-second private members' statements were introduced (now down to sixty seconds), and the time for speeches was again reduced.[64] Around this time, a private member's ability to delay legislative proceedings was lost because a single member should not be able to thwart the government. Today the House of Commons standing orders comprise a detailed bilingual document that runs more than two hundred pages.[65] For example, an entire chapter is devoted to spelling out types of parliamentary committees, of which the most prominent are the standing committees that generally mirror the names of government departments. A long list of rules encompasses procedural minutiae such as the election of committee chairs.

The evolution of the standing orders reflects a historical pattern of members agreeing to cede power to leaders and government business. The foremost remaining procedural power for a private member is withholding unanimous consent, which is necessary to bypass normal House rules or practices,[66] and an MP determined to participate in debate irrespective of political parties' subjugation must engage in the parliamentary tradition of "catching the Speaker's eye."[67] Further retrenchment is on the horizon given that some MPs want Friday sittings eliminated.[68] Similar patterns of self-marginalization are found in provincial assemblies. It remains to be seen whether recent experiments in virtual meetings take root and, if so, what the implications are for the role of private members.

In Canada, the accountability function of responsible government leaves little room for legislators to dissent from their party's position. The confidence convention holds that a government's core policies, particularly the budget, must have the support of a majority of parliamentarians. Losing a confidence vote results in the prime minister asking the governor general to dissolve Parliament; likewise, a premier asks the lieutenant governor for an election if the provincial government is defeated. The confidence convention therefore plays a pivotal role in discipline, especially for governing parties. The party's leadership can exploit it to whip votes on lesser items, causing some to believe that a separate non-confidence motion should be required if a budget bill is defeated so that governing party backbenchers can vote against a budget.[69] Discipline need not be as exacting in opposition parties, particularly in the aftermath of an election defeat or during a party leadership contest. As well, some parties are more ideological than others, which fosters natural cohesion. Yet any party can split into factions during an internal struggle.

The decline of the autonomy of members of legislative bodies co-incides with the ascendency of the party leader as the chief public spokes-person. Extraparliamentary parties are such small outfits in Canada that the leader fills a power vacuum as the main connection with the parlia-mentary group.[70] In 1919, the Liberal Party of Canada held a leadership convention so that party delegates could select the leader, effectively ter-minating the practice of an outgoing leader or members of the caucus making that decision. The Conservatives followed suit in 1927. Subsequent developments have seen parties use televoting and online voting that broaden leadership selection away from party delegates to the masses. Charging fees for party membership is being replaced with signing up supporters to populate the party database and ramping up rhetoric in digital fundraising. The result is leaders accountable to a somewhat amor-phous extraparliamentary group, whereas members of the parliamentary caucus might believe that the leader is accountable to them.

A monumental change occurred with amendments to the Canada Elections Act that came into effect for the 1972 federal election.[71] Up to that point, federal election ballots featured the name, address, and occu-pation of each candidate. The legal recognition of federal political parties set the groundwork for the regulation of party finance and the introduction of party labels on election ballots. Formally listing a candidate's party af-filiation reflected a desire among the parties for their candidates to be identifiable as well as to reduce confusion should people with identical names contest a seat. It resolved the problem of prime ministers, minis-ters, and party leaders using those titles on ballots in their electoral dis-tricts.[72] As well, henceforth the only candidate who could campaign as a representative of the party would be the party's nominated candidate.[73] The leader was granted the final say over who is nominated, causing incumbents to face discipline from above and below because a dissatisfied leader can refuse to approve a nomination while local party members can mobilize to nominate a different candidate. To avoid criticism of the leader for overruling a decision by grassroots members, the party manipulates the nomination process to shun undesirable candidates, such as the subtle announcement of cut-off dates for membership submissions that only the preferred contestant hears about.[74]

Party officials scrutinize the suitability of Canadians who express interest in being an election candidate. Vetting applicants for the party nomination grants the leadership a pre-emptive veto to reject undesirables, a process that doubles as a mechanism to ensure that future parliamentarians yield to discipline imposed by the party hierarchy, headed by the leader. For example, the Green Party of Canada promotes grassroots representation. It shuns whipped votes. In theory, Green MPs may vote as they wish. In practice, the party screens out aspiring candidates whose beliefs do not align with its values, thus increasing cohesion before any votes are cast. Vetting affects party unity: when legislators are beholden to a small selectorate in the extraparliamentary party hierarchy – that is, registered party members and party officials potentially loyal to the leader – they are pressured to satisfy that oligarchy instead of voters.[75] Conversely, formal accountability of parliamentary party leaders is beyond the grasp of the caucus (but see below), with the exception of a crisis that ruins the leader's public legitimacy, in which case extraordinary action is taken to push the leader out. In such moments, presenting a unified front to protect the party brand is at the forefront and demonstrates the upper limit of a leader's control.[76]

Avenues now exist in Ottawa for a caucus to act as a formal fail-safe over the party leader's power, provided its members opt in. The Reform Act, 2014, amended the Parliament of Canada Act to require that MPs in a parliamentary group with official party status (twelve MPs) hold a series of internal votes in their first caucus meeting after a federal election.[77] The decisions are in effect until Parliament is dissolved. The first of four voteable items authorizes one of the caucus or the leader to expel or readmit an MP. If the caucus opts in, then a member can be expelled only if 20 percent of the caucus submits a written request for a secret ballot vote and then a majority votes the colleague out. A second provision is to choose whether the caucus should have a say in the process of installing and removing the caucus chair. A third option concerns a process for the caucus to initiate a leadership review. A fourth involves electing a temporary leader. To date, Conservatives have voted to select the caucus chair and to be the ones to decide about expulsion, but voted against empowering themselves to overthrow the leader, with many rationalizing that the extraparliamentary party should decide.[78] The Bloc Québécois caucus did likewise. Liberal and NDP caucuses have been slow to follow the requirements and voted against all four options, seeing the Reform Act as a Conservative instrument.[79]

Party Values, Constitutions, and Platforms

The conformist behaviour of Canadian legislators has been seeping out of Canada's legislatures into all aspects of public life. In the 1970s, a veteran Member of Parliament (MP) observed that mavericks could criticize their party as long as they voted the party line, because the leadership would "tolerate loose talk more than they can deviation in voting."[80] Things changed by the late 1990s. Docherty writes in *Mr. Smith Goes to Ottawa* that "not voting with the party is acceptable; however, speaking in a way that brings the party into disrepute is a far more serious matter. Members cannot allow the integrity of the party itself to be questioned."[81] There is even less tolerance of message dissymmetry in the twenty-first century, particularly where the virtue of the party leader is concerned.

Politicians' acceptance of party discipline is anchored in their support for a political party's core principles. Every parliamentary group has a cast of characters, from staunch partisans and careerists to agitators and plotters.[82] They draw on political ideologies to conserve mental energy and speed up the process of evaluating political choices. Their belief systems, often deeply held, are reduced to values that influence attitudes and behaviours.[83] Adhering to shared convictions is what bonds a political party in the pursuit of a common cause. Party values guide policy decisions, election platform content, and message development. They underpin the policy resolutions approved by delegates at party convention meetings. Party leaders used to be bound to promote those policies on the campaign trail. Today leader loyalists might screen draft motions, and the leader might vow to disregard a contentious motion passed by delegates. A party's election manifesto reflects diverse sources of information, ranging from public opinion testing to consultation with experts.[84] Cost estimates are calculated, and the pledges are collated into message planks. The platform of the party that forms the government becomes a moral contract with voters. Policy commitments do not include disclaimers that delivery depends on private members who vote in sufficient numbers or that members might have pet projects.

Major political parties systematically weed out non-conformists. They recruit people who connect intellectually and emotionally with a political vision. Their vetting processes disqualify people whose values differ, particularly if opponents are likely to dredge up an intolerant comment. A nominated candidate is welcomed into a social unit and gains a greater prospect of being elected but forfeits many political freedoms. After the election, the intensity of partisanship sinks in further as newly sworn-in parliamentarians prepare to take their seats in the assembly. The full range of the leader's surrogates comes into focus, as does the esotericism of legislative proceedings. A paucity of written rules about a caucus means that private members learn about party discipline through observation and scuttlebutt. They come to accept the principle of negotiation log-rolling, whereby mutual advantage results from exchanging favours and accepting trade-offs, with the understanding that support for a group position will be reciprocated by colleagues on something else. They settle into the multifaceted role of lawmaker, caseworker, and brand ambassador (i.e., party representative).

Canadian political parties set some extraparliamentary parameters around discipline. During Justin Trudeau's tenure, changes to the Liberal Party of Canada's constitution updated its principles and assigned more power to the leader.[85] That constitution makes no mention of how MPs should vote. The party pledged in the 2015 election to restrict party discipline to matters concerning the "electoral platform; traditional confidence matters such as the Speech from the Throne and significant budgetary measures; and those that address the shared values embodied in the Charter of Rights and Freedoms."[86] Some interpreted the commitment as offering Liberal backbenchers more independence than other parties offer. That democratic spirit carried over to the 2019 Liberal platform, which asserted that MPs ought to be "free" to "be the voice for their communities, and hold the government to account."[87] In practice, there are far more disciplinary subtleties than the party lets on.

First, whipping votes on all bills related to implementing a party's electoral platform is a broad statement. Governing party members are expected, if not required by the leadership, to support cabinet initiatives. This holds even though a government bill can be different from what the party promised in the campaign. As well, whereas backbenchers must publicly support all aspects of the platform, the cabinet can reverse course. Backbenchers are compelled to defend the flip-flop even though they played no part in reneging on a campaign pledge to constituents, and they risk embarrassing the leader if they publicly apologize for the turnabout. Conversely, parliamentarians become frustrated when a free vote is announced on an election commitment that they passionately support.[88]

Second, cabinets interpret confidence measures to their own liking. In Canada's early years, the government often lost votes but did not resign.[89] In the twenty-first century, governing parties sometimes follow the British three-line whip system (see page 53).[90] Their members must always support the throne speech and budget; if not, then they cease to be part of the governing party's caucus because they are expressing utter disagreement with the leadership. The government can fiddle with confidence votes by burying items in a budget omnibus bill that bundles many proposals. Furthermore, a cabinet can argue that anything involving money relates to the budget. It can even decree that a routine motion is a judgment of its suitability to govern.[91] The threat of a snap election is ever present.[92]

Third, party discipline is fragile on issues that weigh on a parliamentarian's personal moral compass. In Canada, the constitutional protection of the fundamental freedoms of conscience and religion can chafe against the freedom of thought, belief, opinion, and expression, as well as with certain rights, notably equality rights. Debate on these highly charged issues risks tearing a party apart. Capital punishment, abortion, same-sex marriage, and medically assisted death are some high-profile morality issues that have exposed fissures. Other flashpoints encompass diverse topics from provincial self-determination in separatist referendums to the national firearms registry. On occasion, leaders back off to permit private members to vote as they wish. At other times, a leader demands conformity on a highly charged issue.

The Conservative Party of Canada constitution accords slightly more individual agency. A policy document declares that "all votes should be free, except for the budget, main estimates, and core government initiatives," and that Conservative MPs should consult with their constituents "on issues of moral conscience, such as abortion, the definition of marriage, and euthanasia."[93] What constitutes a core initiative and what soliciting constituent input means for voting are unspecified. In any event, consecutive leaders have decreed that the Conservative Party will not reopen the abortion issue and shall consider same-sex marriage a settled matter, topics that are nevertheless sources of wedge politics. Conservative parties in Canada often struggle to unite on social issues.

The New Democratic Party is the only major federal party that mentions party discipline in its constitution. A section titled "Discipline" briefly disentangles disciplinary responsibility between its federal and provincial parties.[94] Discipline is implied because New Democrats share ideological commitments to social democracy, and the party has formal alliances with the labour movement. One recent survey of NDP MPs found that their party's position was a significant, and sometimes the only, consideration in deciding how to vote in the House.[95] Despite party nomenclature that champions democracy, the New Democratic Party's constitution, policy declaration, and election platforms are conspicuously quiet about the rights of elected representatives.[96]

Niche parties can be less regimented. The Bloc Québécois's founding principles state that its MPs are not subject to voting discipline as long as they remain united on core party values.[97] That is an ideal that fell away over time.[98] The Green Party's constitution establishes its core values as a "basis of unity."[99] The Green leader once presented a private member's bill to curb a leader's authority over nomination papers, which she maintained is "an undemocratic tool for discipline and control over MPs."[100] Issue-based parties offer flexibility on topics for which party ideology might not have clear application, such as whether to reduce the voting age.

Notably, party constitutions and platforms do not specify the consequences for saying or doing something inconsistent with party values. For many new entrants into party politics, it is not obvious that they will be scolded for something as innocuous as clicking the "like" button below the Facebook post of someone affiliated with another party. Serious disruptions are generally dealt with by the disciplinary process outlined in Chapter 10. The rigours of party discipline cause some to wonder whether representation in parliamentary legislatures would be better off without political parties.

Politics without Political Parties

Politicians' use of prescribed messages is a symptom of their dependence on party affiliation. Just 4 to 5 percent of the Canadian electorate prioritizes candidate factors in elections, a percentage even lower in urban areas, among less informed voters, and outside Quebec.[101] Voter assessments of local candidates matter to the outcome of elections in only 10–14 percent of seats.[102] This means that candidates make a difference in close races but otherwise have no practical bearing on who wins or loses. If political parties did not exist, or even if party labels did not appear on the ballot, then voters would be more attuned to their local representatives.

Parliamentary politics without political parties might result in a greater medley of candidates. A slew of Independents would generate innovative, responsive policy ideas. The political polarity that divides society might tone down – or it might ramp up. Regardless, the absence of structure would bring complications. Without visible political coalitions, it would be hard for voters to differentiate between political choices.[103] Interest groups would have considerable influence, and legislators' votes could be bought. Periods of paralysis would likely result from mass bickering, personality conflicts, grandstanding, and vote trading. Factions would emerge, possibly dominated by regional loyalties, with the most populated areas exercising their voting muscles. Forming an executive, distributing resources, and ensuring that legislators are present to vote would be daunting. The electorate would lose their bearings in the political sphere, unsure of which policy agenda is on offer or whom to hold accountable.

Occasionally, a message of prioritizing constituents inspires the electorate. In the aftermath of the First World War, many suffragettes worked outside the male-dominated two-party system. The National Progressive Party formed as a coalition of anti-party agrarians, reformers, and westerners to rally against the "big interests" dominating party politics.[104] The Progressive movement nominated grassroots candidates to run against the lawyers and professional politicians whom it alleged were beholden to party and donor obligations. Many Progressives were motivated to "destroy" the centralized control of a parliamentary caucus over the party.[105] In the 1921 federal election, the Progressives won the second most seats. Their anti-partyism was so resolute that they refused to form the official opposition. As with all MPs, the conflicts inherent in weighing constituent, regional, national, party, and personal interests beset them. Initially, Progressives lined up to support economic policies that favoured their provinces. Ultimately, on most bills, they voted together.[106] Internal division followed. In a minority government, it was apparent that only "a tightly organized group" could hold the balance of power, but policy disagreement impaired the Progressive caucus,[107] and a number of Progressives switched parties.[108] Suffragettes gravitated toward working with the established political parties, and the movement fizzled out.

An effort to do away with partisanship is under way in the Senate of Canada.[109] It is an ambitious task given the unelected chamber's history as a landing spot for party loyalists, some of whom a judge found to be "robotically marching forth to recite their provided scripted lines" during Prime Minister Harper's tenure.[110] Justin Trudeau's commitment to appointing unaffiliated senators promises to stimulate thoughtful examination of public policy. Senators now question ministers, and they amend government bills with greater frequency than their predecessors did. Independent senators do not have a whip to discipline their voting. There is a scroll meeting instead of an order paper, and they put their names forward to the Speaker instead of the party whips controlling who can speak. A senator with the title "government representative" learns about government messaging on bills by attending the Cabinet Committee on Agenda, Results and Communications chaired by the prime minister. The applicable minister and public servants debrief senators about a government bill. Parliamentary secretaries – the government-side legislators assigned to assist ministers – lobby them, as do ministers.

There are recognizable practices even as overt partisanship recedes in the Senate. A "government liaison" tries to identify how senators intend to vote and provides them with information to convince them to support the cabinet. Senators with shared values form affinity groups around geography, profession, background, and socio-demographics. Many like-minded senators congealed into the Independent Senators Group. In the 42nd

Parliament, its members voted with the government representative on 86 percent of bills because, they said, the appointed upper house should respect the will of the elected lower house.[111] Senators who leave the Independent Senators Group have their seats moved to the back corner of the chamber. At the start of the 43rd Parliament, some appointees formed the Canadian Senators Group and the Progressive Senate Group, demonstrating that legislators are inclined to work in like-minded teams. As well, familiar communications tendencies arise: senators stonewall the media during a controversy, and sparring on social media occurs among senators and their staff, including during committee proceedings.[112] More time is required to see how the Senate experiment turns out.

For evidence of the parliamentary system functioning without political parties, we only need to look at the consensus system of government in two of Canada's territories. There are exclusively Independents in the legislatures of the Northwest Territories (nineteen MLAs for 45,300 citizens) and Nunavut (twenty-two MLAs for 37,800 citizens). In those territories, after a general election, the MLAs use a secret ballot to choose a premier and the cabinet. Power shifts from the executive branch into the hands of elected representatives, and there is more cooperation than conflict. On the surface, the setup suggests that parties are not required for a Westminster system of government, at least not in places with small populations.[113] Looking deeper, though, there are complaints that the cabinet is too weak and that excessive power is concentrated in the head of the government. The public has little say in selecting their premier. An opposition still forms. Private members can become upset with closed-door decision processes and believe that the cabinet pays insufficient attention to their opinions.[114] Indigenous communities likewise have governance structures without political parties. With consensus-based decision making, Indigenous leaders are not slotted automatically into positions. They can have vigorous debates before coming to general agreement. Nevertheless, significant challenges arise in Indigenous governance, such as issues of accountability and transparency.[115]

Political parties are also absent from (most) Canadian municipal politics.[116] As in the Northwest Territories and Nunavut, seating arrangements tend to place representatives in a circle or horseshoe, which is less adversarial than the parliamentary practice of grouping the government and opposition on different sides of the debating chamber. The mayor is directly elected, and candidates run on their own recognizance, giving them greater incentive to be responsive to public opinion. Without the ideological tempering of parties, there are more candidates holding diverse points of view. However, it is difficult for most citizens to discern a municipal mandate. Public interest is limited; voter turnout is low. Citizens lack sufficient knowledge to judge candidates' policy positions and cannot substitute party labels as information cues. They might defer to other cues, such as name recognition or family dynasties, making incumbency a barrier to entry for new politicians. As well, some municipal politicians have well-known partisan affiliations, and sometimes candidates present themselves as a united slate. Others engage in private bargaining once in office as they form alliances, organize into coalitions, and trade votes. The absence of parties complicates the electorate's ability to keep individual members of a municipal council accountable for decisions.

Small-scale legislative assemblies can evidently operate without party labels. The House of Commons and provincial legislatures can have spurts of all-party cooperation, particularly when there is a public emergency. The predicament for most of the occupants is about trying to optimize their influence in normal circumstances. That means playing by entrenched codes and rules that are often concealed from public view.

RESEARCH METHOD

The purpose of this book is to disclose the many facets of discipline in Canadian parliamentary politics, particularly those devoted to communications. The research describes party discipline in an integrated digital environment. It presents the architecture for identifying ways that parliamentarians can be strong representatives within the constraints of message conformity. In the following pages, I present the objectives of the study and the types of data.

Canadian Research

Literature on party discipline in Canada is surprisingly enduring. Canadian MPs interviewed in 1962 talked about ambition, wanting to avoid the label of malcontent, frustration with the binding confidence convention, and the need for unity. One MP remarked that the "party system simply does not tolerate MPs who disagree publicly with their party," while another believed that cohesion "strengthens the image of the party in the eyes of the public."[117] In the 1970s, scholars found that party cohesion exists because of rules and peer pressure, not because of rewards or punishments.[118] In 1985, the Special Committee on Reform of the House of Commons, chaired by MP James McGrath, reported that communications technology contributes to a lesser role for private members in legislative business and a greater role as constituent ombudsmen. An MP quoted by the special committee foreshadowed the connection between legislative votes and the party brand, particularly for the party in power, saying that "the longer a government is in office the more every vote is maybe not a vote of confidence but a vote of reputation, which is close to confidence, and therefore you have to have uniformity."[119] The 1991 federal speech from the throne acknowledged that impressions of "excessive party discipline and over-zealous partisanship, of empty posturing and feigned outrage," were eroding respect for Parliament.[120] In 2003, an MP complained that party discipline turns backbenchers into "potted palms" who adorn the background and that freedom of speech is "forbidden."[121] Such observations are just as relevant, perhaps more so, in a digital communications environment. Yet despite decades of concern, the internal details are largely undocumented because they involve secretive business that politicians are unwilling to betray. Research on party discipline in Canada is wanting.[122]

The two main academic examinations of party discipline in Canada conduct statistical analyses of division roll call votes that identify how each Member of Parliament voted. Empirical testing in *Party Discipline and Parliamentary Politics* of a model dubbed "loyalty elicited through advancement, discipline, and socialization" propelled scholarly thinking about why MPs rarely dissent.[123] *Lost on Division: Party Unity in the Canadian Parliament* documents the evolution of parliamentary party unity in Canada through a historical review of voting in Parliament, concluding that parliamentary reforms will not resolve party discipline because "parties will always find a way to maintain their influence in the legislative process."[124] Despite these works' considerable insights, analyzing votes has some limitations, such as an inability to account for parliamentarians who express dissent by missing a recorded vote or that like-minded politicians cluster together irrespective of party label.[125] We know little about private deliberations that computer software cannot measure, such as the inner workings of party caucuses, or the undisclosed ways that governance bleeds into the legislative branch. In particular, we lack information about how communications management intensifies party discipline in Canada.

A growing canon of Canadian research shows that a fixation on marketing infuses the parliamentary system with communications discipline.[126] In *The New NDP: Moderation, Modernization, and Political Marketing,* David McGrane documents the federal New Democratic Party's adoption of message discipline protocols.[127] At the turn of the millennium, the leader's office exerted minimal control over parliamentary business. Messaging was devised during roundtable discussions at caucus meetings, and MPs managed their own interview requests. When the leadership introduced more formalized processes, MPs' ideas for Question Period had to be pitched by email, and the leader and House leader selected topics that might get the leader on the news. The leader's staff wrote questions. They designated MPs to rehearse with a QP preparation team. They used a central spreadsheet to manage the distribution of speakers and topics. Staff tracked MPs' media appearances. Private members' bills and motions were vetted through the leader's office and caucus; sometimes topics originated from staff. MPs relinquished their independence as they ceased to prioritize their own pursuits in favour of issues of interest to the leadership circle. As McGrane puts it, the use of political marketing was a choice of "discipline and order over freedom and discretion for MPs."[128] Discipline seemed to translate into electoral results when the NDP formed the official opposition in 2011 for the first time.

The micromanagement of Members of Parliament by their party's leadership is now routine in Canada. We still have a lot to learn about the hidden practices that lead Canadian politicians to behave as "skilled ideological chameleons" and party messengers.[129] Little Canadian-wide information is available about party discipline in the provinces despite similar parliamentary, electoral, and party systems. Academic study of discipline in a digital communications environment is especially limited.

Research Objectives and Data

How would you describe party discipline? Only parliamentarians experience it, but it is so vast that even party whips might not grasp its full scope.

A component in the pursuit of power is only part of the story. In this book, I reveal ways that party-affiliated members of Canada's House of Commons and provincial assemblies are conditioned to prioritize party interests and are infused with reminders to stay on-message. In particular, I comment on the absorption of governing party backbenchers into the government's publicity apparatus, a practice that diverts them from critical commentary. My objective is to document the inner workings of party discipline and to show that communications are integral to how we understand it. Through the richness of qualitative research, I intend to explain who is involved, what it is, where it reaches, when it occurs, why it exists, and how it happens. Given that there is so much secrecy involved, a description of the goings-on in private political quarters promises to be an exhibition of "how social research attempts to make the invisible visible."[130]

Gathering information about political secrets is exacting, especially when a study delves into the caucus principle of confidentiality. Hansard records of legislative debates are insufficient because party discipline and caucus management are off limits in Question Period.[131] Access to information legislation does not apply to the political executive or parliamentary parties, and in any event sensitive information is shared verbally. Caucus meetings consist of oral reports with "no printed agendas, no minutes, no recorded votes, and no press releases."[132] The only thing in writing is the internal email informing members of the time and location of a meeting.[133] Everything is shredded when a politician leaves office, and a computer specialist wipes digital files; Library and Archives Canada mandates only that ministerial records related to departmental matters must be preserved.[134] This is why one former chief of staff in the Prime Minister's Office (PMO) believes that studying how a caucus works is more difficult than studying the cabinet. As he points out, at least the cabinet makes formal records publicly available after a holding period of twenty to thirty years.[135]

Interviewing people who have experience in party politics is the best way to reveal confidential information about what happens in private settings off limits to outsiders. Refusals to provide basic information belie political secrecy. Politicians who agree to speak with a researcher can become silent when asked about what happens in the caucus[136] and some require anonymity for fear of retribution.[137] A staffer in the chief government whip's office in Ottawa explained to me that a whip's work is too sensitive to discuss, even in the abstract.[138] Consider the following attempt to identify the MPs who belonged to an all-party democracy caucus created in response to reports by the Samara Centre for Democracy about former MPs' disillusionment with party control.[139] The Parliament Hill office of the Liberal who chaired the all-party caucus offered the following reply when I enquired by email about the group's membership.

FROM: Alex Marland
TO: MP's Office
SUBJECT: Request for list of All-Party Democracy Caucus members
I am looking for a list of the MPs who are members of the all-party democracy caucus. I wasn't able to locate this online. I would be obliged if you could provide me with this information.

FROM: MP's office
SUBJECT: RE: Request for list of All-Party Democracy Caucus members
This is to confirm I have received your email, and am working on putting together a list of names!

FROM: MP's office
SUBJECT: RE: Request for list of All-Party Democracy Caucus members
Thank you for your patience, I looked into getting the names of the all-party democracy caucus members, and realized the reason for its absence online is because this kind of information is not disclosed to anyone for privacy reasons.

FROM: Alex Marland
SUBJECT: RE: Request for list of All-Party Democracy Caucus members
Thank you. However, I'm confused. What are the privacy reasons?

FROM: MP's office
SUBJECT: RE: Request for list of All-Party Democracy Caucus members
No problem! It is for confidentiality.[140]

The culture of secrecy means that much of our knowledge about the practices of parliamentary parties is anecdotal, unsystematic, and/or dated.

My priority in this book is learning from practitioners who are or were in the cut and thrust of political action. National-level politics in Canada is my main unit of analysis, supplemented by provincial-level information. Collecting data from Ottawa and ten provinces responds to a methodological problem that studies of party cohesion usually examine one legislature.[141] For the purpose of readability, I identify a person's position at the time of the quotation, and I sometimes need not explicitly differentiate a federal or provincial source. Instead of naming provinces, I sometimes distinguish between large places where operations are more professionalized (e.g., House of Commons, Ontario) and smaller places with fewer formalities and resources (e.g., Manitoba, Prince Edward Island). Because of space limitations, and to keep the focus on Canada, I integrate information from other countries sparsely. The main exception is the British Westminster system when insufficient Canadian information is available, such as *How to Be a Government Whip* written by a then-British MP.[142] American sources have limited application, in part because the independent-minded communications of American politicians are alien to those of MPs.[143]

Using multiple methods to gather qualitative data about party discipline across parties, jurisdictions, leaders, and time enables general observations. The first of three sources of data is publicly available information. I scoured Canadian political memoirs and consulted academic publications. I reviewed reports about how to fix Parliament. I read countless Canadian news stories, many of which were published by the *Globe and Mail* and the *Hill Times,* which I supplemented with historical and contextual research for specific information using the Google search engine and the Newspaper Archive and ProQuest subscription news databases. I conducted purposeful searches of Canadian legislatures' websites including those of the Parliament of Canada, Hansard, and House of Commons procedural documents, and sometimes submitted emails requesting additional information. I looked for details via government and political party websites, in the political texts archived by Laval University on Poltext, and in political ephemera on file in my office. I transcribed content from two documentary films on party discipline and some televised news stories, political podcasts, and YouTube videos. I inspected some transcripts of Library of Parliament archival interviews, four of which were with party whips who served in the 1970s and/or 1980s. A fifth with James McGrath concerned the afore-mentioned special committee that he chaired. Some limited quantitative data are part of this review, such as the prevalence of party candidates who retweet their colleagues (see Table 4.1). I examined social media only when an applicable item was mentioned in a news story, in which case I tracked down the original post.

The primary source of data comprises 131 semi-structured, in-depth interviews held between 2018 and 2020 with current and former Canadian politicians and political staff, many of them involved with the 42nd Parliament. Conversations lasted from twenty minutes to over two hours. Some required follow-ups. People with experience as prime minister, premier, minister, House leader, parliamentary secretary, opposition party leader, whip, caucus chair, backbencher, senator, or as a defeated election candidate were interviewed. Political staff included current and former members of the PMO, premiers' offices, ministers' offices, caucus research bureaus, MPs' offices, and leadership and election campaign personnel. Appendix 1 lists the main people interviewed for this book. To respect their requests for confidentiality, some names are withheld, and attribution sometimes obscures whether the participant held the stated job title at the time of the interview. Original quotes are interspersed with quotes found in publicly available information. Appendix 2 documents the sampling and recruitment methods, including a breakdown by high-est position attained and party (Table A1) and by province and gender (Table A2). Participants received a discussion guide, also included in Appendix 2. In addition, I communicated informally in person, by tele-phone, or by email with approximately a dozen other politicians and staff to obtain specific information related to their sphere of expertise.

I asked many of the participants about the best way to obtain private files on party discipline. As might be expected, they emphasized that in-ternal politicking goes undocumented or unsaved. Instead, they shared personal experiences, role-played, or read out party messaging from their smartphones. Although certain topics remained off limits even when I developed rapport, some people shared internal emails, photographs of documents, and in one case a flash drive of internal messages. As a quality control measure, I obtained feedback on draft chapters from some current and former parliamentarians as well as some political science subject area experts.

A third source of data comprises transcripts of in-depth exit interviews with 131 retiring MPs conducted by the Samara Centre for Democracy. The policy institute's corpus encompasses MPs who exited during or on conclusion of the 38th Parliament (2004–06) through the 41st Parliament (2011–15). Interviewers asked about motivations for entering political life, the work of an MP, connections with civil society, and advice for future parliamentarians. The controlling nature of party discipline arose often.[144] Among the Samara Centre's findings was "a deeply held view that anything other than absolute message control would make a party unelectable" in Canada.[145] I read transcripts of the organization's lengthy interviews with retired party whips, and I examined the entire collection of interviews for more than three dozen terms to isolate information about specific topics that needed fleshing out. Some searches were fruitful (e.g., ninety-six of the former MPs mentioned the whip) and some less so (e.g., just five mentions of candidate vetting). Multiple terms routine in the House of Commons precinct did not appear, such as "duty whip," "lobby desks," and "vote sheets." The transcripts were mostly used to verify information, as were the Samara Centre's publications, such as *Tragedy in the Commons: Former Members of Parliament Speak Out about Canada's Failing Democracy*.[146] We interviewed a small number of the same people, and I am careful not to overstate that input. Advice for parliamentarians gleaned from the transcripts is presented in Figure 12.1.

PLAN OF THE BOOK

The chapters that follow reveal strategic mindsets and internal management practices in Canadian politics. Much of this information takes parliamentarians years to learn; many never do grasp it.

In Chapter 2, I look at political representation. I begin by examining the invasive vetting of prospective election candidates by Canadian political parties. I summarize some theories about styles of representation before disentangling the functions of government-side backbenchers. The story of a Conservative MP whose frank conversation with constituents appeared on YouTube animates the real-world challenges of representation in Canada. I explain that, as government expanded, backbenchers evolved from lawmakers into caseworkers. As emphasis on communications unity grew, they became brand ambassadors. A missive from a New Democratic Party MLA in Alberta outlines the constraints on parliamentarians absorbed into a government message machine. We learn about a Liberal MP who used social media to build a personal brand that became a source of tension with the Trudeau PMO.

In Chapter 3, I emphasize how partisans are integrated into a political team. To understand caucus mindsets, I look at the social psychology of group behaviour, including the famous Stanford University prison experiment. Applied to politics, we see that self-discipline arises from membership in a party whose shared quest requires group cooperation and sacrifice. This gives rise to the parallels some see between political groups and competitive sports teams. We learn how Brian Mulroney, Canada's prime minister from 1984 to 1993, built personal loyalty throughout the Progressive Conservative (PC) Party. Coupled with information in Chapters 4 and 7, the story of his extraordinary interest in caucus solidarity helps to solve the puzzle of how Mulroney remained popular in his party despite political upheaval and public disapproval. The chapter marks the first of several forays into the work of the party whip by looking at human resources functions.

I provide an overview in Chapter 4 of the political communications arena. I examine the media ecosystem, including the ways that journalists cover political news. The disruption wrought by digital communications technology has tightened party message control in Canada. Political correctness and populism are two notable phenomena that pull message conformity in different directions. I explain how parliamentary parties exploit media interest in caucus division and use the threat of media drama as a reason to close ranks. The practices of message amplification, wedge politics, and trap votes are discussed. Vignettes include a distressed MP who voted against a motion about compensating hepatitis C victims and the Liberal communications machine exploiting a Conservative MP's quip about abortion.

Chapter 5 is about message discipline. I look at how a secretive atmosphere and an aversion to surprises increase the appeal of message consistency. I touch on how non-stop campaigning and political marketing influence a relentless effort to control information, including through the deployment of branding. Next I summarize how party values, anecdotes, and public opinion research inform the construction of concise messages. Communications strategists urge message repetition, but they warn about robotic delivery as they encourage speakers to convey an image of authenticity. I conclude the chapter by observing that the quantification and centralization of data collected on citizens are further ways that political parties exert influence on elected representatives. Strategic thinkers from the Harper PMO and Trudeau PMO are among those who share wisdom.

Chapter 6 presents insights on discipline coursing through the political executive in Canada. Management of the cabinet and centralized coordination of government communications are profiled, as are ways that the executive branch exerts control over government-side backbenchers. I touch on the formidable role of staff in the PMO, premiers' offices, and ministers' offices, including the types of planning meetings they engage in. I explore the work of staff who station regional desks to act as liaisons with governing party backbenchers. The ability of politicians to put differences aside in a public emergency is discussed in the context of the COVID-19 pandemic when partisan silos fell away but message discipline grew.

Chapter 7 is a journey into the clandestine world of a parliamentary party's caucus meetings. I tackle the internal dynamics of caucus gatherings, including variations in format and how prime ministers have run their meetings. Leaders say that caucus is the place for parliamentarians to make their voice heard, but leaders and their inner circle may not grasp the intensity of social and institutional forces that cause many backbenchers to fall silent. I give attention to sub-caucuses, notably regional caucuses. I also examine the divisive topic of staff attending caucus meetings, whose presence has become a permanent fixture. The attention paid to social media in Ottawa caucus meetings is particularly illuminating.

In Chapter 8, I delve into the communications work of parliamentary caucus research bureaus, and profile that of the Liberal Research Bureau. These publicly funded units of political staff play an underappreciated role in providing parliamentarians with messages. Although messaging is essential for MPs to do their jobs, the practice invites questions about whether a bureau works for the caucus, as intended, or whether the staff are agents of the leadership and the extraparliamentary party. A bureau can also become integrated into public administration. I provide examples of internal messaging circulated to Liberal MPs that show how government-side backbenchers are encouraged to be government messengers.

Chapter 9 presents new insights on how message discipline affects what parliamentarians do in the legislature. I offer a brief history of behaviour in the House of Commons to dispel notions that representation was necessarily better in the past or is beyond reproach today. After profiling the interlocking work of the House leader and whip, I acquaint readers with communications facets of members' statements, Question Period, government orders, and private members' business. I review the ways in which political parties exert control over MPs in the House of Commons, including the conflicted roles of standing committees as organs of the party leadership versus checks on the executive. I discuss how party whips manage attendance and deliver votes. For the first time, non-MPs will get to see what a party whip's vote sheets look like. Readers will also gain an appreciation for the digital interactions between the whip's office staff and MPs during committee proceedings.

Chapter 10 discloses how discipline is exacted when a partisan goes off-message. I begin the chapter by delving into conflicts within a caucus. Process, policy, and personality disputes sometimes escalate into arguments, coarse language, and tantrums. I touch on bullying and harassment, which appear to be less prevalent in parliamentary politics than some might think, at least by political standards, with the notable exception of power imbalances between senior and junior political staff. The steps that disciplinarians follow when dealing with a breach of unity are profiled, as are the types of punishments. I conclude the chapter by identifying how rare it is for Independents to be elected at the federal or provincial level in Canada.

Chapter 11 is about the SNC-Lavalin controversy. The events comprise a pivotal case of party discipline, for they expose the mayhem that results when immovable positions spill into a public disagreement. In 2019, the Trudeau Liberals went into a bunker mentality over controversy about the PMO's attempt to persuade the attorney general to cut a special deal so that the Quebec-based engineering and construction company could avoid criminal prosecution. Tracing the policy dispute sets up a summary of cascading events, followed by perspectives shared by some Liberal MPs and PMO staff. There are many layers to the story. This version focuses on a standoff that, among other things, divulges Justin Trudeau's management style of delegating unparallelled authority to senior PMO personnel.

Chapter 12 concludes by presenting ways that parliamentarians can be compelling advocates within partisan boundaries. It differentiates the stereotypes of team players and political mavericks from party robots who act on command or troublemakers who bristle at receiving orders. I channel suggestions from parliamentarians into maxims that offer promise for rejuvenating the relevance of private members within the restraints of party discipline. The chapter concludes with a return to the research objectives and suggests best practices, such as adopting a caucus code of conduct. A few areas for further research are identified.

In the pages that follow, readers ought to keep in mind that rules, processes, and actors are subject to change, as is the emphasis that a leader places on message control. As well, political parties and leaders routinely make commitments to legislative reform that do not amount to anything. We should therefore be suspicious about Prime Minister Trudeau's ministerial mandate letter to the government House leader urging more time in the 43rd Parliament for private members' business, to "eliminate the use of whip and party lists" that guide the Speaker when recognizing MPs, and to further limit when backbenchers must vote with the government.[147] As this book makes clear, in Canada the culture of discipline penetrates party politics far deeper than promises of reform or what goes on in a legislature.

SUMMARY

The political institutions that make Canada a model democracy simultaneously undermine the democratic functions that they are supposed to perform. Party discipline draws out compromise to accomplish a shared political agenda. It is rooted in a culture of secrecy necessary to foster trusting relationships, compromises, and smooth workplace operations. Its potency evolved as political parties formalized and as party leaders gained more authority. Gradually, parliamentarians transformed into party soldiers following orders in a command hierarchy. The encroachment of the confidence convention has become a significant impetus for solidarity among governing party backbenchers. As will be shown, the power emanating from party discipline intensifies as it spreads into message discipline.

2

Representation

What are the implications of party messaging for political representation, particularly for governing party backbenchers? How do Canadian political parties weed out non-conformists from the party fold? In Canada, even the most adamant constituency advocates and independent thinkers can develop an image as party enthusiasts as they succumb to a system that incentivizes them to communicate central messaging.

CANDIDATE VETTING

Understanding political representation in a digital environment requires awareness that scrutiny begins the moment that an aspiring candidate expresses interest to a party official about representing the party in an election. The immediate objective of subjecting a prospective candidate to rigorous vetting criteria is to assess the danger of causing embarrassment to the party. Campaign strategists take measures so that the party's candidates are not the source of a "bozo eruption" or a social media post that generates negative headlines.[1] A deeper purpose is to get the individual to submit to the party's authority beyond the election. Candidate vetting has become a tool for engineering party discipline, but we know little about it because the process is "utterly opaque."[2] This section shines light into a dark area of importance to political representation in Canada.

Evolution of Party Screening of Candidates

Candidate vetting enables a party's hierarchy to reject someone seeking nomination to run as a party candidate. It can be done without disclosing the reasons for the disqualification, which can be explained away as something as innocuous as an outdated party membership.[3] The practice originated in earnest as a response to the scandalous behaviour of some MPs during Brian Mulroney's tenure. In 1988, two Progressive Conservative ministers announced that the party's Quebec candidates were being interviewed.[4] Discussions focused on assessing honesty and morality by urging the candidates to disclose any ethical lapses and crimes. The ministers did not disclose the vetting questions.

The western-based Reform Party advocated a higher standard of representation in that election and into the 1990s. Its belief in decentralization was embodied in its softer title of caucus coordinator rather than whip.[5] Reformers promoted citizen-initiated plebiscites, wanted the MP oath of office to affirm allegiance to constituents, and pledged to hold caucus votes after which the majority view would be the caucus position.[6] Vetting by the fledgling party in the lead-up to the 1993 federal election applied judgments on candidate quality. Reform subjected its prospective candidates to criminal record checks. The party asked applicants if they had participated in illegal strikes or been rejected by a church or synagogue. It also sought medical details from doctors and information about physical exercise regimens.[7] In the aftermath of that election, controversy surrounded candidates from various parties who embellished their education credentials. Public protests over one such misrepresentation resulted in the banishment of a Liberal MP from the governing party's caucus.[8]

Throughout its existence, the Reform Party contended with bozo eruptions from some candidates and MPs who espoused xenophobia, sexism, racism, and homophobia. Top-down control was necessary to minimize damage to the party brand.[9] But central oversight cut to the core of the party's mission of decentralization and grassroots representation, while screening processes stirred internal anger about interference with local selection.[10] Ultimately, the image problems were so acute that Reform rebranded as the Canadian Alliance Party. It later merged with the federal PC Party. The enduring lesson for all Canadian parties was to rigorously screen their prospective candidates and impose top-down messaging. It also highlighted the value of opposition research, known as oppo in political circles. Some information is held for years, waiting for an opportune moment to destabilize an opponent.[11]

Digital communications increased the possibility of a bozo eruption derailing a campaign. Furnishing the media with a controversial digital remark can stir up pressure for a leader to disassociate from the offender. A Liberal in the 2015 federal election resigned from running in a Conservative stronghold when opponents unearthed offensive social media posts that she had authored as a seventeen year old: "If [political parties uphold] the standard of being perfect online, they'll have fewer and fewer candidates every year," she later reflected. "The person you were on social media doesn't necessarily mean the person you're becoming or the person you are now. I go through my posts at age 13 and I think: why did I post that? It was so lame. People change all the time."[12] Political parties do not care. They vet prospective candidates for precisely this reason.

As social media footprints become bigger, society is trending toward greater tolerance of politicians who apologize for past behaviours while keeping the bar high for recent actions. Midway through the 2019 campaign Justin Trudeau accepted the public apology of a candidate who had tweeted racist and sexist remarks seven years earlier.[13] The candidate went on to win, showing why candidates in safe seats are less likely to be dropped, whereas long shots in unwinnable districts are expendable, especially if the deadline to nominate replacements has passed. When *Time* published photographs of Trudeau wearing blackface before he was an MP, he admitted hiding his actions from Liberal vetting committees when he first applied to run as a candidate because he was "embarrassed."[14] The earlier failure of anyone to unearth the photos in school yearbooks underscores that scrutiny is foremost a digital exercise. To avert public humiliation, political parties investigate the backgrounds of prospective candidates and require them to sign a contract.

Candidate Contracts

Centralized processes immediately confront a political rookie in Canada. Canadians interested in running for a political party receive an extensive application form, including a contractual obligation to behave as a party representative. Federally, the wording dances around the Canada Elections Act, which stipulates that a candidate cannot sign a campaign pledge that makes a "demand or claim ... to follow a course of action that will prevent him or her from exercising freedom of action in Parliament, if elected, or to resign as a member if called on to do so by any person or association of persons."[15] The probing questions on the form aim to identify what opponents might discover as well as to prepare both the party and the candidate for embarrassing information that might become public. Parties are concerned about applicants who exaggerate on their resumés, hide controversial details, or lack comprehension that opponents will dredge up negative information. For instance, a question about whether the applicant plagiarized in school appears to be excessive, but even controversial remarks made as a student in a university seminar discussion can end up in the news more than a decade later.[16] Few are aware of the hypocrisy that the parties' vetting forms contain copied information. In 2004, a Liberal Party official said that the party's questionnaire was based on one used by a provincial law society for screening lawyers.[17] Asking applicants if they had "been charged or convicted of plagiarism, cheating on examinations or other conduct that was the subject of academic discipline" appeared verbatim on Liberal forms for years as well as those of many other parties.[18] Scrutiny of candidates can sometimes be a case of do as I say, not as I do.

A standard requirement is authorizing the party to conduct a credit check. A certificate of conduct from the police might be required. Some parties collect a good conduct bond and return the money if the individual does not publicly criticize the party during a specified period. A growing number request an applicant's social media passwords. Prospective candidates might notice a mysterious digital follower, an avatar of a party staffer who reviews their online history, and might be advised to shut down their accounts and start new ones.[19] In response to the #MeToo movement, the Conservative Party added a question about whether an applicant had ever been accused of improper sexual behaviour,[20] and the United Conservative Party of Alberta requested usernames for online dating sites and asked whether an applicant had ever engaged in sexting.[21] Vetting can branch out from candidates. The United Conservatives created a database of citizens barred from becoming party members for communicating intolerance online.[22] The People's Party of Canada required members of its electoral district associations to submit a resumé, a criminal record summary, and social media details. They signed a pledge not to embarrass the party and committed to supporting the party's principles and platform.[23] The party gave the information to an external firm specializing in background checks. However, relying on public records only goes so far. For example, it can be difficult to verify someone's claims of Indigenous identity, and thus parties must decide if they can trust what applicants tell them.[24]

The Liberal Party of Canada and some provincial Liberal Parties use nearly identical application forms. A detailed candidate contract affirms that the applicant supports the principles outlined in the party's constitution and will hold party business in strict confidence. Commitment is assessed by asking whether there are any party policies to which the applicant objects. Most of the paperwork features intrusive questions about the applicant's life history. Figure 2.1 summarizes some of the topics. The applicant authorizes party officials to collect additional information from any source. The reckoning is an assessment of an applicant's candour if party officials uncover compromising information that the applicant did not reveal. The parties treat the process as a job application, with little regard for civic literacy. Nomination packages do not test knowledge about the role of a parliamentarian or educate the signee about the toll of politics on family life.

The Liberal paperwork contains legalistic statements to improve the veracity of supplied information. There is a declaration that the completed form "is of the same legal force and effect as if made under oath and by virtue of the Canada Evidence Act."[25] A notary public or commissioner of oaths must initial or sign the pages. The involvement of a party lawyer provides the assurance of confidentiality under solicitor-client privilege while conveying the seriousness of the process. Other commitments include submitting disputes to the party's appeal committee and promising to waive legal recourse. Potential nomination contestants must submit the completed forms, a $1,500 non-refundable application fee, and documentation concerning their credit and criminal records.[26] A member of a Liberal Green Light Committee reviews the application and at least one probing interview with designated party officers occurs. As in other parties, an interviewer implores the prospective candidate to come clean with anything that could be a source of embarrassment and, depending on the circumstances, might ask brusque questions: *"Are you clean? You got*

> **FIGURE 2.1**
> **Vetting topics in Liberal Party candidate nomination package**
>
> - any outstanding judgment or garnishment
> - breached any tax or immigration statutes
> - campaign debts or liabilities
> - charged or convicted of any election or party rules
> - conduct that was the subject of academic discipline
> - declared bankruptcy
> - defendant in a court martial or similar proceeding
> - denied entry, landed immigrant status or citizenship
> - denied or had revoked a licence or permit
> - disciplined by any professional association
> - misappropriation of funds or fraud
> - name changes
> - object to any of the party's policy positions
> - outstanding taxation liabilities
> - resigned a public office
> - tax filings not up-to-date
> - anyone campaigning with you investigated for breaking campaign rules
> - any complaint about campaigning for or holding public office
> - charged with or found guilty of any crime, offence, or delinquency, including sexual or other harassment
> - discharged, suspended or asked to resign from any employment
> - disciplinary action by any tribunal, organization or society
> - dispute with a public body or civil court proceedings about fraud as part of business dealings
> - involved in any breach of trust or rules of a private organization
> - involved with a business that is the subject of a charge or indictment
> - matrimonial or custody proceedings
> - subject of any legal proceeding, inquiry, or investigation
> - suspended, expelled, or required to withdraw from a post-secondary institution
> - unfair or illegal employment or labour practices
> - written anything that was published or distributed online
> - anything else that could be used by opponents

Source: Synthesis of Liberal forms used for candidates in the 2015 Canadian federal election, the 2018 Ontario election, and the 2019 Newfoundland and Labrador election.

luggage? Any skeletons in your closet? Have you ever declared bankruptcy? Have you ever beat up your wife? Has your wife ever beat you up? Have you ever crossed the street or pissed on the wrong side?[27] The recruiter explains that the purpose is to make the applicant feel violated in anticipation of the public scrutiny that occurs during a campaign.

A potential candidate whom the committee believes should be rejected is "red-lighted," and the matter is brought to the party leader for a decision. The application form anticipates this possibility by requiring a signee to agree to support whoever becomes the Liberal candidate in that electoral district. The agreement furthermore commits the applicant not to run as an Independent or with another party anywhere else in that election or a subsequent by-election. There is no public record of the number of unsuccessful applicants or the reasons for their rejection. This raises the possibility that the process is a facade when a leader hand-picks candidates.[28] Furthermore, there is little allowance for youthful indiscretions, thereby eliminating a swath of Canadians: "If everyone who is going to be standing for office needs to demonstrate they've been perfect every step of their lives, there is going to be a shortage of people running for office," Trudeau remarked when the blackface images surfaced.[29] His defence echoed the protests of the young Liberal banished from the previous campaign.

Applicants who go on to secure the nomination immediately receive party messaging. They are granted access to the party's constituent database for the electoral district in which they are running. Tutelage includes attending candidate training schools where sticking to approved messaging is enforced under penalty of the party's endorsement being rescinded. Candidates are told that someone somewhere is observing everything that they say or do. By now, it is clear that staying on-brand involves taking a cue from whatever the leader is saying. During the campaign, an initial trickle of party messaging becomes a flood. Candidates learn that they must not distract from the leader's tour and that part of their role is to clap enthusiastically at events.[30] Their campaign team leverages economies of scale by using party templates and adhering to brand specifications. For instance, the Liberal nomination package commits an approved candidate to using a micro-website provided by the party and to purchasing products from its riding services package of party buttons, banner stand displays, posters, and volunteer badges. As well, a party might require that an aspiring candidate sign over a proportion of any election campaign expense rebates, which weakens the political muscle of the electoral district association.[31] All of it constitutes training for what to expect as an elected representative, including the unwritten code of never contradicting the leader in public: "I'm a new MP. I don't know how all this works," said one freshly elected newbie: "I would refrain from talking about areas I disagree with my leader until I get to meet him at the caucus table."[32] By the time they arrive in the legislature, Canadian party politicians have learned to be cautious about speaking out publicly, and they are on their way to voting as a partisan bloc.

DILEMMAS OF REPRESENTATION

There are many styles of democratic representation. Some representatives champion a macro-issue such as mental health, the environment, or public finance because they care about addressing a topic that affects society. Others choose to pursue local matters such as cleaning up a harbour, retrofitting public housing, or paving roads in the district.[33] Politicians might be outsiders who venture to the capital city to channel the views of constituents. Alternatively, they can behave as insiders who represent the government and the legislature to constituents – what Reform Party MPs used to call being "Ottawashed."[34] Whatever the preferred style, members of Canadian legislatures face institutional pressure to behave as "party delegates" who promote party interests.[35]

Representation in Theory

A common starting point in the theory of political representation is eighteenth-century British philosopher Edmund Burke's belief that parliamentarians should be deliberative thinkers who put the national interest first. His position was that representatives should not pander: "Your representative owes you, not his industry only, but his judgement; and he betrays you instead of serving you if he sacrifices it to your opinion," the Whig MP wrote to constituents in 1774.[36] Burke's views reflect a standard dilemma that confronts politicians. Are they mainly trustees with a mandate to determine what they deem to be in society's best interests? Or are they delegates with a solemn duty to follow the wishes of the people who elected them? Consider how a former Liberal MP who served as the chief government whip looks at the national interest:

> I was on a committee amending the Elections Act. An opposition MP was saying we should put in the Act that the prime responsibility of a Member of Parliament is to their constituency. I looked at him and said: "You may think that. But people elected me to Parliament. They think

and expect my prime responsibility is to my country." As a representative, a constant challenge was to rationalize the interests of my constituency and my country.[37]

Contrast that national imperative with that of Elizabeth May, the longtime Green Party leader, who who articulated that party discipline inhibits the ability of parliamentarians to put their constituencies first:

Members of Parliament are elected to represent their constituencies. Party discipline tells you that you're a mere cog in a machine. You got elected because you're wearing a brand t-shirt, and that brand is the leader. You do whatever you're told. That's destructive; it's a perversion of the Westminster system of parliamentary democracy. Backbenchers with the governing party don't hold the government to account. If they ask a question in Question Period, it's scripted by the minister's office and put to a minister who praises the questioner. It's awful.[38]

The trustee versus delegate model is fanciful when it comes to Canadian parliamentary politics. It assumes that representatives are free agents, which partisans are not. Burke's views preceded pontification about parliamentary government by other British philosophers, including Jeremy Bentham, John Stuart Mill, and Walter Bagehot.[39] Their theories of representation, as with Burke's, did not anticipate the practical limitations of government-side backbenchers in Canada's party-centric and leader-focused system.

Although it too has finite application to Canadian politics, a topical perspective comprises the four typologies that American political scientist Hanna Pitkin theorizes in *The Concept of Representation*.[40] Pitkin presents descriptive representation as the idea that the socio-demographic makeup of an assembly should mirror society. Many advocates of equality latch on to the ideal that members are champions of the people with whom they share characteristics, such as gender or race. That objective holds value but is reductive: proponents of descriptive representation rarely champion other underrepresented groups, for as Pitkin observes there is little desire for the cognitive abilities of an assembly to be proportionate to those of society overall.[41] Formalistic representation is concerned with the legitimacy of authority. Its advocates want accountability mechanisms to ensure that institutional actors and voters can reward or punish a politician. They support existing rules as long as the democratic process is fair, an assessment that is open to interpretation. Substantive representation refers to a utilitarian who takes action to advance changes to public policy and/or attend to the needs of constituents. It is imprecise because representatives hold competing interpretations of who their constituents are. Some believe that a parliamentarian has legitimacy to represent an electoral district; others think that a parliamentarian has a duty to represent underrepresented voices everywhere, irrespective of electoral boundaries. Finally, Pitkin's view of symbolic representation is that constituents derive meaning from perceptions of a politician. Confidence is related to what their representative stands for. In this way of thinking, whether constituents accept a parliamentarian is what matters.

We can see how these styles of representation clash when a parliamentarian raises issues within a parliamentary caucus in Canada. A former government-side Member of the House of Assembly (MHA) in Newfoundland and Labrador tells of how school board administrators lacked policy tools to address a situation involving a male student accused of harassing female students off school property. The issue caused a public uproar.[42] The school is located hundreds of kilometres away from the electoral district the MHA represented, and she was criticized in the caucus for championing a cause that was not germane to her constituents: "I was told by a couple of my male colleagues, 'Well, what does that have to do with you anyway? It's not even in your district,'" she recalls. "The belief that my voice was limited to representing my own constituents is a flaw. It is problematic that my voice as a woman, representing women and young girls who are in vulnerable situations, was quieted because it involved an issue outside of my district. I thought it was very offensive." After some introspection, she decided to continue to raise issues in the public interest, which spurred further clashes in the caucus: "For a while, I felt that I could only speak to things that were related to my constituents. Then I realized that I'm also there to implement policies for the entire population, and I need to advocate on behalf of my own lived experiences. But I was still often reminded it wasn't my place to raise an issue because it wasn't in my district, and so it didn't have to do with me."[43] She believes that party politics being an old boys' club was a contributing factor. In that assembly, some women felt that the safest place to meet with women from other parties was in legislative precinct bathrooms,[44] a location that women ministers have used to exchange information after a federal cabinet meeting.[45]

Pitkin likewise struggles with the many conflicts and dilemmas of representation – constituents are not a monolithic group, for instance – which brings her to question whether democratic representation is a myth that disguises the main act of political parties competing for office.[46] As she would concede, representation does not bundle neatly into archetypes (including those depicted in Table 12.1). The thrust of representation theory is that the ideal legislative assembly is composed of a diversity of people, elected in a fair manner, who put the public interest ahead of self-interest, and are held to account by voters. But in Canada the constraints of party discipline create a representation paradox: the inability of constituents to assess whether their representative is advocating on their behalf behind closed doors can result in perceptions that hard-working exponents are behaving as party representatives. Without the ability to claim credit, there is little or no electoral payoff for causing internal upheaval, whereas compromises might be negotiated if the representative follows orders. A former minister summarizes the quandary:

> A representative needs to have the freedom to tell her constituents, on almost any issue, that I have raised that issue for you. When you join a caucus, and even more so a cabinet, you make a conscious trade-off. You accept a level of scrutiny about what you say publicly in order to have a greater say within caucus or within cabinet. You have the freedom to speak contrary to what your party wants with the result that you might then be excluded from caucus or from cabinet. You always have the freedom; you have to take into account the consequences.[47]

It is up to every parliamentarian to decide what representative role to play, especially those who are with the governing party.

The Peculiar Role of Government-Side Backbenchers

Most government actions do not require authorization by a legislative assembly. People might not understand that the only members of a legislature who are part of the government are those in cabinet. The cabinet answers to the Crown; in turn, the legislative branch holds the cabinet accountable. The government seeks support from the people's elected representatives on broad plans to tax and spend and presents draft legislation for approval.[48] This means that it is up to private members on both sides of the House – not just the opposition – to demand that the cabinet justify its decisions. Here is how some experienced MPs make the distinction:

> I don't think enough people understand that the governing party's caucus is not the government. The government is the cabinet. They're two different things.[49]

> You'll hear a backbencher saying "my government." No, it's not your government. The government is the executive council, the cabinet. We're parliamentarians. We're members of the governing party, but we're not the government. There seems to be increasing linkage between the two. There's a difference.[50]

In the Samara Centre for Democracy's transcripts, one former MP recounts an exchange with a parliamentary secretary who believed that they had to vote together on a standing committee because they were the government. Parliamentary secretaries are rarely part of the cabinet. The MP retorted that they were indeed part of the governing party's caucus – but as private members they were certainly not the government.[51]

Role confusion abounds. The House of Commons standing orders refer to "the government party."[52] Government-side backbenchers are encouraged to refer to "our government" when trumpeting accomplishments.[53] Backbenchers join ministers at policy and funding announcements, sometimes with government novelty cheques in hand.[54] Staff can be complicit in failing to recognize that the separation of the executive and legislative branches: "If they're MPs, they're members of the government," said a staffer in a minister's constituency office when confronted about the problem of Liberal MPs using the government of Canada wordmark logo in their advertising.[55] The media amplify the misunderstanding, such as by referring to the "government's" Indigenous caucus, which implies the government and caucus are synonymous,[56] or publishing op-eds penned by a former deputy prime minister stating that "the caucus is actually part of the government" and that the caucus is "empowered to act on [the] cabinet's executive direction."[57] Such wording nuances reflect a belief that all parliamentarians affiliated with the governing party are part of the cabinet's team.

Backbenchers in the governing party have a peculiar role. Instead of asking critical questions of the cabinet, they might ask planted questions so that the minister can highlight government achievements. They rarely, if ever, critique the government and might avoid associating with opposition members or interest groups that do so. If a member should contradict the cabinet, then a rapid clarification is issued that the member misspoke.[58] Bernard Lord, the former premier of New Brunswick (1999–2006), recognizes that representation is demanding for a governing party's parliamentarians, particularly when faced with supporting unpopular policy decisions:

> Sometimes very practical issues come up, such as closing a hospital in a community where it's part of an overall government plan. As a candidate, the member agreed that the government needed to balance the budget and find efficiencies in health care. That's fine in theory, until in practice they learn it's the hospital in their riding that has to close. They live in that riding. They may have friends and family who work in that hospital. They support the party, but on that issue they weigh a need to represent their community and not represent the government.[59]

The involvement of government-side backbenchers in the late stages of the policy process (see Figure 2.2) requires them to show initiative if they want to represent constituents' interests. Cabinet secrecy means that private members are rarely privy to inside information. In fact, the public service can stonewall them if they pose questions, and inquisitive backbenchers get redirected to political staff in the minister's office who feed them a mixture of messages. The first time that private members see the finer details of government plans is often when information becomes available publicly. Generally speaking, the political system in Ottawa and the provinces encourages complacency and suppresses inquisitiveness.

Some heads of government involve backbenchers in certain cabinet deliberations to compensate for a lack of agency and to guard against caucus

Note: Communications environment terms used in Rathgeber (2014), 178.

insurrection.[60] In some governments, notably that of Prime Minister Paul Martin (2003–06), parliamentary secretaries attend select cabinet meetings. Premiers can invite backbenchers to sit on cabinet committees, even chair them. Allan Blakeney, the former Saskatchewan premier (1971–82), set up caucus committees to review cabinet proposals. The Blakeney cabinet designated decisions either as class A, which all ministers were required to defend in the caucus, or as class B, which ministers could debate freely within the caucus.[61] In Alberta, Premier Ralph Klein (1992–2006) created a system of ministerial caucus advisory committees that the Harper government subsequently used. Ontario Premier Doug Ford (2018–) set up caucus advisory teams to quell backbench unrest.[62] Such configurations earn the respect of the caucus for sharing power. Parliamentarians perceive the consultation mechanisms as a democratic act, such as a former minister who credits Saskatchewan Premier Brad Wall (2007–18) for going "out of his way to ensure there was as little daylight between the legislative arm and the executive as possible."[63] As well, ministers can initiate their own caucus consultation mechanisms. In contrast, public servants fret over an information breach,[64] and academics worry about "executive creep."[65] These are among the many institutional reasons that government-side backbenchers are viewed as cheerleaders in the communications machinery of the government.[66]

Representation in Practice

Canadian parliamentarians practise multiple styles of representation. In *Representation in Action: Canadian MPs in the Constituencies*, political scientists demonstrate that private members exercise free will when abiding by party norms and figuring out ways to represent constituents within the constraints of party discipline.[67] In their electoral districts, MPs are part sentinel, part salesperson. They connect with people through policy discussion, by emphasizing service, by communicating shared values, and by establishing party links. For instance, the authors profile a governing party MP sharing information about policy initiatives at a local town hall. He lavishes praise on the prime minister, the party, and the government. Faced with criticism, he empathizes with constituents and pledges to talk with the applicable minister during the national caucus meeting.[68] Through such observations, the authors conclude that an MP seeks to "inform, persuade and correct" while simultaneously amassing feedback to bring to Ottawa.[69] The study shows that private members represent an astounding array of perspectives and interests that must be reconciled within partisan boundaries.

Amateur YouTube video adds to their research about the paradox of political representation in Canada.[70] In 2012, Conservative MP David Wilks held court with some constituents at a restaurant table in Revelstoke, British Columbia. One of them asked for Wilks's permission to video-record the conversation. The MP agreed, believing in transparency. The video depicts constituents agitated by some policies that the Conservative government is proposing within a 425-page budget omnibus bill. Wilks tries to educate them about how parliamentary government works. He explains the three-line whip system. A level one whip is a free vote. A level two whip occurs when the cabinet supports the bill and the leader has not indicated a preference. Government-side MPs have a choice, though they are urged to side with the cabinet. A level three whip requires backbenchers to vote in solidarity with the frontbenchers under the penalty of severe reprimand. A budget bill is a confidence issue and therefore an obligatory level three vote. If Wilks were to vote "nay," he would become an Independent. His ability to access the spoils of office would vanish; his prospects for re-election would be bleak.

The constituents are astonished. They complain that something is wrong with how parliamentary parties operate. They want to know if their representative thinks that the lack of free votes is a problem for democracy. They speculate that opportunities must exist to discuss matters before the vote is called. Wilks informs them that backbenchers have ten minutes to put questions to the prime minister at national caucus meetings on Wednesday mornings in Ottawa: "It certainly concerns some of us backbenchers that decisions are predominantly made by cabinet, and then they come back to us informing us how this is going to move forward," he says in the video. "Some backbenchers, including myself, will meet with [the finance minister] ... but at the end of the day, in my opinion, they've made up their mind. And this is how it's going to move forward. One person is not going to make a difference, one MP ... If Canadians want it changed, then enough Canadians have to stand up to their MPs and say 'no.'"[71] The constituents try to grasp why a governing party's backbenchers do not receive the budget bill before the media do. They argue that a protest vote by their MP would show that he believes in democracy. Wilks advises them that the budget will proceed unless multiple Conservative backbenchers break ranks.

When the video appeared on YouTube, the news media began filing stories about dissent in the governing party's caucus. The whip's office phoned to instruct Wilks to go home immediately, stay off the telephone, and not talk to the press. He was told to skip a funding announcement that afternoon in his riding. Next the chief of staff called. Wilks would have to apologize, say that the remarks were taken out of context, and publicly endorse the budget. He agreed, as most backbenchers would.

The next morning a statement appeared on the MP's website affirming his support for the budget.[72] At a local Chamber of Commerce meeting, Wilks repeated that he would vote for the bill but complained that "Ottawa is run by a ton of 20-something bureaucrats who know that in three years my term is up and they will still be there."[73] On returning to Ottawa, he reported to the whip's office, where the whip asked that they talk through the episode. The MP clarified that he was merely trying to enlighten constituents about why it is pointless for a governing party backbencher to vote against the budget. Although he did not escape punishment, he received the benefit of the doubt in part because he had built a reservoir of goodwill with the whip's office for substituting on standing committees at a moment's notice.

The video was fodder for the commentariat, including CBC TV's "At Issue" panel on *The National*. Host Peter Mansbridge was among those who found Wilks's comments refreshing: "It's not the kind of phony stuff we see there in Question Period or outside of Question Period, at the microphones," Mansbridge said to the panel. "This is a real guy trying to deal with a problem that his constituents, his voters have, [and he is] trying to answer it."[74] Opposition MPs kept the controversy alive by mentioning the video during Question Period and in their members' statements. Protesters chanted some of Wilks's remarks outside Conservative constituency offices as a pressure tactic to urge Conservative backbenchers to vote against the budget. During a late sitting of the House of Commons, Prime Minister Harper called Wilks aside. They sat at a back table in the lobby for a few minutes. The MP retold what he was attempting with the constituents and assured the prime minister that he would vote for the budget. Harper nodded and said that he understood what the MP was trying to do. Eventually, Wilks voted "aye" on the budget bill. The whip shuffled him from a committee that he enjoyed to one in which he had little interest. Gradually, he worked his way onto two committees that he liked.

Two years after the episode, Wilks opened up on Facebook about his indignation with message discipline.[75] He expressed abhorrence that MPs cannot be forthright. Whereas candour is respected in municipal politics, he saw how honesty in federal politics can cause offence and turn into a news story. He went on to lose his Kootenay–Columbia seat by a margin of less than half of 1 percent. Reflecting on his time as a Member of Parliament, Wilks believes that power hierarchies dismiss the life experiences of private members: "The biggest concern I have about federal politics is that, if you're a backbencher, you're there for one thing, and that's to vote," he says. "You can get the odd thing done. I did get some things in the budget for my riding. But I don't like being treated like a schoolchild who just does what the teacher tells you to do. Sometimes you have to respectfully speak your discourse. You may not like what I have to say, but you should at least respect it."[76]

Whether persuading constituents of the government's position, or pressing caucus colleagues to take action on an issue, government-side members face special pressures of representation. The story of David Wilks is one component of how message cohesion surfaces. Another is what happens behind closed doors in caucus meetings. Two divergent post-austerity cases show that a governing party's caucus can be powerful when it is united and weak when it is deadlocked.

In the first case, lobbyists pressed the federal government for a share of public funds after dramatic cost cutting in the mid-1990s. Representatives of the medical research community communicated with public office holders and sought meetings with them. At a late-summer caucus meeting in 1997, a number of Liberal MPs remarked on the importance of the government of Canada funding research, and support galvanized at a caucus meeting in the new year. The 1998 federal budget ended up allocating considerable funds to the Medical Research Council. A member of that caucus recalls that the lobbying of backbenchers was successful because it occurred on an individual level:

Each year two of the most important caucus meetings happen in August and January before the House comes back. In August, there is an intense discussion about what goes into the budget, and in January it is a last-minute opportunity to get a word in. One year at both those meetings, funding for medical research was raised by a large number of MPs. Lobbying had a big impact because constituents who were involved with medical research or affected by it met personally with their own MPs. A good lobbying effort also communicates with MPs on all sides of the House. That way, if the government doesn't act, the opposition is more likely to challenge the government on the issue.[77]

The second case shows how a head of government who exerts primacy on budget priorities can jolt backbenchers. A former Alberta MLA recalls how Premier Klein convened a special day-long meeting of the caucus in 2005 to discuss an unexpected budget surplus.[78] The caucus spent the morning deliberating how to carve up the funds. The premier's desire to provide money to taxpayers was contentious. They failed to reach a consensus and broke for lunch. While the MLAs were lining up in a cafeteria, and as they continued to mull over policy options, they overheard Klein announcing his unaltered populist plans to the media: Alberta's tax filers would receive four-hundred-dollar cheques, tax free. Unlike the Medical Research Council case, which suggests that a government-side member has clout when there is caucus unity, the "Ralph bucks" and Revelstoke video incidents point to the futility of representation in Canada when there is real or implied caucus division.

ROLES OF PRIVATE MEMBERS

In *How to Be an MP*, then Labour MP Paul Flynn offers tongue-in-cheek tips for surviving the British House of Commons and handling constituency work. Private members are encouraged to pick from dozens of roles. They can become a constituency evangelist, or perhaps they would like to be a procedural buff. Communications roles are available for mantra chanters who repeat slogans, for robots who read scripts, and for media tarts who like to be quoted in news stories. There are sleaze busters, committee loyalists, single-issue eccentrics, comedians, international statespersons, and people who are a thorn in the party's flesh. MPs who fancy themselves as lawmakers have the most distinguished work: "Legislators are the aristocrats of backbenchers," Flynn suggests.[79]

In both the UK and Canada, backbenchers trying to figure out their role in the parliamentary system is a consequence of strict party discipline. Prime Minister Pierre Trudeau (1968–79, 1980–84) could be callous about the role of the opposition, as heads of government are inclined to be. In one exchange in the House of Commons in 1969, he taunted: "I think we should encourage members of the opposition to leave. Every time they do, the IQ of this House rises considerably."[80] Then he lobbed an infamous quip: "When they get home, when they get out of Parliament, when they are 50 yards from Parliament Hill, they are no longer hon. members – they are just nobodies, Mr. Speaker."[81] Some backbenchers believe that they are nobodies outside the caucus room; others believe that they are nobodies in the capital city but somebodies in their constituencies.[82] The chair of the 1985 Special Committee on Reform of the House of Commons had this to say about the aphorism:

> Mr. Trudeau made that comment about Members of Parliament when they get 50 yards from here, they're nobodies. The fact of the matter is the reverse is true. Members of Parliament are somebodies when they're out there in their constituencies. It's here in Ottawa that they're nobodies. They have no clout, no power. They've lost the power to hold up supply in the House, they have no control over government spending anymore, they have little if any influence in the legislative process.[83]

Ultimately, Trudeau thought that it is up to governing party backbenchers to establish what their roles ought to be: "I think that there's a double role. It's because the conflict between them hasn't yet been resolved by the MPs themselves that there's perhaps a bit of confusion," he once said. "Is he mainly a legislator, or is he something less and more than a legislator? Is he what I call that link between the executive, or the administration, and the people?"[84] The nobodies remark resonates for a reason. Half a century later, obscurity also applies to some ministers given that many Canadians are unfamiliar with them as well.[85]

The importance that parliamentarians attach to their varied roles fluctuates depending on their circumstances, including the stages of their political careers.[86] New parliamentarians are thrust into a job unlike anything that they have experienced. According to one former MP, the role requires them to "combine the research techniques of a graduate student, the tact of a diplomat, the compassion of a social worker and the organizational skills of a CEO in a medium-sized business."[87] By the time that they are sworn in, their political beliefs have been tested by interacting with voters, and they know to stick to party messaging. At their first caucus meeting, they are exposed to a boisterous group of people from assorted backgrounds, industries, communities, and cultures. People whom they would never interact with are now their colleagues: "Sitting there the first thing I understood is we come from all different places, towns, cities," reflects a former Bloc Québécois MP. "We are very different, but we have to all come together. That's what makes representation important."[88] They learn about regional identities and diverse perspectives and thereby gain a better sense of citizenship.

It can take years to comprehend parliamentary processes. Even if a determined parliamentarian were to learn off the standing orders, there is a sizable history of Speakers' rulings, as well as practices and customs, the sum of which makes it rare for an elected official to become a procedural wizard. Some private members complete their parliamentary careers having never understood the system, let alone mastered it: "No manual is given to you when you're first elected saying here's how things work. You've mostly got to figure it out for yourself," relays a former MP.[89] A couple of sitting MPs go further about the lack of training:

> There is no rigorous conversation with candidates about what it will be like to be a Member of Parliament. People are surprised about the tremendous pressures on family life. They don't really understand the daily work of an MP. There is a little bit of a vested interest in withholding that information so you can attract people to run. Also, the executive branch likes to keep power, so they don't really want backbench MPs to understand their role.[90]

> You spend the first two to three years trying to locate the bathrooms. Because Parliament operates under largely unwritten conventions, it is

an enormous task to get up to speed as a new MP on how the place operates. There is a compendium of procedure and practice for the House of Commons, but it's a massive bible that takes a while to get through, and there's no easy way to navigate your way through the House itself. Most new members just try to find their legs.[91]

When the House is sitting, a typical workday for an active MP on Parliament Hill leaves little time to examine bills and motions, let alone read up on the finer details of procedure and practice (see Figure 2.3). No two days are alike, though there are routines. One day, a backbencher meets with interest group representatives, attends a parliamentary committee and Question Period, and serves on House duty for an emergency debate late into the evening.[92] Another day might bring caucus consultations, a meeting with representatives from the MP's electoral district, an evening reception, and an all-party caucus meeting. Wednesdays feature the national caucus meeting; on Fridays, many MPs have left Ottawa to engage in their constituencies. Whatever is on their schedule, a commonality is that the lack of job clarity exacerbates the struggles of private members to perform critical tasks. Conflict over how to advocate on behalf

FIGURE 2.3
Example of government-side backbench MP's Ottawa workday

Pre-8:30 a.m.	Check social media, email, and news headlines Review news digests and message lines from caucus research bureau
8:30 a.m.	Engage with office staff
8:45 a.m.	Attend to correspondence and review committee materials
9:30 a.m.	Meeting with college president and dean from electoral district
10:20 a.m.	Meeting with life insurance industry group
11:00 a.m.	Meeting of the Standing Committee on Finance
1:15 p.m.	Lunch in parliamentary cafeteria
2:00 p.m.	Members' statements
2:15 p.m.	Question Period
3:00 p.m.	Routine proceedings (e.g., introduction of bills, committee reports) Government orders (e.g., business of supply, government bills) Private members' business
6:30 p.m.	Dinner with organization providing mental health support for veterans
7:30 p.m.	Reception hosted by international humanitarian aid organization

Sources: Adapted from Calis (2016); Pessian (2016).

of constituents leads to interpersonal tensions, missed work, and media coverage that is superficial or confused.[93] Furthermore, a disciplinary ethos means that work in the legislature is becoming less and less of a private member's primary function.

Lawmakers

Traditionally, the work of a private member has revolved around contributing to legislation, attending to constituents' problems, and holding the executive accountable.[94] A 1960s study of Canadian private members found that a majority of them self-identified as lawmakers who influenced legislation.[95] Today few incentives exist to prioritize legislative activity. News coverage of parliamentary business has declined, and a host of changes has eroded parliamentary autonomy. The process outlined earlier in Figure 2.2 causes the tabling of a bill to arrive as a baked cake requiring no further ingredients; the only thing missing is the icing to make it look appealing.[96]

Two documentaries filmed decades apart profile the moribund role of parliamentary lawmakers in Canada. In 1971, the CBC televised *The Noblest of Callings ... the Vilest of Trades,* a journalistic study of the roles of backbenchers during Pierre Trudeau's first ministry. It opens with a government-side MP confessing futility: "I might tell you that, since I've been elected, for at least two years I've felt useless for the first time in my life," the MP says.[97] In a parliamentary office, a group of Liberal backbenchers strategize in preparation for the national caucus meeting. They are angry about an unspecified government policy. They deliberate the pointlessness of vocalizing their concerns at the meeting because the prime minister will agree to look into the matter or strike a caucus committee – and then nothing will happen. One of the MPs recommends that they lobby ministers directly:

> You confront the prime minister in front of all his ministers. But I think you've gotta hit the regional caucuses. You've got to pinhole the ministers individually. I think we've got to decide that we're going to make appointments to see the ministers after this is done, after we've put the problem in the lap of the prime minister in front of the whole caucus. Then you've gotta go after each minister.[98]

Another MP complains that governing party backbenchers' law-making functions eroded as the public service expanded and professionalized and as the leader became more dominant: "Members do not make legislation now," the MP says. "They put their rubber stamp on legislation that has been drafted by the civil servants and approved by the cabinet. So the role of legislator has basically gone."[99]

The scene of the 1971 documentary turns to a former mayor of Toronto who is downcast about his insignificance as a governing party MP: "As backbenchers, nobody even asks us for the correct time," he declares. The MP had grand visions of playing an important role in policy decisions and delivering captivating speeches. Yet only a corporal's guard was present in the House of Commons to listen to his oratory. MPs busily signed correspondence or read publications while he spoke. He also learned that the executive was uninterested in backbenchers giving policy talks: "Officialdom views you with suspicion when you come up with new ideas. The general concept is you're supposed to behave yourself," he says.[100] Another MP remarks that public servants are unconcerned when they receive a letter from a governing party member because they know that the writer is unlikely to embarrass the government. Conversely, they treat with urgency a letter from a member of the opposition.

A second documentary produced decades later exposes provincial lawmakers' displeasure with party discipline. In *Whipped: The Secret World of Party Discipline,* journalist Sean Holman probes why Members of the Legislative Assembly vote the party line in British Columbia. The 2013 film profiles former MLAs who despaired about voting against their beliefs. They recall how colleagues do not oppose the party line because doing so would jeopardize the possibility of a cabinet appointment; that draft legislation is provided without enough time to read it; that there is more genuine debate in municipal politics; and that it takes courage to say "no" to the leadership. One member recounts how, in an interview with a local newspaper, he called a government decision stupid. Multiple ministers telephoned him to chastise him for implying that the premier was stupid. Then they gave him the silent treatment.

The frustrations of the BC MLAs and their 1970s Ottawa counterparts are striking. Over and over, parliamentarians have been saying that the system needs to give backbenchers a greater role in policy making. Caucuses have more diverse memberships today and can make their opinions known on social media, yet they seem to follow a common message track more than ever before. The work of a backbencher now centres on providing assistance to constituents and participating in party-initiated public relations (PR) activities. Their ineffectiveness in the House makes their role as a legislator seem like a lost cause that interferes with other obligations: "When the House is sitting, I have 30 hours of wasted time every week, if you include Question Period, which I do. I have to squeeze in everything else around this parliamentary stuff," says a parliamentary secretary.[101]

Constituency Caseworkers

Some private members are less interested in law making or parliamentary procedure. They believe that constituency work is key to their re-election prospects.[102] Some of them are therefore content to serve the needs of their electoral districts without the burden of further responsibility and make room for local demands by reducing the time spent in the legislative precinct.[103] Gradually they become more knowledgeable about policies than many of their constituents.[104] Improving a voter's life circumstances is more satisfying than the abstractness of voting the party line on an obscure bill or reading a speech prepared by a staffer. As one former politician puts it, "you say yes, over and over, until one day you realize casework is all you're doing."[105]

As government has expanded, parliamentarians have evolved into caseworkers who are likened to liaison officers, intermediaries, ombudspersons, and advocates.[106] Their expanding role as assistants and advocates is reflected in growing offices. In the 1950s, many MPs remained in Ottawa for months at a time because they did not have budgets to travel home.[107] Some of those who operated constituency offices from their homes relied on their spouses for help.[108] Parliament Hill office suites housed two MPs, one telephone line, and one secretary.[109] The members took messages for each other and tapped on a colleague's door to use another phone. The secretary and/or the other MP would go for a walk when visitors arrived for a private meeting with the officemate.

The joint offices became crowded when private members were assigned individual secretaries in the 1960s. Full-time constituency offices followed in the mid-1970s. By 1976, each MP had one secretary stationed in the constituency and three staff in Ottawa.[110] Gradually, policy analysis replaced secretarial support, and each MP had one or two researchers by the 1980s.[111] Rural members honed a particularly well-deserved reputation for attending to constituency service.[112] Today a Member of Parliament employs four to six assistants, most of them in the constituency.[113] During parliamentary recesses, some MPs redeploy their Ottawa staff to their constituency office(s) to deal with the heavy caseload and volume of enquiries. Many of those offices have become unofficial government service centres that receive walk-in traffic.

Constituency staff assist with resolving an assortment of problems. Queries fall outside system processes, such as helping to get a constituent's family member into an emergency shelter, locating a lost bus pass, or fixing an error on government paperwork. People have novel questions for even the most experienced staff. A former minister is emphatic about the importance of constituency personnel: "Constituency assistants perform absolute yeoman service. They are brilliant at managing day-to-day issues, and they occasionally fill in at meetings or ceremonial events," he says. "They deflect difficult issues, they act as a buffer, and they help manage your time. They are incredibly important, absolutely invaluable, and a critical part of the whole apparatus that sometimes gets overlooked."[114] As we will see, constituency staff working for a Liberal MP can store information in a central database that familiarizes users with a constituent's case history. They integrate approved talking points into correspondence by accessing a central party database of stock phrases that guide speedy replies to enquiries.

Publicizing the member's local engagement is a flourishing aspect of constituency work, especially in light of the need to generate visual content for social media. A constituency assistant might accompany a parliamentarian to a local event to take photographs and record video. For many, drafting newsletters has shifted to filling in templates with collages of local photographs. As well, MPs often designate assistants as social media liaisons to manage online interactions and process requests to post information.

Looking at an MP's social media activity, a constituent might think that the representative is in the constituency, when in fact staff are the ones posting content.[115] The digital publicist function of constituency assistants reflects a side of representation that is growing.

Brand Ambassadors

Political scientists lump legislators' work into the categories of lawmaker and constituency caseworker, with recognition that representation straddles both worlds.[116] The conventional dichotomy warrants a rethink in light of the party leadership's treatment of parliamentarians as messengers and public perceptions of them as brand ambassadors.

The Samara Centre suggests that Canada's parliamentary parties are experiencing "disintermediation."[117] That is a business term for rendering intermediaries obsolete when suppliers can connect directly with buyers. The think tank suggests that the role of backbenchers is diminishing to the point of obsolescence, hurried along by digital communications that enable parties to bypass go-betweens. The proposition predates the internet. In 1969, the federal Liberals held a weekend caucus meeting to discuss the role of governing party backbenchers. The opening address drew a parallel with automation.[118] Parliamentarians were said to no longer be important people in the eyes of the community because formalized government processes intercepted their traditional function of dispensing jobs and patronage. The resulting efficiencies freed up time for backbenchers to specialize in other areas where their interventions were necessary. From the perspective of the party leadership, that ancillary work involved spreading key messages.

Samara research views parliamentarians as entering into a contractual relationship that renders them party franchisees.[119] R.K. Carty, the Canadian political scientist who initiated the franchise analogy, sees it as an institutional manifestation of mutual autonomy.[120] Franchises are networks of individuals who work under the same brand umbrella. A franchisor licenses a business name and an operating structure in exchange for a fee and royalty payments. Franchisees benefit from a proven business model with brand recognition, professional support, and a customer base. They are subject to the strict contractual terms of their franchising agreement. They sacrifice some autonomy to respond to local markets in deference to a consistent look and customer experience. Corporate office executives are the ones who make policy and operational decisions, ranging from advertising campaigns to supplier agreements. Input from franchisees is considered along with sales figures, market research, and competitive analysis. The franchisor-franchisee relationship is characterized by the view that Canadian parliamentarians are expected to help their party. In return, they receive their party's help.[121]

Party franchising offers efficiency, longevity, reliability, and standardization, including communications consistency.[122] It provides elasticity to accommodate linguistic and regional differences. Although there is no standard set of relationships in a franchisor-franchisee network – that is, one electoral district association can have different interactions with the party centre than another – a commonality is limited opportunity for political franchisees to develop their own personal brands within the party brand. Parliamentarians cognizant of their place in a larger political operation rationalize the benefits of being faithful to the franchise bargain. A veteran MP puts it in layperson terms:

> We've seen how leader-centric the party brand has become. And when you're running under that banner, you have accept that the leadership is going to be the one making some of these calls. Sometimes you have to stay with the party and be prepared to defend some of the things that is going to entail, if you want the benefit of running under that brand.[123]

The fusion of all aspects of the party into a cohesive unit results in an assumption that any officeholder, as well as staff and volunteers toiling in backrooms, is a representative of the party brand including the leader. The public perception of government-side backbenchers as government functionaries means that anything they say can be interpreted as government policy. Even a lone actor who manages an electoral district association's social media can compel a party to urgently practise brand management.[124] The transition to representing the party brand is gradual, explains Jane Philpott, the Liberal minister who became an Independent MP: "Message discipline is somewhat communicated by osmosis and happenstance," Philpott says. "From the start of the candidate process, you hear a lot about the benefits of being on the same page, being part of a team, and that we stand or fall together. There is a huge emphasis on what is good about unity and staying on-message. Then an enormous flow of messaging occurs during the candidate process and gets more intense as an MP."[125] Politicians cannot turn off their role as brand ambassadors. Every public interaction is susceptible to online documentation. The party becomes part of their lifestyles and their public personas.

The trend of parliamentarians who behave as party franchisees conflicts with the view that they should be freethinkers who prioritize their constituencies over party interests and who should influence public policy.[126] The situation gives rise to what Pitkin calls a "mandate-independence controversy" in which members have a mandate to promote their party's agenda yet need space to behave as independent actors.[127] A veteran MP chimes in: "People are not trained seals. At some place along the policy highway, they express their opinions, and they cannot be knowledgeable on every subject out there," he says. "But being a brand ambassador can cut into critical thinking and genuine debate on issues. You need to be able to constructively criticize the position of your party or the government."[128]

Every so often a legislator goes public with a complaint about treatment as an agent of the party apparatus. Resentful of message micromanagement, Robyn Luff, a government-side NDP backbencher in Alberta, alleged that scripting is a symptom of a workplace of hyper-partisanship, bullying, fear, and intimidation. In a 2018 open letter on Facebook (see Figure 2.4), she contended that the leadership decides which backbenchers can speak in that province's legislature. She alleged that debate on proposed legislation is superficial, members' statements are vetted, private members' bills are edited, messaging is provided for Question Period and committee meetings, and parliamentarians are told how to vote. The premier expelled Luff from the caucus within hours of the public complaints.

The newly Independent MLA released a second letter.[129] In it, she relayed that governing party backbenchers are constantly encouraged to share government messaging on social media. They are asked not to talk publicly about certain issues of concern to their constituents. The caucus, Luff alleged, was advised not to publicize information about opposition members who behaved inappropriately so as not to draw attention to their own members' suspect behaviour. The party's MLAs were instructed not to talk to the media about, or communicate with, a member who crossed the floor. Nor were they permitted to be photographed with the federal

FIGURE 2.4
Open letter from a government-side backbench MLA

FOR IMMEDIATE RELEASE

Under the premier's leadership, every power that Members of the Legislative Assembly (MLAs) are supposed to have to be able to represent their constituents in the legislature has been taken away or denied from the start. MLAs must vote at the direction of the leader at all times. Questions from private members are written by ministries and given to them to ask. If a member's statement is deemed to be "inappropriate" then that MLA will lose the privilege to make a statement. Decisions about who speaks in the House and to what bill are all made ahead of time by party leadership. Statements and questions at committee are all highly scripted and agreed upon ahead of time. If MLAs should choose to go against any of these directives, there is a fear that they will lose privileges, such as their seat on a committee or opportunity to speak in the House. There is also a fear that they will be isolated, and that their political career will be finished, that their nomination papers will not be signed and opportunities never given. This has the effect that only two voices are ever heard in the legislature: that of the approved official government party message, and that of the official approved opposition party message. It leads to hyper partisan rhetoric, and to no actual debate on bills. Everything that happens in the House is predetermined, rendering everything that happens there to nothing more than a vehicle for scoring partisan points. It makes a mockery of the proceedings. This is a mockery of representation and a tragedy of democracy. Regularly when ministers and MLAs come into the House to vote they will say: "What are we voting for? Are we for or against this?" They have no idea what we've been talking about in the House – all they need to know is what they are being told to do. Too often I hear from constituents that all politicians are the same, that they don't listen, and that they're all corrupt – that voting won't make any difference. I believe that an MLA's role is to refute this opinion, to be the voice for their constituents, to represent the people to the best of their ability. However, because of the toxic culture that exists, I don't believe that citizens are being represented properly. When I have attempted to bring this up with caucus officers, with the premier's chiefs of staff, and with the premier herself, these concerns have been dismissed as not being a priority. I have had member's statements taken away, and my private member's bills edited until they weren't what I intended. I have had to fight for months for the ability to ask my own question in Question Period, and have been questionably removed from a committee. I have been told by a cabinet minister that my career was sidelined for not jumping when a chief of staff told me to and that the interaction was used as an example of what not to do as an MLA. ... This is a conversation that needs to be had publicly, with all citizens.

Source: Luff (2018); lightly edited.

NDP leader because of a federal-provincial policy dispute. Party incumbents not seeking re-election were struck from the list of people eligible to deliver members' statements. Luff did not seek re-election.

A year later long-time Conservative MP Scott Reid expressed similar complaints in his own open letter about the stifling constraints of party discipline in Ottawa. He wrote on his website:

> Leaders habitually make decisions on behalf of their caucus without full consultation. Votes are virtually never taken in caucus. Rules of order are non-existent. The leader decides what will be done by "reading the room" – when he or she can be bothered – and any person who complains out loud about the abuse of process is ruthlessly punished for breaking caucus confidence ... [The role of an MP is] like a Victorian child, to be seen and not heard, except when they are reading a speech prepared for them by a staffer from the PMO or the leader's office.[130]

These sorts of accusations are a backbencher's refrain about a parliamentary system that has lost its way in a digital world. Luff is resolute when invited to elaborate. She makes a strong case that the role of a governing party's backbencher as a brand ambassador leaves little room for participating in public policy development: "When you get into the nitty-gritty of being a backbencher, very little of what you do is policy. It's pretty much all sales," she says. "We were told multiple times that good casework doesn't win elections. The leader makes a decision. It's your job to go tell your constituents that's what's good for them and then try to raise money and sell more party memberships. It's more partisan and more sales than I ever wanted it to be."[131]

The theatre of the absurd extends to performers in stage-managed political events. Ryan Cleary, a three-time NDP candidate and one-time MP from Newfoundland, makes the following comments: "The moments I absolutely hated most were serving, along with other MPs, as a backdrop when the leader was giving a public statement," he reflects. "Standing behind the leader, you could watch him reading the teleprompter, know exactly what he was going to say, and still have to jump to your feet and give a standing ovation at every second sentence."[132] At an extreme, staff in the leader's office can be so obsessed with staging that they monitor backbenchers who do not rise on cue to deliver a standing ovation for a front-bencher during Question Period.[133] Some of these political actors jockey for the best spot behind a leader and clap without direction, particularly those auditioning for a better part. They might not realize that they are being treated as props to inhibit them from saying something that compels damage control. A former leader's office staffer observes that some private members do not accept that they are poor public communicators:

In communications, a lot of your time is spent with people in caucus who are unhappy, not with the top twenty-five performers but with the bottom twenty-five. They want more responsibility but can't do it. You have to be polite because they are elected. Some people have minimum skills. They should never talk in front of a camera. You cannot tell them that because everyone thinks they are very important and they're very good.[134]

Building a personal brand within a franchise system comes with constraints. Celina Caesar-Chavannes is a case in point of how diversity and a keyboard can change political debate. Between 2015 and 2019, the Liberal MP expressed her opinion on sensitive topics irrespective of the Liberal government's priorities. Initially her parliamentary career involved the same role familiarization that all beginners experience, albeit as a parliamentary secretary. She nurtured an engaging social media presence, such as by posting cooking videos and makeup tutorials. As more Canadians followed her online, Caesar-Chavannes developed the mettle to raise issues and develop her persona. As she explained while an MP,

I am a unique individual in Parliament. Being one chocolate-coloured woman out of 338 people, I have spoken from the perspective of a woman of colour about things that people really didn't talk about before, such as the taboo of speaking about mental health in our community or justice and equity issues. There is an added element of shifting social and cultural community conversations. Once I found that lane, and began to build my brand around calling things out, Canadians started following that brand.[135]

One of her first encounters with PMO message discipline was when she posted a screenshot on Twitter showing that all members of a Canadian board dedicated to promoting diversity were Caucasians. Within fifteen minutes, a PMO staffer phoned to direct her to take down the post. She complied. As she became more willing to challenge societal norms, and as her posts went viral, Caesar-Chavannes became a polarizing figure.[136] She talked about experiencing micro-aggressions on Parliament Hill and about systemic racism. She gained confidence to ignore central messaging and avoided the whip's wrath by voting with the party 99 percent of the time (dissenting on 6 of 929 recorded divisions). The PMO backed off its attempts to micromanage her. However, she encountered the same predicament that many non-conformists face: when a parliamentarian ventures outside approved messaging and attracts public attention on unsanctioned topics, partisans shut that person out: "Party discipline exists in terms of 'here's the script, here's what you say, here is how you vote on a piece of legislation,' et cetera," Caesar-Chavannes says. "Do you need to do that all the time? Yes, if you want to stay in good favour. Is it necessary to stick to the script? Absolutely not. I rarely stayed completely on-message. But unless you are strong enough within the party, and have your own brand, it pushes you out to the periphery."[137]

Her online engagement became a distraction for the Liberal government that professed many of the same political values. She believes that the PMO wanted to distance itself from her rhetoric on racism and intersectional feminism. In particular, inflammatory exchanges with Conservative MP Maxime Bernier about multiculturalism, (white male) privilege, identity politics, and free speech reverberated for weeks online and attracted national media attention.[138] The number of social media followers climbed for Caesar-Chavannes; however, the venom of social media trolls took its toll. She grew frustrated when the PMO and the extraparliamentary party reached out to support a fellow Liberal MP who experienced online hatred but left Caesar-Chavannes to fend for herself. After defying his party's message parameters, Bernier was shuffled out of the Conservative shadow cabinet, and in August 2018 he left the caucus before its members could vote him out. Four days later Caesar-Chavannes resigned as a parliamentary secretary. She went on to sit as an Independent and did not seek re-election. Bernier founded the People's Party of Canada but was the target of a ruthless online campaign to brand him as a racist that the Conservative Party appears to have sponsored.[139] The veteran MP was not re-elected.

Both of these provocative MPs behaved as trustees willing to engage in philosophical deliberation on topics that were not necessarily priorities to voters in their electoral districts or their parties. By challenging public policy, they delivered substantive representation that appealed to philosophically incompatible constituencies across the country. They were also on opposite sides of formalistic representation and especially descriptive representation. Their experiences exemplify that, regardless of representational style, in Canada there are political consequences when a parliamentarian's public discourse strays from the party line.

SUMMARY

In Canada, discipline begins the moment that someone expresses interest in seeking a local nomination to represent a political party in an election. Aspiring candidates enter a franchisee-franchisor relationship that involves signing a values contract to affirm a quasi-legal commitment to the party's political principles as outlined in its constitution. Thinking about styles of representation invites a reductionist conclusion that voting on bills and motions is the main work of a backbencher. It is not, and most Canadian parliamentarians are not free agents. Gradually, attending to constituent service has supplanted a direct hand in designing public policy, and newer duties include promoting central messaging on social media. Projecting a united public image requires group buy-in, the topic of Chapter 3.

3

Partisan Teams

In this chapter, I discuss social, psychological, and institutional forces that underpin why Canadian parliamentarians accept party discipline. I show how easily most humans defer to authority and how social structures bind partisans, nudged along by the leadership's repeated calls for everyone to be a team. How do party leaders promote cohesion? Why do elected representatives obey the commands of the leader's staff? What role do party whips play in fostering a team culture? A predisposition to conformity eases partisans into following the crowd and is a precursor for embracing party messages.

GROUP PSYCHOLOGY

Organizational hierarchies are found throughout society. From families to motorcycle gangs, amateur hobby clubs to the army, group members assume diverse roles. Solidarity is fostered through structures that encourage cohesiveness and endure when any one individual leaves the group.[1] Whether in small associations with few rules, or in large bureaucratic systems, members with a common identity who share a sense of belonging are more likely to stick together. Cohesion is natural when people share social attachments and common objectives.

Trust is a key component of solidarity. Relying on other members of a group is imperative when a lot is at stake, such as during a military operation or in a hospital operating room. Trustworthiness is a vote of confidence in the group. It spurs cooperation. Those who are cautious about dispensing trust can work well with others; however, it is when unconditional trust is attained that relationships flourish into friendships and groups transform into teams.[2]

Classic social psychology research has examined the effects of groups on individual behaviour. In the early 1950s, Solomon Asch conducted a seminal experiment on group conformity.[3] Groups of students were presented with three lines of different lengths. All but one of the participants were in on the ploy: to insist that an obviously shorter line was the longest line. Asch sought to study the effect of false information proffered by the majority on the judgment of the lone innocent participant. That participant sided with the rest of the group's blatantly erroneous claims in a third of the cases. When the experiment was repeated multiple times, a quarter of the innocent participants never succumbed to group pressure, but the rest conceded at least once. The test established that some people are impervious to group pressure, whereas many are susceptible to believing a clearly false proposition. The power of suggestion and persuasion evidently enables people and circumstances to influence others.[4]

Another social experiment around this time has obvious connections with reward structures in parliamentary groups. Herbert Kelman found that small groups of people are more susceptible to opinion conformity when only some of them are guaranteed a reward for conformity and when they have some flexibility to deviate.[5] Somewhat counterintuitively, conformity in such low-restriction circumstances is greater than in high-restriction conditions when everyone is promised a reward as long as they agree with a stated position. Kelman reasoned that competition for finite rewards motivates members of a group to express more enthusiastic support as they try to outdo their peers. As well, people who are undecided have a reason to fall in line. Finally, the experiment showed that top-down pressure can provoke dissonance because people value free will.

A decade later Stanley Milgram set up a famous ruse in which participants followed commands from a scientist in a lab coat instructing them to administer what they believed to be increasingly painful shocks to a victim, to the point of danger.[6] Whenever they expressed concern about the victim's well-being, the scientist replied that the experiment required them to continue. The majority of participants complied with the instructions. Their sense of obligation to follow orders enabled them to overcome personal anguish as they subjected someone to potentially deadly punishment.

Milgram showed that people go against their moral tenets when an authority figure says that they must do so. Responsibility for personal actions is redirected to the person in charge.

The Stanford University prison experiment further examined group power dynamics.[7] In 1971, researchers renovated the basement of a university building to simulate a penitentiary. They randomly divided student recruits into role-playing as prison guards or inmates. Guards were equipped with wooden batons and authorized to impose sanctions arbitrarily. The prisoners were assigned uniforms with identification numbers. From the outset, they were subjected to degradation, oppression, and depersonalization. During their mock incarceration, the prisoners became more passive in response to the commanding style of the guards.

The Stanford "guards" repeatedly assembled the "prisoners" to conduct head counts that chipped away at individualism. Prisoners who disobeyed rules or conveyed disrespect were required to do push-ups, which became a more upsetting form of punishment as the experiment endured. A rebellion broke out. The guards summoned reinforcements, applied more punishments, sequestered the ringleaders in solitary confinement, and granted special privileges. Some of the congenial prisoners were dispersed with members of the rest of the rebellion. Prisoner solidarity eroded as suspicions arose about possible informers roaming among them. The prisoners themselves were now carrying out behavioural enforcement. A newly introduced prisoner, appalled at the guards' treatment of inmates, went on a hunger strike in protest. Rather than support the protest, most of the prisoners dismissed the newbie as a troublemaker. Meanwhile, the guards formed trusting relationships as they united against an unruly common foe.

Individual identities eroded as time passed. When a prisoner fell ill with emotional distress, the guards had the rest chant in unison that he was a bad prisoner, prompting the ailing man to want to return to prove his mettle. Guards behaved as rule keepers, softies, or disciplinarians (some as sadists). They flaunted control over underlings whom they conditioned into subservience by turning necessities, such as bathroom breaks, into privileges that could be withheld: "Power can be a great pleasure," reflected a guard when the researchers called off the experiment after six days.[8] Stripping away individualism, role-playing, dispensing privileges to reward desired behaviour, treating non-conformists as troublemakers – as we shall see, these actions exist in a partisan environment of authority and compliance.

Human behaviour transforms in group settings even in the absence of uniformed authority figures. The 1957 film *12 Angry Men* depicts sequestered jurists who deliberate the fate of an accused murderer. The movie dramatizes groupthink, peer pressure, deference, prejudice, and standards of reason. A lone holdout seeks to persuade fellow jurors to question whether the state proved its case. The jurors who want to get on with their lives consider the contrarian a nuisance for interfering. As the contrarian stirs up reasonable doubt, the jurors stress over the execution of the accused if they render a guilty verdict, and one by one they swing to acquittal. The scenario depicts that group tensions escalate in deliberations when the stakes are high.[9] The corollary is that group members are more willing to acquiesce to others when they perceive that the stakes are low. Building consensus begins with discussion, then gets some doubters onside, followed by more discussion that convinces a critical mass, until holdouts surrender to pressure to overcome their internalized belief systems.

Sometimes pressures for conformity lead to inconsistency between a person's beliefs and behaviours. This is known as cognitive dissonance. Landmark research in the 1950s by American social psychologist Leon Festinger argued that humans dislike this uncomfortable mental state. To alleviate their anguish, people will take action to reconcile the cognitive dissonance or avoid exposure to stimuli that aggravate it. If they do something that goes against their private opinions, then they are likely to adjust those opinions to align with what they did, thereby achieving cognitive harmony.[10] Festinger showed that exposure to social communication causes people to reconcile their private beliefs with those of their reference groups. If, by virtue of being part of a group they publicly support something that they privately oppose, they rationalize their behaviour to achieve cognitive consistency. However, if the dissonance is severe, then it can be very difficult to prioritize group interests over personal convictions.

Many of these phenomena occur in parliamentary politics. Some MPs notice that social structures influence caucus psychology: "There is praise or rewards for loyalists. There is subtle shaming or shunning of those who are independent. There is a mob mentality that you want to be part of the group," an MP says. "It all keeps people in line. There's an anthropological instinct to be part of the herd."[11] Another MP concurs: "The things that substantially influence parliamentarians are their peers and their colleagues," she says. "It's no different than any other work environment."[12] A third MP adds that "people have a huge tendency towards conformity. So little tension points are reduced to bring down the conflict within small social groups. There is something within the human mind, within social groups, that pushes us towards conformity."[13]

Interactions among like-minded politicians are conditioned by group psychology that encourages conformism. New members are socialized into a parliamentary caucus by imitating how other members act, or perhaps a party stalwart gives a talking-to about the way that things work.[14] For some of them, discipline is consistent with their experiences outside party politics. They experienced it working in business or with a labour union or even growing up in a tight family unit. Either way most new group members quickly behave like everyone else as a condition of membership.

Diversity exposes group members to a range of perspectives. The aforementioned seminal studies of group behaviour occurred when there was greater deference to the authority of heterosexual white men. The same scenarios might produce different outcomes with more diverse participants willing to question established norms. Kathleen Wynne, the former Ontario premier (2013–18), recalls the tensions when the provincial government introduced legislation to align with federal changes in same-sex marriage laws. The caucus was the scene of emotional conversations. At the time, Wynne was a government-side backbencher who shared a unique perspective that infused confidence among those who worried about the political consequences in their electoral districts: "I believe, and was told by some of my colleagues, that my standing up as an out lesbian backbencher talking about the conversations I had with Muslim religious leaders in my own riding helped others feel courageous," she says. "They felt braver going back to their communities saying 'this is what I believe, this is who I am, this is what I'm going to do.'"[15]

Because homogeneity in Canadian politics has been giving way to heterogeneity, coupled with growing interest in descriptive representation, big-tent political organizations are experiencing new challenges with maintaining group cohesion. Incivility is more prevalent in diverse groups, in which the accommodation of differences strains a group's shared identity and common goals.[16] Sometimes differences erupt in public, showing how pluralism can pressure a rethink of the conventions of party discipline. New approaches can expand to testing the traditions of the legislative assembly itself, such as women breastfeeding during parliamentary proceedings and defying professional dress codes.[17]

TEAM STRUCTURES

In Canada, party discipline leverages the social psychology of group behaviour by using the language of teamwork. Team organizational culture is rooted in business management, which treats groups of people as teammates with shared objectives who recognize that more can be accomplished by suppressing individualism and working together. Cohesive teams subscribe to self-discipline. They leverage complementary skill sets, are committed to a common purpose, and hold each other accountable.[18] They celebrate individual accomplishments that reflect positively on the group and rally around a cult of personality. In party politics, reminding people that "there is no *i* in *team*" is a common siren call for collective harmony, and a competitive *us* versus *them* mentality takes hold.

Political Groups

Like a society of chimpanzees, political groups sort themselves into hierarchies, within which coalitions form to enable members to gain more than if they work alone.[19] Parliamentarians defer to people in positions of authority and accord them respect because of their access to power. They are in constant competition with one another to gain resources, win policy arguments, and reach higher stations to reap influence, prestige, and fringe benefits.

A parliamentary caucus would be a motley crew without social structure. Helen Jones, a former British Labour MP who served as assistant government whip, has written that a caucus contains serial rebels, plotters, and crusaders. They dislike the leader, bristle against control, derive power from their celebrity, cause mischief, and/or vote according to their conscience.[20] Type A personalities with large egos are sensitive about their group status, whereas unquestioning loyalists do as they are asked. Loyalists advocate the party line, ask planted questions, repeat party messaging, and tattle on their Janus-faced colleagues. Party diehards are so attuned to the cause that they praise a whip who takes on their disgruntled peers.[21] Their fidelity, Jones believes, leads them to "see every deviation from the official line, however stupid that line may be, as a sign of imminent social breakdown and the precursor of political annihilation, which must therefore be stamped out."[22] Her verdict is that a caucus is a cauldron of ambition that assembles unwavering partisans and backstabbing schemers.[23] A less dramatic characterization differentiates competencies: "There are people who genuinely have something to offer," clarifies a former Canadian whip. "And then there are people who think they have something to offer but may be woefully deficient. Many have thoughts about being the leader themselves. As Napoleon said, every competent soldier has a marshal's baton in his knapsack."[24]

The formations that keep intense rivalries bundled up rely on group psychology. Partisans form bonds as they pass through stages of socialization. Team building develops locally within a national or provincial election campaign. Candidates make fast friends with members of their electoral district association. They develop companionship with the party's candidates in neighbouring electoral districts and the party stalwarts who reach out to them. An experienced candidate reflects on being part of a local support group during a general election:

> Team is the foundation of politics. Even a strong person needs a group around you to help you through the toughest of days. That team isn't just the people on your campaign. It's your family, it's your financial supporters, it's your colleagues running in neighbouring ridings. When your name is on an election ballot, it gives you huge confidence to know that people are looking out for you. There's someone at the campaign office answering calls and helping you deal with constituents, some financial people are helping raise the money, my family is backing me so the house can keep running. A team gives you the support you need to seek elected office.[25]

Campaigning helps future parliamentarians to recognize that being elected requires an extensive support network. Winning a campaign is not an exercise in individualism.

At their first caucus meeting, members form an instant connection with people who just went through a similar electoral journey. It is educational and cathartic to swap stories. They build off each other's experiences. They learn that through group cooperation they can achieve grand collectivist bargains unlikely in an individualist environment.[26] Solidarity is evident in their shop talk: nobody should air dirty laundry in public, everyone needs to sing from the same song sheet, we all have to row in the same direction, it is better to hang together than to hang separately, and so on. Parliamentarians grow dependent on one another. They know that there is someone who can offer guidance if they are going through a difficult time. Years later they will likely have warm feelings for many of the people with whom they shared an incredible experience. Of course, a parliamentary team can also be downcast or bad tempered, such as when cabals of leadership supporters cause trouble.[27]

Political Teams

Canadian partisans have been referring to political teams since at least the 1940s.[28] The party leader is presented as a team leader who presides over the parliamentary party and the extraparliamentary party. Members of non-governing parties formally constitute the opposition (i.e., opponents who resist). The word *team* is a euphemism for group conformity under a corporate brand and is a popular substitute for the negativity associated with *party*. A team philosophy papers over wounds that are slow to heal after a bitter leadership race and binds together people in conflict with one another. It also infuses a mentality of fierce polarity with opponents. Sports metaphors are common when Canadian partisans – particularly men – talk about party discipline.[29] For example,

> I look at it like a sports team. Very rarely will you have players on a hockey team or a basketball team come out and criticize the coach publicly. It may go on behind closed doors. As a political party, you're part of a team. You don't beat up on your own team in public, your own coach, your own captain. If you have those issues, they are usually dealt with in the dressing room. If it's a political party, it's usually dealt with at your caucus meeting.[30]

When party discipline is publicly compromised, it is a major distraction. When it breaks down, you cannot focus on public policy issues or goals that you need to focus on for re-election. You're putting pucks in your own net rather than your opponent's net.[31]

Politics is a team sport, and if you don't want to play a team sport go and play something else. You want to form government? You want to be successful? Think you can determine what the message is? Run for leader and see how hard that is and see how, when you're the leader, what you think about the importance of communicating a unified message. Even if you win, you'll go back to having message discipline because politics is a team sport. In order to govern, you need to have unity of purpose, unity of vision. Otherwise, you won't win, and/or you won't govern very well.[32]

The thrust of sports comparisons is that people join a side in organized competition. Teams form rivalries with opponents who are differentiated by labels, uniform colours, and logos. Coaches advocate an offensive system and a defensive structure. Players are driven by camaraderie and a competitive will to win as they perform assigned roles and stick up for each other. Opponents are trash-talked; banter fills private locker rooms. The conduct of competitors is guided by rules and officiated by referees. Breaking the rules draws penalties or suspensions. As they go on quests, some teams congeal under a common banner, whereas others turn on their coach or one another.[33]

Not everyone agrees with equating politics with sports. Some parliamentarians believe that the caucus is more an army than a team.[34] A less popular analogy treats frontbenchers as management and backbenchers as workers.[35] Criticism of partisan teams is that government-side members become insignificant:

"Team" is code for a trained seal and synonymous with [a] team-trained seal ... If being a team player means being a trained seal and an irrelevant government backbencher, then who wants to be one? The fact is there is no team in Ottawa. When you're on the government side, power is concentrated in the hands of half a dozen people, half of whom are not elected.[36]

Understand that if you are going to get involved it is a team game. You will follow the team rules. If you can't follow the team rules, this level of government is not for you. It is not always what you want to say; it is what you must say. You will support the government, its policies and procedures, and the budget, because you're a team. You may think that you have a free voice. You may think that you are representing your constituents. But foremost you are representing the party. Period.[37]

There are psychological downsides to a system that organizes politicians into combative teams. The political hierarchy wants the game played to perfection.[38] Identifying with a team makes it easier to loathe opponents, hurl insults, and communicate within echo chambers without discussing public policy.[39] The media participate by covering politics as sporting events, ranging from anticipation of a knockout punch in a party leaders' debate to horse-race treatment of party standings in public opinion polls. The resulting game-style media stories about politicians' strategic calculations breed public distrust.[40] Some parliamentarians – particularly women – disagree with the characterization of politics as combative sport:

> I understand the concept of being a team but not a blood sport. It's incredibly problematic for democracy if we're not looking beyond our self-built fence about what we think should be done about particular issues. Political parties can take away from making good public policy when people cannot work with someone else who might have just as good an idea or a better idea. There needs to be a better balance.[41]

> People in party politics say "get thick skin, toughen up, politics is a blood sport." It's not a blood sport! We're there trying to help people. So why are we hurting each other in the process? I've seen a blood sport. It's people fighting in a caged octagon ring, and they come out with broken bones and bloody noses. That's not what politics is. It's about helping people. And, if we're not kind to each other in the process, then what are we doing there? Quit the illusion that you're supposed to be some kind of tough guy in a ring, and get to the work of creating policy that helps people in a bold, transformative way.[42]

Team mentalities can lead to cautious fraternizing with opponents. Some partisans brush off being seen with their counterparts from another party. They hesitate to mingle with them over food and drink. Some turn down breaking bread when abroad; some are advised where to sit in the parliamentary dining hall.[43] In Ottawa, MPs segregate by party when they lunch together in the assigned lobby outside the chamber.

Yet some parliamentarians do form strong relationships with members of opposing teams. People with formal titles find that they can sometimes build a stronger rapport with their counterparts across the aisle than with many members of their own caucus. Backbenchers can recognize the usefulness of cross-party alliances to advance a private member's bill or an amendment. Focused work on a parliamentary committee and travel are opportunities for partisans to be acquainted, says a former government whip: "You can diffuse a lot of potential issues by having MPs from all parties get to know one another in a less structured way than in the House of Commons, which tends to be very adversarial," he advises. "In a strange way, getting together on foreign trips and delegations lends itself to better cooperation once they get back to Ottawa and into the parliamentary cycle."[44] When travelling abroad, partisanship often becomes secondary to a shared Canadian identity.

Some cross-party interactions turn into lasting friendships. Personal connections are curated based on shared interests and by not talking about politics. While waiting to participate in a political panel, politicians chat about their families, swap stories, and joke around: "When you see us debating each other using strong language with simple messages, you wouldn't know that some of us get along very well personally or that we are working together privately on other initiatives or issues," says an MP. "We often have substantive and detailed debates with each other, which is not what you see when we're communicating publicly. The public would be shocked to know that politicians who are ideologically far apart can be talking a lot together to find common ground."[45]

Similarly, federal-provincial party teams can be cooperative or adversarial.[46] Integrated parties reinforce messaging. They share objectives and tactics, though federal laws impose some restrictions on the pooling of party resources. They provide notice of policy disagreement, and they coordinate policy announcements. They use the same party technology, collaborate on election platforms, and assist with candidate recruitment. Databases and candidate vetting forms are among the corporate tools developed by the national franchisor. The constitutions of the national Liberal Party and NDP mention the sharing of workers, information, election readiness, membership lists, and assets with their subnational namesakes.[47] In comparison, the Conservative Party's constitution states only that the party will "maintain relationships" with subnational parties.[48]

Posturing erupts during intraparty feuds. As Luff revealed, Alberta NDP MLAs were told not to appear in photographs with the federal NDP leader.[49] In Newfoundland and Labrador, the PC caucus and staff were given "Anything but Conservative" badges when the premier railed against the Conservative government led by Stephen Harper: "We were encouraged to wear the ABC badge to work as a symbol of loyalty to the leader," recalls a backbencher in that caucus. "It was almost like a little cult, like Jonestown, where the leader says this, and you do it."[50] The button was a visual mark of team solidarity irrespective of lifelong partisan attachments. Federal-provincial integration also ebbs and flows with standings in public opinion polls. Provincial leaders fawned over Justin Trudeau when he achieved global fame on becoming prime minister, but even provincial Liberals hesitated being seen with him when he became unpopular.

Party Leaders

Politicians who demur to a leader-hero who controls their career advancement are the norm in Canadian parliamentary groups. Party leaders attract considerable media attention, which contributes to their prominence in the public evaluation of parties.[51] A leader's importance in vote choice fluctuates from election to election, with negative impressions building over time.[52] Keeping the caucus happy is paramount to avoid rebellion.

There are many types of team leaders in party politics. Those interested in a stately image leave the scrapping for others. They create a collaborative workplace by coordinating activities, managing resources, and setting boundaries for a self-directed group. They want the caucus to feel supported. Kim Campbell, who served as prime minister in 1993, was keen to encourage discussion. She did not equate difference with disloyalty: "I always treated my caucus with respect, I always listened to them, I never made enemies of them, I understood where they were coming from,"

Campbell reflects. "They trusted me. They knew they would always have my ear even if they didn't win the argument. I felt that was very important."[53] Other leaders are commanding. They centralize power structures that lead to high degrees of cohesion, particularly when the party owes its success to them.[54] Their style of presiding over a caucus is more dictatorial than democratic.

A party leader's authority recedes if group members believe that their needs are not being met. Leadership aspirants have a network of allies, some of whom are chomping at the bit for change and are on standby for insurrection to force the incumbent out.[55] A former provincial leader establishes that leaders need to convince followers that they have mutual dependency:

> Party discipline takes a realization by followers that they're part of a group, and to be part of a group you have to follow the rules. Leaders have to realize that leadership is far more than simply saying "go" to get people to go or "jump" to get people to jump. There is no divine right to leadership. You have to persuade people and maintain their confidence. Party discipline is almost irrelevant. It's incidental. It becomes essentially a matter of trying to convince your colleagues that the cause you're advocating is one they should accept and that it may reflect their cause as well.[56]

Inflexible leaders risk a caucus revolt if they have weak personal relationships with backbenchers and the party is faring poorly in public opinion polls. A former minister elucidates: "When different members of the team feel they are not being listened to, or they are not having the ability to guide defining principles or policies, that's when things fall apart," he says. "When a leader is using powers to control policy, to control the decision of a caucus or cabinet, or a political party, there will be disruptions and constant turmoil. You don't have a strong team if a leader is doing that."[57] In the right circumstances, resentment can erupt into a leadership coup, so leaders are compelled to dote on their caucuses. The simple act of acknowledging a parliamentarian's birthday, or neglecting to do so, is noticed.[58]

An astounding case of party cohesion was the fealty of the PC caucus to Prime Minister Brian Mulroney as an election reckoning loomed. His efforts to maintain caucus support were exceptional because of an un-wavering commitment to personal outreach remarkable for its breadth, depth, and persistence. On becoming the PC leader, Mulroney was deter-mined not to repeat infighting that undermined his predecessors: "In the parliamentary system, caucus is the most important piece of the puzzle," he says. "If you are the leader of a party in Parliament, you had better make it your business to ensure that your caucus is behind you all the time. That can be brought about only by personal commitment and personal action."[59] The following exposition shows that camaraderie is strongest when a charismatic leader who embodies the group's values advocates a course of action.[60]

In 1992, the PC government was nearing the end of a tumultuous second term in office marked by a number of polarizing policy initiatives. The caucus was encouraged to think like trustees who prioritize the na-tional interest while the media gorged on public angst and the whiff of scandal. Six PC MPs had defected to form the Bloc Québécois; two former PC MPs were now Independents; another had been sentenced for corrup-tion; by-election losses were mounting; and the Reform Party was siphoning support in western Canada. A majority of Canadians wanted the prime minister to resign, and at one point just 11 percent preferred the PC Party.[61] With political jobs on the line, we would anticipate public sniping and efforts to install a new leader. Quite the reverse: most Tories were steadfast in their allegiance to their leader and party.[62] Mulroney's exceptional efforts to form personal relationships and build trust through inclusion had fos-tered their loyalty. All were made to feel that they mattered. The size of the cabinet grew. Backbenchers contributed through caucus committees and task forces. The prime minister wrote letters to all members of the caucus inviting their input on priority items for the party's election platform.[63]

Mulroney was unshakable in his belief that the caucus must see results if they brought concerns to his attention. Four to five caucus relations staff in the PMO worked with governing party MPs to resolve issues. They offered the assistance of the prime minister when warranted and made MPs believe that the PMO was looking out for their interests. The quid pro quo was a heightened expectation of compliance when staff informed backbenchers that the boss wanted them to do something. Political staff embodied the prime minister's belief that "caucus solidarity is indispensable for long-term success," which requires a party leader who "works at it relentlessly."[64]

On Wednesdays when the caucus met, a handful of PC MPs attended a breakfast meeting at 24 Sussex Drive, the prime minister's official residence. Mulroney took notes while listening to a rotation of three to five of his party's backbenchers from different parts of Canada who might have been steered to a seat next to a caucus adversary. Around 9 a.m., he met in his parliamentary office with the PMO chief of staff (who oversees political staff) and the clerk of the Privy Council (who oversees public servants). As Mulroney tells it, he raised the problems voiced over breakfast and directed that the MPs' concerns be addressed immediately, especially if something involved a localized campaign promise. His determination to inspire commitment was on full display in national caucus meetings, largely celebratory events from which PMO staff were excluded. Afterward, he met again with the chief of staff and clerk and once again relayed concerns from backbenchers. If a PC backbencher complained about an inaccessible minister, then the prime minister arranged for the minister to receive a message that others were interested in the position.

There was more. After Question Period, backbenchers brought people from their electoral districts to meet the prime minister for a short chat and a photograph. On Wednesday evenings, Mulroney placed approximately ten telephone calls across the country to praise his caucus members. The president of a PC electoral district association would field a phone call about how the area's MP had spoken forcefully in the caucus that morning. If the MP's concern was about the need for a new bridge, then the prime minister instructed PMO staff to get the minister of public works to travel to the riding with the member to look into getting the bridge built. Mulroney encouraged the electoral district president to share this information with others. He propped up these types of private remarks by telling journalists about a member's passionate advocacy for local issues.[65]

Efforts to cultivate solidarity went even further. Mulroney spent years nurturing personal relationships by making sure that he knew all of the caucus members, including their families, which amounted to hundreds of people. He connected through flattery and by acknowledging that backbenchers' spouses make sacrifices.[66] He wrote letters to compliment MPs on their speeches in the legislature and their policy presentations.[67] The caucus relations staff kept their boss abreast of humanizing details – who was off sick, who was celebrating a birth or anniversary, who had marital problems, whose mother was in hospital, who was mourning a death. Mulroney – described as a "phoneaholic" – telephoned MPs and their relatives to recognize accomplishments or to express concern if someone was experiencing illness, loss, or tragedy.[68] A former PC MP recounts that "Mulroney would call out of the blue, full of effusive praise and leaving his subject – friend and foe alike – swimming in endorphins."[69] At cabinet meetings, the prime minister updated his ministers about MPs who were celebrating a milestone or going through hardship.[70] A chief of staff recalls that the only time Mulroney became angry was over not being told that a PC MP's wife had broken her arm in a car accident. The lesson for the entire PMO was that, "without caucus cohesion, unity, and loyalty, nothing else mattered."[71] Mulroney also phoned junior political staffers and local party supporters. Surprised staff might receive flowers to mark special life events with a card co-signed by his wife, Mila. He even sent congratulatory notes to MPs' children graduating from high school.[72]

No other Canadian prime minister has paid so much attention to caucus cohesion. Plying caucus members with food and drink is customary. John A. Macdonald, Canada's first prime minister (1867–73, 1878–91), and his wife Agnes hosted dinner parties and kettledrum afternoon teas for ministers, caucus members, and other political notables.[73] Wilfrid Laurier, who was prime minister from 1896 to 1911, brought parliamentarians into his office for a cigarette and asked them about individual constituents and personal interests.[74] Pierre Trudeau held lunch meetings with a rotation of three to four of his party's MPs in the parliamentary dining room.[75] Jean Chrétien, prime minister from 1993 to 2003, hosted approximately fifteen MPs for lunch two or three times a month.[76] Though it could take up to a few weeks to get a meeting, he invited backbenchers to join him in his office for a chat after Question Period and returned their phone calls even when "he might hate your guts."[77] Paul Martin hosted ministers and MPs for a relaxed lunch or dinner. Once a week he attended meals served in the House of Commons lobby.[78] Stephen Harper invited his party's members of standing committees to lunch or dinner at 24 Sussex Drive.[79]

Justin Trudeau's interactions with Liberal MPs were less intimate during the 42nd Parliament. Supporters and detractors alike observe a head of government who does not devote attention to all ministers and all back-benchers. By virtue of his familial lineage and charisma, Trudeau has always had people seeking his attention and, at a young age, he became the leader of Canada's most dominant political party despite a thin resumé.[80] The lack of anxiety about caucus support combined with his considerable success as leader explains his reduced compulsion to engage in meaningful caucus outreach. He is also the first social media prime minister. Liberals receive a stream of electronic information about him that is a digital surrogate for personal contact.

Trudeau prefers to meet with groups while travelling across Canada, such as eating with caucus members when he visits Winnipeg.[81] He prioritizes short phone calls to members of the caucus who have suffered a tragedy, including when he is abroad. He makes small talk with MPs in the lobby during all-night sittings. Personal access is often limited to a backbencher who makes a remark at a caucus meeting or waits a long time for the PMO to set up a meeting. When an MP wants to talk with the prime minister about an issue, his staff attempts to resolve it, and if necessary they schedule a five-minute issue meeting with him for which there is considerable preparation.[82] Access varies: MPs who are friends with Trudeau might get a meeting within twenty-four hours, whereas those on the periphery might wait weeks, while a request from a troublemaker might be ignored. Ministers might likewise experience difficulty securing a meeting.[83]

A concerted effort to have lunch with MPs in Ottawa did not emerge until upheaval several years after forming the government. Faced with caucus management problems during the SNC-Lavalin turmoil, Trudeau's chief of staff announced the formation of a caucus relations office in the PMO and pledged that the prime minister would respond to a backbencher within forty-eight hours on pressing matters.[84] Two staffers were designated as liaisons among the PMO, ministers' offices, and caucus. One was the liaison with ministers' offices and absorbed a new responsibility for attending daily senior PMO staff meetings and regional outreach meetings. From March to June 2019, Trudeau's calendar filled with one-on-one meetings. Members of the caucus who sought a meeting were accommodated whenever possible. Staff sought out backbenchers who might have been too reserved to initiate contact. The prime minister phoned MPs to check in on them: *How are things going? What's happening in the constituency? Are there any issues that we need to be thinking about as we're moving forward?*[85] He attended a rotation of weekly regional caucus meetings in advance of the national caucus meeting. As well, Trudeau hosted lunches in the West Block with half a dozen senior MPs.

Opposition leaders have more time to be collegial. They stop members of the caucus in the hallway for a chat and try to sit together while travelling. Convening lunches with small groups can be a concerted attempt to improve caucus morale, convey a sense of access, and exchange information.[86] Many MPs have dined at Stornoway house, the residence of the leader of the official opposition. Leaders' spouses are sometimes the ones who ensure social opportunities to mingle with caucus members, such as hosting spaghetti dinners or barbecues. Entertaining on Thursday evenings those who have to remain in Ottawa for a Friday sitting is described by one former opposition leader as an opportunity for members "to get to know each other better, to vent any problems and issues, and to establish a sense of comradeship."[87] Leaders of smaller caucuses might host get-togethers at their own homes.[88] Rotating invitees avoids the perception of favouritism.

The Leader's Staff

Direct interactions between parliamentarians and the leader hold particular value when a leader's staff play the role of gatekeeper. The influence of staff can be considerable. They are particularly powerful when they are nestled within a head of government's inner circle, especially when a prime minister or premier freely delegates authority to them.

Senior political staff are indispensable because of their institutional memory and specialized skill sets. Most of them are cognizant of where they rank in the organizational hierarchy. They have a strong sense of their superior's opinion. They check in for guidance. They realize that their jobs are on the line if they overstep their stations or make indefensible pronouncements. As one experienced staffer puts it, "advisers advise, and leaders decide. If I give my best advice and the leader decides to go 180 degrees in the other direction, then so do I."[89] A phalanx of staff performs unglamorous grunt work that allows the leader to focus on more important matters. A former staffer to an opposition leader dispenses with notions of grandeur:

> It's a big job to be a party leader. You need staff. Staff are there to serve. It's not staff controlling the leader, believe me. They do not control the leader at all. Our job is to make sure the leader is taken care of. Someone looks after the leader's bag, coat, makes sure there's coffee, and books a hotel room with a window. The chief of staff tells the leader what is going on, arranges high-end meetings, and takes some of the heat. Deputy chiefs of staff deal with human resources and other stuff. A big communications team is there to help by preparing talking points, reports, and rehearsing Question Period questions.[90]

Politics is turbulent, so it is unsurprising that staff crave predictability and discipline. Their livelihoods depend on keeping their employer out of trouble. With the possible exception of unionized NDP staff, they lack protections from arbitrary sanctions; if they are fired, then their career options are limited. They desperately try to avoid a communications slip-up that compels crisis management. Staff sometimes need to be assertive. In scrums, for instance, journalists ask variations of the same question to identify the party's position on a divisive issue. Staff are there to end the media melee. The staffer who worked for an opposition leader tells of how the leader lingered for an extra five minutes. A slip of the tongue jolted the entire caucus and required weeks of reparations: "The leader said something outside of the message box that was not party policy. We had to deal with it for two weeks. It created chaos within the caucus, a major commotion," she explains. "A lot of time went into persuading MPs of the party line, some of them even facing death threats. Freelancing is not a good thing. People who are good at it want to know the party position first."[91] Other staffers share similar stories of managing self-inflicted wounds when a leader strays from the party message.

Power struggles arise when the leader's staff issue instructions. Most politicians tolerate slights if the staffer offers high-quality advice. Others have none of it. Veterans have outlasted a carousel of staff over the years and push back.[92] Some of them contemplate what is being asked. They bristle at a request to make a day trip during the summer recess or to read canned talking points. Frontbenchers and backbenchers unwilling to act on a staffer's directive might suggest that the leader place the request instead.

Traditionally, political staff avoid public exposure in deference to elected representatives.[93] Things have changed. Many of today's staff are key actors in partisan teams who have used social media to promote messaging during an election campaign. When they are hired, their accounts might go dormant, but more likely they actively amplify government and party messaging. Those at the apex of the political pyramid set standards of message discipline. Senior personnel close to the leader can opine in cyberspace, whereas a backbencher or junior staffer who goes off-message online can anticipate a request to remove the post. As well, a ministerial staffer exuberant about the minister on social media can anticipate being called for not paying adequate attention to the prime minister or premier. Most junior staff have few digital followers, so a minor indiscretion is easily contained. It gets tricky if the staffer made a good point because disciplining or firing the person could be newsworthy.

Team Player Rewards

To further understand why so many parliamentarians follow orders, we need some sense of political motivation. Several academic theories indicate that politicians have an inner fire to make a difference, achieve personal benefits, and boost their egos. Rational choice theory treats them as "strategic utility maximizers" whose actions are explained by their ambition and institutional environment.[94] They pursue the pathway that offers the best opportunity to achieve the results that they want. A related approach is new institutionalism, which holds that parliamentarians' behaviour is a reflection of their political environment.[95] Their choices are constrained by internal and external forces. These institutions range from customs and rules developed by their predecessors to emerging structures adopted in response to societal pressures. Another popular hypothesis is the office/policy/votes model, which holds that partisans' actions are explained by their motivations to occupy higher office to access the spoils of government, their goals of pursuing public policy positions, or their desires for votes.[96] A fourth theory blends the above to suggest that party discipline occurs through the combination of a politician's individual preferences, institutional factors, and sociological pressures. More specifically, a Canadian parliamentarian's behaviour is explained by loyalty that results from political advancement, socialization, and sanctions.[97] Those who do not see a path toward upward mobility gradually rebel and might conspire to install new leadership. Finally, theorists believe that a legislator is chiefly motivated to regain the party nomination because the legislator cannot achieve anything otherwise.[98] A desire for permission to represent the party in the next election is therefore a catalyst for parliamentarians to do the bidding of their leader and the leader's surrogates.

Team leaders and followers have a symbiotic relationship, albeit an uneven one. The leader – especially one who heads a government – wields the power of appointment and disappointment. Deference to the leader increases the chances of advancement, whereas dissent jeopardizes promotion and invites the peril of demotion. A cabinet post is the biggest prize. Government-side members with prior ministerial experience or legal training are most likely to be appointed to the cabinet, as are those who have contended for the party leadership.[99] Competent people can linger as private members, whereas weaker performers are elevated to fulfill regional or demographic obligations. Distributing positions among a large caucus requires careful thought given that there are more veto players with fewer incentives to remain loyal.[100] The competition for so few jobs makes for ruthless surroundings: Brian Mulroney divulges that moments after a minister resigned a backbencher submitted a note casting for a position.[101]

Non-cabinet appointments mollify some government-side backbenchers passed over for the cabinet. Granting title is a proxy for group recognition of individual behaviour. A bevy of parliamentary secretaries is appointed to assist ministers, though it becomes evident that such positions are a tool of appeasement.[102] The quasi-executive appointment is typically a cabinet stepping stone only for those anointed at an early stage of their parliamentary careers.[103] Many like the profile and pay packet; others are attracted to public service. Kathleen Wynne recalls her time as a parliamentary secretary and being assertive with the minister to ensure that work was delegated:

Not everyone has the capacity or the life experience to say "actually, I deserve as much respect as you do. Just because you're a minister that shouldn't stand in the way of me having meaningful work to do." If you don't have the ability to say that, then sometimes you can feel like you're cooling your heels, and you'd be far better being back in your constituency because you're not being given anything meaningful to do.[104]

As well, backbenchers are kept occupied as chairs of sub-caucuses and special initiatives. Titles that seem to be important are created, such as Special Advisor to Prime Minister Trudeau on LGBTQ2 issues. In Ottawa, a suite of official positions brings an attractive stipend (Table 3.1), with executive creep prone to increase the longer a government is in office. Indeed, in the first year of the Trudeau majority government, the cabinet and parliamentary secretaries comprised 35 percent of the Liberal caucus (65 of 184 MPs); by the end of the 42nd Parliament, their numbers were at nearly 41 percent of the caucus (72 of 177 MPs); and, after the 2019 election, they constituted 47 percent (74 of 157 MPs). The appointments buy loyalty to the executive branch and homogenize public thought, all the more crucial for a minority government. The number of private members who see themselves as part of the government is even higher when we consider that many positions are rotated. In the provinces, particularly the smaller ones, fewer governing party backbenchers go without a position that accords them status (Table 1.1).[105]

Inducements other than title are dangled. At the top end, private members can visit exotic places as part of an interparliamentary delegation. Membership on certain committees is appealing if there are policy areas of interest or international trips. The members can be invited to travel with the leader. Perhaps they will be asked to attend a formal dinner with a foreign dignitary or greet an important person at the airport. Being invited to represent the party on a televised political panel is enticing for parliamentarians keen to build their profiles. As one former MP puts it, "it's great to be on the CBC's *Power and Politics*. You feel like the big gal on campus."[106]

Where members sit in the assembly is another non-monetary perk. Those on the front bench get the most media exposure if they sit near the

TABLE 3.1
MPs' remuneration for extra duties, House of Commons (2019, 42nd Parliament)

Title	Extra pay ($)[1]	MPs Liberal	Conservative	NDP
Prime minister/leader	60,600 to 178,900	1	1	1
Cabinet minister	85,500	34	–	–
Speaker	85,500	1	–	–
Deputy Speaker	44,200	–	1	–
Assistant deputy Speaker	17,500	1	–	1
Parliamentary secretary	17,500	37	–	–
Opposition House leader	17,500 to 44,200	–	1	1
Deputy House leader	6,200 to 17,500	1	1	1
Chief whip	12,400 to 31,900	1	1	1
Deputy whip	6,200 to 12,400	1	1	1
Caucus chair	6,200 to 12,400	1	1	1
Committee chair	12,400	23	5	–
Committee vice-chair	6,200	5	23	24
MPs with extra pay (*n*)		106	35	31
MPs without extra pay (*n*)		71	62	10
MPs with extra pay (%)		60	36	76

Note: May 2019 figures. Base pay for an MP in 2019–20 was $178,900.
1 Other forms of remuneration exist, such as an official residence and/or a car allowance.
Source: Compiled from public accounts (Canada 2019). See also Walsh (2017), 196–97.

leader; for the rest, seating assignments might be based on the year elected and alphabetical order by last name. Additional considerations in seating arrangements include status as parliamentary secretaries and, in Ottawa, membership in the Privy Council.[107] Deviating from seating traditions upsets members who lose out on a camera view.

Many other incentives are on offer. Members can lobby the government executive for spending in their electoral districts or for support to advance local projects. There are symbolic privileges, for instance receiving permission to table a minor amendment that the party will vote down. Belonging to a political band offers social benefits, including peer respect for voting with the group in the face of constituent backlash.[108] Rewards come in smaller forms, such as better seats and tables at events or the whip's approval of a request to leave early. More convenient parking and nicer office space might be available. Incumbents interested in re-election can be protected from enduring a contested nomination. During an election campaign, those on good terms with the leadership can access party resources and advertising and get a boost from a visit by high-profile politicians, including the leader. At the conclusion of a parliamentary career lies the prospect of a patronage appointment.

Opposition parties harbour different dynamics because the leadership has fewer goodies to offer. Shadow cabinets are unofficial structures, and thus there is no financial reward for a ministerial critic, with the notable exception of the House leader. The title of critic offers prestige and media attention by imparting a leadership role signalling that the member is cabinet material for a government in waiting. Some opposition members would forgo a committee vice-chair's stipend to be designated a critic because of the public exposure.[109] Others would gladly shed extra work, especially if the leader requires a shadow cabinet to vote as a group without sufficient rewards to offset the anguish, or if they are tasked with monitoring multiple portfolios. In the Bloc Québécois, perquisites are traditionally associated with work roles. A Bloc critic goes on applicable trips involving that portfolio; otherwise, the travel is assigned to the most suitable member of a parliamentary friendship group. The requirement that members submit post-travel reports to the whip for review is another mechanism to change perceptions that all-expenses-paid junkets are gifts or bribes.

Members' desires for rewards can stimulate artificial relationships on parliamentary teams. Some of them play up their friendships with the whip by paying compliments and bringing coffee. They give birthday and Christmas presents. In return, they expect special treatment, such as permission to miss a Friday sitting: "Thursday afternoons, every cabinet minister becomes the whip's best friend," explains a government whip.[110] The friendly texts and tea service stop when someone else gets the title.

PARTY WHIPS

The party whips are perhaps "the most misunderstood" institutional force in parliamentary assemblies.[111] The label implies a fixer who wields power to ensure that a party's interests prevail over those of democratically elected representatives. Occasionally, disgruntled parliamentarians sound off, such as the Independent MLA in Nova Scotia whose private member's bill proposed to ban whips because they interfere with representation.[112] In reality, a party whip performs functions essential to the operations of a legislature, but the work is so delicate that whips can refuse to talk about it. Even party leaders have limited knowledge of the whip's work. This is by design: the idea is to have a low profile and shield the leader from the stresses of caucus management. The only certainty is that nobody wants to be summoned to the whip's office.

At a minimum, the political functions of a whip involve finding out how the party's members intend to vote on bills and motions so that the leader can publicly explain differences of opinion. In practice, ensuring attendance and lining up votes with the House leader's instructions are the main duties, as well as dispensing committee assignments, speaking slots, and trips. A government whip, in conjunction with the government House leader, has the added responsibility of ensuring quorum and delivering on confidence votes. Whips assert more coercion over the parliamentary team than those obligations require, yet the whip is not the power broker that some imagine.

Overview of the Whip

The word *whip* is fearsome. It conjures up brute discipline as a daunting symbol of authority with a punitive commission. To some, whipping anyone or anything is unethical, for it is painful and cruel; others see whipping as practical and cultural, a necessary instrument of control. As a noun, a whip evokes images of a medieval instrument for flogging or a leather cord used by cowboys. Whips are staples in a dominatrix's tool kit used by sadists and masochists. As a verb, whip cracking directs the movements of livestock and steers horse-drawn stagecoaches. Colloquial references to someone who is whipped denotes subservience in a romantic relationship. The general impression is that an authority figure brandishes a whip to gain the compliance of underlings.

In Ottawa, bullwhips are displayed in sealed glass cases in and around the offices of the chief government whip and chief opposition whip (see Figure 3.1). The practice dates to at least 1970.[113] Office staff often hold an informal ceremony to present an incoming whip with a cord in a framed wall hanging. Although a staff presentation is the custom, there are exceptions: an electoral district association might present a display box, some newly appointed whips arrive to find a framed bullwhip already on the wall, and some refuse to exhibit the item. Members of Parliament leaving

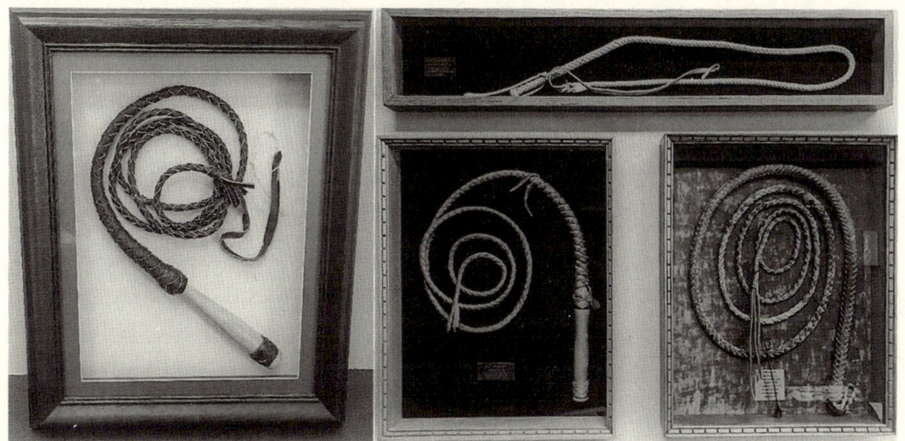

FIGURE 3.1 Whips displayed in offices of the whip, Ottawa | Political staff.

the role might regift the display to their successors or take the souvenirs with them.

Impressions of party whips are bolstered by tropes in popular culture. Politicos are some of the most devoted fans of serial political dramas, including Justin Trudeau, who says of the American series *The West Wing* that "a lot of the interplay – from campaigning, to machinery of government, to the political lens you put on things – is very, very real and [a] very reasonable facsimile of what we're doing."[114] Others believe that the archetype of political puppeteers contrasts with the disarray and indisposition of Canadian politics. Melodramas portray the whip as an arrogant, conniving disciplinarian with no scruples who thrives on outwitting subordinates and enjoys making minions quiver in fear. In the British version of *House of Cards,* the government whip is an ambitious functionary who portends fierce loyalty to the leader and "puts a bit of stick about" to make MPs jump.[115] In the Netflix remake, the US House of Representatives majority whip cunningly leverages political pressure to get representatives onside. Both whips escalate their manipulative actions to murder. Audiences are led to believe that whips are sociopathic browbeaters.

Helen Jones, the former British MP, burnishes an image of whips as oppressors in *How to Be a Government Whip.* As she tells it, a whip must project poise and order, especially when chaos is zapping party morale. Punctuality is needed to ensure that government business moves forward;

attendance is essential to avoid losing a snap vote. Jones remarks that private members interested in promotion "do as they are told and attend when they're asked."[116] Where possible, reprimands are treated as internal, private matters to maintain a public facade of unwavering unity. Her descriptions of Machiavellian routines are dramatized for theatrical effect – for instance, whips are advised to drag out a decision about reallocating office space when an MP dies – while revealing the need for political acumen.[117] "There are occasions when the job requires you to be heartless, not to care about who you humiliate or the damage you may inflict ... Save your kindness for small children and old ladies," Jones recommends.[118]

Looking past the bravado, Jones indicates that a whip possesses greater powers of intimidation than recrimination. She observes that forcing a whipped vote on a divisive issue can create martyrs out of otherwise loyal members.[119] Threatening to leak embarrassing information about an MP to the media can harm the party's brand too.[120] Ignore problems, and the party leadership gets frustrated that legislative business is bumpy; dish out sanctions too freely, and MPs rebel. A whip must be cautious about addressing insubordination while being decisive when sanctions are needed.

These spirited portrayals distort the fact that party whips are collegial wranglers. They are part steward, part human relations manager, and part emissary. Canadian whips are friendly yet firm. Some are affable; some are headmasterish. The position is likened to a mother hen that keeps her chicks in the fold, or as a cross between a high school principal and guidance counsellor. Some parliamentarians use descriptors such as shop steward, coach, linchpin, interlocutor, and grandparent. A chief government whip for Prime Minister Lester Pearson in the 1960s described the role as follows: "The whip is the chief of police of the party ... The whip sits right behind the prime minister, like a bodyguard ... The chief whip is a kind of 'aide-de-camp' or 'contact man' between the private members and the party leader."[121] Whips wear many hats: an agent of the leader, a broker with political staff, a referee for the caucus, a conduit, a confessor, and a defender of the party brand. Whips are liaisons with the Speaker, the House leader, the caucus, and other parties' whips. They are also mentors to rookie parliamentarians.

In large assemblies, especially during a minority government, the government whip and staff meet with their opposition counterparts.

Sometimes the cross-party meetings occur multiple times a day to discuss things such as late sittings and special debates. As one of Pierre Trudeau's whips put it, being able to "zip in and out of Ottawa quickly" matters because the role requires being present in the legislative precinct.[122] This goes some way toward explaining why nearly fourth-fifths (thirty-seven of forty-seven) of chief government whips between the 1st and 42nd Parliaments were MPs from Ontario or Quebec, of which most (twenty-nine) were from Ontario. In small assemblies and tiny caucuses, a single individual might hold dual titles; for instance, the House leader can double as the whip. Phone calls, texting, and emailing can negate the need for formal meetings.

Whips help to manage caucus affairs. In some setups, they defer to the caucus chair, who steers meetings and tends to be elected by the caucus.[123] In other caucuses, the whip operates in concert with the leader, leader's staff, and House leader. Whatever the structure, these officers need to have the pulse of the caucus in order to manage it proactively. Their management styles vary, as illustrated by the following remarks from recent whips and ex-whips:

> The unpleasant, hard conversations that any team has to have amongst themselves – that's what the whip does ... Party discipline is the system, the tools, and the culture that are required to result in successes on House of Commons votes and for maintaining consistency and coherence in messaging while staying focused on the larger team, instead of prioritizing specific individual riding issues which at times can clash with where the larger team has to go.[124]

> You have to find a balance. You have to respect the work of the MPs, the positions, their aspirations, their ideals or values, and you have to listen to them. But at the end of the day you have to also make sure that we move ahead with our agenda, and we do what we're elected for, and in that sense the whip's position is key.[125]

> It's a lot of saying "no." It's a lot of delivering tough news. And a lot of telling people they can't be where they want to be, or do what they want to do.[126]

> I wanted to treat everybody fairly, equally, and with respect. In return, the members treated me the same way. So when I really needed something, they were always there.[127]

> The more a whip can use enticements and rewards instead of demotion or punishment, the happier everyone will be.[128]

Most of the whip's functions concern human resource management, whipping attendance and votes, and taking corrective action. Generally, the best martinets exert force of personality rather than authority of position, and they recognize that private members are not disposable. Members accept the whip as a taskmaster only if they believe that the group is treated fairly. A common theme is that whips must be confident that the leader supports them whether they are right or wrong because the caucus is constantly scrutinizing their decisions. A former whip explains that discipline is an equalizing force:

> You have to act like a team in order for this all to work. Somebody has to pick up the slack if you don't go to a committee meeting or if you decide to leave an hour early. People get quickly disgruntled when they notice that someone is late all the time or has an excuse every single day why they can't stay. They'll say it isn't fair they had to miss a community meeting because someone else left. When you're a whip, the number one word you hear is fairness. Members say, "well, three Tuesdays ago you said this, or you let so-and-so go early to do this." They are watching. An outgoing whip will say to a new whip, "if there's one piece of advice I can give, it's that everything you say and do, your team is watching you." Team is a big part because, if someone is not pulling their own weight, someone else has to cover for them, and people get resentful.[129]

Positivity is often a whip's preferred weapon. Others see manipulation: "The whips use coercion, intimidation, and bribery to affect the outcome of what they want," asserts an MP.[130]

Whips and Human Resource Management

Whips are a parliamentary party's administrative lead with the Speaker's office and other party whips. In Ottawa, they sit on the Board of Internal

Economy (the management board of Parliament) alongside the Speaker and House leaders to decide on resources for parliamentarians. They discuss routine management topics, such as encouraging healthy lifestyles and upgrading technology. They consider exceptional circumstances, such as increasing funds for an MP who incurs extra travel costs in an electoral district contending with forest fires. Whips and their staff participated in planning meetings about relocating offices to the West Block while the permanent chamber undergoes renovation. Whips also manage emerging issues. In the lead-up to the Trudeau government's legalizing recreational cannabis, someone mailed Liberal MPs a gram of the controlled substance. The whip's office quickly phoned around with firm instructions to turn it over to the police.[131]

The whip's office is an immediate stopping point when freshly elected representatives first arrive at a legislature. It is a hub for sorting out office arrangements, hiring staff, securing parking, determining where members sit in the chamber, and which committees they are on. A lot of time is spent on budgeting. In orientation meetings, there is a notable lack of emphasis on asserting parliamentary privileges or the best ways to exert influence within a parliamentary group. A former MP recalls that the first lesson shared is that "Ottawa is the moon, and your home riding is planet Earth. Remember, everything is important back on Earth, not on the moon."[132]

Some whips have the autonomy to assign offices and parking spots. Others are bound to rules about status and seniority, or perhaps allocations are made under the authority of the Speaker's office. The assignment of office space is a disciplinary tool foremost after a general election when turnover requires movement. Factors include square footage, a window view, and location. Incumbents are left alone unless there is a reason to move them, but re-elected private members who pull their weight are likely to end up with nicer offices. In Ottawa, entrepreneurial MPs secure a suite within walking distance of the chamber, whereas during inclement weather a neophyte with an office in the Confederation Building commutes by shuttle bus to the House of Commons.[133] Members of Parliament are entitled to two parking spots (one for them, one for a staff member) whose location can be a bargaining tool: "You want to get the attention of someone who is not being quite the team player that you would hope? Just raise your eyebrow about the member's parking space," says a former whip.[134] An inordinate amount of time is spent on internal workplace issues, such as grievances between members and demands for more resources. Whips assess complaints about a member of the caucus while being mindful of the complainant's motives.

Isolation is a cause of a parliamentarian's dissent.[135] Whips and caucus chairs therefore strive to keep morale high to encourage cohesion. Unifying caucus members nurtures social bonds, with those who support the party leader and enjoy working as a unit being more satisfied than those who do neither.[136] Morale increases when members derive a sense of participation, belonging, personal development, and public recognition.[137] Whips and chairs can suggest work related to members' interests and talents – even simple things such as asking a gregarious member to warm up the room with an icebreaker before a big meeting. They coordinate social activities so that people become acquainted with their colleagues on a personal level. The whip or caucus chair or both plan events for members and their spouses – an office party, a dance, a weekend golf tournament, an impromptu soccer game in front of the legislature. They deploy psychology to perk up the caucus through marks of recognition. Shout-outs in front of a group make people feel appreciated. Birthday cakes are delivered to a caucus meeting. Sometimes customized T-shirts are distributed to build a sense of togetherness and team affinity. Private groups on social media are set up for parliamentarians to interact about social events and offer birthday messages: "The more you can concentrate on improving the morale of the caucus, the fewer problems you'll have with needing to discipline the caucus," relays a former whip.[138] Less proactive whips and caucus chairs concentrate on formalities instead of animating their colleagues.

Whips and their staff recognize that parliamentarians are people with real lives and families. They constantly check in with private members. Politicians are extroverts who post personal information on social media, making it easier to spot implications for their ability to perform as public figures. People ask for time off because they have a medical appointment or a family urgency. A whip is likely to prioritize a request from a member who needs to deal with a personal issue or wants to attend an essential constituency event, with greater leniency granted to a rookie in a marginal seat. Whips become concerned when someone goes silent, leaves the capital on an early flight, or has been inexplicably absent. They listen to parliamentarians who confide their troubles. They absorb stories about problems at home, poor health, a death in the family, tax issues, gambling problems, and substance abuse.[139] Some former government whips explain the types of personal issues that arise:

> Whips are confessors. The whip calls an MP and says "look, you haven't been here for a week. You've missed votes of confidence. What the heck's the matter with you anyway?" The MP starts crying and says "my wife left me." Consoling is part of what whips do.[140]

> There were instances where people came to my office, men and women, and sat down on the couch and sobbed. They had horrible things happening in their personal life, they were stressed. There were also people who would come in who had been told by the clerk [of the House] that they could not sit in Parliament because the necessary paperwork hadn't been filed correctly after their campaign. We'd put the person in touch with a lawyer and tell them to go home to figure it out.[141]

If a member of the caucus is contending with personal problems, then the whip initiates contact to provide collegial support as well as to solicit information. The whip sometimes refers members to counselling services.

An open-door policy is abused when private members ask the whip to relay a political opinion to the leader. If many of them voice concerns about the same issue, then the whip informs the leader's office about a trend that requires attention. Whips attempt to handle issues independently. They are in regular contact with the chief of staff, the director of communications, or a designate to ensure that any extraordinary instructions are preapproved. Smartphones are useful to provide updates about minor matters.

Leaders depend on whips and caucus chairs for information. Those caucus officers might provide a briefing in a routine meeting with the leader or perhaps seek a quick chat on the way to Question Period or in the chamber. A former premier affirms that these officers are crucial to ensuring that a leader is aware of caucus happenings:

> The whip is the eyes and ears of the leader in terms of being able to follow the internal dynamics of the caucus. Along with the caucus chair, who

is a listener and an observer of caucus opinion, they play a really important role in the life of a leader. There are so many demands on your time
and other things you have to worry about. You're not necessarily aware
that someone is having marital difficulties, or someone's father just passed
away, or a range of things that you need to know in order to keep in touch
with people. That's a part of the whip's job that is misunderstood. To
deliver votes, the whip has to be listening carefully.[142]

The whip's updates on personnel issues must be careful about betraying
confidences or naming individual parliamentarians. The managerial role
of whips is in full force when they are strict about attendance or manage
trouble in consultation with the leader's office.

SUMMARY

Parliamentary parties are groups of elected representatives with strong
political opinions. Their public bonhomie runs deeper than a corporate
mask of employees who follow their employer's dictum. The reasons for
sticking together are explained, in part, by the psychology of group behaviour and social pressures of conformity. The bonds of kinship congeal when
a parliamentary group unifies into a team on a quest. Parliamentarians
themselves are behind much of the disciplinary ethos within party caucuses, adding weight to the urgings of leaders, staff, and whips. With experience, politicians learn that self-discipline avoids group trouble. If
they experience problems, then the party whip is there to encourage cohesion and provide human resource support. In the next chapter, we will
see that the external communications environment is a significant stimulus
for party discipline.

4

The Communications Arena

"Party discipline is relentless, and the message discipline is suffocating Parliament," says a former national party leader.[1] If true, then why do MPs put up with it? Why are so few Canadian politicians willing to speak off the cuff? Politics operates at a hectic pace and is fraught with antagonism and controversy. The unrelenting requests for details about diverse topics make it impractical for politicians to figure out independently how to respond, let alone promptly. It is therefore understandable that they want messaging. To discern message discipline, we need to be acquainted with the communications ecosystem. In this chapter, I describe the many facets of the political arena that contribute to party unity.

THE MEDIA ECOSYSTEM

Buried within the defunct Toronto Telegram newspaper are photos of a fifteen-year-old boy who tore up a poster in front of Prime Minister Louis St. Laurent (1948–57) at a 1957 campaign event in Toronto, prompting a Liberal official to push the teenager, who fell down some steps, struck his head, and was knocked unconscious.[2] In today's integrated media environment, digital eyes are everywhere, and visuals of even a minor calamity are shared within seconds. Partisans commonly point to the news media environment as a major pressure for group conformity.

Media Logic and Digital Disruption

Media logic refers to the way in which the media think, behave, and structuralize.[3] Many Canadian journalists value a professional credo of neutrality.

They see their role as reporting things as they are, educating audiences, and analyzing current affairs as detached observers.[4] Many journalists concede that their personal beliefs, their supervisors and editors, and editorial policies affect their reporting. Those slants reflect the fierce pressures to monetize news production, which drives editorial decisions about what is newsworthy and how to present information, as well as the digital marketplace's need for speed and visuals. Packaging public affairs as infotainment is cheaper than intellectual public policy analysis and attracts higher ratings.[5] Snappy sound bites, interesting visuals, and dramatic storytelling are what draw attention.

Pierre Trudeau once remarked that good government is not newsworthy.[6] He recognized that news production is rarely dispassionate or unbiased. For example, a party leader who draws a large crowd can be portrayed as a failure if the news story shows empty seats,[7] and news reports follow adages such as if it bleeds, it leads, or that a journalist should comfort the afflicted and afflict the comfortable. A formula extolled by some Alberta politicians, dubbed the "five Cs theory," holds that stories with controversy, conflict, chaos, confusion, and confrontation are attractive.[8] Another, used in academia, is that the media sensationalize politics by applying a "game frame" that emphasizes high stakes, conflict, strategy, tactics, performance, and celebritization.[9] Furthermore, social media metrics are treated as a popularity barometer, and journalists can rely on digital handouts. Whatever the formula, news storytelling pits protagonists against antagonists, with politicians cast in dramatic roles, journalists as theatre critics, and citizens as the political audience.[10] Suffice it to say that many believe that objectivity in news production is rare because so many journalists editorialize. Reality is distorted when news reporting is not passive or neutral, which has considerable implications for how politics operates. Two MPs from different political parties comment on how their behaviour changes in response to media practices:

> The media often take a stand as though they are players in the field as opposed to reporting what is going on. The media have an opinion about policy decisions. That has enormous influence because they have the tools to communicate with the public more than anyone else. I personally believe that stifles our democracy. We are supposed to be a country about

freedom of choice and freedom of speech. The leadership of a party wants to be seen in a constructive light. So it crafts its messages in a way that will be accepted by the media and tells its caucus that these are the rules of engagement, this is what you're allowed to do, this is what you're allowed to say.[11]

If I'm in front of a hot mic and a camera, and a journalist asks me a question, there might be a misunderstanding. If I don't express myself clearly, it is already playing out, and it's hard to walk back because walking it back might not get the same attention. People might think I don't have any backbone, that I'm not standing by what I said, and so on.[12]

Instead of trying to educate journalists about public policy, Canadian politicians resort to repeating sanitized messages or not saying anything at all. In his autobiography, Justin Trudeau reflects that journalists want a succinct quotation or a four-second sound bite or video clip. He learned as an opposition MP that, "the more I strayed from the core message I needed to convey, the less likely it was that the message would reach Canadians."[13] As prime minister, he worked out that clickbait stories about his colourful socks or Halloween costumes are more economical for the media than conducting a detailed analysis of a government bill. Media biases about how a politician should look or behave disadvantage women and visible minorities in particular.[14] Even the most reticent get a makeover when their physical appearance distracts from talking about public policy.[15] These conventions of media logic are evolving with digital communications.

In Canada, initial optimism that email, blogs, and websites would improve news reporting and political representation was tempered by the realization that political parties insist on message discipline.[16] Instead of democratizing, parties integrate digital technologies to fit their existing practices, a process known as normalization.[17] Major parties simply leverage their resource advantages to maintain their dominant positions. As Canadian political economist Harold Innis foretold, some practices harden instead of changing or innovating. According to Innis, impermanent electronic media contribute to centralization and flatten government hierarchy.[18] With digital media, a political leader has a greater ability to exert authority over a large area. This is possible because, as one Innisian scholar puts it, the internet "enables centralized authority to closely monitor and manage subordinate units wherever they are."[19] Keeping track of politicians in real time propels message conformity.

Partisans believe that self-restraint is essential in a cyberculture of outrage. Online trolls conduct influence campaigns and agitate politicians in the hope of provoking an outrageous response. Pranksters wreak confusion through hoax news releases, spoof websites, and imposter social media accounts. Saboteurs leak information online. They create harsh memes (images with text overlays), spread innuendoes, hack websites, and create bots to circulate fake news.[20] A ham-fisted comment can go viral; even a private telephone conversation with a constituent can end up in the public domain.[21] Politicians learn to be cagey: "If you get a random call from a reporter in a small town, and say something out of sync, there was a time when that might go unnoticed," explains a former minister. "Now, if it's controversial enough, it could be on the national news. Every minister in every party has a sinking feeling after they've given an interview: Is it going to be taken out of context? Is it going to be clipped?"[22] Senior political staffers comment on the practicalities of digital disruption for political communications management:

> With social media, political campaigns can get derailed very, very quickly by things that are said that knock them off-message. It's governments as well. All of the forces are driven by a news cycle that is down to microseconds and lend themselves to more centralization of communications in order to control the message. It is easy to get distracted because there's so many mediums and ways for the message to get out. It's not like you sit around anymore waiting for the six o'clock news to see how your sound bite was treated by a reporter. It's just a constant cycle of this all day long.[23]

> Where are we going to have political debates that include views unacceptable to the broader public? With smartphones, people can come to a constituency association meeting and record everything. Even the average citizen isn't able to express a sincerely held opinion for fear it might be twisted into something negative. We haven't come to grips with it yet. You expect opponents to use things against you. But it is the media that

expresses these things as controversy when the whole objective of political parties is to have debate.[24]

Tweeting a news story before going to bed and waking up to an onslaught of digital anger comprise a hard lesson in vigilance.[25] One MP mentioned backlash to an inflammatory message posted by the young staff trusted to handle her social media.[26] In such circumstances, the leader's office can empathize because even a crew of personnel can make a digital mistake.[27] Everyone is aware that a poor choice of words or double-edged remark can activate an online hate mob.

Political Correctness and Populism

Confrontation about political correctness is another factor in party discipline. The contested term can be pejorative; here it refers to political pressure to avoid language that marginalizes. Its advocates pursue a more equitable and multicultural society by promoting egalitarian policies and word choices. Its opponents see it as a form of Orwellian "Newspeak" imposed by the cultural elite.[28] The orthodoxy sparks a conformity-culture war among conservatives, liberals, libertarians, and socialists. Whatever its merits, this call-out culture is a constraint on politicians' ability to speak extemporaneously. It contributes to the withholding of opinions on sensitive topics and to the pursuit among groups of courses of action that avoid criticism.[29] It motivates political parties to conduct even higher standards of candidate vetting in order to uncover potentially offensive remarks. Politicians learn to delay saying what they think.

Populism somewhat bridges the chasm between political correctness and traditionalism. It too is a misunderstood term, often conflating its proponents' anti-establishment streak with being anti-democratic or always slotting as left-wing or right-wing. Here I refer to populists as anti-elite crusaders. Whether they are socialists, conservatives, nationalists, or of some other political persuasion, one commonality is they are typically charismatic leaders who challenge social norms and portray themselves as the voices of ordinary citizens who distrust institutions.[30] The philosophy is attractive to those who see problems with political parties, who think that parliamentarians should prioritize constituents' views, and who prefer solving problems at the grassroots level.[31] Populist plainspeak strikes many as a refreshing tonic to the party message merchants afraid to cause offence.

There have been several populist uprisings in Canadian national politics. The Progressives, United Farmers, Cooperative Commonwealth Federation (precursor to the NDP), Social Credit Party, and Reform Party are some of the more successful protest parties that have proposed radical changes to the political system. Others have failed to capture the public imagination, most recently the fledgling People's Party of Canada. Populism can also erupt within an established party that goes on to head the government. In the mid-twentieth century, amid years of uninterrupted rule by the Liberal Party, national opposition parties were calling for "restoration" of the authority of Parliament.[32] Progressive Conservative leader John Diefenbaker advocated for the supremacy of private members and for Parliament to reflect the public will rather than being a servant of the government: "I am a House of Commons man," the long-time MP said in his first speech of the 1957 campaign as he placed his hand over his heart.[33] Yet his tenure as prime minister (1957–63) was crippled by his own lack of discipline. His PC government was marred by retrogression, indecisiveness, perfunctory caucus consultation, and high-handedness.[34] Diefenbaker's leadership style exposed the weaknesses of excessive deliberation and contributed to a cabinet revolt. Populist calls for devolution to grassroots representation have proven to be no match for a political system that centralizes power.

A problem with tight messaging acting as an inoculator against public shaming is that scripted politicians whet the public's appetite for outbursts and risqué humour. According to one survey, a sizable majority of Canadians believe that people are too easily offended by language choices and think that political correctness is excessive.[35] As well, most Canadians say that they would be more likely to vote for a candidate who stands up for common people and is unafraid to challenge elites.[36] "Political correctness goes too far," says Maxime Bernier, the former Conservative who sparred online with Celina Caesar-Chavannes and founded the People's Party. "I think Canadians are interested in politicians who say what they believe in and who are real like them."[37]

Populists play off media logic and political norms by making statements that challenge elite compacts. They attract attention to controversial third-rail topics into which the establishment is afraid to wade. They target scapegoats. Populists connect with a disillusioned and disengaged electorate that craves the authenticity of a plain-spoken politician unafraid to be themselves in public – someone who "doesn't use a ten-dollar word when a buck would suffice," as one parliamentarian puts it.[38] A populist's unconventional style enables the rebuffing of calls to dismiss a candidate whose public remarks or social media posts cause offence. The appeal of anti-scripting makes political parties keen to have their messengers communicate in a genuine manner – just as long as brand ambassadors do not contravene party values or criticize the leader.

DIVISION, AMPLIFICATION, AND WEDGES

Many political issues are polarizing. A government decision can have serious implications for constituents. Some policies cause a rupture between urbanites and ruralites. People can be intransigent about financial, social, religious, and human rights issues. International relations can be a source of rancorous debate. Even whether to address or ignore demonstrators chanting in front of the legislature can excite a caucus. A parliamentary group is at constant risk of media reports on rumblings of internal disagreement.

News Value of Division

In Canada, when members of a caucus take competing positions on a high-stakes issue, leaders are rarely characterized as democratic for tolerating healthy disagreement. Instead, the media is prone to either portray downtrodden backbenchers rising up against draconian party constraints and an authoritarian leader, or else the leader is mocked as indecisive and depicted as weak.[39] Either way, caucus division leads to questions about the leader's views, judgment, and suitability to lead. A former PMO communications director observes that "it is news if a party is not able to hold its members together, which is treated as a proxy for an inability to govern, for weak leadership, and a party that's at war with itself."[40]

Decades ago a private member could think aloud publicly. A reporter would call looking for a comment on something controversial, and staff could negotiate the story. Joe Clark, prime minister from 1979 to 1980, reflects on how things have changed: "There was not as much intense attention by journalists as to who was onside or offside on a particular issue in a party," he says. "If several MPs were offside with their party, that became newsworthy. There was an expectation that a number of MPs would be both partisans when it really counted and individuals more often than was the case when Parliament became more contained."[41] Today it is headline news if a little-known backbencher makes an intolerant remark.[42]

Frontbenchers and backbenchers alike report that the potential for bad news creates tremendous pressure for party discipline. Party discord is evidenced by the thinnest of digital deviations: retweeting a controversial post, commenting with a particular emoji or hashtag, or posting a positive remark about a colleague on the outs with the party leadership.[43] Here are some snippets of what Members of Parliament have to say about the ferocity of media logic in Canada:

A dangerous thing the media does is to define us as either trained seals – if we say "amen" to everything the leadership does or says – or as rogue elements if we don't follow the party line to the letter. It's all about ex-tremes when, in reality, we can have opinions that are not exactly the ones advanced by the party, without going against its core values. But the media, as soon as someone deviates from the party line, portrays the party as divided instead of taking it as an invitation to look at something from another angle.[44]

The minute that you have a view that is slightly different from the party orthodoxy, the media uses it as a cudgel to illustrate how poor the leader is, or the party isn't ready to govern, or it doesn't know whether it is coming or going on an issue. You get punished for having different views within the party umbrella. So it's best to hash out those opinions in private within the caucus or within the party to come up with a position and stick with that position.[45]

The fact that Liberals disagree with Liberals is as big, or bigger, of a story than the actual story. The conflict between the politicians is a story in and of itself. The reason they are in conflict is almost secondary. People like the human drama, and they'll pay more attention to it than the actual policy-level discussion.[46]

I find it astonishing, time and time again, why people in the media and others are surprised when party members vote with the party. We were elected as a team, we were elected on a platform. So I don't get why people keep going back to this. By the same token, I don't understand why people are surprised when the odd time people don't vote with the party. It's not really as big a deal as people try to make it out to be, in my opinion.[47]

Division is the easiest story to write. The conflict itself becomes the story. It's like coverage of a hockey game: whenever there's a big fight in the hockey game, they cover the fight first even though it's not relevant to the results of the game, except for penalties. Knowing that, we want to demonstrate coherence, lest people think there are conflicting messages out there.[48]

Arguably, the media are doing their job by shedding light on dissent that politicians try to hide. Reporting about caucus disputes in a dramatic way is fair because heated political conversations are dramatic. The problem for politicians is the lack of room for nuance. They cannot triumph by explaining different interpretations of certain words, getting into a social media debate about policy minutiae, or protesting that filing a story should have waited until they were available for comment. A former minister suggests that parliamentarians realize the benefits of speaking as one in public:

People regulate themselves. The one forum where they are told it is okay to be frank and open is a caucus meeting. But that is on the strict understanding that caucus is secret. It is very clear you must not fall out of line outside of the room. It's not like people have to be disciplined into that. It's that they say "yeah, that makes sense." All you have to do is see one news story where there is a bit of daylight between two members of the same caucus, in any party, and the story is about conflict and disagreement. You realize you're not going to get anywhere with a media story like that. I saw politicians, including myself, take on board the idea that you must stay on-message. Not because somebody is telling you to but because it's the only practical and efficient way to get stuff done.[49]

Without the sense of order derived from message consistency, a parliamentary party contends with the chaos of negative press and internal disarray. Conformity is even more necessary in a milieu of digital agitators.

Amplification

Which came first: the media dramatizing division within political parties or political parties urging message cohesion? The origins of message unity are impossible to establish. Evident are displays of outward-facing insularity by partisans. Less obvious is the backroom manoeuvring to coordinate brand cohesion.

Canadian political parties use social media mainly as a broadcast medium to push one-way messages.[50] Sharing what someone else posts online validates the remarks to a wider audience. A CBC News examination of retweets by party candidates of other candidates throughout the 2019 federal election found them amplifying posts from members of the same political family (Table 4.1).[51] Whenever Liberal candidates retweeted other candidates, 99.2 percent of the time it was fellow Liberals; similarly, for the Bloc Québécois, it was 98.8 percent, for the Conservatives 98.4 percent, for the New Democrats 97.3 percent, and for the Green Party 95.5 percent. This expression of like-mindedness reflects instructions from the party centre to boost party messaging. Avoiding engagement with opponents is a natural defence against criticism or potential saboteurs who try to spread disinformation. Such indicators of discipline can conjure up myths of powerful party bosses who spread terror about the consequences of division. There is some truth to that perception. A less sinister explanation is that most message unity is organic behaviour intrinsic to a political club, especially one that uses extensive vetting processes to select loyalists.

Political staff participate in digital discourse by building amplification networks to push messaging. Extraparliamentary engagement with the 4 percent of Canadians who are members of a political party is increasingly digital.[52] Staff regularly send electronic messages to citizens in the party's database. As well, personnel dig through social media monitoring reports, private Facebook groups, and email lists to assemble online communities of party activists.[53] These mobile partisans receive snippets of counterintelligence and facts about which to write. The online nomads sustain the

TABLE 4.1
Candidates' retweets of other candidates (2019 Canadian federal election)

	Retweets (%)				
	Bloc	*Conservative*	*Green*	*Liberal*	*NDP*
Bloc tweet	98.77	0.02	–	0.01	0.03
Conservative tweet	0.25	98.35	0.61	0.59	0.66
Green tweet	0.10	0.02	95.47	0.06	0.36
Liberal tweet	0.74	1.40	2.34	99.23	1.56
NDP tweet	0.10	0.19	1.38	0.05	97.25
(*n*)	(2,040)	(18,157)	(4,919)	(31,778)	(7,884)

Note: Data for candidates whose Twitter accounts were listed on their party's website. People's Party of Canada data account for the remainder in order for the columns to total 100 percent.
Source: Courtesy of Roberto Rocha.

message during off-peak periods and ramp up during a controversy: "We have amplification networks as part of digital campaigning," a party staffer divulges. "Facebook groups and specific email listservs are sent messages and asked to please amplify this message out on the interwebs. It is sent to both central and local party people. It's one way that we get organic traction."[54] Staff send emails to politicians and constituency assistants requesting that they share and retweet select messaging, such as entertaining memes or snappy infographics, or perhaps messaging within a news story. An MP's social media assistant explains that recipients in turn ask the same of their local networks: "Many MPs have their supporters amplify messages," she says. "You have an email list with members of your riding association and people on the communications team for the next election. A blast is sent asking those people to share on Facebook and retweet on Twitter. An email includes the links for sharing, suggested posts, ways to encourage friends."[55] Political staff throughout the executive and legislative branches of government contribute to the amplification using their social media (see Figure 4.1).

Hyper-partisans use social media pseudonyms to feign grassroots support and to spread negativity about opponents. The online subterfuge can escalate to paying supporters to participate in amplification; to purchasing online followers, likes, and view counts; and to criticizing opposing voices through robot accounts.[56] "The dark side of amplification is paid

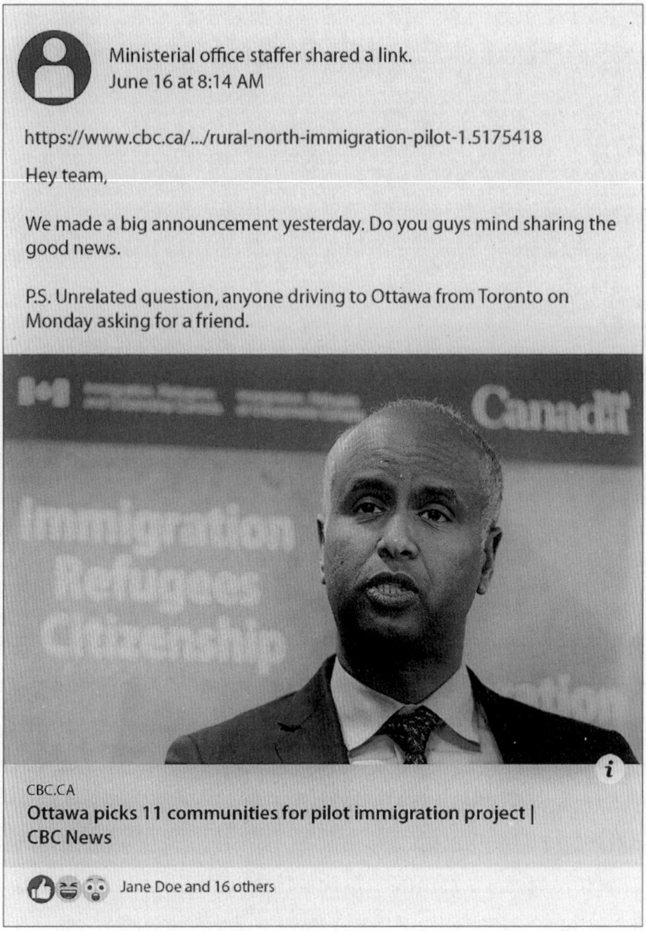
Ministerial office staffer shared a link.
June 16 at 8:14 AM
https://www.cbc.ca/.../rural-north-immigration-pilot-1.5175418
Hey team,
We made a big announcement yesterday. Do you guys mind sharing the good news.
P.S. Unrelated question, anyone driving to Ottawa from Toronto on Monday asking for a friend.
Immigration
Refugees
Citizenship
CBC.CA
Ottawa picks 11 communities for pilot immigration project | CBC News
Jane Doe and 16 others

FIGURE 4.1 Social media amplification of a government news story | Canadian Press/Frank Gunn.

trolls. People are paid to comment negatively, and sometimes hatefully, on news stories and social media posts about other parties or even on their livestreams," the party staffer declares. "They amplify the party's attacks and are unshackled from being politically correct. The idea is to create such a toxic atmosphere on those threads that people who think differently and want to counter those attacks won't bother because it's so hateful and gross to engage with. So then, to anyone reading the comments or threads, it seems like the negative side is winning or the attacks are working and are unopposed."[57] The practice of amplifying or dampening online discourse is becoming automated with political bots, which are hard to identify or attribute. Digital dark arts offer constant reminders to public officeholders of the benefits of sticking to party messages.

That said, digital enthusiasm ignores that much political communication involves the same people talking to each other. As well, the news stories that partisans amplify expose their preference for distinct news organizations. The above CBC News examination of candidate retweets found contrasts in retweeting of news outlets and journalists by Liberals (who retweeted CBC News most often), Bloc Québécois (*La Presse*), Conservatives (*National Post*), New Democrats (*Toronto Star*), and Greens (*Maclean's*).[58] Enthusiasts also overlook that many citizens do not pay attention to digital politics. One survey found that a majority of Canadians have never shared a political opinion online, and less than a quarter of internet users are prone to "like" a political post.[59] "Social media doesn't have an overwhelming influence in my constituency," relays an MP for a rural riding. "As one lady said to me, 'You know, I have a telephone. You could just phone. I don't do that computer thing.'"[60] Even so, digital politics is an entrenched form of partisan sorting that has yet to reach its ceiling.

Wedge Politics and Trap Votes

Framing the debate and discrediting opponents are among the arsenal of communications tactics that politicians deploy to advance an agenda. As strategic utility maximizers, politicians minimize communications risk by not taking a public stand on divisive issues that would put them on the wrong side of public opinion. However, ambiguity is incompatible with targeted political marketing and the call-out culture of digital politics. Joe Clark reflects on how parties now think in terms of how each other's core supporters will respond to a policy stance: "There was an era in which major political parties would seek votes from whomever might be inclined to give them. They were quite open parties," Clark says. "Now there is this sense of 'who is my base?' There is a tendency to speak to a base that, on the one hand, reinforces party discipline from the top because the message has to be the same and, on the other hand, reflects a different attitude towards the role of an MP who is a little less independent."[61]

A leader confident about group solidarity can take a blunt public stand on a polarizing topic to energize the party's support base.[62] The topic is raised at every opportunity to bait an opponent to state a clear position. A wedge creates a policy quandary. It stokes caucus unrest and gives rise to a media spectacle. The leader of the targeted party is compelled to contain internal fissures while opponents mobilize to sustain the pandemonium. Drawing attention to such differences can frame ballot box questions.

In the legislature, parties introduce "trap votes" to frame the image of an opponent on an area of weakness. Omnibus bills, motions, private members' bills, and other types of votes can all be a tool of wedge politics. The unstated purpose is to exploit disunity, draw public attention to a controversial topic, and differentiate one brand from another as the strategic game of gotcha politics generates controversial headlines that inflict more distress. Individual members become attuned that how they vote can be used against them in messaging and targeted social media advertising.[63] More broadly, a trap vote tests the solidarity of a caucus grappling with a philosophical conundrum, and forcing the caucus to take a side on a double bind situation exposes stark cleavages. Simply putting notice of a motion on the notice paper can generate news stories about policy contrasts and plunge a caucus into emotional debate.[64] Most motions have no legal force, but the symbolism does force a leader's hand. An MP divulges how wedges and traps strive to exploit an opponent's Achilles heel:

> Solidarity is a weapon. Many governments deliberately try to find private motions, private members' bills, or government legislation that seeks to find a weak spot within a caucus that will divide the caucus to show there's disunity or that not everyone in the caucus believes in the leader. If an election is about the leader, something incredibly powerful is to be able to say "look, all of his people don't believe in him either." On social conservative issues, the Liberals put together motions to try to divide the Conservatives, and the Conservatives look at fiscal issues and focus on ridings that are blue Liberal rather than NDP leaning. It is using law-making to try to score political points. It gets to the importance of a leader showing caucus solidarity because if you don't show solidarity it will be continuously tested by opponents.[65]

The politically charged issue is often a false dichotomy that presents a choice between good and bad. Trying to explain that the issue is complex or complaining about hidden motives implies that politicians are on the wrong side of the either/or fallacy. For many legislators, stepping out of the chamber for a cup of coffee when the vote is called is better than providing an opponent with political ammunition.

Trap votes are games of political one-upmanship that can require skilful dodging. A prominent case occurred in 2006 when Prime Minister Harper upended a Bloc Québécois motion to recognize Quebecers as a nation. Instead, Harper introduced a countermotion that the Québécois form a nation within a united Canada, turning a separatist volley into a federalist win. The wedge still resulted in collateral damage. Michael Chong, the Conservative intergovernmental affairs minister, resigned after Harper introduced the plan at a caucus meeting without consulting him beforehand.[66] Another way to deal with a trap vote is for the leader to exit when a motion is presented. In 2019, Prime Minister Justin Trudeau and the minister of defence left moments before the House unanimously supported a call for the government to apologize to the vice-chief of defence staff. The opposition presented the motion after the Crown stayed a charge of breach of trust against the public servant who had allegedly leaked cabinet documents.[67]

A government attempt to drive a wedge between members of the official opposition in 1983 offers a peek into a leader's uniformity mindset. It was Brian Mulroney's second day in the House as the Progressive Conservative opposition leader. A Liberal backbencher rose to ask Prime Minister Pierre Trudeau a planted question about the government's support for the French language in Manitoba. The prime minister expressed interest in co-sponsoring a motion with the opposition leader, knowing perfectly well that official bilingualism was a divisive issue in the Tory caucus, particularly among Manitobans. Mulroney was determined to fortify caucus solidarity: "If I allowed that split, I knew the Liberals could then campaign in the next election by making the case that if the new Tory leader couldn't even hold his own caucus together on the sensitive issue of language in Canada, how could he keep the country together?" he later reflected.[68]

The new leader assembled the PC caucus to outline the trap. He explained the need for unwavering public unity: "Using the saltiest of language, I told my MPs to keep their mouths shut. The media, I warned them, were waiting outside to ambush each and every Tory MP. All it would take is one anti-French comment from any of them, just one, and eight-column headlines would trumpet the remark in newspapers from coast to coast the next day," Mulroney recounts.[69] A wavering MP was told that the party's ability to form the government would be compromised if even one Tory voted against the motion: "I will personally expel from caucus any of my members who propose to vote against the resolution," he warned the waverer. Mulroney sprung a countertrap by securing agreement from the prime minister for party leaders to register a vote on behalf of their entire caucus. The move spared vexed MPs from voting. The PC leader received a standing ovation in the caucus for delivering a passionate speech in the House of Commons in support of French language rights. Neutralizing the bilingualism wedge set in motion a recasting of the party as unwilling to tolerate anti-French bigotry.[70] Today the Conservative constitution declares a belief in English and French equality of status, rights, and privileges.[71] Of course, the wedge politics and trap votes continued. Soon afterward, the PCs devised a plan to divide the Liberals on a debate about pensions, whereas the Liberals countered with medicare to divide the Tories.[72]

The federal cabinet is on the receiving end of a wedge on designated opposition days when the opposition controls the agenda. A notable case of exploiting the confidence convention occurred in 1998 when the Reform Party moved that the government should compensate thousands of additional people infected with hepatitis C through a tainted blood supply. Prime Minister Chrétien announced in the House chamber that the proposed $1 billion compensation package would be a confidence vote. Liberals would be required to vote against it. In a caucus meeting, government-side backbenchers complained that the health minister had not consulted them. They doubted the public service's financial analysis. When a backbencher said that he did not want to be in a caucus if people could not speak freely, the prime minister rebutted that perhaps the MP should resign and chastised the group for not applauding the health minister: "There is no regard on the front bench for the backbenchers," a Liberal complained.[73]

At the time, Carolyn Bennett was a first-time Liberal MP. The family physician was a founding member of the Hepatitis C Society of Canada. The government whip directed the new MP to fly back to Ottawa from committee travel to help vote down the opposition motion. It was defeated 155 to 144. Bennett was brought to tears: "I'll be fighting for it tomorrow morning in caucus," she vowed after the vote.[74] At least one distressed MP voiced second thoughts about being a parliamentarian: "If I could do it over again, I would not get involved in active politics," said a Liberal back-bencher who had been advocating for hepatitis C victims.[75] Bennett stuck it out. For years, she contended with being labelled a hypocrite. She rose through the ranks to become a full minister under Justin Trudeau. Along the way, her willingness to speak out reflected her varied roles until she became constrained by cabinet solidarity, at which point her public remarks became more reserved.[76] Decades after the hepatitis C controversy, the political veteran remains pained by her vote and is bothered that party discipline trumped her personal conviction.[77] Little wonder that governments try to minimize the impact of opposition days, such as by scheduling them on a Friday when most MPs have returned to their constituencies.

Politicians evidently can have long careers after conforming on trap votes, though they might endure lasting personal consequences. Private members struggle when faced with a party position diametrically opposed to their own. A senior colleague might be the one to persuade them that it is better to vote with the party. An MP recounts the cognitive dissonance that a trap vote causes:

There was a non-binding motion. My perspective was close to my constituents,' and I wanted to vote "no." However, I understood our overall national objective and that the strategic purpose of the motion was to stereotype our party. I struggled. I talked to the whip. I talked to the leader and to other members. A veteran MP who is a bit independent-minded like me said "you know, you would probably be allowed to miss this vote, and if you absolutely must vote 'no' you can do that. But let me tell you that you are early on in your career, and one day you will need the team. You need to make your choice now on this non-binding vote that has no practical impact and factor in your knowledge about all of the political and strategic considerations." I struggled and struggled.

And then I voted "yes." It is a trust thing. You prove whether or not you are going to be with the team on difficult issues.[78]

Whereas trap votes are planned in advance, many wedges involve unplanned opportunities that one party seizes to divide another. Abortion is a sword issue for Liberals in part because it is a shield issue for Conservatives. Justin Trudeau, who is pro-choice, is firm that Liberals "must speak with one voice" on women's reproductive rights.[79] In contrast, the Conservative Party attracts both pro-life and pro-choice advocates. The party's leaders have struggled with the division. They permit debate about the medical termination of a pregnancy while signalling that Conservative MPs will be encouraged to vote down any private member's bill that proposes to restrict access to abortion services. Occasionally, anti-abortion supporters in the caucus make a public display and put the party on the defensive.

During an otherwise innocuous Question Period in 2018, Prime Minister Trudeau remarked that his government "will always be unequivocal in standing up for a woman's right to choose."[80] A Conservative MP chirped "it is not a right." The Conservative might have been referring to a legal nuance; regardless, the message was anti-abortion. Conservatives exiting the chamber avoided reporters or said that they did not hear the remark. The governing party's communications machine got to work. Staff in the Liberal Research Bureau collaborated on messaging with the PMO and a designated minister's office. Two senior PMO staff tweeted their support for the prime minister. A photograph of Trudeau with the text of his remark, followed by a video clip, appeared on the party's Facebook and Twitter accounts (see Figure 4.2). A blitz of posts encouraged people to share, like, and retweet that the Liberal Party is pro-choice. Social media lit up; news stories appeared online. Liberal MPs received the following messaging, along with links to a tweet and a Facebook post for sharing:

> It's unacceptable and disturbing that 30 years after the Supreme Court of Canada affirmed a woman's right to choose there are some members who still refuse to recognize that right. While Conservatives stay stuck in the past, our government knows women have the right to decide what

to do with their own bodies. The government will continue to be un-equivocal in standing up for women's rights. We will always stand for choice and will work to ensure that women have access to reproductive health options no matter where they live in the country.[81]

Message repetition was in full swing. A Parliament Hill staffer told me that in the next day's Question Period she watched as some ministers "were answering unrelated questions with talking points about a woman's right to choose – they read the same talking points over and over indifferent to what the question was."[82] The Liberal Party emailed supporters asking for donations to support its efforts to defend the Charter and followed with an email blast deploring the Conservative leader for evading media questions. The messages steered recipients to a party web page requesting an email, name, and postal code to "stand with us and support women's rights."[83] The Liberal Research Bureau was on standby to document how many Conservatives had voted against abortion access. They were prepared to deploy pro-life blog posts authored by Conservatives and release photographs of Conservative MPs attending pro-life events.

The Conservative leadership closed ranks. The only public statement about it from leader Andrew Scheer was that he spoke with the MP about an internal matter.[84] Privately, he asked another MP to advise the heckler

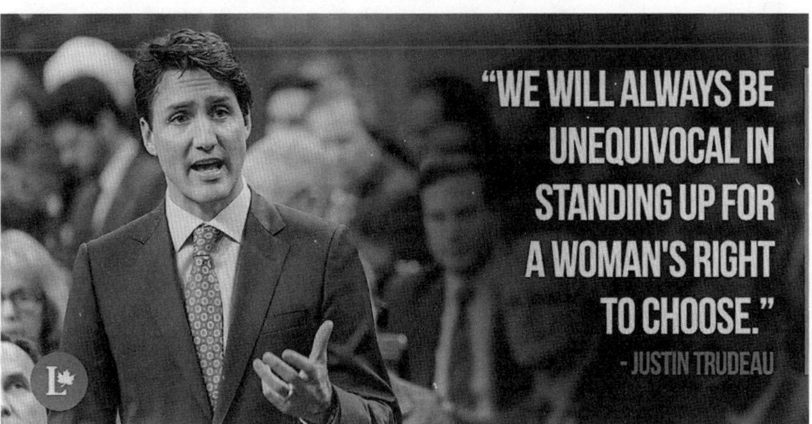

FIGURE 4.2 **Abortion as a wedge issue, Liberal Party Twitter graphic** | Liberal Party of Canada (2018d)

to stay away from the media.[85] It was standard thinking that controversy fades away if a story is deprived of new information. The public outrage galvanizes the leadership circle to caution for the umpteenth time that a single misstep does serious harm.

SUMMARY

The communications environment sets parameters for how political actors behave. In Canada, division within political parties is newsworthy, and the media landscape is fraught with danger for politicians. Political adversaries exacerbate communications hazards by exploiting controversy through wedge politics, trap votes, and combative behaviour. Partisans learn to stay within their digital echo chambers, but their caution only serves to contribute to the appeal of populism that challenges language policing. The circumstances establish a desire for message discipline, the subject of the next chapter.

5

Message Discipline

Party discipline and message conformity are formidable aspects of Canadian parliamentary politics. The drive for tight messaging responds to a citizenry that processes slivers of self-selected information, journalists who take remarks out of context, and political opponents who pounce on errors. How do message lines develop? What is the strategy behind communicating them? In this chapter, I delve into message discipline by establishing the strategic basis for communications consistency. I look at ways that messages are created and delivered. The gold standard is for messengers to convey the brand promise in a manner that reaches intended audiences and resonates with them on an emotional level.

MESSAGE CONSISTENCY

Mute politicians who stand like mannequins behind a leader have become a fixture of media event stagecraft in politics: "I am here to represent people. I don't want to be a flower pot in the legislature or a message machine in my riding," says a backbencher.[1] Such thoughts are common among neophytes whose enthusiasm to represent their community clashes with the premise that they are party representatives. The corporate strategy that instigates unoriginality or silence among parliamentarians is grounded in a desire to prevent them from interfering with planned strategic communications. A core tenet of message control is secrecy.

Political Secrets

Limiting public consumption of political information is an operating principle of Canadian parliamentary government and party politics. Secrecy enables the government to operate smoothly even though it centralizes power structures and ruffles democratic principles of transparency. In opposition, politicians call for open government and can be chatty. Once in power, the same politicians become taciturn.[2]

The most strident political secrecy is vested in members of the Privy Council for Canada. Privy councillors take an oath on appointment to "keep secret all matters committed and revealed to me in this capacity, or that shall be secretly treated of in Council."[3] Members of the federal cabinet are sworn into the Privy Council, as are a variety of senior federal officeholders such as chief justices and former governors general. Some government whips – including all three who served during the 42nd Parliament – are added to the Privy Council's ranks so that the government House leader can share pertinent information available only to the cabinet. The leader of the opposition might need to join, such as for the purposes of receiving a national security briefing. Normally, the only privy councillors eligible to attend federal cabinet meetings are the prime minister and ministers. Public servants in the Privy Council Office (PCO) support current members of the cabinet, with priority given to the needs of the prime minister and the PMO. These national standards inspire comparable oaths, concealment practices, and executive supports in the provinces.

A member of a federal or provincial cabinet commits to engaging in opinionated but secretive debates. The Supreme Court of Canada has ruled that democratic government is at its best when cabinet members can speak their minds during the secret deliberations without concern about the public perception of what is said.[4] The resulting cabinet confidence privilege means that unauthorized disclosure of cabinet discussions is unlawful, including information in memoranda, discussion papers, records of deliberations, communications between ministers, and draft legislation.[5] This includes not revealing the specific contents of a government bill until it is presented in the House. Members of the cabinet are warned to be vigilant about carrying documents and about electronic eavesdropping.[6] A minister who reveals confidential information risks being investigated and charged under the Criminal Code of Canada for breach of trust by a public officer and, if convicted, faces up to five years in prison.

Cabinet solidarity and collective responsibility are the heartbeat of parliamentary government: a minister of the Crown who publicly expresses disagreement with the cabinet must resign the post. Accordingly, ministers can get into intense arguments in cabinet meetings and then present a public image of camaraderie and vote as a coterie in the legislature.[7] The solidarity principle is so entrenched that it unofficially extends to ministers who publicly agree with the prime minister or premier on party matters as well, including who should be a member of the caucus.

The commitment to safeguard secrets passes through the ranks. Parliamentary secretaries in Ottawa promise "not to disclose or make known, without due authority in that behalf, any matter that comes to my knowledge by reason of my holding that office."[8] A minister can therefore share information on a need-to-know basis even though a parliamentary secretary is not a privy councillor. Government of Canada public servants take a similar oath to "not, without due authority, disclose or make known any matter that comes to my knowledge by reason of such employment."[9] Those who require access to classified information or sensitive places, including the legislative precinct, must go through a security clearance process. Employees are trained to engage in secure exchanges of information with people who are "trustworthy, reliable, and loyal."[10] The Security of Information Act regulates the communication by federal public servants of any information that could harm the interests or safety of Canada.[11] Requiring select employees to sign a non-disclosure agreement increases awareness of their obligation to comply with the Act.[12] Whistle-blowers chance dismissal and a criminal investigation.

The culture of secrecy leads to obfuscation. Delays, redactions, and refusals characterize the management of access to information legislation obliging the release of certain government records.[13] Some political personnel and public servants avoid disclosure by opting for verbal discussions over written records. They use peer-to-peer messaging, exchange texts over personal phones, and use private email accounts to avoid exposure. Scrutinize everything with the litmus test that it could become a news story or used in a deposition, politicos are told. Their caution reduces the potential for public controversy.

Private members are bound by an unwritten code that replicates the spirit of the cabinet confidentiality practice. As part of the candidate nomination process, most if not all of them signed a contract agreeing to hold in strict confidence any information concerning the business and affairs of the party. Once elected, they take an oath or affirmation of allegiance to the monarch. They begin attending in camera caucus meetings. Participants who voice opinions in the caucus do so with the communal understanding that the deliberations are not discussed in public. In a safe and trustworthy environment, they can argue with the assurance that they will emerge united irrespective of what is decided. Upholding the gag order allows the caucus to become a conclave for "external secrecy and internal frankness" and a forum to manufacture consensus.[14] A further practice that mirrors cabinet confidentiality is that an MP must withhold the details of a private member's bill until it is presented to the House.[15] Caucus members can be incensed if these codes are broken.

No Surprises, No Freelancing

A rule of no surprises permeates the public sector, in which political actors believe that nothing is "worse than a surprise decision, not having consequential political information, or being caught off-guard."[16] In a legislative assembly, notice must be given for many actions, such as debate on a bill. In the caucus, a private member who springs new information can cause embarrassment. In public, going off script can wreck a planned policy announcement and give opponents a reason to blast alarmist electronic messages urging their political base to make financial contributions. Message discipline is so steeped in the Canadian political psyche that it must seem to freshly elected parliamentarians that communications management was always this strict. In fact, the clampdown on public opining has become more restrictive with the diffusion of digital communication.

In 2003, the United States was preparing to invade Iraq. Jean Chrétien's deputy prime minister instructed Liberal MPs not to criticize publicly the policies of President George W. Bush. Nevertheless, a Liberal backbencher voiced some strong opinions about Bush in a post-caucus scrum. Then, away from the designated scrum area, a reporter's microphone picked up her exchange with an anti-war colleague: "Damn Americans, I hate those bastards," Carolyn Parrish was caught saying.[17] Asked to comment, the whip and ministers told the media that the outspoken MP was free to express herself. One minister said that "it certainly does not reflect my view, but we have free speech in this country."[18] That afternoon Parrish apologized. The prime minister rebuffed calls to remove her from the caucus. The only punishment was self-imposed when she decided that it was not viable to continue as chair of the Canadian NATO Parliamentary Association.[19]

Flash-forward to when Donald Trump became president. In late 2016, Justin Trudeau held a one-way conference call with the Liberal caucus to instruct them not to criticize publicly his American counterpart.[20] Trudeau cautioned how things turned out for the MP who critiqued the previous Republican president. The warning confused Parrish's offhand comment with subsequent events that resulted in her banishment under Prime Minister Martin; regardless, his message about serious career consequences for any commentary was clear. Liberal staff were instructed not to mention Trump on social media, including their personal accounts. The PMO created a Canada-US relations war room to steer digital diplomacy and coordinate public remarks from across the government.[21] Liberals on the public and party payroll appear to have adhered to the prime minister's directive. Had any of them done otherwise, it is improbable that anyone would have invoked free speech to qualify the recusant or that the anti-Trump commentator would avoid swift justice.

In Canada, "freelancing" – the term used for expressing opinions in public irrespective of the party leader's official position – is now viewed as a serious problem.[22] Lower-ranking politicians who show off their personalities and become sideshows disrupt political teams. A message to get on-message can be delivered in a searing manner, says one experienced operative:

In severe cases, I've been the person who had to call a candidate who went off-message, and my edict to them was very simple: "Dig a hole and get into it. When you're done, take the shovel and put it through your phone. If you don't do that, I will dig a hole, put you into it, and you will never get out. You can't be talking a divisive issue that will drive us off-message for three or four days when we're trying to tell the Canadian public how we plan to run the government. If you can't stay on-message, then you won't be a candidate for this party." A version of that has been told to everyone who has worked in politics, particularly communications people.[23]

The attitude toward conformity persists after the election, by which time parliamentarians are the ones urging communications solidarity: "Freelancing ... is an unacceptable challenge to the caucus, to the leader," says an MP.[24] Another MP warns that a colleague who goes off-message is "distracting from what we're trying to do as a team."[25] A third MP adds that "it's up to us as politicians to make the public discourse better, but message discipline is important because we want our ideas to be expressed coherently, comprehensively, and for everyone to be on the same page."[26] A centralized communications operation introduces streamlining processes to replace the mixed messaging of freelancers with consistent commentary from topic specialists.[27] It is a similar story for provincial parliamentarians, often with less rigidity. A former premier used to counsel his caucus to "always say what you think – as long as you understand the difference between saying what you think and everything that runs through your head."[28] Even a one-member caucus can face message constraint. Controversy in a provincial fishbowl can lead party leaders elsewhere in the country to call and voice their concerns about message disagreement, and the extraparliamentary party executive can exert pressure to fall in line.

These are among the many reasons that parliamentarians are keen to know message parameters. They appreciate access to succinct statements that reflect their values. A former MP avows that thoughtful messaging is helpful:

> Messaging helps me to be compelling and convincing. It helps me speak to Canadians to help them see why what I believe in is a good thing. I'm so grateful for messaging on issues. It helps me better express my passion for a more just society. But only when it's in the context of those political values. Not garbage about how can we win and how can we outsmart our opponents.[29]

A former chief of staff to a premier concurs that parliamentarians crave talking points: "The main complaint I've seen about messaging is when caucus members were asked a question by a reporter or a constituent, and they didn't know what the party's position was, so they didn't know what to say. The caucus is a very hungry consumer of messaging," he says.[30] Exasperation with scripting surrounds being handed messaging without an opportunity to participate in its development or understanding of the strategic rationale. Others find the whole practice insulting: "I think it's disgusting to think that I should be told what to do, what to say, and how to represent the people of my riding based on emails that are sent to me by political operatives," says Jane Philpott, the former minister. "Not all MPs repeat the messages. It's not out of spite or some sort of rebellious feeling but a respect for Canadians that they deserve to not hear speaking points."[31]

Some parliamentarians and political staff subvert message control by covertly sharing inside information with a journalist. An unspoken rule is that only the leader or a source acting on the leader's behalf is permitted to betray confidentiality. A high-ranking political staffer can spin information to generate positive news coverage and the head of a government sometimes authorizes the strategic leak of cabinet information to sound out public reaction to a proposed course of action.[32] Leaks can be crafty, such as Chrétien's staff leaking budget commitments to limit the finance minister's options.[33] Conversely, the leadership fears unauthorized leaks. Kathleen Wynne comments that

> leaks are not helpful. It's so disrespectful. It undermines any attempt at having an important confidential conversation. Having said that, governments do strategic leaking. You always hope that there's a reason for a leak, and there usually is. As the government, you live in horror of a leak that undermines what you're trying to do.[34]

Leaders who get side-swiped by leaks lose control. Some ministers in Pearson's cabinet were so cozy with journalists that his complaints about leaks in cabinet meetings appeared in the evening newspapers.[35] Backbenchers who mobilized for new leadership positions excused themselves from Clark's caucus meetings to feed information to reporters.[36] Chrétien once threatened his cabinet to stop leaking information, or he would pluck the names of two ministers from a hat and dismiss them.[37] To quell rumours of internal division a leader or caucus officer can boast about how energized everyone was in a meeting.[38]

When people break confidentiality principles, they undermine the leader's authority and the ability of the caucus to sway public opinion.

Those who want to bring down a leader and/or are upset with their own stations are motivated to disclose confidential information. An Ottawa joke goes thus:

Q. What do reporters call governing party MPs who don't make it into cabinet?

A. Anonymous sources.[39]

The hunt to identify an unauthorized leaker involves systematically disclosing confidential information to a rotation of suspects to narrow down the source. Documents can contain subtle variations so that they can be traced back to the leaker. Other ways to regain control are mentioned in Chapter 7. The best way to manage a surprise, of course, is to prevent it from happening by cultivating an organizational culture that abhors insolence.

Permanent Campaigning and Branding

When a parliamentary assembly convenes after a general election, party leaders declare in the caucus that votes are won in ridings, not in the capital city or the legislature. Campaign architects assume senior staff positions in the leader's office. These hyper-partisans are authorized to wage a so-called permanent campaign of non-stop communications by harnessing all available resources to win every battle and every news cycle.[40] Seized by a rapid response mentality, they try to anticipate issues, selectively present information, push counterpoints before journalists file stories, and sweep an unfavourable topic from the news.

Among the outcomes of permanent campaigning are "new limits" on backbenchers, portrayed by the media as an insignificant category of politician.[41] Members of the governing party are absorbed into campaign readiness infrastructure. Digital visuals are generated at "echo announcements" at which they join a prime minister or premier, a minister, and/or other politicians to flog the local aspects of a larger government policy. Information can be repackaged multiple times to reannounce it in order to reach new audiences and maximize positive media coverage. Message discipline ramps up when an election is on the horizon, particularly during a minority government.[42] Ministers and parliamentary secretaries make a flurry of announcements – events celebrating details of local community grants are a favourite – in targeted regions.[43] Political staff encourage a backbencher to register a "local win" by taking credit for government action, which portrays the representative as working hard to influence cabinet decisions, irrespective of reality.[44] Claiming responsibility for pushing the government to make the decision helps to offset perceptions of being a media prop.

The dark side of permanent campaigning is opposition research. Staff in caucus research bureaus constantly unearth, check, and archive remarks made by members of other parties.[45] What representatives say in the legislature and how they vote can be used against them. Scrutinizing social media posts is a favourite pastime. Staff informally eavesdrop at political events and coffee shops, looking for any political advantage. Party whips remind members to always be alert: "In caucus, especially after an election, I would caution new MPs about having a dinner conversation with a fellow MP: 'Don't ever think the person sitting a few feet away from you playing with their phone isn't recording every word you're saying,'" says a former government whip.[46] Parliamentarians are mindful that chatter in taxis might be recorded, and they are careful what they read on airplanes.

Branding introduces calm into this turbulent atmosphere. A political brand is the sum of tangible and intangible impressions.[47] It promises to consistently fulfill wants and needs in a way that resonates. A strong political brand attracts enthusiasts who form an emotional connection when they are satisfied that the promise of the brand has been delivered. Their psychological attachment causes them to value the brand above alternatives, even when it falters. Branding inundates how Canadian politicians think about party discipline, which they see as "the recognition that we are elected as part of a team, under a brand and under a platform," says an MP: "Discipline is more than voting. It has to do with attitudes, with comments, engagement."[48] Brand messaging becomes a talisman for a politician under pressure who searches for safe ground. For example, a politician ambushed by journalists who seek immediate comments can stall with stock phrases. In a siege mentality, political managers prefer non-answers to admitting fault, and spinners dodge questions by repeating key messages irrespective of the question posed.[49] The brand becomes a compass to stake a credible position.

Skeptics advise that it is not the information that an organization puts forth that warrants attention; rather, we should look at what branding evades, suppresses, and hushes.[50] Branding increases the tendency of politicians to frame or spin facts while suppressing dissenting views and obscuring things that they want to hide. It can make a political party look anti-democratic, because a repeat-remind philosophy depersonalizes parliamentarians whose own personal brand must align with the master brand. There is a danger that targeted audiences will tune out the blather of message repetition, dismiss politicians as one and the same, and crave authentic representation. A critical flaw is that politicians can be boxed in when a message factory cannot adjust quickly enough to a fast-moving public predicament. When a party is engulfed in controversy, there is no time to test messaging in focus groups.[51]

Public administration subscribes to branding as well. Governments save time and money by standardizing their communications.[52] They maintain strict standards for the consistent use of government symbols, logos, and wordmarks; and they use internal planning templates to coordinate messaging. Journalists might be encouraged to submit questions by email, which enables government flaks to recycle approved phrases and avoid deeper probing. Being economical with information aligns perfectly with a branding mindset.

MESSAGE CRAFTING

As mentioned, party politicians see many positives about messaging. They are constantly reading the public mood to discern whether public unrest is real or exaggerated.[53] They begin as generalists who need to learn about complex issues while considering the written and unwritten policy books of their party. What is their position on combatting the destructive mountain pine beetle in western Canada? What should be done about vaping? Child protection legislation? Regulating hunting at night? Religious symbols in the public sector? There are countless public policy issues to become acquainted with in a hurry, many of which do not appear in the party's election platform and intersect with different levels of government. The craft of message development draws on street-level anecdotes and public opinion research to communicate brand values succinctly. Further sources of input include the extraparliamentary party and its election platform, the government, and the parliamentary caucus.

Brevity

People draw on snippets of information when they are unwilling or unable to exert effort to become more informed. Social scientists refer to these processes of searching for information as heuristics, cognitive shortcuts, and memory-based versus impression-driven decisions. Invariably, people form political judgments anchored by images of political parties and their leaders, especially during a crisis.[54] Doing so saves citizens time and mental energy, at the risk of forming an opinion based on the likeability of the communicator and making a deficient decision.[55] Nevertheless, many citizens are content to ignore most policy problems. Their "rational ignorance" about politics and government allows them to get on with their lives.[56]

Political strategists use information tidbits to connect with inattentive citizens. Catch phrases, witty one-liners, visual cues, and emotions all take on added importance. Condensing information into short, memorable, and inspiring messages is a tactic of persuasion that highlights positives and glosses over undesirable information. To connect with a distracted electorate, strategists stress brevity, consistency, standardization, and amplification. Patrick Muttart was a Conservative strategist during the Harper era and a pioneer of political marketing in Canada. He believes that message discipline is related to the ability of the political marketplace to absorb information:

> People are bombarded with so many messages, from so many different sources, often simultaneously, particularly with the advent of social media. Within government, within the party, we had an informal rule. We called it "the three-second rule." We believed that people only give a message three seconds before they decide whether to move on. We came to that view by testing political materials, watching people in focus groups, observing how they behave, considering consumer research about how long people look at pieces of mail, and looking at data about social media usage and the behaviour of consumers as they go through their Facebook newsfeeds. You basically have three seconds to imprint a message into

somebody's mind or to convince them to keep reading, watching, or listening.[57]

The more time that marketers spend in politics, Muttart says, the more they realize how little bandwidth most citizens have for political news and commentary: "When you're producing political creative, the shorter it is, the harder it is to write," he says. "A one-page narrative is hard. A paragraph is even harder, one sentence even more so. The Holy Grail is to get one word that captures a message."[58] Consequently, message design focuses on capturing interest in as few words as possible, perhaps in visual form. A shopping list of policies can be bundled within a theme or a buzzword-saturated catchphrase. Details of a policy are narrowed to core selling points, and sound bite zingers are crafted to attract media attention.[59] Whatever the length, a message must align with the party's values.

Party Values

A party's messages stem from the values and principles articulated in its constitution. That bedrock informs policies, the election platform, the party's purpose and mission, and the leader's vision for the party. They constitute the foundation of the party's brand. Experienced politicians such as Paul Martin are adamant that members of a caucus must support the party's core values: "Good people go into public life because they have strong views and convictions, and they want to carry them through to fruition," Martin says. "It is important that those views conform in essence to a political party's underlying principles. There should not be deep dissent from the underlying principles that a political party believes in, but there can be dissent on their application."[60]

The party's belief system is an essential component of brand symmetry. Message indoctrination begins with the candidate contract that secures a personal commitment to party values: "At the nomination, you sign a document with the party's core principles and which says you will uphold the party's policies. Did you sign it? Yes? Okay, well, then shut up because this is what you agreed to," says David Wilks, the former Conservative MP. "It may never come up again, but it is made very clear to you in the nomination process that these are the party's core values; here are the policies as per the party's annual general meetings. You must sign this, you must agree to it. If there's something you don't agree with, don't sign it. If you don't sign it, you know what's going to happen."[61]

Campaign platforms are the basis for messaging throughout an election period and, if the party is successful, for the government. Candidates might receive talking points to keep them in line with broad policy parameters as they wait for the party to release a platform.[62] The standard of a detailed manifesto was set in 1993 when the Liberal Party of Canada distributed a 112-page policy "red book" itemizing specific pledges, including a promise to give MPs a greater say in the House of Commons.[63] Platforms have since become corporate strategic plans. They outline a vision, propose courses of action, identify progress benchmarks, and offer competitive differentiation.[64] For some partisans, supporting all aspects of the platform post-election is an accountability measure, says a former government whip:

> A fundamental principle that I go by about the role of Members of Parliament is that we run for a party, our party runs on a platform, and we shouldn't be running for that party unless we support that platform. If you say to voters "if my party is elected and forms government, this is what we will do," then people have to be able to then hold you accountable for doing what you said you were going to do.[65]

Unwavering support for the party platform can compromise a parliamentarian's ability to represent constituents. A former MP suggests that party candidates who promise fierce representation are dishonest. Instead, they should say the following to voters: "I will support the party position and thereafter attempt to persuade you of the correctness of that position, because if I stray from the party position I will be out of the caucus and off the team, and I can do more for you inside the caucus than I can from outside the tent."[66]

Street-Level Anecdotes

Message crafters are tasked with humanizing the legal tenets of party constitutions, the policy guidelines of campaign platforms, and the details of public policy. Party strategists recognize that parliamentarians are a tremendous unscientific resource for figuring out the public mood. Elected officials interact with constituents in local shops, on the doorsteps, at community events, and on the phone. They receive an influx of communication via their constituency assistants, email, and social media. They chat with businesspeople, the presidents of union locals, and local activists.[67] A former premier reflects that some of the best street-level intelligence comes from interacting with retirees or the unemployed who linger as part of weekday coffee clubs:

> The coffee shop is the best measuring stick. They all have their groups that meet every single morning. They all talk about politics, and they all talk openly. There will be six or eight women and men sitting in a corner, so you pull up a chair. One morning I'll go to one group, the next morning I'll go to another, and I'll say to them "what do you think of this?" They'll ask "what's this about?" or "did you mean what you said?" They're quick to provide their advice and input while having a cup of coffee in their group discussions. Without doing polling, without knowing what the whole world thinks, you get some of the best information from the coffee shops. Grocery stores are much the same way.[68]

The political value of street-level information should not be underestimated. Justin Trudeau periodically phones Canadians who wrote to him. Listening to the opinions of a cross-section of ordinary citizens helps him to construct messages. Sometimes he develops "the heart of my public narrative in tangible conversations with a real person" and by talking through an issue without the trappings of "the common lingo and the common accepted realities" of the Ottawa "bubble."[69]

Politicians in dense urban districts are often astounded by how connected their rural counterparts are. A politician who visits a rural bakery conducts an impromptu town hall with constituents; a representative who steps into an urban coffee house finds customers who are as diverse as the menu, many from neighbouring electoral districts. Some are tourists. In comparison, everyone at a rural event might have lived in the community their entire lives. They can be on a first-name basis with their representative, who knows their schools, their employers, their families. Urban and rural representatives contend with different policy priorities. A politician in a metropolitan area might report hearing about the need to combat global climate change, whereas a rural representative might contend with the toxic runoff from an abandoned mine poisoning the local water supply.

Political message crafters pay special attention to smoothing out urban/rural and regional variances. Historically, brokering English/French ethnic and regional cleavages has been a considerable factor in the ideological coherence of Canada's federal governing parties.[70] Federalists and sovereigntists tell tales about deep ideological divides in Quebec: "The stakes are extremely high, the highest they can be," says a former Quebec premier. "The experience of fighting for national unity magnifies the importance of party discipline because success depends very much on the ability to deliver a unified message."[71] Regional values are believed to be less pronounced today than are policy cleavages.[72] That view differs from how Canadian politics is organized. The regional imperative is vibrant in federal political offices and parliamentary party caucuses, and on the campaign trail. Partisans know that the single-member plurality electoral system can both suppress regional differences and exaggerate them.[73] In a country as vast as Canada, it is essential that regional cultures and perspectives feed into central messaging, particularly when caucus suggestions differ from how the media are framing a story and members can quantify what constituents are saying.[74] The party brain trust investigates when many parliamentarians say that an issue is coming up on doorsteps in their riding. If communications staff are struggling with issue wording, then they can consider what parliamentarians say works with constituents, and a pollster can test the language in focus groups.

Another source of unscientific input is the leader's confidants. Friends and family members are a useful sounding board. Jean Chrétien placed great value on political advice from his wife, Aline, who weighed in on everything from spotting potential cabinet ministers to deciding whether her husband should seek re-election.[75] Technology now enables a spouse to offer communications advice in real time, such as texting a directive to the leader to stop fiddling with a wedding ring while on camera.[76]

Public Opinion Research

Empirical research is essential to message design. To some parliamentarians, polling data are mechanical and inhuman and cannot replace in-person interactions that force politicians to evaluate their internal belief systems. To others, data collected using scientific principles are invaluable for better communication. They derive assurance from a pollster who makes a persuasive case that a message will connect with audiences and weaken opposition messages.[77]

Political strategists source public opinion research to shape political debate by recasting language and evoking metaphors.[78] Surveys and focus groups help them to locate optimal words and catchphrases as well as test message tones and arguments. Shades of difference between political parties are embellished for strategic gain because strategists know that audiences respond differently to frames. Party leaders, campaign platforms, and websites substitute *team* or *movement* for *political party*. Instead of using the neutral language of increases or decreases to discuss public finance, politicians use emotive words such as *cuts, investment, tax grabs, bailouts,* and *waste*. Conservative opponents of a carbon tax claim that the government is putting its hand in people's pockets; Liberal supporters of a price on pollution advocate for a clean economy. Researching word choices has added importance when communicating in more than one language, Bernard Lord explains:

> Some translated words may seem to say the same thing, but sometimes there are nuances. Using the right words to say the right thing in each language is very important. The normal, maybe lazy, thing to do is if you have a word that sounds the same, it's almost the same, so you use the same word in French and English. But sometimes they don't exactly mean the same thing, or they don't generate the same emotion with voters. It isn't literal translation from one language to the next.[79]

Although disparities in political vernacular portray the parties as diametrically opposed, it can be little more than jargon that sets them apart.

The role of opinion research is critical to communications. Tracking surveys show how messaging is resonating. More sophisticated analysis of polling data enables message targeting by segmenting voters into like-minded cohorts.[80] In strategy sessions, pollsters and political staff explore demographics and voter attitudes to develop a profile of the desired coalition of voters. They build inventories of strengths and weaknesses and identify lines of distinction that juxtapose the party from its opponents.[81]

Some pollsters become full-time party or government employees.[82] Their proximity enables regular presentations to political personnel in different offices to help ensure that messaging is aligned across policy and communications units. Research findings are shared at cabinet retreats and in response to requests from chairs of caucus committees. What pollsters say can be a wake-up call. They can show that what politicians are talking about differs from the most important issues to citizens. Research might also reveal that citizens are giving credit for a policy decision to a different party or level of government.

There is little that parliamentarians can do to rebut a pollster's findings. A former minister explains: "Individual members of caucus don't have any way to counter the staff around the leader who are informing the caucus: 'This messaging works; we're going to use it. This messaging doesn't work; we're not going to use it.' You pretty much have to take this stuff at face value," he remarks. "If they say 'don't say this because it doesn't have the effect you think it has, it actually has a negative impact, we've tested it,' then you assume that's reasonable." Moreover, "even with messaging you don't particularly like, you find out it works when you try it out on some constituents. So you do it because the leader's people have professional heft that no individual politician could possibly have. Otherwise, you need the confidence to rely on your gut instinct to challenge the leadership."[83] Deference is compounded when a backbencher who takes the initiative to commission a public opinion survey is labelled as disruptive.

MESSAGE DELIVERY

Where have all the characters gone? What happened to the gifted orators? Politicians of yesteryear remember when Canadian politics was more colourful. Before the televising of legislative proceedings, there were unpredictable personalities who spontaneously expressed opinions. They were indifferent about whether the leader liked it or not. Those personas have all but vanished and been replaced by scripted performances that strike many as senseless. One veteran parliamentarian alleges that party "messaging has become narrow and repetitive, with every activity of the candidate a rote repeat of prepackaged, whitewashed slogans. Defining the opposition in as vicious and dogmatic a way as possible is now more than half the game. The other half is repeat, repeat, repeat the message that has been crafted as your brand."[84] There is considerable truth to the belief that many of today's politicians are a bland extension of the brand, though as we shall see political staff urge authentic delivery in order to disguise the repetition.

Scripting

Many politicians skilfully word their rhetoric to have an emotional punch.[85] They take pride in a Hansard historical record of what they say in the legislature. Others find public speaking arduous. They rely on prepared notes when addressing the assembly. They worry that opponents will search the public record to use words against them. In opposition, Justin Trudeau used to grumble about message scripting: "I think Canadians are tired of politicians that are spun and scripted within an inch of their life, people who are too afraid of what a focus group might say about one comment or a political opponent might try to twist out of context, to actually say much of anything at all," he said as a private member. "And I don't think that in our parliamentary system, which thrives on countering arguments and robust back and forth around debate, that we are well served when everyone is trying to be as bland as they possibly can be."[86] As his career progressed to party leader, and then prime minister, Trudeau came to appreciate the functionality of prepared lines. Heads of government live by the adage that poor communication can sink good public policy. A former premier elaborates:

> I cannot overemphasize how important it is to have good communications. So many of the problems that develop internally that I have been called upon to tackle as a leader are communications related. Sometimes you're so devoted and earnest at developing public policy positions that you forget about how equally important it is to develop good communications in the most thoughtful, intelligent, and respectful way possible. As a leader, you've got to spend a lot of time working with your caucus, working with your team, and developing relationships so you can properly communicate. Focusing on getting the communications done well is at least as important as development of the policy itself.[87]

Parliamentarians are thrust talking points with the force of officialdom and attack lines that carry the sting of a partisan jab. Instead of trying to comprehend the topic or question the lines, some politicians mindlessly repeat the script, often in hurried circumstances under pressure. Others are irritated when staff spoon-feed messaging. Some push back against staff requests, whereas others acquiesce to them:

> I didn't want to just talk about the budget. That's boring! Who wants to listen to that? If someone asked me to give a speech, I'd say "tell me three points that I must say before I get off the stage. Then I'll write my own speech about whatever I want. But I'll get your three points in. That's the deal."[88]

> I was force-fed lines to memorize. I felt ridiculous reading the lines in the House. It is BS for soundbites. It may be relevant to people in ministers' offices but for most Canadians, it's ridiculous.[89]

> I said to staff "no, no, don't just give me talking points: you're going to give me a briefing note, I'm going to ask you questions, and I won't say anything unless I have a good reason to say it. There are other people who are talking heads who can only say those five or six things, so, fine, don't ask them to have an independent thought." Too many people don't want to be bothered with the details. We're too much about the sound bite, and some don't want to give a fulsome answer because of extra sentences someone could take out of context. So they keep it short, sweet, and simple. Things get dumbed down, and the messages lack substance.[90]

A political staffer counters that agreement on political values is what generates messaging buy-in: "It's not about being punitive. It's not about an action and a punishment. Elected colleagues are not going to be invested in our messaging just because we threaten them. That's not collegial, that's not nice," she says. "People are going to repeat a message or stay within a message box when they believe in it, when they believe in the values that underlie it, when they understand it, when they feel like they were part of creating it. That's what positive message discipline is within a team."[91]

Politicians are taught to use transitional phrases to answer an unrelated question with key messages. They begin with a value statement about what

FIGURE 5.1
Message box

Us on us	*Us on them*
• Our team has a strong plan to get government spending under control and get our economy back on track • Lower taxes • Spending within our means • More jobs and economic growth	• Our opponent's reckless high-tax, high-spending agenda is ruining our economy • Higher taxes • Out-of-control spending • Weak economy and fewer job opportunities
Them on them	*Them on us*
• Our team has a responsible plan to grow the economy through smart government spending • Economic opportunities for everyone • Making the rich pay their fair share • Strong social programs	• Our opponent has a mean-spirited agenda to slash government programs and services • Supporting the rich and big business • Cuts to social programs • Loss of good government jobs

Sources: Inspired by Faucheux (2002, 80), Richler (2016, 55-56), and an NDP document.

the party stands for. Some insert a positioning statement that calls attention to a problem with their opponent. A stock phrase is followed by a supportive remark highlighting how their party addresses the problem differently. Public figures can achieve equivocation by using rhetoric that repeats core messages irrespective of what they are asked. One practice is packaging lines within a message box, common in the NDP. The box organizes positions into four quadrants that can anchor any commentary (see Figure 5.1). Partisans seek to control the public conversation by steering the discussion above the line in the message box. It helps them to avoid issues below the line that expose their party's weaknesses.

Lines that are more perishable are circulated as messages of the day and social media graphics. Accessing a party database of stock phrases is another tool. A low-technology activity is distributing key message cards. Three-and-a-half-inch by two-inch business cards are convenient for parliamentarians to review cogent messages that blend positives about the party and negatives about opponents. The Saskatchewan Party caucus used to receive updated cards every quarter with messaging that they could carry around in their pockets.[92] MLAs feathered the orientation statements into speeches, members' statements, and interviews. When backbenchers do not have messaging they can turn to what frontbenchers are saying in the news, in press releases, and on social media.

Repetition

Most Canadians claim to pay attention to politics.[93] However, they might not recall a given policy announcement or a political accomplishment. They might never see or hear a message, let alone remember it. Consumer behaviour research suggests that people who pay close attention to commercial messages and/or are brand enthusiasts begin to tire of a message after hearing it three times.[94] Similarly, political research has found that electors tire of seeing mailed reminders to vote after five or six exposures, leading authors of one experiment to conclude that "messages may become tedious when delivered repeatedly in a consistent format."[95] Frequent exposure to messages in a variety of formats is necessary so that limited awareness evolves to learning.

The repetition mindset in politics surfaced in the 1990s when changes in communications technology and the proliferation of political marketing contributed to a sharp uptick in the use of partisan words.[96] Strategically, the objective is to provide citizens with fragments of information in order to cue memory recall and create selective contrasts with opponents. Tactically, politicians are taught to deliver the same message in different ways in order to break through in a busy media universe. Supporting each others' remarks minimizes the number of topics competing for public attention and shapes how those issues are framed.[97] Consequently, Canadian politicians learn to say the same things ad nauseam:

> The basic rule is you say something until you are absolutely sick of saying it, and then you say it another thousand times. Being consistent on messaging is as important for candidates and parties as it is for laundry detergent. How many times have you heard that Tide gets clothes clean? They've been saying it for decades. The question is how you can maintain consistent brand messaging around your political party – which matters for electoral success – at the same time as create room for candidates and MPs to be individuals who bring their own thoughts and ideas to public service.[98]

There is great encouragement around certain phrases. You can tell when a party's MPs have been encouraged to use a particular tagline because you'll hear it over and over again. The counting of words is monitored.[99]

Keep it simple. Policy debates are for losers. Focus on what is most likely to sink in with a distracted electorate: slogans, scandals, personalities, pictures, image. Find whatever works, then repeat it relentlessly.[100]

Every caucus meeting you're given the current version of the message box, which is the main points and the key phrases we're using right now. It's drilled into your head that your job is to go out and say these things as much as possible. If you're starting to get sick of them, then you know you're doing the right thing. If you feel like you've been saying the same thing over and over again, and you're starting to get tired of hearing it, then the public is starting to hear it, and you need to say it more. It's your job to be a message-disseminating machine. It's your social media, your community newsletters, the speeches you give. You need to put the key messages into everything so people are hearing them as much as possible.[101]

In legislatures, parliamentarians sometimes repeat identical lines and expressions or reuse talking points from past years. A parlour game of detecting repetition in Hansard and cyberspace then ensues. A *Toronto Star* examination during the 42nd Parliament found considerable "centrally coordinated political messages or slogans in constant rotation" among MPs of all parties.[102] Messages repeated word for word online are discovered, such as the party shills who posted similar comments on a CBC Facebook Live platform during a party leaders' debate.[103] An MP discloses what to look for: "Watch what people are tweeting. A lot of times they're tweeting word for word what's sent out," he says. "If you find five or six or a dozen MPs who are tweeting the same information out, well, you can be sure that's a provided message."[104] Politicians can feign plausible deniability if they are caught repeating a digital script. However, the limit of conformity is reached when someone leaks internal instructions about which text and photos to post.[105]

Authenticity and Storytelling

Repetitive language is counterintuitive to those who believe that the currency of politics is realism. Communicating information with sincerity conveys good faith, incorruptibility, and trustworthiness.[106] Citizens relate better to grassroots honesty than they do to politicians whom they cynically view as institutional mouthpieces, and they want politicians who show a bit of personality and are genuine.[107] To be authentic, politicians who are told to be on-brand need to be involved in message development and have the freedom to sound human.

Authenticity can be an illusion given that parliamentarians sometimes endorse things they personally oppose. In particular, government-side backbenchers put their personal credibility on the line when they publicly convey ownership of decisions made by the executive branch. A former party leader voices her chagrin at politicians who funnel a parade of party messages: "Inauthenticity erodes public confidence in the entire political process. Cynicism in politics emerges from a lack of sincerity," she says. "Politicians say certain things to get elected and then act like a trained seal when they become part of a government because they are vying for a cabinet position. I think that creates a huge amount of distrust in politicians. It isn't healthy for democracy."[108] Political strategists counsel not to memorize lines because robotic delivery kills the message and because politicians who repeat messaging verbatim are mocked.[109] Rather, politicians should comprehend information before putting it in their own words.

Astute politicians realize that talking points are information aides, not scripts. Key messages should inform original speech: "When you're speaking to a journalist, tell those stories differently. You don't have to be a robot repeating things line for line," says a former MP.[110] Trudeau Liberals are told that message lines are starting points. Philpott explains how scripting evolved in the Liberal government to encourage artistic licence to rephrase messaging:

> There is a lot of talk about the benefit of everyone going out on the same issue on the same day using similar messages and infographics. They got some pushback, not about sending out messaging, but because some MPs were cutting and pasting into their social media. It looks ridiculous

that people have the same thought. So they emphasized that MPs are supposed to use their own words drawing on the general message and the provided bullet points.[111]

A former Liberal communications strategist elaborates:

You are in a precarious position as a government, as a party, and in op-position when message control starts at the top and is too rigidly disci-plined and focused. What we would often communicate to candidates and MPs is this: "Okay, you've seen the key messages you're getting? Never go out with those. Stop. Take a break. Read them over to yourself. Then say them aloud in your own voice. If the lines are difficult for you to remember, or you don't agree with them, you should definitely talk it through with senior communications and policy staff." We don't want them robotically repeating messaging.[112]

Advocates of authenticity are probably unaware of the social psychology behind rewording. People who improvise a speech proclaiming support for a topic that they oppose are more likely to change their opinion about the topic than are people who recite a script.[113] In effect, a person's efforts to come up with persuasive arguments and play the role of issue advocate cause a rethink of that person's disagreement. Political operatives are far more concerned with getting the attention of distracted online audiences. Staff counsel parliamentarians that personalizing the messaging will expand their social media reach, particularly if they package it in storytelling.

Governments and parliamentarians have become news services that release a stream of digital images accompanied by pithy remarks that tell a story. At the turn of the millennium, perusing official photographs of the Canadian prime minister required a visit to the official archives in Ottawa or browsing a coffee-table book.[114] A decade later the PMO issued a single digital photograph of Prime Minister Harper on most days when the House was sitting and intermittently otherwise.[115] Improved bandwidth and social media platforms remedied the technological hiccups of clogging email inboxes with image files. Soon, in a blatant display of permanent campaigning, the PMO was creating scripted video newsmagazines that documented behind-the-scenes moments with the prime minister.[116] At the time, some journalists saw propaganda that enables evasiveness and content manipulation. They overlooked that digital visuals nourished Conservatives across the country with central messaging that encouraged partisan parallelism.

The Trudeau PMO takes things further by connecting symbols with visual messages in a story arc. Symbols are shortcuts for information that in another form takes much longer to discuss or process. A visual icon evokes the main message and contributes to imagined realities. Trudeau elaborates: "When you talk in policy, or you talk in numbers, you sound good but you don't connect," he says. "The stories we tell about who we are, where we're going, it happens in narrative form."[117] He adds that he sees "images as a way to communicate" and that visuals are "a way of connecting directly with the people."[118] Leaders nowadays know that their communications staff need visual content that can be transformed into internet memes, GIFs (static and animated images, such as short video clips), TikTok lip-syncing, and other short-form creativity that can be viewed on a mobile device.

The PMO official photographer has an office two doors down from Trudeau's office. The photographer nips into meetings when the door is closed. He weaves among security detail and bypasses non-disclosure agreements thrust on the media.[119] The prime minister often helps by commenting on lighting, considering angles, and repositioning himself during government activities: "When I hear his shutter, I say: 'Okay, is he getting a good shot?' And I'll turn to give him a better shot," Trudeau discloses.[120] Throughout the day, the PMO photographer edits photographs on a smartphone. Visuals posted to the prime minister's social media accounts are chosen with senior communications personnel.

Kate Purchase, who served as Trudeau's communications director, says that the digital visuals are woven together as part of a story: "In a campaign, in opposition, and in government, we've always taken the approach of sort of 'digital by default.' And the way you tell digital stories is through pictures," she says. "It's not just about the policies. The photo is able to cut through all of it in a very simple way."[121] Purchase adds that Liberal MPs are similarly encouraged to turn written information into visual stories:

Something that MPs could do more of is harnessing stories. At every public meeting, after every interaction, write down stories after you hear them. Often in media training they learn about the structure of an answer to a journalist: start with the values base, go to the core policy ten-second answer, and then pivot. That's the right way to do it in a short scrum with a journalist, but the piece that's missing is the story – how it connects back to a person. It's so much more effective if you say "I know this is going to affect Nancy and her three kids because they're going to get fifty dollars more every two weeks from this policy." Real-world examples are more effective for communicating with Canadians and are a better way to get yourself clipped on the news.[122]

The Liberal Research Bureau channels that desire for local storytelling, discussed in Chapter 8. Relatedly, the Privy Council Office hiring of an employee with the job title of master storyteller embodies the Liberals' imprint of a storytelling style on government.[123]

Taking this lead from the top, political staff advocate that information needs to be presented in a minister's or backbencher's own voice. Parliamentarians and their assistants are taught to use social media to celebrate positive forces in the community: a prominent citizen who stops by the constituency office, a local photograph about Crossing Guard Appreciation Day, images of local Special Olympics athletes, video of the MP helping to clean up the community fire station. When communicating with constituents, instead of mentioning that the government is going to spend $8 billion on infrastructure, ministers and governing party backbenchers are encouraged to highlight that a local bridge will be repaired. The storytelling formula adds a dollop of authenticity, which increases the potential of getting audience attention in a busy media landscape. With any luck, some otherwise disengaged constituents might notice.

Databases

Updating databases is a hidden side of party discipline. In Canadian party politics, the main type of political database is used for partisan purposes to identify supporters contacted for money, volunteer labour, and votes. Constituency assistants use another type as a filing system to keep notes about constituents. A third type is a searchable repository of key messages and images (InfoLib, discussed in Chapter 8). Some parties are more data savvy than others. Integrated federal-provincial parties are at an advantage by pooling voter information in a shared database. Weak parties with their own systems can flounder when they change leaders, whereas backbenchers can be empowered by using their own parallel data storage systems. Pertinent here is that the centrality of party databases further absorbs parliamentarians into the party apparatus.

Party databases begin with contact information in the electronic lists of electors that election agencies are responsible for updating. Major Canadian parties are relentless in their searches for additional data, which contribute to centralizing power in the party hierarchy.[124] They buy lists from commercial data providers, employ telemarketing, and create mail-back questionnaires that appear on parliamentarians' constituency newsletters. When door-knocking or placing phone calls, local partisans input information into mobile phones or tablets synchronized with the database. Invitees to local political events submit data when they register online. Social media advertising urges people to take action by clicking, which leads to a request to provide contact details and give money. The data are refined as people participate in online petitions, contests, and local days of action. If someone donates to the party, or takes a lawn sign, then the information is added to the party database to customize future correspondence. The parties can enhance these digital inventories with data on supporters' purchase behaviour, social media activity, navigation of websites (clickstream data), and online browsing history (cookies).[125]

Party databases are essential for fundraising, event promotion, digital advertising, fieldwork, and narrowcasting. A party can tabulate which issues interest its supporters and rank their support levels, enabling sophisticated precision of messaging, mediums, and geography.[126] Lists of social media influencers can be generated. Responses to variations of a message generate data on which calls to action and wording prompt preferred reactions.[127] An emerging trade is the use of mobile phone numbers for peer-to-peer texting. As party databases are integrated with other technologies, they transform into political engagement platforms that enable direct connectivity with voters. In addition to monetization and stealth communication, party databases serve a crucial electoral purpose. They fuel the microtargeting of exposing selected audiences to selected messages, which in turn firms up loyalty to the party brand.[128]

Party databases have turned central oversight of constituency outreach from anecdotal to empirical. In the early 1970s, rewards and reprimands were distributed based on backbencher performance, which included an assessment of their constituency work: "We do follow the members in their constituency. We're not spying on them. But we like to get reactions from the standview [sic] of their constituents," a chief government whip said.[129] With social media and party databases, parliamentarians who are lackadaisical about constituency service can no longer pretend to be attentive. Today some caucuses have regular reporting mechanisms to disclose how many doors parliamentarians have knocked on, how many local phone calls they have placed, how many events they have attended, and how many times issues have come up. Intra-party competition to keep updating the central database provides senior personnel with evidence of who is participating in active outreach and who is not. A Conservative strategist confides that

> MPs feel like someone is watching them. Which is true: we call them up and say "you haven't put anything into our database in the last few weeks. What's going on?" Most hate door-knocking, with people slamming the door in their face or wanting to talk about wastewater. The ones who complain about central monitoring are usually not doing any work. Even when they're in the fight of their lives, some of them hate going door to door. It's not about message discipline so much as enforcing some level of activity.[130]

The nagging helps to ensure that parliamentarians stay in touch with their constituents. During canvassing, they inquire about what is on people's minds: *How are you doing? How is your summer going? Are there any particular issues that you feel aren't being addressed? Are there any issues that we've been working on that you're happy with?*[131] Staff trot out frequency counts of constituent interactions to motivate other members of the caucus to become active in their communities. Party leaders can assert that they will not sign nomination papers if incumbents do not collect enough data. Liberal MPs who wished to be renominated for the 2019 election were required to participate in mass mobilizations of supporters by telephone, on doorsteps, and at local events; knock on 3,500 doors or place five thousand phone calls; and sign up donors. Many of them believe that the requirement was reasonable. Achieving the targets was "difficult," said one MP, but it involves work that "we should be doing anyway" and "there's no reason for MPs to get a free ride."[132] Others struggled to achieve all of the party's requirements: "I'm a committed Member of Parliament to my constituents. That's first and foremost," said an incumbent. "My job is not to raise money. My job is to represent these people."[133] The central tracking is likely to expand as other parties replicate the Liberals' data criteria for renomination.[134]

Liberalist is the Liberal Party's central voter contact database. It is divided into political and partisan components that require separate levels of authorization. The first of two main components of Liberalist is a constituent relationship management (CRM) contact database. The interface has a casework module that stores information about constituents and manages correspondence. When a constituent interacts with a Liberal MP's office, an assistant uses the name, telephone number, or address to look that person up in the system. The staffer becomes familiar with the case history, including whether the constituent has been rude or threatening, and can update the case notes: "It is helpful to have the casework information that we're inputting on the CRM side in one place," says a constituency assistant. "If one staffer is looking after a file and that staffer is away or leaves, all the information is still accessible to the constituency office. You can seamlessly continue to help the constituent even if that staffer goes."[135] There is an ethical wall to inhibit MPs or their assistants from using the records for partisan outreach. Otherwise, personnel whose salaries are funded via the legislature would be conducting private party work, not to mention the lack of informed consent: "When you're entering casework into the CRM part of it, there's a clear distinction around that just being used in the office. We would never use any of that information on the political side," the assistant adds.[136] Nevertheless, slippage sometimes occurs when industrious MPs or their staff engage in partisan communications with constituents. They can leverage information to ask for donations, refuse services if someone did not vote for them, and block people on social media.

The second and better-known component of Liberalist is for the private party work of election readiness. A Liberalist user agreement outlines the terms of use, including acknowledgment that all data belong to the party. Authorized clients, including nominated election candidates, can look up individual profiles for political purposes. The software is used to promote events, mobilize volunteers, and manage phone banks. It features out-reach tools such as telemarketing scripts to recruit volunteers, survey questions, and "impersonal pushed communications" (i.e., email and voice mail blasts).[137] Liberalist enables crosstab analysis to isolate specific infor-mation, such as demographic profiles of donors in each electoral district. The metrics assess the performance of parliamentarians, pinpoint com-petitive advantages, optimize finite resources, and monetize citizen inter-actions. Data can also propel the terrain of psychographics and predictive modelling. In testimony to a House of Commons standing committee, a Liberal-affiliated data scientist explained that, through advanced statistical analysis, political parties can leverage their databases to forecast supporters' behaviour.[138]

The obsession with big data makes some backbenchers think that what they say in the caucus is of little interest. Gut instincts and local stories are up against quantification: "In caucus, members of the PMO are sitting there listening to an individual MP complain about an issue and might say 'well, that's a nice story, but data is data. According to the data we have, that's not the number one issue in your riding,'" relays an MP. "They match email addresses with Facebook users in your riding. They accumulate likes, shares, and retweets from your riding. They look at the traffic in emails and householder mail-backs."[139] Database statistics complicate the ability of parliamentarians to represent individuals on the margins. Senior staff look at inanimate numbers, whereas politicians interact with real people with real concerns. The MP continues that "I get the people who are falling through the cracks. Every piece of data has a story attached to it. Technology allows the party executive to diminish the individual mem-ber."[140] As well, party databases further erode the traditional function of MPs who lobby for political patronage. Under Justin Trudeau, political staff consulted Liberalist for background checks on prospective government appointees, including the vetting of a potential governor general, judges, and senators.[141]

Central databases foster dependency on the party and increase the ability of higher-ups to treat non-compliant representatives as disposable. Access to casework or political information can be rescinded at any time. If a Liberal MP switches parties or sits as an Independent, then the MP and staff lose casework notes if they do not have an external backup drive or the constituency office did not maintain its own system. The party's replacement gains instant access to Liberalist data and digital infrastructure. Conservatives have a bit more independence. When a Conservative MP recruits a local donor, the national party does not have access to donor information uploaded to its database. The separation respects that MPs should have their own pools of financial backers. Nevertheless, party personnel can attempt to interfere with parliamentarians who manage private databases by insisting that information be contributed to the central database. Those who resist demonstrate a lack of commitment to the team: "If they get mad at you and don't want you to access your own data, you're done," reflects a former MP.[142]

Party appropriation of data adds a new layer of party discipline overtop the struggle to control voting on bills and motions or what parliamentarians say. The fixation on metrics creates unpleasant circumstances for anyone who values self-reliance, and it promises to be grounds for new tests of party dominance over elected representatives: "The greatest way to get disconnected from the centre and excommunicated from future ambition is to say 'sorry, you can't have access to my data,'" says a former PMO director of communications. "The greatest act of political treason you can commit today is to say 'hands off my data, you can't have it.'"[143]

SUMMARY

The price that parties pay for incoherence or dissonance motivates tightly knit formations. Developing messages involves a concoction of brevity, party values, street-level anecdotes, and public opinion research. Candidates and parliamentarians are encouraged to deliver messages with sincerity as part of a story. The sales function of private members is especially fierce for those on the government side. Information about citizens is a valuable commodity in a digital world and party databases are yet another institutional structure that prioritizes party interests. Keeping caucus communications united is beneficial for the government given that it has an agenda to implement, as we shall see in the next chapter.

6

Government Centralization

Familiarity with the executive branch of government is needed to help us understand its relationship with the legislative branch. How are strategic communications centralized in government? What is the role of prime ministers, premiers, the cabinet, and ministerial staff in message coordination? Entire books are devoted to the topic of executive power in Canada.[1] In this chapter, I touch on the communications aspects of cabinet meetings and the coordinating functions of government political staff.

THE POLITICAL EXECUTIVE

In Canada, government operations orbit around prime ministers and premiers.[2] They are a government's most important spokesperson. The way that they run cabinet meetings, how they manage the media, and how central agencies coordinate messaging all set the tone for the caucus.

Cabinet Management

Private members who see salvation in a cabinet appointment might not realize that the thumbscrews get tighter. The cabinet is filled with powerful people who advocate ideas and jockey for resources. A new minister grapples with the quantity of intense deliberations about difficult decisions with real implications for citizens. Ministers discover that the policy system is like peeling a metaphorical onion.[3] "If you think there is central control on caucus and parliamentarians, try cabinet! That's where you'll see the strings pulled and greater restrictions," says a former minister. "You think you'll be able to do what you want to do, but you can't."[4]

The cabinet has tiers of communicators. A cadre of capable ministers is trusted to manage files competently. These ministers constitute an unofficial inner cabinet with more sway than those on the fringes. So-called super ministers and/or regional ministers hold powerful portfolios and sit on, if not chair, influential cabinet committees.[5] They might have a special arrangement to vet their own staff, whom the PMO would otherwise blacklist.[6] They can read a room and adjust their message delivery to communicate in an authentic, adroit manner by personalizing their talking points. They draw on their experiences or integrate what they are hearing from citizens. Some of them treat speaking notes as advice rather than directives: "If it happens to be written in the script, I skip it, and if I'm doing my own stuff, I don't use it," a minister in the Harper government once said about a PMO-mandated slogan.[7] Another tranche is so feeble that without messaging vetted by the centre they do not challenge the bureaucrats in their departments.[8] These ministers are prone to bungle a policy announcement, fail to question advice, are paralyzed waiting for political staff to manage a file for them, and are poor communicators. They constantly seek guidance from senior personnel and rarely assert their independence. Straddling the extremes are some competent ministers who are semi-outcasts because of leadership ambitions, personality conflicts, and other strains.

Many of the communications facets of running a cabinet meeting are mirrored in caucus meetings. In both forums, the leader presides over a structure that briefs group members and invites their input. The gatherings are bound by time constraints, and deliberation is referred to smaller groups. Without sufficient preparation, valuable time is wasted, personality conflicts flare up, and some policies do not receive appropriate consideration. Issues not on the agenda that require urgent attention, known as "drop ins" or "walk ins," can lead to poor decisions because of insufficient time for reflection.[9] When a decision is made, the members emerge publicly united. In both cases, a prime minister or premier must take care not to shower individual ministers or cliques with preferential treatment because overt favouritism leads to jealousy and resentment among the rest.[10]

Cabinet systems are "a very personal choice" that reflect the leadership style of the head of the government.[11] A few leaders preside for such long times that they witness ad hoc approaches being replaced with formalized processes as the volume of administrative decisions increases, as occurred with William Lyon Mackenzie King (prime minister in 1921–26, 1926–30, 1935–48).[12] Some heads of government treat the cabinet as a board of directors that does not require consultation, as Prime Minister R.B. Bennett did (1930–35).[13] In contrast, John Diefenbaker was indecisive. He listened to every minister and offered plenty of opportunities to exchange opinions.[14] Issues were deferred to the next meeting when the cabinet was not unanimous. Diefenbaker was so averse to arbitrary decisions that his cabinets sometimes met twice a day for days on end, including weekends, causing ministers to abscond duties in their departments because of prolonged meetings. Inevitably, the government was criticized for delays, procrastination, and inefficiency. Lester Pearson combatted this problem by requiring that issues be deliberated in cabinet committees first.[15]

Some traditional actors permanently lost influence during Pierre Trudeau's tenure when central agencies expanded and pollsters commanded more attention. In the 1970s, Liberal extraparliamentary executives jostled with PMO staff for supremacy, for instance experimenting with a political cabinet composed of the full cabinet and party officials.[16] The party officials wanted both parliamentary and extraparliamentary executives to endorse the party's election platform and, furthermore, urged the government to consult with them before making major announcements. Those announcements, incidentally, were made by ministers on the floor of the House of Commons instead of at a packaged photo op that is the routine today.[17] The demands went unheeded. Instead, delegates to Liberal Party conventions received reports tracking the progress of the government in implementing the party's policy resolutions, and the prime minister created party troikas composed of a regional minister, a provincial party president, and a backbencher that met weekly to channel information between Ottawa and the extraparliamentary party.[18] In the cabinet, polling data constituted evidence of the best course of action, which ministers had difficulty refuting.[19] The meetings were six-hour seminar deliberations. Fewer committees made their members more powerful, which led to an inner cabinet of influential ministers who navigated a more interconnected government, many of whom had regional support bases.[20]

It was clear by the time Brian Mulroney became prime minister that a few core cabinet committees were the engines of cabinet deliberation. Three of them – Government Operations, Priorities and Planning, and Treasury Board – endure in some fashion today. Mulroney's government marked a further expansion of the central agencies of the Privy Council Office, Department of Finance, and Treasury Board Secretariat.[21] Coordination centred on policy cohesion and authorization of ministerial requests. When the cabinet met, Mulroney moved through the agenda and delivered "a pre-caucus pep talk" that foreshadowed his weekly motivational caucus speeches.[22] Subsequently, Jean Chrétien shortened cabinet meetings into forums for decisions and interrupted ministers to get to their points.[23] He largely left ministers to manage their departments, but his reputation as a "friendly dictator" grew as the PMO's central coordination functions expanded.[24] To wit, when departments prepared cabinet speaking notes for their ministers, they shared the notes with central personnel, including the prime minister.[25] For his part, Paul Martin moved cabinet meetings from earlier in the week to Thursdays so that ministers would have the Wednesday national caucus meeting fresh in their minds.[26] The cabinet meeting lasted two to three hours, a bit longer than Chrétien's meetings. Ministers participated in open-ended conversations. In contrast to his earlier resolve as the finance minister, Martin was portrayed as an indecisive prime minister, a peril of consultation and deliberation.[27]

Stephen Harper's cabinet meetings differed strikingly. They were short, apposite, and discouraged comments.[28] In 2010, the Conservative PMO set up caucus advisory committees to ensure that ministerial plans were shared with designated caucus members.[29] The setup preserved cabinet confidentiality by assigning each parliamentary secretary to chair a group of six backbenchers and three senators. Ministers were required to consult the applicable committee as part of drafting a cabinet proposal, thereby ensuring that backbenchers had an avenue to provide input while providing the government with a regional lens, assistance with communications, and reduced dependence on Ottawa-based bureaucrats. Committee members received a briefing and could voice concerns about the proposal. The minister needed to take the proposal off the table for a rethink if sufficient friction arose at the advisory committee level. The minister's office, the cabinet, and senior public servants obtained valuable feedback from the backbenches, and the PMO received monthly summaries. The mechanism reduced caucus friction, firmed up party cohesion, and reduced outbursts from backbenchers when a cabinet decision was announced.

The most notable aspect of Justin Trudeau's cabinet formation is a commitment to descriptive representation by ensuring that half of his ministers are women. He renamed the Priorities and Planning Committee as Agenda, Results and Communications, a change that reflects the importance of strategic communications planning. In cabinet meetings, Trudeau is a stern time manager who urges concision in order to move through the agenda and hear from as many people as possible.[30] He surprises some ministers with his grasp on the details of the annex items on the cabinet agenda normally not discussed. Under his watch, the PMO urges ministers to communicate with the caucus and warns of potential anger from private members. At a cabinet retreat early in the government's tenure, two ministers talked about their experiences as backbenchers who tried to get a private member's bill passed and shared stories about their past interactions with ministers' offices.[31] Caucus consultation typically occurs in an ad hoc manner once a decision is made, such as when a minister hosts a pizza party after hours or arranges a legislation debriefing meeting that feels rote. One minister achieved success by setting up a feedback process that designated interested MPs as "caucus champions" (see page 313).

Members of the cabinet must be agile when a meeting concludes. In Ottawa, journalists linger outside the cabinet room, hoping to spring questions on those coming and going, known as cabinet ins and outs.[32] Prime Ministers King, St. Laurent, and Diefenbaker were scrummed by journalists waiting to nab the prime minister for a conversation.[33] Pearson tired of pushing his way through and left via a back door.[34] As journalists became more adversarial and security tightened, Pierre Trudeau avoided scrums by holding weekly news conferences; Mulroney cherry-picked questions as he ascended a stairwell; and the Chrétien government corralled the media to designated waiting zones and then set up a pooled microphone outside the cabinet room. The Harper Conservatives ended that practice and did not announce when or where most cabinet meetings were held.

Justin Trudeau's Liberals resumed announcing cabinet meetings but maintained a ban on access to the third floor of the Centre Block. The press gallery obtained permission to install a shared access microphone outside the cabinet room. The PMO directed that pooled press audio, video, and lighting be set up downstairs in the second-floor foyer, a setup that allowed the PMO to select ministers that it wanted available for public comment. As well, the media were deprived of the dreadful optics of a member of cabinet scurrying away as questions were lobbed or the confrontation of scrums that Kate Purchase, the Trudeau PMO communications overseer, has described as so "chaotic" that they "affect the shot."[35] Some provincial cabinets face the opposite problem because of dwindling press gallery membership. In Nova Scotia, a pooled microphone is set up so that journalists can call in questions remotely.[36]

Jostling persisted when the House of Commons chamber was relocated to the West Block in 2019. Journalists interrupted ministers who entered cabinet meetings in the new locale. Members of Parliament avoided the media by entering the interim chamber via a maze of corridors and exiting via a back door off limits to journalists. Initial proposals from the press gallery about gaining more access were rebuffed because of security concerns and interference with members' ability to get to meetings on time.[37] Another change is that during the restoration work the prime minister occupies a West Block office with a private staircase. In 1968, Pierre Trudeau used that exit to avoid reporters when he went to ask the governor general to dissolve Parliament.[38] It is unclear whether his son has used it to escape media scrutiny.

Central Communications Coordination

The number of communications personnel in the Prime Minister's Office, the Privy Council Office, and throughout the government has steadily increased.[39] Central oversight of ministerial activities intensified with technological change and a twenty-four-hour news cycle. In the 1980s, Prime Minister Mulroney's ministers were counselled to focus on core policy objectives and largely left to manage the media themselves. During a controversy, they had to reassure the PMO that the situation was under control. Occasionally, a minister was summoned to meet with the deputy prime minister.[40] Publicly, Mulroney defended ministers who made controversial comments, causing the ministers to realize that it was in their mutual interest to avoid repeating such comments; privately, they knew not to cross him.[41] Message coordination was blossoming with the distribution of talking points by fax machine to MPs' offices or to a staffer waiting in a hotel lobby.

Central approval processes increased under Prime Minister Chrétien as communications connectivity sped up. Several events caused him to require that ministers obtain preauthorization for public remarks, including the 1995 Quebec sovereignty-association referendum, the 2001 terrorist attacks in the United States, and a 2002 leadership struggle.[42] Aside from controlling the message, the central review added scrutiny to a speech-writing process that began with public servants who produced academic-sounding treatises that were finessed by ministerial staff and that ministers had little time to examine.[43] As well, during the 2001 attacks the PMO was unable to locate or assemble ministers spread out across the country, so it instituted a travel authorization policy whereby ministerial travel required preapproval by the PMO and the PCO.[44] The central oversights endure today, with travel authorization now essential for centralized communications planning.

Perceptions vary about whether executive offices coordinate or dictate. While mobilizing to succeed Chrétien as prime minister, Martin gave a renowned speech lamenting the growth of executive power, the erosion of influence of individual MPs, and the alienation of Canadians from democratic institutions. His concern about how to get things done in Ottawa was synthesized in seven words: "Who do you know in the PMO?"[45] As prime minister, he introduced some prescriptions for parliamentary reform, including the three-line whip system. Looking back, Martin believes that the government is so vast that ministers must be trusted to manage files, while adhering to the PMO's central guidance:

> Ministers should run their departments, which is one reason why the public service and the minister's staff are so important. There are simply too many issues out there that require real understanding for needed answers to be controlled by a small group of people at the centre who are not fully involved. Ministers should have a basic understanding of their party's convictions and, where there are differences, be able to

explain them. PMO's role is to ensure that the government's main thrust is carried through while making sure that no other minister's department or view is ignored. One of the main roles of PMO is to ensure coherence in government. Should PMO be a blocking agent? Only rarely. Should PMO be a coordinating body? Yes. PMO also has to be a body that drives files and a vision that may be the party's but may not have historically been the public service's.[46]

Nevertheless, some backbenchers during Martin's tenure became frustrated with the power of unelected advisers in the PMO: "If you don't talk to them, they won't have any influence," vowed one disgruntled Liberal MP.[47]

The advent of social media and Stephen Harper's interest in communications control prompted intense central oversight. Much has been written about the Harper Conservatives' disciplined focus on strategic communications, political marketing, issues management, and rapid response, and how they bypassed the press gallery and ruthlessly debranded opponents. The intensity of message discipline in that government is embodied in the requirement that ministries submit a "message event proposal" form with copious details about any planned media activity for vetting by the PMO.[48] Communications were so micromanaged that it took sixteen communications personnel to coordinate a reply to a Canadian Press question about a type of algae[49] and some MPs apparently worried about what clothing to wear to the office.[50] The unprecedented centralization was a symptom of a permanent campaigning mentality and a government under siege.

Determined to do things differently, Justin Trudeau's government initially trusted ministers with communications management. The Treasury Board amended the government's communications policy to devolve decisions on approval to departments. This resulted in departmental communications planning templates. However, some opted to integrate aspects of the Conservative message event proposal, and major communications items ranging from sensitive issues to those in a ministerial mandate letter still had to be routed through the centre.[51] The pinnacle of ministerial freedom was the first year of office while the PMO was preoccupied with hiring decisions. Ministers were able to collaborate and advance files before the system tightened up. Gradually, political staff became more assertive about pushing scripts. Now they nitpick word choices: "There's a maniacal focus on message discipline," says one Trudeau minister. "Ministers and MPs have more experience than the message mafia, but they are dissuaded from having opinions that might have one syllable inconsistent with the centre."[52]

The Liberal PMO and the PCO continued the practice of maintaining a central communications calendar. The campaign-like timetable lists fixed events, such as public holidays, and a floating schedule of planned events.[53] Information about a minister's travel plans and proposed announcements must align with central scheduling, thereby requiring PMO approval. Purchase observes that the corporate calendar is essential for strategic planning and coordinating announcements:

> Message coordination is a much more complicated beast than people realize. For example, the organizing force of a corporate calendar for announcements can be frustrating. Ministers' offices regularly complain that they want to set an announcement date, but PMO is saying to pick another day because there are already sixteen other things going on. There are just so many channels, so many messages, and such limited public interest in politics that it is essential to have a coordinated message and to be disciplined. It's not about enforcing specific words so much as "today our primary topic is X" and not topic A, B, or C. That coordination is more important than ever.[54]

A newer stratum is the PMO's obsessing about using social media to reinforce a message of the day. Some digital posts involve thirty or more people as part of a multiple-step vetting process that blurs partisan and non-partisan communications.[55] Personnel in ministers' offices complain about the delays that result from seeking central approvals from political staff.

Politicians of all party colours can be railroaded to conform when a government representative is on a larger stage. Prime Minister Trudeau calls on Canadian leaders to deliver a "strong and cohesive message" on international agreements to strengthen Canada's bargaining position.[56] The federal government issued talking points for provinces and territories about renegotiating the North American Free Trade Agreement, and the prime minister held conference calls with premiers to shore up messaging.[57]

His minister of defence adds that "a nation needs to speak with one voice" on international relations, irrespective of party affiliation.[58] Accordingly, a government department stipulated that an opposition MP who participated in an international forum must turn down media requests and follow the minister's lead, but relented when the diktat was mocked.[59] Canadian diplomats have tried to coordinate messaging when signing books of condolences,[60] and some former ambassadors to China have been asked to check with the Department of Foreign Affairs before making public remarks.[61] When brought to light, such message exuberance can prompt media stories about government muzzling.

POLITICAL STAFF IN EXECUTIVE OFFICES

An immense amount of work goes into crafting messages to communicate a policy announcement. The volume of interconnected files in digital, global, and legal environments behoove government executives to delegate tasks. Inevitably, power struggles erupt among senior political staffers, ministers, and backbenchers.

Staff in the Prime Minister's Office and Premiers' Offices

Senior political staff are high-ranking intermediaries. They coordinate the government's agenda with ministerial political staff and the senior public servants who serve at the pleasure of the executive. They strive to align messages and their delivery. They negotiate compromises among ministers, stickhandle backbench complaints, manage political personnel, and collaborate with ministers' offices.[62] At least one senior staffer attends cabinet meetings and possibly cabinet committee meetings. The highest ranking among them, particularly the chief of staff, know or estimate what the head of the government wants done. As a result, political staff are portrayed as camarillas who politicize governance, exerting such considerable influence that some refer to a political service as complementing the public service.[63]

In Ottawa, political staff working for the prime minister or a minister are known as exempt staff. The moniker refers to government employees who are not subject to normal hiring processes or job security. Many exempt staff develop their political bonafides on election campaigns. They generally follow an operating principle similar to the public service edict of offering their best advice and implementing whatever their political master decides. Nevertheless, an exempt staffer's proximity to power is disconcerting. A typical view, expressed in a *Globe and Mail* editorial, is that "unelected advisers in the PMO treat MPs as life-support systems for votes in the House of Commons, cabinet ministers as devices for transmitting talking points, parliamentary committees as rubber stamps, and deputy ministers as political enablers."[64] A former whip comments on senior political staff carving away influence from the caucus:

> Power does not exist in a vacuum. It comes from other institutions and the individual autonomies of MPs. The PMO is involved in increasing levels of detail and is micromanagerial in order to coordinate and manage centralized messaging. The PM [prime minister] is paramount. All other messaging and activities are subordinate to maintaining the broad appeal of the brand. That has consequences for MPs' aspirations, their personal beliefs, and their ability to represent constituents. Power isn't infinite: you have a pie, and the smallest slice by far is with MPs as individuals.[65]

Support is even more essential when a leader travels a lot and has a young family, as Justin Trudeau does. He took things to a new level at his first caucus meeting as prime minister when he asked his chief of staff and principal secretary to join him at the podium and informed the caucus that they speak on his behalf.[66] Consequently, people who interact with the Trudeau PMO assume that staff have the final word.[67] Staff involvement is essential for time management reasons; however, it slows down the process of approval, redirects authority, and alienates people on the periphery of power.

Exempt staff blister at complaints about their work. They counter that Parliament is a significant restraint on prime ministerial power and that the PMO merely synchronizes the government.[68] Mapping out cabinet meetings, assisting with cabinet committees, planning for budget meetings, preparing for leaders' summits, and undertaking other activities keep the government's political agenda moving forward.[69] To them, anxiety that top-down messaging is a sign of authoritarian-style governance is unwarranted. After all, steering coordination is different from imposing control.[70] Staff do not necessarily crave power; for example, they can be flustered that ministers and backbenchers choose to go through them instead of communicating with each other. Complaints must be balanced with acknowledgment that executive-level staff perform an essential role.

The intensity of politics increases the need to engage staff in executive offices. Much like a campaign operation, a middle tier of staff in the centre of government is divided into separate but interconnected spheres of strategic planning and reactive communications.[71] Strategic agenda work concerns proactive planning to communicate topics that the government wants to advance. These staffers are forward thinkers who look to deliver calm and carefully timed messaging. A political strategist elucidates:

> Overlaying a media communications group and the policy group is what we call scripting in a campaign and, in a government, what we call strategic communications. This is a group who pays no attention to what we're saying today or in five days. They are preoccupied with what we will be communicating a week from now, in a month, and in some cases a year from now. That is the source of message discipline. The people who communicate with the media or send out all the materials aren't the ones deciding what we are communicating. They just implement what the strategists were planning.[72]

To optimize positive publicity, a strategic agenda group identifies message themes for each week and day. The staff play a coordinating role in scheduling and planning the communications roll-out of announcements. This is where the master corporate calendar comes in. Figures 8.2 and 8.3 are examples of strategic agenda outputs.

Issues management is reactive and chaotic. It involves campaign-style rapid response to address criticism, refute misinformation, and practise crisis communication. Issues managers employ the same types of combative tactics used in communications command centres during an election campaign. They spin information and hurriedly generate key messages, including public comments that hold the line without delving into the issue. They manage the fallout of bozo eruptions and capitalize on adversaries' missteps. They practise rapid response on social media in a hard-hitting, politicized manner that contrasts with slow-moving, risk-averse bureaucratic approaches.[73] They buy time for the organization to regroup and/or for the media to move on to a different story. Specialized units are struck, such as the Trudeau PMO's aforementioned Canada-US war room to manage social media diplomacy with President Trump or the Alberta government's war room to rebut misinformation about the province's oil and gas industry. Figures 8.1 and 11.2 are outcomes of issues management.

There can be greater opportunities for executive-level staff to exert influence in the provinces. Ministers might pause the start of a meeting until the premier's staff arrive, whereas staff can exclude ministers from conversations concerning their portfolio(s).[74] Here is a typical backbench comment about one especially brazen chief of staff in Ontario: "He is the one who is really in charge. He controls everyone and everything – staff, cabinet, caucus, appointments. It's his way or the highway. He yells at people, controls our social media, and questions our loyalty constantly."[75] Although an extreme, these types of allegations underscore that heads of governments trust high-ranking staff to wield the authority of the office, which some brandish in a confrontational manner.

Subordinates can perceive staffers as having more power than they actually do. They presume that staff act on explicit instructions or at least keep the head of government informed. They can also be susceptible to interpreting a casual suggestion as a command. A staffer in a premier's office confides that he has asked the cabinet secretariat a question out of intellectual curiosity, and then the item has inexplicably appeared on the cabinet agenda accompanied with background information.[76] Another staffer relays how, as a junior PMO employee, he made a friendly comment to a minister about her recent travel; the next day the chief of staff contended with the minister, fretting that the PMO was scrutinizing her travel spending.[77] There are no lab coats or prison guard uniforms in executive offices, but even innocuous comments from representatives of the head of the government carry the force of authority.

Staff in Ministers' Offices

Ministers' offices work with central agencies to ensure message consistency. The staff are liaisons among central political staff, politicians, and the public service.[78] In Ottawa, the Prime Minister's Office oversees the appointment of ministerial chiefs of staff who might in turn oversee the recruitment of exempt staff in the minister's office. Awareness that the PMO is involved with employment decisions contributes to ministerial staff prioritizing central directives.[79] A former government whip comments on the centralized hiring:

> It isn't that backbenchers don't have enough power – ministers don't have enough power! Even the choice of staff in the ministers' offices is dictated by the PMO. When I was in Jean Chrétien's cabinet, the PMO approved the minister's chief of staff as well as the director of communications to make sure that the communications policy was all the same. But the PMO did not exercise hiring authority over ministers' senior policy advisers or directors of parliamentary affairs. I hired 100 percent of my own staff. It is vastly different today.[80]

If a minister falters, then a senior staffer from the PMO or premier's office might step in to manage the situation or assume a senior position in the minister's office, thereby ensuring compliance with the centre.[81]

Long workdays for communications personnel in a federal minister's office begin with morning strategy phone calls before leaving home and gravitate toward issues management that stretches into the evening.[82] The day starts with a digital communication scan to see what news broke overnight, followed by a perusal of media summaries. The PMO coordinates an early morning conference call to run through major news stories and message lines. Afterward, the caucus research bureau emails a synthesis of the stories that arose so that everyone is clear which departments are responding to which issues (see Figure 8.1). Time is spent detecting and correcting errors circulating online. Throughout the day, ministerial staff help to resolve requests for information from backbenchers and their assistants. When there is a big issue, the minister's office reaches out to caucus members to debrief those whose constituents are affected: "It's not so much about message control as making members of caucus feel that they aren't being blindsided," explains a director of communications for a Trudeau minister.[83]

Staff can conspire to manage a minister's media availability. Internal emails authored by a premier's deputy chief of staff revealed plans to marginalize a government House leader for going off script: "I know we have this preference to put out elected officials," she wrote to the premier's press secretary. "But strike him off the list. This is the second time he's done this."[84] In another province, a staffer told a story about her minister's unplanned comment that the government would conduct a policy review.[85] The premier was irate. Without the minister's knowledge, staff in the premier's office and the minister's office decided to route media enquiries through the premier's office for clearance. Keeping ministers in the dark about such backchannelling can breed mistrust and contempt while strengthening alliances among staff.

Four Corners Meetings and Stock-Take Meetings

In Ottawa, two high-level discussion forums have been incorporated in recent years to assist the PMO and the PCO with central coordination, information exchange, accountability, and interdepartmental cooperation. These informal approaches bend reporting structures so that the PMO is involved in policy oversight. They are also indicative of hidden processes within government that constrain a private member's ability to advance a policy idea.

"Four corners" meetings were introduced under Stephen Harper and continue under Justin Trudeau. Exempt staff and public servants meet in the Prime Minister's Office or the Privy Council Office to prepare for cabinet meetings. The purpose of four corners meetings is to coordinate files that are intricate and a PMO priority. PMO, PCO, ministerial staff, and department executives work out a policy issue or a communications matter without anyone from the cabinet present. The meetings enable the sharing of information, which contributes to unity of direction and quick action.[86]

"Stock-take" meetings are less entrenched. On forming the government, the Trudeau Liberals created a results and delivery unit in the Privy Council Office to track policy implementation, ensure that cabinet decisions are implemented efficiently, and fulfill election promises.[87] Stock-takes are a progress-reporting mechanism that leverages the presence of the prime minister to create a sense of urgency. Policy benchmarks are measured against outcomes to assess whether targets have been met. Trudeau periodically chairs an issue-themed stock-take meeting with ministers responsible for certain policy files, their chiefs of staff, and any ministerial staff involved with the issue. Other attendees include deputy ministers, senior PMO aides, senior PCO personnel, and sometimes non-government experts. Ministers provide a briefing; discussion ensues. The PMO chief of staff, Katie Telford, has described the format:

> It's an opportunity to sit around the table with some of the ministers involved in a particular theme, with senior staff from various parts of government on both the public service side and the political side, and to literally do that, to take stock. The idea of those meetings is not to get into reading out PowerPoints or anything like that. It's actually to say "where are we stuck on this file? Let's talk about how we get past where we're stuck" ... When the prime minister calls a meeting, a lot can happen from that.[88]

A senior member of the PCO has added that stock-takes "accelerate progress on complex horizontal issues."[89] For example, during the coronavirus disease (COVID-19) pandemic, Trudeau met with senior PMO staff, the clerk of the Privy Council, the president of the Treasury Board, and a number of academics to assess the economic implications of winding down emergency government measures.[90] Although ministers appreciate the opportunity to update Trudeau, they question the value of meeting if he does not offer much feedback, and they are flustered if they think that suggestions are unhelpful.[91] The technocracy is likely mysterious to most people, including public servants. However, that personnel in the centre of government exert influence through horizontal coordination is widely recognized.

Regional Desks

Members of Parliament and their assistants steer their questions about government to internal hotlines staffed in the PMO and ministers' offices, known as regional desks. Questioners are routed by electoral district, grouped as British Columbia, the Prairies and Northern region, Ontario, Quebec, and the Atlantic region. The political staff who station the desks are familiar with regional dynamics and key political actors in the area. They liaise with all levels of the government, interest groups, local stakeholders, and local politicians as they coordinate events and messaging. The gate-keeping system prevents private members and their staff from obtaining information from public servants directly and is a function of centralized control over government communications. An MP first elected in 1957 reminisces about access to federal public servants when MPs could hold up the budget estimates by continuously talking:

> As a consequence of having that power, ministers were responsive to you, very responsive, much more than they are now. But even more important, bureaucrats were responsive. If you picked up the phone and called a deputy minister, he returned your call pronto. Or if the minister would say "you go and see my deputy," I mean the red carpet would be put out there for you, and you were really a big shot. Because they knew that you had the power to really give them trouble on the estimates.[92]

Regional desks originated in 1968 to attend to localized political tasks, gather information for the prime minister, act as caucus liaisons, and fill voids of representation.[93] At times, MPs have been so angered by PMO staff acting as a buffer that the desks have been discontinued.[94] Others, though, have welcomed the desks as another avenue to get the attention of the prime minister.[95] Today regional affairs advisers – part of the PMO outreach group – perform central coordination functions in Ottawa and are central contacts for the ministers' regional offices that house political staff and public servants in thirteen provincial cities and one per territory.[96] In addition to fielding questions from MPs, they reach out to constituency assistants when there is a significant concern in the electoral district and especially if a visit by the prime minister is planned.

In a minister's office, regional desk personnel are the initial contacts for additional information, special assistance for constituents, or supple-mentary message lines. For instance, if a constituent is trying urgently to get a family member to travel to Canada, an MP's assistant might contact the applicable minister's office regional desk to advocate fast-tracking the paperwork. Desk staff exchange information with their counterparts to synchronize the PMO, ministers' offices, and caucus research bureau. Sometimes a single staff member manages more than one regional desk.

FOCUSING EVENTS (CORONAVIRUS PANDEMIC)

Government operations become even more centralized in the upheaval of a public emergency. Politicians pull their partisan punches in the immediacy of natural disasters, terrorism, industrial accidents, economic catastrophes, and health scares. These types of crises that abruptly command society's attention and vault to the top of government agendas are known as focusing events.[97] As the media report on human suffering, political leaders coordinate an emergency response that relies on the expertise of public servants, and statesmanship replaces partisan sniping. Moments of public mourning also briefly break down party walls. In these circumstances, message unity is spontaneous. Political rancour returns as the urgency of the focusing event subsides.

The COVID-19 pandemic is a case in point. Canadian society was upended in March 2020 when provinces and territories declared states of emergency, physical distancing measures were implemented, stock markets plunged, and workers were furloughed or laid off. Solidarity with different levels of government took hold as public officials, including Prime Minister Trudeau, held daily media briefings. Collaboration replaced acrimony in a first ministers' meeting conducted by teleconference, and as federal ministers and senior public servants held daily all-party technical briefing conference calls with MPs and senators.[98] Parliamentarians across the country amplified public health advice as their constituency casework surged. Centralized federalism was epitomized when PC Premier Doug Ford – demonized by the Trudeau Liberals in the preceding federal election campaign – said "I would never break ranks with the prime minister or other premiers."[99]

Hectic circumstances bring diminished parliamentary scrutiny of government. House leaders, whips, and senior staff negotiated swift passage of supply bills to authorize funds for existing obligations, such as paying public servants.[100] In Ottawa, they agreed to rush the Canada-US-Mexico free-trade agreement through both chambers. Parliament was suspended. Next the House officers arranged for fewer than three dozen MPs to convene in the House of Commons to approve sweeping financial measures.[101] Opposition leaders received an embargoed draft of the COVID-19 Emergency Response Act to enact $82 billion in economic aid. The Conservative House leader cautioned her Liberal counterpart that "there can be no surprises."[102] But there was a surprise, so a Conservative leaked the bill "to apply some strategic pressure" on the Trudeau government for overreaching on powers of taxation and spending without seeking Parliament's approval.[103] This meant that journalists reported on the draft bill before some backbenchers saw it, a breach of their parliamentary privilege.[104] Despite considerable pressure for unanimity, MP Scott J. Reid broke ranks by blogging his intent to defy the Conservative whip's plea to stay away for the vote and threatened to refuse the unanimous consent necessary for fast-tracking, on principle.[105] Ministers responded by conveying urgency but backed down when the media reported on a power grab, and a revised bill passed with oversight measures.

At the peak of the crisis, most backbenchers embraced the role of caseworker as they exchanged information with government officials, and as they and their staff engaged with constituents on social media and in electronic town halls. In Ottawa, a federal cabinet committee on COVID-19 included the deputy House leader who shared information with the national caucus via daily conference calls.[106] The five parties' House officers agreed that a higher proportion of frontbenchers should be permitted to attend sittings while physical distancing measures were in place.[107] The in-person meetings were uncharacteristically civil, as was the first virtual sitting of the House of Commons.

Interparty consultation offered stability in four provinces where minority governments had a tenuous hold on power. In British Columbia, an existing written agreement stipulated that the Greens would support the NDP government as long as principles of "good faith and no surprises" and confidentiality were observed, including "access to key documents and officials."[108] The BC government's confidence and supply agreement secretariat coordinated consultations between the two leaders and caucuses. Left out, the Liberal leader took measured potshots at the premier. Impromptu arrangements arose in three Atlantic provinces where premiers created ad hoc cabinet committees that included all opposition leaders.[109] Members of New Brunswick's all-party cabinet committee on the novel coronavirus took a formal oath of secrecy, whereas the confidentiality principle was used for Newfoundland and Labrador's joint public health response committee and for members of Prince Edward Island's situation response table. Each executive setup had its own nuances that were fluid.

The committees convened via regular conference calls and included, to various extents, the premier, a handful of senior ministers, select opposition members and, unofficially, chiefs of staff. Public servants, such as the chief medical officer of health, and other political staff occasionally participated. Ministers and deputy ministers routed information through the premier and his committee. Inter-party engagement was highest in PEI where the leaders engaged with three cabinet working groups, the finance minister collaborated with her predecessor who was now the third party House leader, and the government whip chaired a task force comprising the opposition whip and a third party MLA.

That such unconventional all-party structures emerged in the three smallest provinces adds weight to an argument that the parliamentary system can operate without political parties in small places, as it does in the Northwest Territories and Nunavut. The all-party cabinet committees enabled a swift, united response by providing oversight of the government's strategic priorities, decisions, and actions. When a premier was presented with a high-level decision, he consulted the other leaders, and when required he sought approval from the cabinet. The committees received briefings from senior civil servants and built consensus on such topics as a pandemic operational plan, declaration of a state of emergency, school closures, postponement of municipal elections, emergency sittings of the House to approve legislation, and phased re-opening. Backbenchers were encouraged to exchange information with government officials, for example through a hotline to the premier's office or a minister's executive assistant holding conference calls with all constituency assistants. That the governing party had a minority of seats was a central variable given that premiers in Nova Scotia and the Yukon refused the opposition's requests to create similar all-party cabinet committees.

In those Atlantic provinces, party leaders who had been at loggerheads were suddenly cooperative and sometimes gushed with compliments for one another. There were partisan cracks, with opposition leaders occasionally going public to apply pressure on government and exert independence. If Canada's easternmost province is any indication, some backbenchers on both sides of the House were confused why government information was available to opposition leaders but not them. Independents in particular were excluded. Although they were frustrated, slighted, and unhappy, they said nothing because bickering would be insensitive and disruptive. As elsewhere, the focusing event highlighted that parliamentarians without title are on the periphery and that it is unusual for them to challenge ruling cliques.

Across Canada, unity of action dissipated as public health restrictions loosened, and the media focused on global anti-racism demonstrations. Inordinate government centralization relaxed: the opposition parties denied unanimous consent when the Trudeau Liberals proposed another emergency response bill; the prime minister's weekly calls with premiers became testy; and public conversation turned to the problem of systemic racialization. Focusing events can be opportunities for political actors to advance their agendas, sometimes with multi-party support, but the convergence of media attention on a single issue subdues the topicality of other policy areas. Whatever the circumstances, frontbenchers and backbenchers alike must be attuned to the political winds in order to navigate the public policy pressures illustrated in Figure 2.2.

SUMMARY

Government communications are both coordinated and controlled from the top. Institutional structures such as cabinet processes, central agencies, staff meetings, and regional desks mean that there is little room for backbenchers to propose a new policy direction or challenge a government decision. Their role as information conduits is especially evident during a focusing event that requires an emergency response from government. In the next chapter, we peek inside the caucus room to observe information exchanges between the leadership and backbenchers.

7

Parliamentary Caucuses

Members of a caucus are part of a partisan club whose meetings are the "hidden chamber" of a legislature.[1] Caucus meetings are the primary forum for internal information exchange between party leaders and private members. The private gatherings provide a venue for group identity, or they can be the site of unravelling cohesion. What happens inside the caucus room? To what extent does group conformity persist away from the public eye? When do backbenchers feel the most free to speak up – and when are they the most likely to clam up? In this chapter, we peek inside parliamentary caucus rooms across Canada, where confidentiality is sacrosanct.

CAUCUS MEETINGS

A caucus meeting is a sanctum for elite bargaining. The intellectual sparring sessions can feature vigorous debates about contentious topics and communications.[2] Parliamentarians might enter the room with a firm opinion and leave it with a different stance as they learn that what matters to them is not a communal priority. Caucus meetings double as social events. They are one of the few settings in which elected representatives' comments are not on the public record and party communication is not rote.

Meeting Format

Caucus meetings are routine in the parliamentary precinct when there is an immediate need to prepare for House business. The meetings range from a tightly managed gathering of a large number of busy politicians to informal conversations among a small number of private members. Some structures present the leadership's position as a *fait accompli;* others require internal consultations before a matter is brought to a vote. Accomplishments are lauded: a minister who did an extraordinary job with legislation or a private member who organized a successful rally are singled out for applause. Large caucuses require formalities similar to those of a business conference meeting. The leader sits at a head table with the caucus chair and other officeholders. A sound system with microphones doubles as a way to limit speaking time and facilitates language translation where needed. The whip's office staff work in the background to operate the audio switchboard and audiovisual displays. The meetings of a small caucus are much more intimate. The leader presides over a roundtable or seminar format in which members are encouraged to participate in the conversation. In caucuses of all sizes, respectful discussion is welcome, but embarrassing the leader is taboo.

A fundamental precept of caucus meetings is that they are private. Periodically, the caucus is reminded that whatever is said must not leave the room. A former minister explains why secrecy is paramount: "It starts to have a corrosive effect if you believe you can't go to the mic and say what you believe and not have it appear in the media," she says. "You need to build those relationships of trust. Teams have to be cohesive. And it is trust that helps build that cohesion."[3] An MP adds that "it is very important to respect the privacy of caucus, and the rights of my colleagues to freely express themselves, and their opinions on behalf of their constituents. You're united, and you're united in a purpose."[4] Solidarity erodes when caucus information leaks into the public domain.[5] Unauthorized leaks undermine collegiality, violate trust, and poison relationships. Members feel betrayed. They become nervous and second-guess making comments. The caucus speculates about the identity of the leaker. Anger mounts as the ability to effect change is hampered along with the re-election prospects of members. Everyone becomes paranoid; the caucus goes into lockdown. The unknown source might be called on to come forward and re-establish trust as measures are taken to ensure the supremacy of caucus secrecy.[6] A confidential document was leaked to a reporter? Stop circulating documents.[7] Journalists are lingering in a hotel lobby hoping to catch someone entering or exiting an off-site caucus meeting? Ask the police to remove the journalists.[8] A member of caucus has been talking to the media? Request that the member stop taking notes and/or suspend meetings.[9] A parliamentarian is writing about the caucus on a blog? Expel the blogger from the caucus.[10] Members are using smartphones to transmit information from inside the caucus room to reporters? Ban the devices.[11] Leaking information from the caucus and feigning outrage at the deceit comprise a shrewd way to undermine a leader. Consequently, many parliamentarians immediately shun a colleague who breaks the confidentiality principle.

In Ottawa, the governing party's caucus, including ministers, must leave their digital devices in an adjoining room. The official reason is to avoid distractions.[12] The political reason is to inhibit leaks through recording or livestreaming. There is also a legitimate security risk. Spyware can end up on smartphones, tablets, and laptops, thereby enabling hackers to activate the microphone remotely. A leader of the Bloc Québécois was shocked to learn that caucus meetings were susceptible to electronic eavesdropping:

> The Royal Canadian Mounted Police [RCMP] told me that people can eavesdrop on caucus conversations even when electronic devices are turned off. I was surprised. I told the caucus there would be no more cellphones in caucus and explained why. They didn't believe me. So I contacted the RCMP who came to the table and proceeded to repeat what different members had said in the caucus room. It was a huge lesson. I was grateful to them for telling me. I wasn't scared about other parties being able to hear us. I was worried that journalists would listen and report that one member was criticizing another member, which would damage confidence within the caucus.[13]

Some parties do permit electronic devices in caucus meetings. Inevitably, members' attention wanders as they check their phones.

Sometimes leaders shake up the format of caucus meetings. Convening them outside the capital city generates news coverage while fostering camaraderie. A team-building planning retreat might be timed for parliamentarians returning to the capital after a long adjournment. When members are in their ridings, a conference call can be coordinated for the leader to deliver an urgent message without fielding questions.[14] As a general election approaches, meetings can become campaign readiness seminars, and private members can be engaged in platform deliberations.[15] Attendance can expand temporarily to include former and/or aspiring parliamentarians. Defeated members with special expertise might offer feedback on pertinent policy proposals, including election platform development. In Ontario, a "super caucus" integrates the party's nominated candidates, exposing them to the intricacy of group policy deliberations and socializing them into caucus customs. The candidates make friends with counterparts whom they might otherwise never meet and develop familiarity with the roles of parliamentarians. Candidates who violate super caucus confidentiality can have their nominations rescinded.[16] Where formats differ the most, though, is between the governing party caucus and an opposition party caucus.

Governing Party Caucus Meetings

A governing party's caucus meetings are a vital intersection between executive and legislative branches of the government. Members of the governing party have a greater responsibility to emerge with united public positions on issues of the day, but the imbalance between in-groups and out-groups is a serious complication. Members are divided into different classes, with a minister having considerably more power and status than a backbencher, a chasm straddled by private members loyal to the executive such as parliamentary secretaries and whips. A further unity challenge is that the governing party represents the largest number of electoral districts.

In Ottawa, the governing party's national caucus meets on Wednesday mornings for two hours. Time is allocated so that the leader, House leader, whip, caucus chair, and ministers can make reports; for backbenchers to make comments; and for the prime minister to close the meeting. The House leader and/or ministers update the room about the government's legislative agenda, the whip provides an administrative summary, and the chair coordinates reports from caucus committees. Occasionally, outsiders, such as the extraparliamentary party executive and PMO staff, present on a topical issue. A sixty-second speaking limit for backbenchers – down from three minutes in the 1970s and ninety seconds in the 1990s – imposes constraint during the open mic session.[17] The prime minister listens intently, sometimes interjecting in response to a provocative remark from the floor. The meeting typically wraps up with the prime minister updating the group and fielding questions. A prime minister explains why he or she agrees or disagrees and identifies which, if any, actions will be taken in response to the caucus input. The closing remarks are also an opportunity to inspire enthusiasm.

The cabinet has a policy agenda to implement that requires caucus support. Ministers jeopardize their positions, and even face the possibility of recriminations, if they do not uphold confidentiality. As mentioned, it is a serious offence to violate cabinet confidences; if a breach of trust is suspected, then the head of the government is likely to immediately remove the minister from the cabinet and request a police investigation. Because of cabinet secrecy and solidarity, ministers keep their backbench colleagues in the dark and rarely inform them that changes were made because of comments raised at a caucus meeting.[18] An MP who served in the Harper cabinet explains the balancing act of divulging information to non-ministers:

> Members of cabinet have to sell their own caucus members on what is happening in the government. You cannot necessarily tell them ahead of time what's in proposed legislation because that's a breach of parliamentary privilege. A minister is not allowed to divulge the contents of a bill until it is tabled in the House of Commons. You can talk about the issues and what you plan on doing, but you cannot pass around draft legislation to your caucus members. It's not allowed. You can only share information with your parliamentary secretary.[19]

Without a formal internal process to ensure caucus engagement, and out of respect for the parliamentary privileges of all members of the House, governing party members might hear of the government's plans for the first time at a caucus meeting or when the plans are publicly announced.[20] A lack of consultation can be a flashpoint.

A head of government can mitigate rifts by insisting that ministers pay attention to backbenchers. Ministers are motivated to be accessible when they fear complaints and caucus backlash.[21] At best, they might have to withdraw a policy proposal, make changes to it, and present it again. At worst, criticism might be levelled because of their prickly style or an aversion to consultation, and the disgruntlement can jeopardize the minister's continued place in cabinet. Possibly, backbenchers calculate that making a minister look bad contributes to freeing up a cabinet position.[22]

A snapshot of how some Canadian prime ministers have run caucus meetings suggests that all of them have been keen to listen to what backbenchers have to say in that private forum. When King and St. Laurent were at the helm, Liberal MPs absorbed information in caucus meetings rather than debated.[23] King saw the forums as an opportunity for the cabinet to identify the "views and opinions" of the public as expressed by their elected representatives.[24] His ministers believed that caucus meetings are the place for disagreement, after which the group must be united. Bennett might have had a reputation for being an autocrat, but he busily took notes when Conservative MPs spoke.[25] Diefenbaker faced insurrection, leading to his wisecrack that in his experience the difference between a cactus and a caucus is that a cactus has its pricks on the outside.[26] He also claimed that Pearson once said that government-side backbenchers "are as useful as an udder on a bull."[27] The crudity referred to caucus consultation falling out of favour under Pearson because leaks caused ministers to be concerned about confidentiality.[28] As mentioned, Pierre Trudeau experimented with ways to include the Liberal Party executive and the caucus in government decisions. In caucus meetings, he was joined at a head table by the caucus chair and by ministers, and MPs addressed the prime minister and not them.[29] Trudeau said nothing until the end, when he concluded with clever responses and presented an overview of the week ahead.

Brian Mulroney believed that the "caucus is the heart of the machine."[30] We saw in Chapter 3 that he lavished personal attention on his caucus. He made it clear to PMO schedulers that it was a personal priority for him to attend a caucus meeting unless an international leaders' summit required him to be out of the country. Meetings began with a standing ovation when he entered the room. He listened attentively for up to two hours and took notes about concerns raised by backbenchers and senators. No staff were present, which enabled free-flowing conversation, and MPs would hand him notes in order to bypass normal gatekeeping processes.[31] Parliamentarians were encouraged to be critical. Anyone brave enough to criticize him risked admonishment in front of the group, sometimes from a backbencher who rose to the leader's defence.[32] To conclude the meeting, Mulroney delivered a passionate motivational speech to drum up enthusiasm for the government's agenda and to nurture feelings of a political family. He spoke for up to an hour. The talks were entertaining barnburners as he switched between English and French. He told stories about the interesting people whom he had met in his travels over the past week, taking care to weave in the names of caucus members. The light fare warmed up the audience for serious comments about public policy. The prime minister energized his audience with plans to persuade the electorate about the government's transformative actions. Progressive Conservatives were made to feel that they were revolutionaries who were part of something special that would improve Canada. Big-ticket items, they were told, might be unpopular but historic. They should anticipate polling numbers to dip when a government does something bold because citizens are averse to change. They were encouraged to look past short-term negativity and toward future laudatory headlines.

Mulroney implored his caucus to be "key salespersons" and instructed them that they "must have the same message, the same themes, the same defence. There can be no divergent views."[33] He warned that opponents had designs on becoming ministers, that MPs had no friends beyond the caucus room, and that the media would not help them. He exhorted the caucus "don't do it if you don't want to read about it in the *Globe and Mail* the next day."[34] Those fearful about not being re-elected got an earful about the shallowness of their opponents: "If you don't like the numbers you can get the hell out," Mulroney challenged naysayers.[35] Backbenchers were reassured that he would look out for them. He, in turn, expected them to support ministers who spoke on his behalf.

The prime minister took great pains to maintain morale when the government backtracked on a policy. He spent hours preparing caucus remarks to explain one such decision. Blaming adversaries, accepting personal responsibility, offering assurances that a media storm would die down, and reinforcing the important role of an MP all featured in his summation. He concluded with a rallying cry: "You are why we were elected in the first place and why we shall be again. I am handing the Liberals and NDP a gun with which to shoot me. I would rather apologize, retrieve the gun, and proceed to shoot them."[36] No matter how low the party was in public opinion polls, or how anxious ministers and backbenchers were about the latest controversy dominating the news, Mulroney soon had them cheering and laughing. They exited the meetings feeling reassured, encouraged, flattered, entertained – and above all reminded that caucus unity is essential. "We were at 22 percent in the polls, and Mulroney was in full oratorical flight," reminisces one of those MPs. "When the caucus meeting was over, if he'd called an election that day, we'd have cheered him for doing it! He was such a terrific motivator. He was absolutely genuine in caucus."[37]

In contrast, unity is a struggle amid leadership factions and party infighting. Before occupying the top office, Chrétien cautioned that a caucus risks becoming "more marginal, more expendable, and at the mercy of the leadership. Certainly fewer backbenchers will be prepared to give their leaders frank advice or tell them to go to hell if they know that they can be replaced."[38] As prime minister, he told the caucus that "this room is open. When you're mad at us, open your mouth and talk to us – not to the press! You can say whatever you want here. It's the way that the messages from your constituents [are] coming."[39] He listened carefully to MPs and made some of them feel that their input mattered to him.[40] He instructed the cabinet to keep backbenchers happy and made a point of ensuring that ministers saw him taking attendance at caucus meetings.[41] Meetings followed the traditional format whereby chairs of regional caucuses, the women's caucus, and special committees made concise reports. Backbenchers wanted the chairs to hurry up so that there would be more time to talk about an issue of the day or a recurring topic. During tempestuous periods, they sometimes called on the whip to ensure vote unity, as a whip from that caucus recalls:

A whip who is too slack is subject to criticism from their caucus. At the caucus meeting, a backbencher will say to the group "look, we've got to pass this bill, and it doesn't please everybody. However, when it was my turn, you got a bill passed that wasn't good for me in my riding. In the spirit of all of us working together to accomplish the program that we put forth in the last campaign, I voted with you. So, whip, do your job!"[42]

Chrétien likewise discloses that backbenchers were so angry when one of their own voted against the government that they urged him to get tough with non-conformists.[43] Despite some initial goodwill, backbenchers who vocalized disagreement were labelled as unreliable agitators.[44] Occasional outbursts cast Chrétien as a bully, prompting several MPs to leak details to the press, which required media management to regain the confidentiality principle.[45]

Paul Martin could be more patient with caucus because, unlike Chrétien, he did not have to manage a disruptive faction agitating for new leadership. After listening carefully in caucus meetings, Martin convened ministers by region to discuss concerns raised by area MPs as well as by provincial governments. He also periodically met with regional and provincial caucuses, affording backbenchers personal time to bring concerns to his attention: "We talked about all the pressing issues facing our ridings and found the prime minister to be very responsive. It was a pretty frank discussion," said an MP after one such meeting.[46]

Caucus meetings with Stephen Harper followed the conventional pattern of listening to grievances and concluding with a short speech.[47] The meeting began with caucus members singing the national anthem. The prime minister, caucus chair, House leader, whip, and Senate leader sat on a dais at the front so that attendees could see them. Each of them made a report. Harper began with a summary of activities since the previous meeting and outlined the government's agenda. The House and Senate leaders talked about legislative business. The whip's report concerned voting, attendance, changes to administrative and procedural rules, and any issues causing consternation for more than a couple of disgruntled members. Conservative MPs lined up behind two microphones on the floor during an hour-long open mic session. The chair alternated from one microphone to the other and decided how many speakers would talk on an issue in the allotted time. Ministers mentioned upcoming legislation. The prime minister's remarks at the end were the focal point, especially when there was a controversy. Harper summarized what he had heard, addressed any negative comments, and motivated the caucus. He briefed the room about how he intended to look into a specific concern, perhaps by striking a committee, or by meeting with a group of interested MPs to try to work through it, or by delegating a minister or parliamentary secretary to do so. If concerns were well articulated, or there was significant pushback, the prime minister withdrew the issue for further contemplation and occasionally reversed his position. MPs could also provide feedback via ministerial caucus advisory committees. The consultation contributed to the Conservatives' reputation for top-down message discipline given that engaging backbenchers earlier in the policy-making process reduces the potential for public dissent.

Justin Trudeau returned to relying on ministers to attend caucus meetings to listen to policy feedback. At his first caucus meeting as prime minister, he implored MPs that "your one job, that you cannot ever forget, is to be a strong voice in service of the people who sent you here from your constituencies."[48] Trudeau advised them that their first obligation is to their families, their second obligation is to the people who elected them, and their third obligation is to the government in Ottawa.[49] He informed the caucus that they were expected to vote with the government on certain matters and that they should notify the whip if they felt compelled to dissent. He counselled that the leadership requires an opportunity to try to reconcile any differences so that the MP ends up siding with the government or not voting. As mentioned, he also openly designated the two most senior PMO staff as his surrogates. As we shall see, his staff have a significant presence in Liberal caucus meetings.

On his way to a caucus meeting, Trudeau often offers a remark to waiting journalists.[50] He opens the meeting with a comment, followed by reports from regional chairs and sub-caucuses (Indigenous, rural, women's). There is an open mic session for MPs, encouraged to speak freely, and ministers "get raked over the coals all the time."[51] The PMO is fond of using the meetings to discuss ways that MPs can digitally amplify government messages. Certain Facebook feeds are profiled as a best practice, or Trudeau points to an interesting way in which an MP used social media.

Some Liberals believe that the prime minister and his senior advisers frown on criticism. Backbenchers are sensitive that PMO staff are judgmental of vocal critics, who might not be considered team players worthy of promotion: "No one wants to speak up when you are worried you'll be insulted in front of the whole caucus," says a Liberal MP. "We don't really have a frank, honest, open discussion on issues in our caucus."[52] There are also complaints that ministers and parliamentary secretaries do not schedule enough time to listen: "We'd like to be brought into the conversation," says another Liberal. "When I see things that make me cringe, I say 'well,

I wish they'd asked me.'"[53] A third adds that "there's never enough consultation. There's always [a] need for more and more and more."[54] As mentioned, unrest led the PMO to make changes to pay more attention to individual members.

Opposition Party Caucus Meetings

Opposition caucuses face less pressure to present a united front because they do not reflect the government. They can be a dishevelled bunch, ranging from an assortment of former ministers to a small perpetual rump, or they can be a cohesive group preparing to form the next government. An opposition caucus meeting is an opportunity to figure out which issues to advocate and to urge caucus officers to negotiate with their government counterparts.

The leader's circle tries to hold the caucus together as it deliberates differences tearing segments of society apart. Notes are taken and questions answered.[55] In some camps, meetings are haphazard, and members see little evidence that what they say makes any difference. Ex-ministers who have only ever served in the cabinet can have trouble adapting to caucus collaboration. Other opposition leaders encourage meaningful input through structured processes and/or informal personalized attention. Small caucuses often include backbenchers in decisions, but that approach can be replaced with a formalized process under new leadership, as occurred with the New Democrats in the early 2000s.[56] During that period, the NDP leadership circle worked to build a united position in response to the Harper government's plans to scale back the national firearms registry. The opposition chief of staff at the time recalls the considerable effort to achieve caucus consensus:

> It was a lot of talking. A lot of listening. A lot of negotiating. We had caucus meetings where we discussed it. We had meetings with different stakeholders. MPs were meeting with different people. It took up a lot of space, a lot of oxygen. It was necessary, and we were eventually able to develop a position that might not have been completely satisfactory to everybody's view on the matter, but it unified the caucus around an approach and a strategy.[57]

A noteworthy difference about NDP national caucus meetings is the presence of a representative from the Canadian Labour Congress who acts as a liaison with organized labour.[58]

Whether in government or in opposition, a leader must match the caucus mood: a parliamentary group that craves sensitivity can shun a disciplinarian, whereas a caucus tired of upheaval can welcome one. After over a decade in government, Wilfrid Laurier ran opposition caucus meetings with charm and calm. He offered suggestions and advice. It did not occur to MPs to question the former prime minister.[59] Conversely, as leader of the third party in the House of Commons, Justin Trudeau organized a disciplined group that revolved around his leadership and sometimes made policy announcements without consulting the caucus.[60]

MESSAGE DISCIPLINE WITHIN THE CAUCUS

Caucus meetings are structured political rituals with a pattern of social norms. Some private members pipe up; others say nothing. Institutional and social pressures condition members to go along with the crowd even though the caucus is a private sanctum in which they are encouraged to speak their minds.

Speaking Up in the Caucus

Private members are convinced that the best way for a leader to stay abreast of political situations is to listen to them in caucus meetings.[61] They bring forward perspectives that might be overlooked otherwise. They spot oversights and mistakes as they draw on varied life experiences and humanize policies with stories about constituents. They recommend key stakeholders to consult. Leaders value the feedback, if only because they require caucus support.

Backbencher input is crucial because it helps to prepare the leadership to speak publicly on behalf of the group. Leaders use caucus meetings as a sounding board and radar system; as Bernard Lord puts it, "caucus meetings are a great time for leaders to listen. Caucus is its own focus group for the leader."[62] Another former premier agrees that information exchange with backbenchers is important: "Caucus is a place for people to express themselves, to be heard, to understand the reasons if what they are saying is not consistent with where the party is going to go, and to understand what their options are for expressing their idea," Kathleen Wynne says.[63] As she moved up the ranks, Wynne felt a responsibility to speak in the caucus when something needed to be said; as premier, she encouraged others to do the same. Figuring out what to say and deciding whether to say it were always on her mind:

> When I was in municipal politics, someone said it would be some of the best years of my political life because you are able to say what you need to say. You can be an agile group of people who are able to act. Later, when I was first in the Liberal caucus, I remember thinking "okay, now I have to sort out what I can and can't say." I always felt as a backbencher and then as a minister that I had a responsibility to speak up when I felt there was something I needed to say or there was a gap in what was being talked about. It was never about dominating caucus meetings. Then as the leader I always tried to create the opportunity for others to speak up.[64]

If enough backbenchers raise concerns, then the leadership must assess the depth of internal division, which can prompt a rethink.

Some members treat caucus meetings as cabinet auditions. To them, caucus is a networking forum. These members can annoy the rest of the room by wanting to talk every week and by fawning over the leader. Other members want to deliberate policy. They believe that forceful advocacy requires emotional debate, possibly using salty language. Coalitions of backbenchers reinforce their points by speaking in succession, some as a voice of reason, others with a fiery temperament.[65] They turn up the theatrics by thundering with excitement, sobbing, and making passionate appeals. A former MP pulls back the curtain:

> Particular behaviours elicit certain responses. You get up to the microphone, you rally the troops, and then there's applause! Sometimes you have a temper tantrum because something isn't going the way you need it to go, so you do this theatrical piece where you yell and scream. There are other theatrical moments where you cry and bring a moment of sadness that will hopefully get everyone to agree that your issue is important.[66]

Some parliamentarians struggle to contain their exasperation. An MLA who was banished from his party's caucus describes perceptions of "a tyrannical dictatorship that expects unquestionable loyalty to the nth degree in an environment where reasonable questions or observations are viewed as an attack rather than a critique."[67] Occasionally, a meeting descends into "a bitch session" or a "gripe session" in which parliamentarians "let off steam."[68] Unhappy members might not hold back, calling a minister a "f*cking coward" or declaring that their leader is "worse than Hitler."[69] Such performances render the meetings unpleasant for some if more entertaining. Venting can enable party unity because the caucus feels heard, even when their opinions do not hold sway.

"The Spiral of Silence"

A backbencher's ability to exert policy influence is related to the leader's style and the political circumstances facing the party. Even though members are urged to share opinions, most of the time a caucus is deferential, particularly that of the governing party. Caucus culture is that they will prevail only if everyone rallies around the leader.[70] Joe Clark recalls a time when, as leader of the opposition, his colleagues were engaged in prolonged conversations about aspects of the 1982 Constitution Act. Bad weather delayed his arrival, and a caucus meeting proceeded without him. Debate on a contentious issue got out of hand. When Clark arrived, the group yielded to his opinion because of his status:

> When I repeated many of the arguments that had been made, we were able to move towards consensus. It wasn't personal, it was official. It had to do with status, the fact that I was the leader. There is respect for a leader's role and the authority of a leader, even in times when that leadership is under contest on other fronts. It was not something I dictated, not something I could whip. I walked into a situation when we were slipping more towards dissensus than we had been for a while, and without being brilliant in my arguments, simply by being there as the leader, we were able to bring it back.[71]

A veteran parliamentarian comments on the leader's influence over the caucus: "Whether it is real or implied, there's always that heavy hand from the centre looming," the MP says. "You hear in a caucus people talking behind the scenes that something is a serious issue, but nobody is bringing it up to the prime minister. That subtle, underlying hand is putting pressure on you not to undermine the team."[72] Members sometimes observe colleagues who side with the leader despite previously advocating a different position. A meeting can erupt into a political rally even though malcontents entered the room determined to call for new leadership.[73]

Speaking up in the caucus is fundamental to democratic representation when party discipline is intense. The latter is prone to prevail over the former because many private members hold their tongues while others flatter those in charge. Saying nothing is equated with tacit support: "Sometimes Members of Parliament, particularly newer ones, believe they need to be as disciplined message-wise inside the caucus room as outside," says a Trudeau minister. "They need to realize that inside the caucus room you need to speak your mind. Caucus is not the time for talking points."[74] Conversation is dampened because brutal honesty has negative implications, and more energy is required to challenge a group's position than to offer passive support. A chill is cast if a leader berates someone for expressing a blunt counterview, making sociable politicians morose. They bottle up opinions out of concern that what they say might be used against them. They might advise a brooding colleague to stay quiet.

Reticence is substantial because of the stark consequences of group isolation compared with the perceived benefits of aligning with the group. In *The Spiral of Silence: Public Opinion – Our Social Skin,* German political scientist Elisabeth Noelle-Neumann theorizes that people who hold a majority view tend to voice their opinions, whereas those holding an unpopular view keep their thoughts to themselves.[75] Those in the minority can lack the conviction to challenge the majority, so they withdraw from debate. As the majority position becomes more popular, some dissenters abandon the feelings of rejection for the joy of inclusion, further bolstering the majority. A spiral of silence results as advocates of a minority position cascade into a splinter group. Translated into a parliamentary caucus, those in the upper echelons promote a dominant view stoked by supporters and bandwagoners. Backbenchers who refrain from speaking up implicitly sanction both the process and a proposed course of action. The few remaining vocal dissenters face the wrath of the leadership and group isolation. Leaders and backbenchers alike recognize that this encumbers democratic representation:

> Holding power as leader of the opposition or as prime minister, you have an ongoing imperative to control your caucus. But that imperative contradicts the representative function of your MPs. This is a conflict at the heart of parliamentary democracy. And it can only be changed by something that's unlikely, which is party leaders saying: "Okay, representative democracy matters so much that we're going to let our dogs off the leash."[76]

> When I got elected, I naively expected that caucus was the place where MPs could have a free and frank discussion of issues of the day. The biggest single disappointment upon becoming an MP was finding that caucus meetings were structured to begin with the head table sort of providing us with our marching orders.[77]

The absence of written rules about caucus engagement makes everything murky. The Albertan who penned open letters about message discipline believes that the opaqueness causes people to err on the side of saying nothing: "In caucus, the rules aren't clear. No one comes out and explicitly says 'these are the things you can say, these are the things you can't say, and these are the consequences there would be for doing this,'" Robyn Luff explains. "There's never a discussion about what the rules are and how the rules are applied. It's an overarching unseen social pressure which makes it difficult to ascertain what you are able to do."[78] A veteran MP agrees: "There is no handbook for caucus. None. There are no written bylaws. You show up to your first meeting, and you go along with the flow," he asserts.[79] Many private members reason that speaking up hinders their ability to advance another file or be promoted, and they recognize that being a contrarian offers limited personal benefit because their fortitude cannot be publicized. They see how policy holdouts irritate the rest of the room, which – much like the jurors in *12 Angry Men* – wants to move on to the next item of business. A government-bench-side MP theorizes that social structures condition elected representatives to internalize their views:

When you have a disagreement publicly over an issue, it causes a lot of problems for people who can't personally handle that stress. Nobody says anything because no one likes conflict. You ask questions, then you're punished, and you can't figure out why you're the only one. I have met people with very strong opinions. Sometimes they'll keep it to themselves, or they'll speak quietly among colleagues. But they won't voice their opinions at a national level or even independently. I think our system can't function with people who are into non-conformity all the time. There needs to be a balance. Currently, if you ask a question, some people think you're criticizing them when you are just looking for information.[80]

The forces of silence mean that it would be an error to mistake tranquility for enthusiasm, particularly if someone has been vocalizing opinions outside the caucus room. Encouraging an upset member to share opinions can generate a good conversation that brings the person onside or causes a policy rethink. A leader who expresses an honest interest in listening to counterpoints nurtures cohesion, and guards against a public outburst. In return, backbenchers who think that the leader values their opinions are willing to assist the whip and the party.[81] Those who feel ignored, taken for granted, blacklisted, or otherwise rejected by the caucus are more likely to reject the caucus back.

REGIONAL CAUCUSES AND OTHER CAUCUSES

When a large caucus convenes, there is not enough time available for its members to speak, let alone get into a philosophical debate. Caucuses of all sizes can get off track, so breaking up into smaller groups that examine specific issues and lobby ministers allows members to have their say. Sub-caucuses provide backbenchers with a framework to exchange perspectives while building consensus. Without the leader present, they have more freedom to strategize, discuss public affairs, and share opinions. They deliberate taking action on an issue with the full caucus or media and might generate policy proposals. Participation in small groups gives them a sense of purpose, importance, and inclusion. They can gain familiarity with other issues, legislators, and electoral districts.

As is so often the case in Canadian politics, sub-caucuses stand to make more progress if they speak with one voice and if they repeat messages.

Members who speak forcefully in small forums might defer to chairs when the full caucus meets, enabling business to move ahead more smoothly. The chairs become point persons for the leaders. Prior to a meeting of the full caucus, an executive committee of chairs might exchange information, and then one of them might brief the leader about what to expect. The leader's staff can be in regular contact with chairs of powerful caucuses to explore how to approach an issue and to solicit opinions about messaging. Leaders and ministers sometimes make an appearance at smaller government-side caucuses, and exempt staff take notes.[82]

An opposition party has fewer members who are busier readying for the legislature. For instance, an opposition committee might review bills with ministerial critics, and then the leader's office will email the committee's position to the full caucus.[83] During the 42nd Parliament, the Conservatives had about a dozen caucuses, and the NDP had four.[84] In contrast, the governing Liberals maintained more than thirty caucuses on topics ranging from aerospace to youth, of which regional caucuses are the most prevalent.

Regional Caucuses

Geographic caucuses are among the most powerful blocs given the likelihood of splits along regional, provincial, urban, suburban, and rural lines. In Ottawa, regional caucuses can break into clusters, represent a single province, or reflect a geographic area where the party has a heavy concentration of MPs. Thus, in the 42nd Parliament, with approximately eighty Ontario MPs, the Liberals had a plethora of regional sub-groups. This included the golden horseshoe caucus (an area in southern Ontario), the 416 and 905 caucuses (referring to telephone area codes for urban and suburban Toronto, respectively), and issue-specific groups populated with Ontario MPs such as the auto caucus and the Ontario immigration caucus.[85] The influence of a regional caucus waxes and wanes. For instance, Atlantic MPs were persuasive with Pierre Trudeau.[86] Under Jean Chrétien, they felt ineffectual.[87]

Regional chairs typically raise a couple of issues at a national caucus meeting. To prepare, regional caucuses tend to meet the day before or the morning before the full group does. A governing party's regional caucuses are folded into the government's communications infrastructure. The PMO periodically asks the chair to inform other members about the party line on a key issue and to keep caucus officers informed about anything brewing. Regional desk staff might attend meetings and act as designated liaisons: "It's usually at the regional caucuses that the eruptions occur," a former government whip says. "It's the responsibility of the chairs of each regional caucus to privately inform the whip's office and the caucus chair of the regional rumblings. The challenge is to nip them in the bud and have an effective solution under way which is communicated back to the aggrieved person or group before it becomes contagious."[88] In some parliamentary parties, the regional chairs are not obliged to share information with the leadership, instead opting to discuss an issue with a minister. The primacy of region is evident when a leader asks a regional caucus to make a recommendation about whether to expel a member from the party, as Justin Trudeau did during the SNC-Lavalin affair.

Other Caucuses and All-Party Groups

An assortment of other sub-caucuses brings parliamentarians together to make progress on issues of shared concern. Some of the most prominent caucuses assemble people based on Indigeneity, gender, or race. For example the chair of the Liberal Indigenous caucus believes that it is a "starting point" for soliciting Indigenous perspectives.[89] Parliamentarians from other demographic cohorts sometimes attend these caucuses to learn about the concerns of members of marginalized communities. A larger number of groupings are based on issues, such as the Conservative hunting and angling caucus or the Liberal early learning and child-care working group. There are also task forces whose members conduct research, conduct consultations, and present a final report to the main caucus.[90] Definitive lists of sub-caucuses, their membership, and their functions are not publicly available.[91] In some cases, the name is obvious only to those involved. A case in point is the Liberal prompt payment caucus, which to the uninitiated appears to be a caucus social fund. In fact, it refers to the topical policy problem of ensuring that contractors in the construction industry are paid in a timely manner. The backbenchers examining that issue are ineligible to sit on a parallel government-industry working group tasked with exploring solutions. The sub-caucus is a route to offer the minister's office and industry some perspectives that would otherwise be missing.

A women's caucus has a particular reputation for cohesion and an ability to move files forward. Its members can be especially keen to solve problems by using a conciliatory style instead of a confrontational style. A former MP says that she felt liberated to speak about issues of concern to women:

> You're always a little careful about what you say. The only place I never felt that I had to be careful was women's caucus each Wednesday at noon. I always felt I could be completely open about what I thought and what I felt. Talking about feelings in any other context would not have been easy. I could blow my stack, I could laugh. I knew it would never come back to bite me outside of that room. We had huge influence on huge issues.[92]

When united, the women's caucus can form a powerful bloc. The chair might also belong to an informal all-party women's group that brings together her counterparts from other parties. The chairs then relay information back to colleagues in their own caucus. The cross-party collaboration can include organizing women-centric events and speaking out on an issue of shared concern. It also invites new ways of thinking about political teams: "One of the good things though about having an all-party women's caucus is that a lot of discussions can happen when you build trust ... across party lines," says an MP.[93]

As this suggests, backbenchers belong to all-party groups that operate outside of formal systems. Some of these unofficial groups attend to sobering issues, such as climate change or diabetes, and might be a function of lobbying activity by government relations firms, charitable organizations, and not-for-profits. Some, such as the parliamentary beer caucus, are social avenues with connections to industry advocacy. Inter-country groups also form. The existence and membership of all-party bodies are mysterious, as I found out when my attempt to identify the MPs on the all-party democracy caucus was rebuffed. We do know that they are a source of personal fulfillment for MPs, even though their advocacy work is constrained by party discipline.[94] None is a venue for parliamentarians to speak freely because the potential for political sabotage always looms.

For those keen to network within their own partisan family, a small caucus can be fortified by reaching out to politicians of the same label in other jurisdictions. The Liberal Black caucus hosts events with the party's Black MPs, senators, and Liberal members of provincial legislatures to discuss issues of importance to Black communities.[95] Other private forums for information exchange between partisans include parliamentary offices, fundraising events, electoral district association meetings, and hospitality rooms at party conventions. Because nothing is ever truly private in politics, partisans must be on guard that a comment made in any encounter can find its way to the whip's office, a journalist, or social media.

LEADER'S STAFF AT CAUCUS MEETINGS

The presence of a leader's staff influences behaviour in caucus meetings, particularly where the Prime Minister's Office or a premier's office is concerned. A small cadre of staff discuss senior appointments with the leader, have many opportunities to influence public policy, and can persuade the leader to agree to a backbencher's request for resources.[96] Their authority, both real and perceived, is elevated by their social media personas. As a result, some parliamentarians are keen about opportunities for the leader's staff to listen to them. Others believe that the leader's handlers stifle free expression in caucus meetings, particularly if criticism reflects on staff performance.

Role of Staff in Caucus Meetings

There are good reasons for a leader's staff to attend caucus meetings, especially if the party is in government. The staff are part of a managerial group and share the leader's desire for caucus harmony. They take notes when someone raises concerns, and they encourage the leader to spend time with disgruntled members as well as greet members in the lobby on the way in for a contentious vote. Likewise, the leader might ask an assistant to go for coffee with an outspoken member.

A caucus benefits when staff grasp issues because comprehension leads to improved execution: "Staff need to understand the mood of the caucus," a staffer says. "You've got to make sure everybody is satisfied, everyone's happy, and knows they have a role to play. If staff do not go to caucus, then it is staff running the show."[97] Caucus meetings are the only regular opportunity for them to interact with parliamentarians. They want to build relationships, learn what is on everyone's mind, and identify stressors:

"Caucus is your best focus group, it's your best polling," says a former chief of staff. "If you fail to listen to what they're saying, it's not going to work."[98] Information discussed by the caucus is crucial to personnel involved in advancing policy, spotting problems, and assessing how messaging is being received on the ground.

The speed of digital communication means that staff cannot afford the time lag of waiting for a briefing about caucus events. An MP who used to be a political staffer elaborates:

> Staff need to be at caucus meetings because of the fast feedback loop in communications and information. It's a balance to ensure confidentiality and security so caucus members can have rigorous exchanges of ideas and perspectives, and frank conversations, which is important for the team dynamic. Caucus members do need some measure of exclusivity to engage with each other. On the other hand, there is huge value in at least senior staff being present to hear decisions and background first hand in order to operate efficiently and effectively. We're in a world where parties need to respond to a crisis or an opponent almost immediately. If staff are back in their offices waiting to get updates from the House leader's office, a lot of time can go by before they are working on the decisions made in caucus, which involves executing multiple things quickly.[99]

Staff are embedded in caucus meetings in Ottawa in which discussing digital communication is an integral component. They present examples of recent social media posts that gained online traction. Here is how MPs in two different parties describe the leader's staff celebrating digital activity at caucus meetings:

> We're marketing managers. Staff in the leader's office tell us at caucus "we're tracking how many times you're retweeting the leader's tweets and how many of you have reposted the leader's Facebook posts. Some of you haven't been doing it enough." They employ a series of inducements and dissuasion. If you're good, you get praised: "Look at these Facebook posts!" They beam it on the screens at the front of the room to show all the grown adults how great so-and-so is because they did all this wonderful

stuff online praising the leader. Otherwise, you aren't helping the team. This happens every week, ad infinitum.[100]

I know they are monitoring our social media because often they will come to caucus and present something off someone's Twitter or Facebook and say "oh, look, this is what so-and-so tweeted on this day. We want to see more of those kinds of positive messages going out." Or "this is what someone posted on Facebook after being in their riding. They got fifty comments. This is great PR! We want to see more MPs doing that and promoting the work that the government is doing."[101]

The staff encourage MPs to draw inspiration from their digitally savvy colleagues. They urge everyone to focus on the intended audience when rewriting messages. They show examples of what not to do online. In between meetings, they might send enthusiastic messages about how many likes and retweets a post achieved or communicate delight that the leader gained more online followers.

Senior staff recognize that discretion is paramount. They are trusted because of their loyalty to the leader, who benefits from stability. Lower-ranking staff, especially those in the whip's office, understand that speaking about caucus meetings is a fireable offence. Political staff in the legislative precinct and in constituency offices do hear dribs and drabs about caucus happenings. The main source is senior staff who boast at planning meetings about the private members whom the leader praised for doing something well. Information is divulged about publicity ideas as a way to inspire staff to create interesting social media content.

Some parliamentarians counter that the caucus should be restricted to elected representatives. They worry about confidentiality when staff are spotted mingling with journalists. More significantly, they are more willing to voice concerns about staff in the leader's office when those staff are not present.[102] They realize that staff hold grudges. In extreme cases, a chief of staff stifles dissent by making an example of any backbencher who questions the government's plans, portraying the questioner as a dissident who undermines the team.[103] The dressing down aggravates backbenchers' isolation and adds to the spiral of silence: "It's not about the leader taking notes or following up," an MP says. "It's about the integrity of that body and its ability to do its core job, which is to speak truth to power, provide honest feedback, and maintain an atmosphere of trust. You don't have that when too many outsiders are permitted inside that forum."[104] Many political staff empathize. They realize that their names were not on ballots. They know that they do not face the public pressures that parliamentarians do.

Occasionally, parliamentarians prod the leader to exclude staff from caucus meetings. The agitation reflects a buildup of resentment over philosophical differences with the leader's office and the treatment of backbenchers. A leader can be sympathetic to a request for staff to leave, especially one with experience on the backbenches who wants the caucus to be a place of candour. Staff might be asked to exit a meeting when sensitive topics are discussed, such as disciplinary measures or caucus resources. In the NDP, unionized staff are not present for collective bargaining discussions. Staff themselves can reason that it is counterproductive to attend caucus meetings. The presence of communications personnel can prompt complaints about communications, a crutch for avoiding gruelling discussions: "Sometimes, if the communications person is in the room, saying we need a better communications strategy is an easy out from having the argument about what the position is or what the policy is or what you need to do to make something better," Kate Purchase says.[105]

PMO Staff and the National Caucus Meeting

National caucus meetings without the prime minister's staff present are no longer viable because of the tempo of social media. They did not normally attend caucus meetings led by Pierre Trudeau, Brian Mulroney, Jean Chrétien, and Paul Martin.[106] Chiefs of staff or principal secretaries would do so in exceptional circumstances. Chrétien's parliamentary secretary took notes, and PMO personnel exited after making a presentation or taking a photograph.[107] The only person from Martin's PMO who regularly attended caucus meetings was his executive assistant. That person arrived while the prime minister was delivering a concluding summary in order to take notes so that the PMO could ensure that any commitments were upheld.[108] When other staff began appearing, the caucus sometimes urged Martin to keep the meetings off limits. That evolved with Stephen Harper, who wanted his chief of staff to attend. One or two other PMO personnel joined them with varying frequency, sitting to the side in deference to the rest and taking notes whether the prime minister was present or not. The chief of staff joined caucus officers in Monday caucus steering group meetings. He also prepared the first draft of Harper's opening remarks for Wednesday's national meeting.[109]

Staff are a fixture in Justin Trudeau's caucus meetings. As mentioned, from the outset his trusted advisers have had a significant presence, to the point that MPs have wondered whether a meeting will have much impact if a senior staffer is absent. Up to a dozen personnel from the PMO and whip's office attend, led by the chief of staff. Some PMO and ministerial staff attend a portion of the meeting or do so for a specific purpose, such as communications personnel who discuss a budget roll-out or a researcher who summarizes the latest public opinion data. The whip's office staff put up visuals on a projector screen and take notes on what is being said. MPs are told that staff attendance is positive because it enables information exchange and follow-ups. Initially, veteran MPs complained, but the many rookies did not know any different.

Discord can surface if PMO staff confront private members in the caucus. In 2017, the Liberal government pushed forward with a small business tax policy despite concerns vocalized by regional caucus committees. The cabinet entrenched its position, but disagreement spilled into the public domain, and the bad publicity led the government to backpedal. Finance Minister Bill Morneau held a conference call with MPs to urge message cohesion in public.[110] At a caucus meeting, PMO staff presented poll data to show that public awareness of the policy had increased because some backbenchers had complained publicly: "Don't try and blame us," a veteran MP said to a senior staffer. "The fact is you never goddamn well listened to what your caucus was saying, so we had to come out."[111] Caucus outbursts caused the Trudeau PMO to become more aware of the reasons for resistance to staff presence. Their number dipped slightly after the turmoil of the SNC-Lavalin affair in early 2019.

SUMMARY

Caucus meetings are the primary forum for parliamentarians to exchange information. Confidentiality is paramount. Formats range from tightly run weekly meetings at which the leadership updates backbenchers to smaller seminar-style strategy conversations. The resulting public image of unanimity blurs caucus conviction and internal division, including the concealment of tension caused by the power of the leader's staff relative to that of backbenchers. Solidarity is boosted by the communications work of caucus research bureaus, the subject of the next chapter.

8

Caucus Research Bureaus

Caucus research bureaus are the workhorses of permanent campaigning. In Ottawa, where they are officially known as national caucus research offices and are funded by the House of Commons, the bureaus help Members of Parliament to contend with the unshakable public expectation that representatives be informed about all public affairs and parliamentary business. In practice, caucus research bureaus are a public relations department for the parliamentary leader and a communications pipeline for the PMO and ministers' offices. How did these communications functionaries emerge? How do they disseminate messaging? In this chapter, I look at the unseen role of caucus research bureaus in transmitting messages to Canadian MPs.

ORIGINS AND COMMUNICATIONS FUNCTIONS

Researchers in parliamentary libraries have access to a trove of legislative materials and regularly assist parliamentarians and political staff with specialized requests for policy analysis.[1] They proactively circulate news headlines and legislative summaries and, on request, they check the veracity of information. Legislative librarians do not perform partisan tasks. As well, they lack knowledge of a party's policy positions and often cannot produce information with the immediacy that parliamentarians sometimes require. Caucus members must turn elsewhere for assistance with strategic communications.

The Liberal Research Bureau (LRB), Conservative Caucus Services (previously known as the Conservative Resource Group), and NDP Caucus

Services operate out of downtown Ottawa in conjunction with other staff in the leader's office. The number of people the bureaus employ fluctuates. In the 41st Parliament, the NDP official opposition had more than 100 research bureau staff.[2] Conversely, in the 42nd Parliament, there were 37 in the LRB, 63 in the Conservative bureau, and 47 in the NDP bureau.[3] With ten MPs, the Bloc Québécois did not qualify for funding; however, the Board of Internal Economy made an exception and authorized "caucus coordination" funds that pooled part of Bloc MPs' office budgets.[4] The growing centralized partisan communications functions of these publicly funded offices deviate from the original intention that bureaus would prioritize research support for private members.

Purpose of Caucus Research Bureaus

Funding from a legislature for political assistance is normally proportionate to the number of elected representatives in a caucus. In large caucuses, there can be so many employees that the legislature houses them in a building separate from that of the parliamentarians. In small caucuses, staff can be housed in and around the leader's office or situated among the parliamentarians and their assistants. Caucuses can also rely on interns.[5] As indicated, parliamentary groups without enough members for official party status do not qualify for additional funding to support extra staff, nor do Independents.

In Ottawa, national caucus research offices emerged in response to a need for well-resourced, high-quality partisan research. In the early twentieth century, the Conservative whip oversaw a literature bureau that circulated printed materials, and the caucus appointed a committee of MPs to review speaking invitations received by party headquarters and to decide who should address public gatherings.[6] After the First World War, the party ran a research and publicity bureau to investigate topical issues, collect information about electoral districts from MPs, and build a mailing list of supporters to bypass the mainstream media.[7] These sorts of ad hoc arrangements changed when Pierre Trudeau became prime minister. The 1968 throne speech promised a "new provision" so that parliamentary parties could "cope more effectively with the heavy load of action and decision each session."[8] Prorated funds for caucus research bureaus became available to political parties with official status in the House of Commons, which was deemed to be twelve MPs.

The intended purpose was to provide private members with assistance that legislative librarians could not offer or that a policy caucus committee was unable to perform. Bureaus initially employed young social scientists who conducted policy research for chairs of standing committees and wrote speeches for opposition private members.[9] They assembled information for use in the legislature, the caucus, and members' constituencies. Support services centred on research as well as technical assistance with media training and mail-outs.[10] Other supports ranged from providing MPs with packages of newspaper clippings to storing research about political opponents in filing cabinets.[11]

Bureaus keep private members apprised of the leadership's position on public issues. Staff analyze public policy, prepare issue notes, and deliver presentations. In opposition bureaus, they work with ministerial critics to monitor government initiatives and stakeholder activism.[12] They generate talking points that criticize the government and sometimes promote alternative policy options, often in concert with the shadow minister. They help the opposition House leader and whip to prepare for Question Period, standing committees, and other legislative business. An opposition bureau also participates in the sort of work conducted by regional desks in the government, such as event planning with MPs and stakeholders. Political strategists have described the bureaus as follows:

> Some parties focus more on short term Question Period and daily news and issue response preparation, as a focus for the research teams. Others give them longer-term campaign development, issue development research responsibilities; often a combination of the two, depending on circumstances.[13]

> They're the people who have uncovered the stories through ATIP [Access to Information and Privacy], through research, through brown envelopes from disgruntled employees ... And a lot of times the very words that members are speaking were crafted by members of the research bureau, so it's very important.[14]

It's where most of the leg work is done by parties, both to prepare for elections and to prepare for House performance ... Theoretically, they're not supposed to be used during elections with campaigns themselves.[15]

Our research bureau continues to provide a variety of services to our caucus members, including translation, policy, research and communications, but as these are internal services, we do not discuss them publicly.[16]

In theory, bureaus are available to help interested MPs tackle an issue. In practice, staff can be selective about providing support. For instance, their response to an MP who requests research assistance for a private member's bill might reflect whether the leader's office endorses or opposes the topic. In essence, bureaus have a hand in conditioning private members to behave as the leader's surrogates.

Communications Functions

Bureaus began to transform into centralized message brokers when their reporting oversight shifted from the caucus to the party leader.[17] Work expanded from research assistance to encompass translation services, media training, and drafting of news releases. Bureau staff drafted op-eds and letters to editors for MPs. They circulated speaking notes and talking points to increase awareness of issues and to ensure that "members are on the same message track."[18] Gradually, the leader's office assumed more authority over a bureau's operations, causing some clients to accuse a bureau of overemphasizing central messages and question whether MPs have service priority over what the leadership wants.[19] Bureaus can be exuberant about communications oversight, a staffer concedes:

Things can get a little petty. There's a degree of control for its own sake. Being cohesive and tight, playing politics as a team sport, that's important for getting your message out. But discipline can get excessive when it becomes more about the control than ... about the team. Some people try to control things to build their little empires, saying "do it my way, there is no other way." It's rare, but you see it.[20]

Naturally, communications functions in the opposition bureaus differ from those of a governing party's bureau. Opposition staff prepare news releases and reality checks, file access to information requests, generate content for social media using the tone and language appropriate to the digital platform, train MPs' staff, and ensure that communications products "follow strict messaging and branding guidelines."[21] The Conservative opposition circulates a "talking points master file" document that contains over three hundred topics, a summary of issues, and a bullet list of key messages.[22] Some topics include a subset of "if pressed" messages to be used only if additional information is required beyond the main key messages.

A governing party's bureau promotes government accomplishments. Staff fine-tune messages about policy developed with the benefit of public service expertise and then convince MPs' assistants to participate in spreading government messaging. Staff want to protect the government, achieve buy-in from MPs if it is the first time that they are hearing about something, and provide a sense of rhetoric on both sides of the debate. The bureau tries to educate MPs about issues, justify the government's position, and provide communications tools for MPs to sell that position to the public. Central coordination reduces the possibility that a private member will accidentally go off-message and enables the detection of someone who betrays the party line.

A governing party's bureau works with ministers' offices to provide governing party MPs with information packages. Bill kits are distributed to prepare for legislative debate and a vote, consultation kits help MPs to collect information from constituents for provision to a government department, and budget kits are resources for parliamentarians to raise public awareness of budget initiatives.[23] In the 1980s, budget kits featured "information to rebut opposition criticism, a list of groups consulted on the budget, sample questions and answers, model radio and television speeches, a summary of media commentaries, and a set of 'good news' economic indicators."[24] In 1983, governing party members leaving Ottawa for the summer received a plastic suitcase containing a vinyl record, speeches, and a document recommending that they seek local media opportunities to promote government policy.[25] As we shall see, there is no longer a summer reprieve for government-side MPs because of the need to replenish their social media.

Both governing party and opposition bureaus achieve marketing economies of scale by creating graphic design templates for MP outreach funded by the House of Commons.[26] Members of Parliament are entitled to use a portion of their operating budgets for advertising, printing newsletters, and creating a website. Partisan advocacy is allowed. Bureau-produced templates save members considerable time and effort and opting-in ensures compliance with rules set by the Board of Internal Economy and alignment with the party's position. The standardization is particularly helpful for freshly elected members. A political staffer discusses the templates:

> All parliamentarians using their member's operating budget have to follow a certain set of guidelines. We provide templates that we pre-clear through printing and material services to ensure they are coherent and compliant. We ensure the information about policies that are outlined is factually correct. Our assistance could be anything from helping a group ad buy, it could be in a newspaper or a magazine, it might be for a cultural community 100th anniversary program. We help ensure it's looked after, and we have graphic designers on staff that help place it as per design specs and make it visually appealing.[27]

Central production offers a more professional design, layout, and general look. MP offices can choose from text boxes provided by the bureau and insert their own local photographs. Rolling news banners that scroll centrally produced headlines can be added to MPs' websites, as can event pages so that constituents can sign up to attend a local event. An MP retains the option to hire a local graphic designer or to have an office assistant create the materials. Most MPs' staff adapt central messaging to suit regional contexts.

Bureaus respond to the pressure on MPs to have a presence on social media. Most politicians and their staff struggle to create interesting posts and worry about causing offence. Bureaus condense information into visually appealing digital content. Under Stephen Harper, the Conservative research bureau followed the three-second rule – "the idea that you need to communicate in bite-size chunks that can be absorbed within three seconds or less," as Patrick Muttart, the former PMO strategic planner, puts it.[28] A decade later bureaus were wrapping messaging into a graphic or photograph for sharing via Facebook, Instagram, or Twitter. Bureau staff slip into technical lingo when talking about how they supply social media shareables with plug and play. Static content, such as text at the bottom of a digital template, mixes with customizable content, such as an insertable photograph. Sometimes bureaus support a backbencher by creating digitals for use by the rest of the caucus that highlight that person's work or accomplishments. Staff urge the use of a common hashtag, which facilitates tracking. The MPs benefit from attracting more social media followers for the next campaign.

Some bureau activities delve into grey areas. Partisan negativity in mail-out templates has been controversial.[29] Bureaus convince MPs to turn over their free mailing privileges, known as franking. A number of New Democrats from the 41st Parliament had to repay the Board of Internal Economy for partisan mailings, which upset Ryan Cleary, the one-time MP:

> I was fairly new as an MP. When the party comes and they ask you to do something, you generally try to do it because you don't want to be seen as disagreeable or not a team player ... The whole scenario left a bad taste in my mouth. I felt like the party kind of took advantage of younger MPs. At the time I was furious, [since] my name was associated with this supposed scandal and I had nothing to do with it except following the wishes of the party leaders.[30]

The publicly funded bureaus engage in extraparliamentary work, such as providing talk show pundits with key messages. Staff monitoring of online activity can inform psychographic profiling and replenish party databases, while software programs scrape social media in order to understand public sentiments and inform MPs what citizens are saying online.[31] At the extreme, bureaus engage in black-ops practices, including video-recording a leader at events and anonymously tweeting a minister's divorce records.[32] Mistakes arise, such as when a bureau violates government policies on nonpartisan communications by adding the party logo to digital communications about government initiatives.[33] The dividing line between caucus support and supporting other entities is especially ambiguous with respect to the bureau's treatment of private members as brand ambassadors, particularly those who sit on the government side.

THE LIBERAL RESEARCH BUREAU

As indicated, the governing party's bureau undertakes to raise awareness of government activities. Staff see their purpose as helping MPs and their assistants – and, by extension, constituents – to learn what the government is doing. Liberal Research Bureau employees describe work under the government led by Justin Trudeau:

> We're the main office that supports Liberal MPs, and that ranges from assistance with communications products to research above and beyond the available resources from the Library of Parliament.[34]

> I produced communications products to support MPs and their staff. It involved acting as a liaison between the research bureau, caucus, the Prime Minister's Office and ministers' offices. The work encompassed digital communication, social media strategy, micro-targeting tactics, multicultural outreach, and caucus relations.[35]

> We are like a little PR team for the government and a caucus PR shop. What are the good stories we can help to tell? What are the fun and interesting things that a member otherwise wouldn't be able to do on their own? We're a place where you can bring your stories to try to stitch them together. We are an important amplifier for the work the government is doing and for turning members into amplifiers for the government messages and announcements. We are also a bit of a voice to ministers' offices or to the PMO to ask how they can make so many parliamentarians be part of the story or carry it forward. They're not always thinking that way.[36]

The LRB performs a variety of communications-related services. A significant facet in standardizing messages is a searchable repository of talking points and model correspondence, known as InfoLib. The password-protected databank provides MPs and their assistants with access to approved English and French messaging, template position statements and stock phrases, as well as high-resolution images to customize. The digital hub offers convenience to personnel who prepare constituent correspondence, public remarks, and social media posts: "Suppose I'm going to speak on a panel outside the country," a Liberal MP postulates. "I can go into the InfoLib system to look for the talking points and some background on those issues. That's really helpful to me."[37] Some use the information as guidelines, whereas others use the stock phrases verbatim. InfoLib includes updated contact details for regional desks across the government so that users know whom to contact to obtain further information. When standardized replies are unavailable, or if the lines are outdated, office staff might advise a constituent that the MP needs to speak with the minister. If the minister's office receives enough enquiries, or if a talented constituency assistant suggests original messaging, then the bureau might add some boilerplate responses to InfoLib. This hidden digital tool plays a formidable role in delivering consistent messages across the country.

The bureau engages in issues management and strategic communications. Its director might attend PMO communications meetings and caucus meetings.[38] The staff identify items in the government's budget to pair with promises made during the campaign, and discuss topics resonating in data metrics. Back at the bureau's office, information obtained at the PMO meeting is shared so that staff can prepare for upcoming announcements. The bureau's work transitions to strategic planning, such as figuring out how to coordinate messaging from members of the women's caucus on International Women's Day. At other junctures in their day, bureau staff consult with the PMO when planning advertising buys for the caucus or convene in ministers' offices where they sometimes pitch suggestions. Extraordinary activities might be planned; for instance, in the 42nd Parliament, the LRB organized mandatory anti-harassment training for Liberal MPs and staff.[39]

Bureau personnel participate in central coordination by gathering local intelligence from constituency assistants and requesting a list of events that MPs plan to attend. Mirroring the PMO organizational setup, inbound information requests are channelled through bureau regional desks. The staffers discuss problems and upcoming events in regional meetings and in conference calls with parliamentary and/or constituency assistants. They alert the PMO and the relevant minister's office when a regional caucus or an individual MP wants to publicize an issue, which can lead to exempt staff running interference, though it is up to MPs to decide whether to accept the interference or ignore it. Ministerial staff sometimes become confused about whether bureau personnel outrank them.

The immediate priority of the bureau's issues management functions is keeping Liberals, including those in executive offices, informed of political developments and identifying who is authorized to comment publicly. A sample of internal emails in 2018 shows how message discipline is coordinated in a digital environment. In the early morning, bureau staff isolate a few issues in the news, and they contact the director of communications in the applicable minister's office to request message lines. The PMO is often consulted. They want Liberal MPs and staff to begin their days by perusing a "daily issues briefing" news digest (see Figure 8.1). A bureau staffer emails them the InfoLib summary in the morning and follows with another digest of major issues in the afternoon. The electronic briefings specify the lead department for each story and provide a bullet list of key messages: "Please note this is reactive messaging only, and not for proactive use," the email begins. Instructions state that MPs are to contact the bureau if they receive a media request.

A special update with talking points is circulated if there is an urgent situation (see Figure 11.2).[40] The rapid response messaging heads off requests for guidance and reduces the possibility that someone will misrepresent the party position. It is also a regular reminder to toe the line. When Liberal MPs discuss the InfoLib emails, they inevitably remark that the information helps them to establish messaging goalposts to guide their public comments and lack thereof:

> We get a daily reminder from InfoLib, such as saying there will be a caucus call with one of the ministers today about their ministry. We get a debrief on when the call is going to happen, what the general issues are going to be about, and whatever information summaries are public. We also get a daily issues briefing. So now, if I want to do a tweet, I can look at it and say "okay, anything within this framework is fair game, I can say it." If there's something they don't want you to comment on, like President Trump, they'll say here's information for you, but either nobody is going to comment or only the minister will comment. We get lines daily on all the topics that are important.[41]

Strategic communications follow for MPs to amplify government messaging. Bureau staff integrate information into visually appealing digital

FIGURE 8.1
Daily issues briefing, Liberal Research Bureau

From: InfoLib
Sent: May 15, 2018
Subject: Daily Issues Briefing

[le français suit]

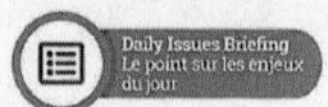

In response to caucus requests, LRB will be sharing our government's messaging on some of today's most pressing issues making headlines. Please note this is reactive messaging only, and not for proactive use. Contact us for more information or if you receive a media request on these topics.

Palestinian death toll rises in protests against U.S. Embassy opening in Jerusalem
[*link*]

Lead: Global Affairs Canada

Summary: Palestinians clashed on Monday with the Israeli military at the fence dividing the Gaza Strip and Israel, leaving at least 37 protesters dead from gunfire and overshadowing a historic opening of the U.S. embassy in Jerusalem hailed as a new chapter in U.S.-Israel relations. The death toll was the largest in a single day since the Israeli army fought a conflict with Gaza rulers Hamas in 2014.

- Canada is deeply concerned by the recent violence in the Gaza Strip.
- We are saddened by the deaths and injuries that occurred yesterday and have occurred over the past several weeks.
- Canada is a steadfast friend of Israel and friend to the Palestinian people.
- Canada's longstanding position is that the status of Jerusalem can be resolved only as part of a general settlement of the Palestinian-Israeli dispute.
- This has been the policy of consecutive Canadian governments.
- We are strongly committed to the goal of a comprehensive, just and lasting peace in the Middle East, including the creation of a Palestinian state living side-by-side in peace and security with Israel.
- We continue to support the building of conditions necessary for the parties to find a solution.

Source: Interview participant (three other news items not shown).

graphics such as memes, gifs, and other visuals. They send out InfoLib emails trumpeting major announcements, including hyperlinks to ministers' social media posts. Much of the content is duplicated in government media relations products. They also distribute shareables for MPs and their assistants to customize (see Figure 8.2). Another InfoLib email, using the subject line "PLEASE SHARE," is a specific announcement that the

FIGURE 8.2 Social media shareables, Liberal Research Bureau |
Liberal interview participant

government wants to highlight (see Figure 8.3). It offers a bulleted list of key messages, including one in bold font that recipients are meant to prioritize. In addition, Liberals receive a message of the day that features a feel-good story about the tangible benefits of a government policy, possibly

FIGURE 8.3
Government announcement messaging, Liberal Research Bureau

From: InfoLib
Sent: May 15, 2018
Subject: PLEASE SHARE: Historic federal investment to expand Calgary's
             public transit system

[le français suit]

Historic federal investment to expand Calgary's public transit system

Today, the Prime Minister announced [*link*] a major investment of up to
$1.53 billion for Calgary's Green Line Light Rail Transit project.

PLEASE SHARE
• Prime Minister's Facebook Post [*link*]

KEY MESSAGES
• Today's historic investment in Calgary's public transit system will make it easier for
  people to get around and connect to the services they need, make our air cleaner,
  and create thousands of jobs for Canadians.
• **This is the largest contribution ever made by the Government of Canada to an
  infrastructure project in Alberta.**
• Construction of the first stage of Calgary's Green Line is expected to begin in spring
  2020 and be completed by late 2026. An estimated 20,000 jobs will
  be created to support the system's design and construction, with a further
  400 long-term jobs forecasted for the operation and maintenance of the
  Green Line when it opens to the public.
• Once in service, the Green Line will provide hundreds of thousands of transit riders
  in the city's north and south-east communities with a direct route to the downtown
  core. It will also improve connections to public services.

Source: Interview participant.

by profiling citizens in a specific MP's electoral district. Once again, a list of key messages is accompanied by shareable image files. Recipients include all Liberal MPs, Parliament Hill assistants, constituency assistants, ministerial staff, the PMO, and bureau personnel.

When constructing these messages, instead of getting into the details of new legislation or programs, bureau personnel try to emphasize how citizens benefit. Messaging authored by the public service is precise, but the requirement for conformity to government communication policies contributes to a lack of imagination or emotion.[42] Political staff distill the academic style of official statements by drawing out feelings and themes, sometimes sacrificing accuracy. Messages are reworded to be straightforward using the active voice with fewer facts: "We kind of strip down messages coming out of the government," says a bureau employee. "What are we trying to accomplish? What difference will this make to people in their day-to-day lives? What's unique about our approach compared with our political opponents? How can we draw contrasts between us and other parties? Ultimately, we want to persuade Canadians that we are making the right decisions and that the outcome we are working towards is preferable to what our opponents would do."[43] Providing concise information is partly a response to MPs who complain when messages are too long, too frequent, and too technocratic. Another strategic parameter is to package messages within whole-of-government messaging. For instance, InfoLib messages of the day tell a story about how a policy will help Canadians. The story features one or more government catchphrases that the prime minister and ministers regularly use.

When MPs and their assistants receive the InfoLib messages, they scroll to identify whether a suggested post is a good fit. They integrate select content into their social media when it is relevant to the electoral district and/or of personal interest to the member. A Liberal MP explains how he manages the bureau's requests:

> "Please share" is what the email says. My staff either picks one of the sample social media messages with the graphics and puts it online, or they ask me to pick from the list. I don't do my own Facebook, my staff does it for me, so they send out what the party suggests just to amplify the message. I do my own Twitter; maybe I shouldn't. The messaging is very coordinated, and it's informed. If you disagree with it, party discipline structure provides you with an opportunity to raise those concerns internally rather than in the press.[44]

MPs need to be prepared to comment on what is posted in their name. Lenses are applied to identify which supplied messaging is irrelevant or incendiary, and sometimes private members discuss a shareable at a regional caucus meeting to see what colleagues think. Ultimately, they and their assistants delete most shareables – filtering that is a microcosm of diverse representation. For instance, MPs who represent workers participating in the Quebec Pension Plan have little need for messaging about the Canada Pension Plan. Those who celebrate an increase of twelve dollars a month in pension payouts are mocked online for their hyperbole, which causes the MPs to be wary the next time. Another example is upbeat back-to-school shareables after Labour Day, which would be derided in a province experiencing a teachers' strike or in ridings where some schools did not open because of unsafe buildings. The randomness of sharing digital content minimizes the potential for online sleuths to detect parroting. Rewording also combats being part of a party soundtrack as well as the digital snafu of party content appearing on social media with "insert content here" cues intact.[45]

The LRB offers digital skills training to help MPs and their assistants customize the shareables, navigate InfoLib, and engage online in an authentic manner. In-person sessions are offered in June and December so that staff can time their Ottawa visit to attend the prime minister's garden party and caucus year-end social events. Webinars are also available and explain how to use the Liberalist constituent relationship management software, a useful option for new staff, volunteers, and interns. A constituency assistant summarizes the types of online training offered:

> Every month a list is circulated that outlines live upcoming online training. For instance, it could be an update from Immigration, Refugees and Citizenship Canada about how to do particular casework, or it could be an information update from a minister's office and how we can help amplify that message in our own riding. All those trainings and the information from them are available on InfoLib afterwards, such as a slide deck or a live recording of the session that you can listen to.[46]

Bureau personnel coach the MPs' assistants on preparing a media engagement plan to optimize publicity. The assistants are encouraged to talk with their MPs to uncover anecdotes that might resonate online: "Members want the ability to see themselves," says a political staffer. "They're not just trained seals who are parroting back vapid talking points. They're helping to tell a story that connects with members of their community."[47] Suppose an MP has a strong relationship with a child-care centre.

The MP's assistants could organize a panel of local child-care professionals to talk about what a new policy means and integrate central messaging into a local news release about the community event. At the event, constituency staff can take photographs and video, pass around a media release form, and ask constituents for a quotation to include on social media. When a post gets traction, the bureau's regional desk phones MPs' offices with positive reinforcement. *Good job with that community photo! What a great video series! Would it be okay if we share this with other MPs in the region?* The praise can foreshadow compliments at the national caucus meeting. Some ministers sense that MPs tune out at local events because they are preoccupied with thinking about what to post online.[48]

Praising desired behaviour and circulating a stream of messaging are powerful tools of opinion conformity. In effect, the bureau of a governing party acts as the caucus communications unit of the government of Canada, which is compounded by party discipline suppressing the potential for the backbenchers whom the bureau serves from investigating the government. An MP comments on the incompatibility:

> All too often we are given lines defending the party position which can restrict more open thought. The Liberal Research Bureau, when they're in government, tends to take the lines from the bureaucracy without question. In my view, the LRB is not an arm of the government. It should be doing a critical analysis of everything we do. It becomes the defender of the government rather than the thinker or the one involved with constructive criticism on where the government stands vis-à-vis the party position.[49]

Regardless of party, some MPs yearn for more staff under their direct control. Insufficient assistance "often means using sound bites and relying on the leader's office," laments a backbencher.[50] Constituency casework is so demanding that an MP might lack adequate support to research a private member's bill, especially when the leadership does not like the topic.

SUMMARY

Parliamentarians require research assistance and social media supports. They also require messaging to engage in informed debate on innumerable topics while minimizing the possibility that they will become the focus of a negative news story. In Ottawa, the propagation of messaging by caucus research bureaus dampens a legislator's entrepreneurial spirit and is a catalyst for backbenchers to act as brand ambassadors. In particular, the governing party's bureau is so integrated into government machinery that it is simultaneously a publicity unit and a purveyor of message discipline. As the next chapter shows, the forces that compel caucus unity are an extension of party discipline in the legislature, where rules and practices condition parliamentarians to act as party representatives.

9

Legislative Assemblies

Experienced Members of Parliament express despair about the choreographing of legislative debate and warn that Canadian political parties are oligarchies.[1] The dominance of parliamentary parties is a reality for backbenchers, especially so in the legislature. To what extent do these elected representatives have freedom to express themselves in legislative assemblies? How do House officers coordinate a unified stance in parliamentary business? In this chapter, I look at the intersection of parliamentary practices and political communications in Canada.

HOUSE BUSINESS

Over the years, changes to standing orders have improved the productivity of parliamentary business at the expense of time available for individual members. Efficiencies are found by enabling parliamentary parties to assume organizational control. An MP comments on the institutional and social structures that encourage team play in the legislature:

> The peer pressure, the pressure from the whip, the pressure from ministers and ministers' staff, the lack of information provided to MPs about procedure and what is really happening in the legislative process and their reluctance to really want to learn procedure, the last-minute nature of votes, the somewhat artificial nature of debate in the House ... the career ambitions of many MPs, the lack of will – or perhaps time – to actually read legislation and know what is in it and what is not in it, and

so on, all conspire to make it very difficult to be an independent thinker as an MP.[2]

Although there are opportunities for attentive private members to defy the party whip, it can take years to figure out the legislative system. Many parliamentarians have no inclination to do so and/or sit a single term in office. In the following pages, I delve into the inner workings of life on the floor of a parliamentary assembly, including items in Table 9.1. For authoritative information about rules and practices, readers should consult a legislature's standing orders and a guidebook such as *House of Commons Procedure and Practice*.[3]

TABLE 9.1
Party control over party MPs in the House of Commons

Item	Summary	Party control (low to high)
Private members' business tabling	Non-ministers present private members' bills and private members' motions	*Moderate:* The House clerk runs a lottery to identify who gets to present. Party influence on the content requires the MP's agreement. Most business does not pass first reading.
Private members' business debates	Debate on private members' bills and private members' motions	*Moderate:* Party whips identify who speaks to the bill or motion. Members are encouraged to use talking points and vote the party line.
Members' statements (SO 31s)	Statements up to sixty seconds	*High:* Party whips submit lists of MPs to the Speaker's office and can switch out non-conformists.
Question Period	Oral questions up to thirty-five seconds	*High:* Whips provide the Speaker with a list of names and the planned speaking order. Questions and answers are rehearsed.
Government business	Presentation of government bills and government orders by ministers	*High:* Whips line up speakers. Members are expected to follow talking points and voting instructions, especially on confidence votes.
Petitions	Paper and electronic petitions presented by members	*Low:* Petitions are formalities. Rules prohibit members from adding opinions.

Partial sources: Marleau and Montpetit (2000); Stewart (2017), 63.

Parliamentary Behaviour

Romanticizing a "golden age" before intense party discipline can gloss over the fact that representation in Canadian legislatures has always been lacking.[4] In Canada's early years, drunkards talked gibberish during legislative debates and sometimes challenged opponents to fisticuffs.[5] Members interrupted proceedings by making animal noises, singing, and blowing trumpets. They tossed paper balls and books. In one 1882 sitting of the House of Commons, some MPs interrupted orators by throwing firecrackers. When Prime Minister John A. Macdonald expressed disgust, more firecrackers disrupted him.[6] A clampdown on unprofessional behaviour did little to arouse the members who fell asleep at their desks.[7]

In 1951, the leader of the opposition (George Drew) imagined a day that television would expose trained seals in the House of Commons: "I only regret that we have not yet television in Canada, so that the people of Canada could see an imitation of trained seals such as we are seeing in this committee at the present time. The only difference, of course, is that trained seals usually have an intelligent look upon their faces."[8] In the late 1950s, MPs who stood up to be recognized by the Speaker had their voices picked up by microphones dangling from the ceiling. Debates were often spontaneous, with members delivering passionate speeches that incorporated their personal experiences.[9] Private members made outrageous proposals; some of them sought advice from journalists about what to say.[10] Things changed in the 1960s when leaders ceased to attend many legislative discussions, and the Canadian Press stopped filing stories about parliamentary debates and maiden speeches.[11] Interest in what backbenchers said was declining, and the comparison to obedient animals was percolating. In 1976, on Joe Clark's first day as leader of the opposition, Pierre Trudeau repeated Drew's lament when mocking the applause of opposition MPs:

CLARK: Mr. Speaker, let me say that I am proud to be here as leader of the alternative government of Canada.

SOME HON. MEMBERS: Hear, hear!

TRUDEAU: Talk about trained seals.

PC MP: Any more comments?

TRUDEAU: Any more trained seals?[12]

The derogatory label, already in regular use, was a twist on a remark Trudeau had made years earlier that government-side MPs were "trained donkeys sitting in the back benches [who] could be trusted to behave."[13]

Televised proceedings brought structure that further limited MPs' individual agency. In 1977, microphones were installed on House of Commons desks to enable remote control of speaking time, and being on television prompted MPs to be mindful of their words, attire, and actions.[14] They were less likely to read a newspaper, doze off in their seats, or return to the House after imbibing at lunch or dinner. Whips passed notes urging members to wake up a napping colleague. Speaking delivery changed for a mass audience, and heckling grew louder so that opponents could hear when microphones were switched off. Notably, the Speaker needed lists of speakers to cut out the dead time of fumbling through seating charts and trying to recall a member's name or electoral district.[15] Today nestled at the Speaker's feet is a computer screen with the day's proceedings and names of MPs scheduled to address the House. As we shall see, the names are submitted by the whip's office or House leader's office.

Many members find legislative proceedings to be tedious – described by one minister as "mind-numbingly boring."[16] Ministers and private members slouch and fidget. They hold side conversations when the camera focuses elsewhere. They bring signing books prepared by their assistants; perhaps they read the news or a book. Digital devices have introduced additional distractions as members engage with their social media feeds, read and respond to emails, and pass the time by checking the stock market, filling out crossword puzzles, or playing video games.[17] They might break the monotony by heckling an opponent addressing the assembly. Interrupting a speaker can be useful, such as urging a minister to focus on answering a question or trying to correct misinformation. However, jeering or taunting is uncivil, particularly when hecklers refer to a member's body size, physical appearance, language, gender, or age.[18] Whips advise members not to heckle on sombre days, when invited guests are present, and when sensitive topics are on the agenda. They might try to manage members who chat or whisper off camera, which distracts others and is observed from the gallery. Sometimes a whip appeals for better conduct from the whole caucus:

Every once in a while you need a come to Jesus moment. It's sitting in caucus, behind closed doors, and calling people out, saying to them "the things you are doing are unprofessional. If you don't want to be here, nobody is forcing you to be. If you don't think you can maintain the small amount of rules that you're given, then maybe this isn't the job for you." It's reminding them they're professionals, that it's a very privileged position, that they should show respect.[19]

A whip also acts on the Speaker's request to remind members of rules about food, beverages, and phone calls. Such matters of decorum are largely peripheral to the main business coordinated by House leaders.

House Leaders and Legislative Agendas

Every parliamentary party leader designates a House leader. That parliamentarian is responsible for being a master of the standing orders so that the group has the best chance of achieving desired outcomes in the assembly. House leaders often raise points of order. They and their staff field questions from caucus colleagues about parliamentary rules and processes.

The government House leader is the member of the cabinet who sets the agenda for the day's meeting of the assembly. Preparing for Question Period is thus a significant part of the job: "The government House leader is the Question Period quarterback and oversees everything about QP, from preparing ministers for the most likely questions, to chairing the daily QP practice session and critiquing ministerial colleagues' responses, to actually designating which minister, parliamentary secretary, or other government MP is to reply to a specific question," a former House leader says.[20] Input on which bills to prioritize is provided by the prime minister (or premier), the chief of staff, and ministers. There are many considerations, including how convoluted a topic is: "Every minister believes their bill is the most important and should be given priority for House time," he explains. "If they feel the House leader isn't sufficiently agreeable, they often won't hesitate to make their case directly with the prime minister."[21] The House leader confers with the government whip about whether votes can be delivered. An item comes off the agenda if the whip senses caucus resistance or knows that key supporters are out of town. Setting the agenda is the official opposition's responsibility on opposition days (not all provinces designate such days).

Negotiations ensue with the opposition House leaders to finalize the agenda. In Ottawa, the House leaders, whips, and a PMO staffer meet early in the week to identify items that can be included with minimal objection. Horse trading ensues, with the opposition agreeing to the government's requests in exchange for meeting its own demands.[22] The back-and-forth sorts out which bills will appear on the order paper and the time available for debate. The participants behave as diplomatic emissaries by exchanging information in an off-the-record, trusting manner. The meetings can be collegial or hostile, says a former government whip:

> The weekly meeting between the House leaders, the whips, and somebody from the PMO is very cooperative. The government House leader starts off by saying "here's what we want to get done and what we're thinking in terms of timing. How much time do you want to debate this issue?" There's discussion, and you come to agreement. By and large, that's how most of the business of the House gets done. Of course, there are times it isn't quite as friendly as that.[23]

When a civil working relationship breaks down, it is usually a reflection of wider acrimony. A government that tries to rush legislation through with insufficient notice of the agenda can expect the opposition to respond with tactics of agitation.

House leaders avail themselves of procedural tools that stymie an opponent's interests. To move an agenda forward, the government House leader and whip might limit how many of their members speak and for how long. They can adjust the order of amendments to minimize time allotted for debating the controversial aspects of a motion.[24] In Ottawa, subject to certain constraints, the government House leader can use time allocation to limit the length of debate on a stage of the bill. The government can also attempt to force closure so that more than one reading of the bill occurs in succession. As a tactic of delay, the opposition can refuse to give leave to requests and put up speakers to repeat party messages on all bills, including bills that they support.[25] As well, an opposition House leader can coordinate a filibuster to drag out debate.

House leaders and whips in different parties can conspire to best an opponent. A whip in the Martin minority government tells of how the Liberals managed to get their controversial budget deal with the NDP through the House in June 2005.[26] Without enough votes to see it through, the budget companion bill would require the support of the Bloc Québécois, which would be a caustic public relations move. On a Thursday, the House approved a rare government motion to extend sittings indefinitely, and so debate on the companion bill continued into the evening. Some MPs filed out to catch flights back to their constituencies as the government House leader droned on about the government's accomplishments. Instead of heading home, a number of Liberal, New Democrat, and Bloc MPs secretly assembled in different locations around Parliament Hill. Suddenly at 10 p.m., the government House leader called for the division bells to ring to notify members of a snap vote on the government's motion of closure, which would cut off debate. The opposition whip frantically summoned Conservatives to return, some of whom could not make it. The lingering MPs filed back in to outvote the Conservatives, setting up a midnight confidence vote on the budget companion bill, which passed 152-147. In exchange for propping up the government, the Bloc received a written guarantee that Bill C-38, the Civil Marriage Act, would come to a vote before the House adjourned for summer, which legalized same-sex marriage in Canada that July.

Statements by Members

Daily proceedings in the House of Commons begin when the Speaker ensures that quorum is met.[27] A prayer and moment of silence follow. On Wednesdays, members sing the national anthem. Each day approximately fifteen minutes are allocated for private members to deliver statements of up to sixty seconds. Members' statements – known as "SO 31s" because they fall under Standing Order 31 – are opportunities for non-ministers, including parliamentary secretaries, to deliver short remarks about topical issues. The statements are appealing to backbenchers because they are an opportunity to attract national attention to constituency matters. They are used to recognize local achievements, acknowledge a death, draw attention to an upcoming festival, and so forth. They might urge Canadians to support a cause. Sometimes MPs criticize government policy or comment on an international event in the news. Delivering concise remarks can be a big moment for backbenchers, particularly if it is their first statement in the House and constituents see them on television or online. Time for such commentary has diminished over the years, with the current one-minute rule in place since 1986.

The management of SO 31s by the whips and House leaders is a source of tension. Each whip's office submits a list of names to the Speaker's office, which creates its own list of MPs who will be called on in succession to deliver a statement, after which whips may request changes. The whip might want to balance demography and geography when selecting speakers; another factor is whether the member has been complying with the whip's instructions. A further consideration is the perceived suitability of topics. Sometimes parties co-opt the members' statement process by putting for- ward MPs who repeat party messaging, especially so during minority parliaments.[28] Some private members recoil, but there are always some who want to please the leadership or are attracted to the public attention. The result is increased mention of parties and more negativity about op- ponents.[29] Consequently, the involvement of the whip's office can deprive private members of a rare opportunity to speak in the chamber about local matters. Members of Parliament vent at the setup:

> With members' statements, members spend one minute talking about whatever they want, usually within the context of their riding. Sometimes it gets abused because people do a one-minute ad for their party. The whole problem is it is controlled by the whip's office. They want to put the issue of the day out there, and they even up the regional, language, and gender aspects. One of the forms of punishment dished out by all parties is they don't give you a slot to speak. I think this is a breach of my privilege.[30]

> The fundamental heart of Parliament is to talk and debate, but the Speaker acts like a bingo caller who reads names from the list. It's the House leaders and the whips who decide who get to speak. If you haven't toed the line, you don't get to speak, let alone get the preferential slots.[31]

Occasionally, MPs speak out about the whip's control over SO 31s. They complain that the party revoked permission because the topic was not approved or was denied as a sanction.[32] Others find a workaround. Defiantly livestreaming the statement outside the chamber is an option.[33]

Question Period

Private members putting questions to the cabinet is the climax of daily proceedings. Question Period provides the people's elected representatives with a forum in which to seek information related to the administrative responsibilities of the government. Ideally, private members ask thoughtful questions about public policy to which members of the cabinet provide informative answers. It rarely works out that way. Proceedings range from elegant exchanges to a circus-like atmosphere.

Interrogating the cabinet was relatively unstructured in the House of Commons until 1964, when many of the rules in place today were introduced. Since 1997, a thirty-five-second speaking limit has been in use during Question Period.[34] The time constraint resulted in MPs further condensing their rhetoric during the forty-five-minute affair, which begins by 2:15 p.m. Monday to Thursday, and by 11:15 a.m. on Fridays.

To prepare, a House leader convenes with the whip and/or a member of the leader's office to discuss issues in the news and identify who should speak. Brevity leaves little room for error. The opposition wants to emphasize topics and delivery that will get media traction; the government wants to get through unscathed and possibly turn the tables. Ministers, parliamentary secretaries, and ministerial critics rehearse with staff during "QP prep" sessions, sometimes known as warm-up meetings:[35] "You get asked mock questions. When you offer an answer, people opine on how to improve the response," says an MP.[36] In private, rehearsals can involve feigning outrage in front of a mirror.[37] Preparations are warranted because hyperbolic accusations get more attention than monotonous conversations about public policies, and so members read from scripts and animate the delivery. A small number have leeway to speak off the cuff because they are quick thinkers who deliver witty quips.[38]

In small caucuses, there is greater concern for consensus during QP preparation. One approach is for the leader's group to identify topical issues and work out questions with the applicable ministerial critics.[39] Another style is for the leader's group to assemble the caucus to pitch questions. A more systematic process sees members submit suggested questions to the leader's office a day in advance. However, if an opposition leader attempts to decentralize Question Period readiness to the caucus, then members might disengage and lobby the leader regardless, leading to indecision and confusion.[40]

The whips submit names of MPs on paper to the Speaker's office, where staff transpose the information to a list for the Speaker with the order of who will be asking a question in each available thirty-five-second slot. In the 42nd Parliament, on a given day in 2019, there were forty-one questions in Question Period, of which the Conservatives had twenty-four questions (slots 1–5, 10–15, 18–21, 25–28, 31–33, 35, 38) and the NDP eleven questions (slots 6–9, 16–17, 22–23, 29–30, 36).[41] Liberal backbenchers asked three questions in the second half of Question Period (slots 24, 34, 37). As governing party members, they could "ask a friendly."[42] That is, someone affiliated with the executive branch could brag about the government's accomplishments, provide local information, or create a wedge issue with the opposition (as occurred with the official bilingualism example in Chapter 4). That sham is not practised in some provincial assemblies where governing party members do not ask questions.[43] Independents rounded out the final three questions (slots 39–41), which included MPs affiliated with parties without official party status, notably the Bloc Québécois and the Green Party. Members can also submit written questions and formally request government documents.

Non-answers by members of the cabinet and – in their stead – parliamentary secretaries are common. In Ottawa, many ministers bring QP cards containing speaking notes and QP books with top-line responses to ten to fifteen of the most topical issues. Ministers also have access to a fuller QP book with an archive of cards from recent years. Discourse is shameful when they try to embarrass the opposition, epitomized by Stephen Harper's parliamentary secretary repeating PMO lines about the NDP's policy on Israel when asked about Canadian military deployment in Iraq.[44] Some private members see little point in asking questions: "I've been a politician for many years and I must say, why play that silly game?" says a veteran MP. "If I stood up and asked a question I guarantee you 100 percent it will not be answered."[45] Indeed, there is no requirement for the government to acknowledge questions. The cabinet can choose not to rise to answer a question, at which point the Speaker proceeds to the next question.[46] That would be a spectacle, so if a minister is under the media microscope the prime minister or another member of cabinet will answer, and the PMO might direct the minister to miss that day's oral questions.[47]

Prime ministers are not always present for questioning, partly a reflection of the considerable demands on their time and partly because they would prefer to be elsewhere. During the 42nd Parliament, Justin Trudeau spent a number of Wednesdays answering all of the opposition's questions in an experiment replicating the weekly prime minister's Question Period in Britain. Yet he was absent from more than half (58 percent) of Question Periods during his first year in power.[48] Absenteeism is inevitable given that a prime minister is obliged to travel, for instance to represent the government at an international summit. At other times, the prime minister participates instead in photo opportunities in nearby offices or leaves the parliamentary precinct to attend a partisan event.[49]

Routine Proceedings and Government Orders

In the House of Commons, routine proceedings normally follow members' statements and Question Period. Routine proceedings involve business that requires little debate. Documents are tabled, ministers deliver statements to which designated opposition MPs respond, and interparliamentary delegations summarize their findings. Committee reports are presented, as are government bills and private members' bills and motions. Petitions – a form of prayer from constituents who urge government action – ensue. Arguably, the main purpose of petitions today is to harvest personal information about citizens for database marketing.[50] Parliamentarians who feel duty bound as constituents' envoys to introduce petitions might need to be assertive with the whip's office on certain topics. Government orders usually come after routine proceedings, involving business items proposed by ministers. This is where party discipline on votes is most regimented, whether through whipping attendance and votes or through trepidations about the consequences of voting differently from colleagues.

The whip's office distributes talking points by email to coax message discipline in the House. Backbenchers might receive speaking notes moments before addressing the assembly or have to improvise on an unfamiliar topic.[51] They are encouraged to massage the script. They can avoid an issue if they disagree with recommended wording and instead concentrate on aspects that they support. Originality is most prevalent when they relate bills to their own electoral districts by applying party philosophy to local facts.

The parties' control over legislative debate upsets some parliamentarians. The more that Cleary reflects on his time as an opposition MP, the more the resentment simmers: "I wanted to make a difference, I wanted to do something," he laments. "I'm not just a figurehead sitting in Ottawa. I've got my own mind, and I represent my own people. But that's stifled. If they have their way, everything would be stifled. You're a puppet, a little marionette, they pull the strings, you speak when they tell you to speak, you move when they tell you to move. Everything is controlled. Every single question you ask in the Commons is scripted; everything is approved by the party. Everything is."[52] Other partisans have mixed opinions. Some know first-hand that the idealism of representation in the legislature is very different from the reality. A novice MP comments that

> it's easy and idealistic for someone to think their MP can vote however they want all the time. When it's put into practice, to achieve anything as a party with a potential to form the government, it's an age-old problem that everyone's got to sing from the same song sheet more or less. If you don't, you're excluded from media opportunities, excluded from access to the leader and the leadership team, you lose committee positions, you lose critic positions. The leadership team has a significant amount of power in terms of determining your career and providing opportunities to represent your constituents.[53]

Party politicians learn that politics is the art of compromise. Usually, the best opportunity for backbenchers to exert a measure of policy independence is to propose a bill or motion under private members' business.

Private Members' Business

In the House of Commons, about an hour of each day is allocated to presentation of, and debate on, bills and motions by MPs who are not ministers, parliamentary secretaries, the Speaker, or the deputy Speaker. Originally, on certain days, the default agenda was composed of issues raised by private members, though members routinely deferred to government business.

Over the years, changes to the standing orders formalized the dominance of government, so time dedicated to private members is a prized commodity.[54] Studies in the 1970s found that MPs were not taking full advantage of opportunities to introduce a private member's bill or private member's motion.[55] MPs rekindled their interest in the 1980s, occasionally defying the express wishes of their leader and demonstrating the practical limits of discipline in a caucus.[56]

Private members' business is a meaningful, if limited, opportunity for studious parliamentarians to influence government policy and advocate on behalf of their constituents.[57] By sponsoring a bill or motion to make a point, backbenchers can collaborate with advocacy groups who spread the message and achieve media attention. A significant constraint is that private members cannot present bills proposing that the government spend money unless they secure ministerial support.[58] Another limitation is the expertise required to research the policy and to draft legislation, which might require assistance from the caucus research bureau and House of Commons law clerk. As well, a proposal can irritate colleagues. For example, calling on the House to designate a day or month to celebrate a cultural group or activity grants the sponsor some exposure.[59] The sentiments can inflame parliamentarians and constituents of a different cultural or ethnic descent and, to a lesser extent, those who bemoan so many symbolic acts. Another divisive type is calling on the legislature to acknowledge contentious foreign events, such as an occupation or a genocide.

Party affiliation is a further constraint. A party's backbenchers can provide opponents with political ammunition, such as the Conservative whose private member's bill sought to criminalize selective-sex abortions or the Liberal who advocated decriminalizing possession of hard drugs.[60] The less that the party leadership is involved, the harder it is for the media to construe the activity as a stand-in for the party's position, which grants members more freedom to advocate outside partisan boundaries. Nevertheless, the public perception of parliamentarians as brand ambassadors means that opponents can frame a private member's bill as party policy. Proposing radical action can drive an internal wedge that puts the leadership, caucus, and/or cabinet in a tricky situation. Party whips have to gauge whether to manage the upset by doing nothing or clamping down.

The whip lacks direct control over private members' business because the Speaker's office holds a lottery to identify which bills may advance to second reading for debate.[61] Labels with eligible MPs' names are affixed to plastic tags. The tags are deposited in the wooden ballot box used for electing a Speaker. The ritual begins and ends with the Speaker (or other meeting chair) reading a prepared statement. Most of the witnesses present are MPs' assistants. As the Speaker draws a tag, the name is announced, and a table officer calls back the MP's first and last names. House of Commons staff type out names as they are drawn, which are projected onto a screen, and the electronic list is sent to all members. The order of names drawn determines the order of presenting bills; a late selection can mean waiting years or not presenting at all. After that, the party leadership plays a pivotal role in private members' business.

Party control is exerted in various ways. Some House officers vet drafts of private members' bills and motions.[62] The party leadership can co-opt the process by working with compliant backbenchers to sponsor potential legislation in order to test interest while retaining the ability to disavow it. The collaboration might involve proposing a motion designed to drive a wedge between members of an opponent's caucus. A minister can support a private member's efforts by authorizing public servants to generate information and by engaging legal counsel to assist with wording, and might encourage the government to absorb a proposal into an omnibus bill, for which the backbencher can claim some credit. Conversely, the party leadership can impede progress on a proposal that it dislikes. Without the sponsor's knowledge, higher-ups influence whether the caucus research bureau should prioritize offering research support. Interparty negotiation can affirm that other party caucuses will coordinate votes to help defeat the bill or motion; this enables the sponsoring member's leader to announce a free vote without disclosing the duplicity of managing the outcome. Ultimately, the parties pressure members how to vote on an item before the House, whether implicitly or overtly.

The whips concentrate their political capital on consequential items. A government whip can take a hands-off approach to private members' bills and motions, causing ministers and their parliamentary secretaries to be the ones to implore vote cohesion. A former whip and House leader for the Chrétien government recalls that the parliamentary secretary of a minister would come into the caucus room, mention an upcoming private member's bill, and invite colleagues to vote a certain way. The whip would quickly say "I'm not touching this. It's a private member's bill, it's got nothing to do with me." If a minister felt strongly it was bad public policy, well, it's up to you to gather enough votes to defeat the stupid thing. Don't get the whip involved in it. Keep the whip for the important things – confidence votes, government bills, stuff like that – not every little thing that comes around. If every single vote is whipped, and MPs are to carry party discipline on things that don't matter for the party, it can be excessive.[63]

The caucus itself can express dismay at a colleague who avails of a free vote. David Wilks recalls that Conservative MPs, not the leadership, were upset when he rebuffed the party line on a private member's bill:

I was shunned by a lot of my colleagues after I voted for a private member's bill from another party. Before I did so, I went to Prime Minister Harper to let him know this is what I'm doing, and this is why I'm doing it. He was good with it. He said "thank you very much, that's all I needed to know, we just need to make sure that we've got the numbers." I wasn't the only one to vote in favour of it; there were some cabinet ministers and other backbenchers. So I wasn't alone.[64]

Other times a whip follows the leadership's decision about whether the caucus ought to support or oppose a private member's bill. Pressure for group conformity increases with proximity to an election and during a minority government.

PARLIAMENTARY COMMITTEES

Party encroachment is further evident on parliamentary committees. Ideally, these multi-partisan groups of private members engage in arm's-length scrutiny of the government, and they hold authorities responsible for promises and responsibilities. Committee members investigate topical matters, call witnesses, and prepare reports summarizing their findings. The work can be monotonous (e.g., a study of wood products), important but unrecognized (e.g., reviewing the Conflict of Interest Act), or high profile when a hot topic is in the news. Parliamentarians learn about issues and processes while believing that they are contributing.

In the 1950s, standing committees of the House of Commons began examining the government's budget estimates, and the task of reviewing bills was often referred to the entire membership of the assembly overseen by the deputy Speaker.[65] Today there are approximately two dozen standing committees that do so and half a dozen special, joint, and other parliamentary committees. They are often known by acronyms (e.g., Indigenous and Northern Affairs is INAN), which facilitate finding information online about them. In the unofficial hierarchy, finance ranks at the top because members benefit from a high profile, as does foreign affairs because of the international travel and cocktail circuit, whereas the library committee is among the least desired. Few parliamentary committees exist in some provinces, sometimes with limited or non-existent functions.

Party whips assign committee membership. After backbenchers identify their preferences, whips inform them about their assignments – "I could not give you your first choice, but your second choice is okay, and you are on standby for your first choice, so if anybody gets promoted or leaves the committee you will be number one to replace"[66] – and members infer that reassignment is subject to behavioural assessment. A practical reason for the managerial oversight is to replace absent members in order to enable committees to meet quorum. Whips can swap in high performers when a committee is attracting media attention, a practice derided as imposing "goon squads."[67] Party discipline flows when a whip replaces a non-compliant member with someone who votes as per the leadership's instructions. Disciplinary tools include withdrawal of a chair position, reassignment to a less desirable committee, and loss of committee membership entirely.

Committee members elect a chair and, in Ottawa, two vice-chairs. Whips advise their members whom to support for the position.[68] A chair from the government side has a special working relationship with the applicable minister and parliamentary secretary, which involves walking a fine line of blatant partisanship. The presence of a parliamentary secretary on the committee annoys some members who perceive a government agent keeping tabs and coordinating votes.[69] Indeed, the sentry offers information about the government's position and indicates which amendments might be acceptable. Strategic advice is offered about posturing, such as which questions to ask, what to avoid, which lines the opposition pursued in the past, and what can be done to buttress television footage if opponents are grandstanding. Whether or not these ministerial representatives cast votes is an example of shifting rules. In the 42nd Parliament, the Trudeau majority government declared that parliamentary secretaries would no longer vote on relevant committees; however, with a minority of seats in the 43rd Parliament, the Liberals reinstated the voting privileges.[70]

Generally, an hour of committee time requires two hours of preparation.[71] Each whip's office organizes private pre-meetings to ready the party's committee members, including educating them about issues likely to arise and about the party's position(s) in order to set boundaries for what is said. Ministerial staff, and sometimes the minister, attend to communicate the government's positions. Members want to know what the party leadership wants them to do: *What's coming up? Who is going to get to ask questions? Which issues are going to be raised? Which amendments do we want to propose?* The group tries to anticipate how a witness will respond to questions because surprising testimony disrupts what the party wants to emphasize. They practise short, concise questions with the objective of getting a desired answer. This helps to ensure message consistency when members speak, which matters because it is likely on the public record and possibly televised. Nevertheless, members can act in ways not cleared beforehand with their parties. For example, a backbencher might ask questions not authorized by the whip or spontaneously urge a department to conduct a study.

In Ottawa, a representative of each whip's office is assigned multiple committees to observe proceedings, troubleshoot, communicate the party's position, and record attendance.[72] During a committee meeting, the staffer liaises with representatives from the other whips' offices and participates in electronic conversations with the committee members, whip's office, minister's office, or other applicable personnel. MPs seek guidance while a meeting is in progress: *What happens next? What's the parliamentary procedure on this? Can I make a point of order? Do you have a motion? Do you want me to do something?* Staff check in with the whip's office about political aspects or ask the clerk's office about procedural matters.

Standing committees can behave as government offshoots or be treated as an inconvenience by the executive branch, especially when the governing party has a majority of seats.[73] In one notorious instance, the Harper PMO prepared a manual for Conservative chairs to inform them of ways to exploit standing orders for how committees operate.[74] In the 42nd Parliament, Justin Trudeau's ministers sometimes telegraphed that issues were being referred to committees for study within a limited timeline.[75] There were instances of the government announcing a policy while a committee was still researching the topic or providing information to the media before opposition members received it. Ministerial staff contacted lobbyists to warn them not to appear at standing committees or speak with parliamentarians. Most of all, the Liberals followed the standard that a governing party expects its members to do its bidding, or it will install ones who will. "There's a sense of 'here's the directive, this is the decision the government made, here's what we expect you to do.' There's an expectation that you defer to the government's view," a Liberal MP says. "Very occasionally, committees make changes regardless. That's rare. Usually, the changes involve amendments prepared by the minister's office that were passed through different members of the committee [and vetted by the department]. It's a very tightly controlled process, even though it doesn't always appear that way."[76] A governing party member who wants to make an amendment normally consults internally beforehand. Amendments are often at the behest of the minister's office, which has considered new information: stakeholder intervention, witness testimony, social media outrage, et cetera.

A minister's office receives draft committee reports, with the notable exception of dissenting reports. In consultation with the PMO, it provides input on a document intended to encourage the direction of government policy.[77] The government can save face if a committee's report exclusively contains recommendations likely to be pursued. As an election approaches, committee studies are tabled before the assembly rises so that there is no obligation for the current minister to respond. A couple of former ministers in the Trudeau government comment thus:

> The government is required to respond to every committee report. Officials often find a way to merge all the recommendations when coming up with a government response. It feels like it is done because it needs to be. I don't think the committee recommendations are taken with the seriousness that they could be.[78]

There may be some interesting discussions and debates that happen at the committee level. There can be interesting and valuable witness testimony. But we must remember that, if a majority government does not want something to happen, it will not happen, given that under our current standing orders they hold the majority on committees.[79]

Other members of the cabinet have concerns as well. A Trudeau minister confides that "parliamentary committees should be more independent. They should not be branch plants of ministers' offices."[80] Some backbenchers concur, believing that the forums are little more than partisan rituals in which participants are unable to build expertise or act in meaningful ways.[81] They become disappointed by the lack of interest in thoughtful commentary compared with the praise heaped on those who critique opponents, especially if that criticism spills into cyberspace.

Many private members feel differently. For some, serving on a parliamentary committee is a satisfying experience, particularly when there is multi-partisan support for a course of action.[82] They consider standing committees to be among the best settings for meaningful policy debates and feel that the work engenders peer respect and personal satisfaction. They relay that a committee is a good place to express ideas and to voice reservations about an issue of the day or legislation under study: "Committee is really where a lot of the work I'm going to do gets done," says an MP. "It's where I have the most opportunities to speak."[83]

Paul Martin is a strong believer that standing committees are a good forum for a private member to make a mark: "The single best place as a parliamentarian to make your voice heard is in a parliamentary committee," he says. "That's where a Member of Parliament can really establish a reputation, not for the positions they take but in the way they make the argument to support those positions."[84] His convictions are rooted in the consensus building that he forged during the 35th Parliament for the pivotal 1995 federal budget. As minister of finance, Martin was the public face of intense deliberations on getting the government's budget deficit under control. Unhappy ministers pleaded for exemptions to proposed reductions to their budget envelopes. Their complaints went nowhere when Prime Minister Chrétien said in a cabinet meeting that he supported his finance minister's position.[85] Chrétien was furious about media stories of cabinet divisions over financial exigency and lectured ministers about the need for confidentiality, trust, integrity, and solidarity.[86] Martin met with ministers and MPs individually and in small groups. He determined that the House of Commons Standing Committee on Finance should hold public consultations and that he should make public appearances.

The finance committee was a venue in October 1994 for Martin to deliver an economic update in clear language with visuals to press the case for a tough budget. He asked the committee chair to hold meetings across the country. Members summoned witnesses who would have otherwise lobbied finance officials in private. The committee debated policy options. Meanwhile, within the government, a parallel Treasury Board program review committee fielded ministerial appeals.[87] That group of ministers listened to other members of the cabinet plead for special treatment and were authorized to change a given department's percentage budget reduction as long as another department made it up. As one government official expressed, the finance committee's public consultations were "a way to watch a surrogate debate about a variety of budget measures without taking ownership of them."[88] The involvement of private members from different political parties helped to build parliamentary and public acceptance for grim policy decisions.

"Governments often forget that debate is a good thing," Martin reflects. "Budgets shouldn't surprise. I went across the country for a year and a half saying 'here's the issue, we have to deal with it.' It's going to be tough. I asked the finance committee to go across the country. People heard opposite views expressed at the table. If someone said the government should cut something, someone else objected, and someone else defended the cut. People understood that the government was arriving at some difficult decisions, which wasn't being done on a whim." The great advantage of a parliamentary committee, he says, is that people on opposite sides can argue their positions, and the public can see Parliament at work: "What happens in most political debates is that they become excessively partisan. However, real and substantive discussions come through in a parliamentary committee, one that works," Martin explains. "As the minister of finance, when I said that I was going to deal with the deficit come hell or high water, I said that in a parliamentary committee. I knew that a parliamentary committee is really the essence of Parliament."[89]

An indicator of the perceived influence of committee members is the attention that outside interests pay to them. The Lobbyists Registration Act obliges lobbyists to register their interactions with federal public figures as a modicum of transparency. The filings confirm that the executive branch is lobbied more than the legislative branch and indicate that sustained efforts result in better access to the PMO.[90] Government relations PR campaigns focus on ministers, high-ranking political staff, and parliamentary secretaries as well as chairs of standing committees. The registry also shows that MPs are contacted more often than their supposed lack of agency would suggest. The government relations sector sees value in contacting members of influential committees who are accessible, are known to be vocal within the caucus, and have a reputation for communicating with ministers and fellow parliamentarians. A public affairs strategist explains why committee members are of interest to lobbyists:

> Any thoughtful government relations contact plan should involve the backbench members sitting on the committees dealing with the relevant subject area. You may not do the most intense contact with them – maybe one contact every six months or every year as opposed to ten with the minister's office because the file is on their desk – but the bias is only the proximity to the urgency of the decision, not a sort about who is important and who is not.[91]

Committee chairs and members have particular influence when the governing party has a minority of seats. Government control tactics give way to an increased need to collaborate with the opposition, with the Harper Conservatives' so-called manual of dirty tricks being the exception, not the rule: "There's a bit of a conspiracy on the part of the government – all governments – to keep committees in the dark, and off doing busy work," says a long-time MP. In a minority Parliament, he says, that is less likely because, "with opposition members actually having a significant say in the agenda of the committee, there is much greater likelihood that the committees will do work that is of interest to everyone as opposed to just interest to the governing party."[92] Ultimately, the government is interested in ensuring that parliamentary committees do not embarrass it, whereas the opposition takes every opportunity to portray the government as anti-democratic while being careful not to vilify parliamentary institutions.

WHIPPING THE VOTE

A whip's invisible hand is felt throughout Parliament. As set out in Section 48 of the Constitution Act, 1867, the minimum number of members required for an assembly of the House of Commons to proceed is twenty, including the Speaker. Quorum ranges from twenty-one in Quebec to ten in British Columbia, Manitoba, and Prince Edward Island (see Table 1.1). The whips constantly count how many members are present. They and their staff can round up lingering members for a quorum call or a vote.[93] If numbers dip, then the opposition can halt proceedings by withdrawing its members and asking the Speaker to call quorum. Committee meetings must also maintain quorum. In the capital city, members can be substituted, but frantic phone calls result if a committee is travelling.

A government whip obsesses about ensuring that more members are present on the government side than on the opposition benches. Acting as a ringmaster is pivotal when the governing party has a minority of seats. The deputy whip in a fragile provincial government once informed the caucus that, "if you die, you still have to come in. We'll shine you up. We'll get you in there. We'll lift your hand up for the vote."[94] In a majority government, whips have a less compelling argument to engineer unanimity, but the government whip must nevertheless deliver votes to pass bills and wants to avoid media controversy about dissenting members. For these reasons, the whip can nominally outrank everyone to secure votes, including frontbenchers.

Situations arise when a government whip needs to know where all members of the caucus are – even those taking a bathroom break. A government whip who anticipates a close vote can direct ministers to remain in the House and order others to return to the capital immediately.[95] Logistical problems result as the minister's office attempts to reschedule or relocate events, rebook flights, and/or negotiate with the PMO. The government whip must have the prime minister's backing in order to withstand pressure from an unhappy minister. Pierre Trudeau's whip during a minority government has re-enacted the telephone conversations:

[The whip] would say, "You have to come back, I am sorry." They might say, "Well, I am a main speaker at a banquet at the Chamber of Commerce." We would say: "That is too bad. If you do not come back, stay home, we will tell you the election date. So it is up to you: you can address the Chamber of Commerce tonight or an election rally next week, whatever you wish."[96]

Today people continue to warn about the fall of the Clark minority government in December 1979 when some members were out of the country and/or could not be contacted. Few are aware of what Clark's whip orchestrated to deliver votes.[97] The whip's staff phoned daily to see where MPs were. Sometimes intoxicated members required persuading to leave their offices or the parliamentary lounge to vote. To throw off the opposition, PC MPs brought empty suitcases to Parliament Hill, made sure to tell some Liberals that they were flying home, took taxis to their apartments instead of the airport, and snuck back that evening for a vote. Some government-side MPs on an international trip agreed to meet their opposition counterparts for breakfast and secretly flew to Canada the night before.

Some politicians believe that without rules about quorum there would be lower attendance.[98] Certain members are chronically late for an assortment of reasons. An enduring challenge for Canadian whips is that snowstorms can impede the ability of members to get to the legislature for a vote.[99] Whips can also be concerned about the optics of empty seats on their side of the assembly. In small places, the whip and staff scramble to locate people who stepped out of the chamber. Wayward members are discovered giving a media interview, on a telephone call, holding an impromptu meeting, or wandering off for coffee or a cigarette. Members are sometimes found napping in a nearby room. Whips relay stories about people who want to leave because of the room temperature, which prompts a game of thermostat adjustment, seat switching, and opening and shutting windows. Unusual circumstances arise, such as an MLA who came unglued at news that a bird was perched on his car. Having to assess requests to leave puts the whip in a precarious situation because the caucus is always scrutinizing special treatment.

Members of Parliament are told that the whip's office must be notified if they travel more than thirty minutes from Parliament Hill. Here is an example of why that rule exists. On an otherwise routine day in 2016, opposition MPs noticed that they outnumbered Liberals in the House of Commons. They quietly agreed that the NDP MP scheduled to speak on some amendments to a government bill would instead sneak into the lobby.[100] Because debate on the proposed amendments could not proceed, it ended abruptly, triggering a snap vote with thirty minutes of notice. The government whip summoned Liberal MPs in the Ottawa area to rush to the House. A number of ministers were at a community event, and others were at funerals. Some became caught in traffic as they hurried back; one minister was spotted running down the hallway to the chamber. The vote ended in a tie, prompting the Speaker to cast the deciding vote in favour of the bill, which saved the government from falling on a procedural tactic. Some months later, when a new whip was appointed, Prime Minister Trudeau remarked that the work involves ensuring that the party's MPs "are on time and at the right locations."[101]

For these reasons, whips and their staff track parliamentarians' whereabouts. Making members aware that the whip's office is taking attendance throughout a committee meeting can help to ensure that members remain for the duration of it.[102] In small legislatures, there is a constant tally of members' comings and goings. Some whips scribble notes on a seating plan to monitor who is out and the estimated time of return. At caucus meetings, they might require members to initial an attendance sheet or have staff count no-shows.

In Ottawa, parliamentary parties maintain House duty rosters of MPs to ensure that minimum numbers are present.[103] House duty is a block of time for which the office of the whip schedules select MPs to be present in the House of Commons chamber and, if quorum is met, obliges them to stay nearby so that they can be pulled in for a vote. They linger in the adjacent lobby behind their seats where they catch up on reading, take a language lesson, meet with a group, or eat lunch. For a government-side member, House duty might be multiple half days per week when Parliament is sitting (as depicted in Figure 2.3); for an opposition member, it might be a full day. Members must find replacements if they cannot fulfill their House duty obligations.

In the House of Commons, each whip's office staffs a desk in the lobby to provide assistance to its MPs and ensure smooth operations. Parties with official status are designated an area outside the chamber. The opposition side of the lobby is carved out to allocate space to each party, proportionate to its share of seats. On their way into the chamber, members can pick up talking points from the lobby desk or a nearby table staffed by someone from a minister's office or the opposition office, as applicable. The lobby desk is there to field questions about parliamentary procedure, ensure that speakers for bills are in queue, outline the procedure if there is a delay, and be in constant contact with MPs via smartphones. The staffer monitors whether the MPs on House duty are present and helps to ensure that quorum is met. A lobby desk's primary concern is that MPs show up as scheduled.

The whip's staff handle requests from members to be absent. A source of tension is that MPs who represent electoral districts along the Toronto-Ottawa-Montreal corridor have the advantage of being able to visit their constituents and family during the week without missing House duty.[104] Assignments are traded to accommodate schedules; for example, an MP who wants to fly home on Thursday evening might sit late on weeknights on behalf of a colleague who agrees to serve House duty on Friday. MPs notify the lobby desk when they negotiate a swap with a fellow caucus member, although switching a committee meeting is more laborious because of the need to be briefed on the party's position.[105] The whip's office is firm with members who shirk House duty because the system breaks down otherwise, and so exemptions are granted in special circumstances, such as when the member is scheduled to attend a committee. MPs who are flexible about trading House duty assignments can build social capital and political favours. However, some MPs are reluctant to accommodate others or forget that they owe hours.

Whip's office personnel meet with members on House duty to review the legislative agenda. A duty whip is appointed from among the MPs on that day's House duty roster. The designated MP covers the responsibilities of the House leader, whip, and their deputies if those officers are not present. The duty whip leads the duty group in line with the strategy of the House leader and whip (e.g., managing attendance, keeping debate going). The practice gives private members experience with caucus management as they advance the group's strategic objectives and attempt to thwart opponents' sly procedural manoeuvres. Although the House duty system helps to ensure that sufficient numbers are always at hand, it can mean that a skeleton crew is present in the chamber, requiring that someone from the whip's office reminds MPs to switch seats to fill empty chairs around a speaker. Seat shuffling improves the optics on television and provides an MP's office with the option of circulating a YouTube video clip.

Where feasible, whips trade absent votes by pairing members from either side of the legislature. A whip's authority is undermined if a minister contacts an opposition whip's office to invite a critic to go along on a trip or if a member whose travel was disallowed by the whip tries to arrange pairing. Whips collaborate with one another to prevent such circumvention. They also exchange information about how many speakers they plan to put up for a debate on a bill. When the opposition filibusters, the whips implement rolling shifts and manage breaks. They keep track of which sleep-deprived members are napping in cots in the lobby or went home to refresh. The government whip has the added pressure of not being outnumbered in the middle of the night.

When a vote is looming, the whip needs to know how many members will be present and how they intend to vote. The whip contacts members to say "the vote's on. Are you going to be there? If not, why not? We really need you to be there for this particular vote."[106] Creativity might be necessary. One whip required anyone who missed a vote to donate fifty dollars to the caucus Christmas reception.[107] The tactic was probably unsuccessful given that whips who try to levy fines give up when people do not pay them. If attendance is slipping, then the leader urges members to be more diligent and might remind them of times when governments fell.[108] Whips and their staff are reputed to have long memories of people who cause attendance problems. The staff exert political acumen to encourage turnout, says a former federal whip: "It's the whip staff who really have the relationship with members to say 'I know you stayed late last week, but can you do it again this week?' or 'you've got House duty on Friday; we're really counting on you to be there because the opposition could pull some procedural shenanigans,'" she explains. "It is that personal relationship of the whip's staff that is so essential. A whip is only one person."[109]

Whipping the vote requires that House officers communicate the party line. In small legislatures, the volume of business and the number of members are low enough that backbenchers can meet before heading into the chamber. Governing party members might convene in the morning and again in the afternoon so that a staffer can debrief them about legislative activities. Afterward, the staffer or a parliamentary secretary briefs the premier's office. Any significant concerns are relayed to the applicable minister(s) and/or the premier.

Vote coordination is more systematic in large legislatures, where the number of parliamentarians and the volume of business are higher. In preparation for a vote, Members of Parliament receive bill summaries from the Library of Parliament synthesizing the proposals.[110] Ministers' offices prepare supplementary information packages distributed at caucus meetings or available to governing party MPs who ask for them. A bill kit – sometimes known as a package – includes a copy of the bill, a detailed backgrounder, a news release, a questions and answers sheet, and supportive comments from stakeholders.[111] The news release might be a template for MPs to customize. How ministers and private members are encouraged to vote is stated on a whip's vote sheet (see Figures 9.1 and 9.2). Bill kits are essential for educating backbenchers about a proposal so that they can engage the whip and/or minister's office if they have concerns.

There are two types of internal vote sheets in the House of Commons.[112] Procedural clerks use the first type to prepare an official record of decisions. While seated at the table in front of the Speaker's chair, the clerk or a deputy writes on a seating chart to record how MPs voted on a bill or motion. The procedural notes are sent to the Journals Branch to inform the preparation of the House of Commons *Journals,* the official record of decisions. The second type is a partisan vote sheet prepared by the whip's office, sometimes moments before the vote occurs, and placed by House of Commons pages on MPs' desks in the chamber. It is also available via lobby desks.

A whip's vote sheet identifies the party line on each motion and should not surprise attentive MPs. For the debate on the Budget Implementation Act, 2019, vote sheets prepared by the Liberal government whip's office and the Conservative official opposition whip's office followed a template identifying the number of a bill and the leadership's "position" on supporting

FIGURE 9.1
Vote sheet, chief government whip

	House of Commons Office of the Chief Government Whip	
	VOTES Wednesday, June 5, 2019/Le mercredi 5 juin 2019	
Vote total/ *Total de vote*	*Vote description/* *Description du vote*	*Government position/* *Position du gouvernement*
1/8	Motion 1 C-97 (Budget)	OPPOSED CONTRE
2/8	Motion 18 C-97 (Budget)	OPPOSED CONTRE
3/8	Motion 34 C-97 (Budget)	OPPOSED CONTRE
4/8	Motion 44 C-97 (Budget)	OPPOSED CONTRE

Source: Adapted from a photograph provided by a Member of Parliament (2019 budget).

or opposing it. The wording conveyed a guideline rather than a command, thereby respecting the independence of private members to consider available information when deciding how to vote. The Liberal sheet featured a column for a sequence of vote totals, in this case on opposition motions related to the budget (see Figure 9.1). The government's position on a confidence matter was presented without any explanation.

The official opposition's vote sheets had more details. The Conservative form identified the name of the bill, its mover and seconder, a short definition of the bill, and a rationale for the party's position (see Figure 9.2). For private members' bills, it included the recommendation of the critic and identified the whip level as level one (free vote), level two (party line vote), or level three (whipped vote). For committee business, a member's vote sheet can include clause-by-clause recommendations on how to vote.[113] In lieu of such documents, committee members may strategize ahead of time on submitting amendments to the chair via the clerk.

Information on vote sheets is handy for private members when they do not scrutinize proposed legislation, especially omnibus bills. For many, the guidance is essential because of the complexity of the government and

FIGURE 9.2
Vote sheet, chief opposition whip

Chief Opposition Whip	CPC Position
MOTION NO. 1 – Mr. Doe (Carleton), seconded by Mr. Public (Edmonton West) – That Bill C-97 be amended by deleting Clause 30.	SUPPORT
Rationale: Conservatives support this motion as it will remove the media bailout package from Part 1 of the Budget Implementation Act. A healthy democracy relies on an independent press, free from political interference; the government has abandoned this principle and is attempting to stack the deck in their favour.	
MOTION NO. 18 – Mr. Dupont (Sherbrooke), seconded by Mr. Toutelemonde (Beloeil–Chambly) – That Bill C-97 be amended by deleting Clause 198.	OPPOSE
Rationale: Conservatives oppose this motion as we believe in reducing regulation to mitigate the high cost of compliance.	

PRIVATE MEMBERS' BILLS	Recommendation of Critic (Health)	Whip Level
M-174 – Mr. Smith (Timmins–James Bay) – National suicide prevention action plan	SUPPORT	2
Rationale: There is a suicide epidemic. This motion for a study will, we hope, lead to concrete actions that can be taken to resolve the problem.		

PRIVATE MEMBERS' BILLS	Recommendation of Critic (Industry)	Whip Level
M-208 – Mr. Untel (Pontiac) – Rural digital infrastructure	SUPPORT	2
Rationale: It is impossible to ignore the successive Liberal failures on this file. This motion will allow two committees to study an issue that affects rural Canadians.		

Source: Adapted from a photograph provided by an MP (2019). Pseudonyms used.

an individual MP's limitations. One government-side backbencher declares that "MPs are very busy and they don't have time to study every bill, so a lot of MPs just will listen to what the government says on a bill and follow it."[114] Even an MP as determined as Ryan Cleary cannot get through everything:

> Whenever I took my seat in the Commons prior to a vote, there was a sheet on my desk from the party telling me how to vote. I usually knew what most legislation was about; for instance, a budget bill was about the budget, generally. But it was not humanly possible for an MP or their entire staff to read through all the legislation. There simply isn't enough time in the year. I worked harder than most, and still 95 percent of the time even I didn't know what I was voting on. Of course, you either voted the party line or faced the consequences. Democracy is a joke.[115]

Not all parliamentarians are interested in the finer details of draft legislation. The volume of information combined with other priorities and time demands makes clear the indispensability of political staff who prepare summaries. When a vote is called, members who are not paying attention have to ask a colleague what they are voting on. Sometimes they inadvertently vote the wrong way.

Whips keep count of expected ayes, nays, and maybes. They also identify what the other parties' positions are, in part to establish which party's parliamentarians will be standing up first during voting. As a test of loyalty, whips can require that members be present to vote with the party on a low-risk procedural motion and can put private members in a bind by requiring them to be present to vote the party line on a trap vote.

A member who contemplates rebuffing the party line is of great interest to the whip's office. The whip or a surrogate reaches out to members who voice concerns at caucus meetings or rant to colleagues. The whip's office might initiate a conversation or coordinate a brigade of people invested in the proposed policy to speak with the member to reconcile differences. Advocates of the party line express empathy when attempting to persuade a vexed member to stay onside and chatting with "maybes" to find out what is upsetting them can lead to their siding with the party. Unlike on *House of Cards,* disciplinary threats are avoided if possible. As one government whip puts it, "a good whip doesn't whip ... A good whip pulls people together and gets them onto the same page."[116]

 Anyone determined to vote differently from the party might have an entrenched point of view. Conversations with additional caucus members ensue. A whip encourages dialogue between the backbencher and the applicable officeholders, ranging from ministers to ministerial critics and/or senior staff. A whip might work on getting informal caucus leaders to be influencers.[117] If a member is emphatic about voting, then the whip gives the minister or critic a heads up, strategizes with the chief of staff, and/or alerts the leader. The headstrong member is cautioned not to cause embarrassment. Private back-and-forth negotiations can go right up to the division bells ringing, at which point the leader might be the one pleading with the member to stay onside or come down with the diplomatic flu.

A member who cannot be restrained is asked to consider not voting. Stepping out of the chamber, faking illness, or being out of town are preferred over signalling disagreement by formally abstaining. Securing permission from the party leadership to stand down involves an agreement not to speak publicly about the policy: "There is often pressure to stay away. Caucus colleagues who don't want to openly dissent will not show up for the vote," says a former MP. "It is a well-known mechanism of leadership and the leader's circle to convince people to take a walk on a particular day. On quite a number of occasions, a leader would say to me 'look, at least take a walk, don't vote against us.'"[118] The whip can find a reason to send a recalcitrant member on an overseas trip to avoid the debate. Sometimes absenteeism is not viable, such as during a minority government or on a contentious topic.

There is safety in numbers. Occasionally, a cluster or even a mass of parliamentarians disobeys the whip. Government-side members can be emboldened to rebuff a minister's instructions to a parliamentary committee, and they can defy the government's position that is stipulated on the whip's vote sheet.[119] A burst of group independence is overpowering because disciplining multiple private members is impractical. The leadership spins the spurt of anti-partyism as democratic temperament – whereas a lone wolf incurs disciplinary measures.

SUMMARY

Organizational management is essential to optimize the limited time available to a legislative assembly for a heavy volume of bills, motions, and debates. Messaging and vote guidelines are indispensable to busy or apathetic parliamentarians who would otherwise be overwhelmed. However, relying on party cues reduces private members to voting machines, bringing into question why backbenchers must be physically present to vote in the House. The dominance of parliamentary parties will persist as long as private members are ill-equipped to mount efforts to change internal practices or lack incentive to do so. Managing individuals who threaten group unity is the topic of the next chapter.

10

Managing Trouble

Canadian democracy is at its best when politicians participate in robust conversations about public policy. Debate can – and should – escalate into respectful argument when philosophical convictions clash or grave real-world implications are at stake. As we have seen, a spectacle results if private deliberations become public or if a politician is at the centre of a *cause célèbre*. What happens when parliamentarians violate expectations of message conformity? How do the leader's agents try to contain someone who springs a surprise or causes a disruption? In this chapter, I outline how the leadership of a parliamentary party manages trouble from within.

INTERNAL CONFLICT

By now it should be clear that parliamentary groups are an eclectic assortment of personalities whose behaviour is structured by social and psychological forces. Members of a caucus are guarded, even rivals, and veterans might be unwilling to share information with rookies.[1] Innumerable factors determine whether a parliamentarian resorts to public defiance. Maybe a policy or a consultation process causes irritation. The party's stance on a given issue could be someone's bottom line, or a disagreeable parliamentarian might have obstinate personality traits. Perhaps they value free will, causing them to seethe in a team environment that devalues individualism and to chafe against a system designed to elicit obedience. Politicians who feel slighted, are passed over for promotion, have other career options, or are not seeking re-election have fewer barriers to iconoclasm. Those who lack a personal attachment to the leader, such as a parliamentarian who won the local nomination over the leadership's favoured candidate or has leadership ambitions, can become a serious threat to group harmony. Sometimes online commentary emboldens them to speak up; at other times, social media comprise a gauge to tone things down. Leaders are acutely aware that a caucus is a potential powder keg that requires careful management.

Process and Policy Conflict

At any given time, members of a caucus are irritated. Some of them complain about insufficient opportunity to offer input, or they can be bothered that colleagues do not stick up for principles or parliamentary privileges. At a caucus meeting, someone who raises excellent points forces the leadership to decide whether to accommodate or rebut them and can become upset if the leader shrugs off fair comments, especially if others echo the remarks. An intraparty dilemma about sticking to principles versus pandering is exactly the kind of division that opponents hope to elicit with wedge politics.

Within the caucus, an impassioned member who makes spirited and convincing arguments about why a position is outrageous can attract a swath of support if the leader is steering the group outside its lane. A champion of party philosophy who embodies the party's values is very good at this. A prominent non-conformist in the New Democratic Party points to the Catch-22 of strong representation within the boundaries of party affiliation:

> One of the greatest challenges you have to wrestle with is the extent to which an individual member of caucus can take a strong stand. What are the boundaries? How much freedom does that individual member have to take a position which may be challenging politically for colleagues but which reflects the member's personal values or, more importantly, issues that reflect the values of the party but which are unpopular? I probably have the dubious distinction of being fired by more leaders than anybody else for dissent. That is what I always wrestled with: how do you balance the tension between an individual member who believes strongly and passionately in issues and the discipline of a

caucus which is saying "that's all well and good for you, but by taking that stand you're hurting us"? I don't have an answer.[2]

A trailblazer who advocates a contentious position that is true to party values can nudge the party to adopt it against the wishes of the leader.[3] A former Parti Québécois Member of the National Assembly (MNA) recalls his desire to promote the creation of a Quebec constitution.[4] His idea aligned with the party's values of advocating sovereignty and therefore could not be dismissed as taboo, but the proposition polarized the caucus. When the leader chided him in a caucus meeting, the MNA exited the room saying that he would reflect on whether to remain with the party, safe in the knowledge that the party would want to avoid a by-election. The next leader was open to discussing the idea, and the backbencher worked on a private member's bill. Although it did not pass first reading, the extra-parliamentary party endorsed his proposal at a policy convention, and a pledge to develop a Quebec constitution appeared in the party's election platform. The Parti Québécois gained seats in the 2008 provincial election; however, the MNA was not re-elected and the party remained in opposition. The story illustrates how leaders struggle to contain philosophical disagreements when private members are the actors who personify party principles.

A defiant member might be branded a selfish rabble-rouser, yet in reality the vocalizer likely feels horrible about inflicting political pressure on colleagues. An MP who has challenged the party line admits to having greater concern about the reactions of members of the caucus than the responses of party officials: "The whip's office thinks the phrase 'be a team player' is a knockdown argument. It's their go-to reprimand," says the MP. "I don't view the whip as particularly effective in controlling my behaviour. But I do give great thought into how my decision will affect my colleagues. I do try to consult with the colleagues who will be affected."[5] As mentioned, avoiding the wrath of peers is a substantial motivator to stay in the fold.[6] Concern about the political repercussions for fellow members of the caucus is surprisingly common given portrayals of the agitator as selfish.

Excuses and Deception

Some trouble involves honest mistakes. A hot mic (an open microphone that the speaker does not realize is recording) that catches a politician in a frank exchange or a story about a staffer who loses confidential documents can fill a news hole. Some communications calamities can be spun; others end political careers. All of it disrupts group harmony if poorly managed. Politicians who get into scrapes need to be forthright so that communications professionals can sort out the best ways forward in a fast-paced media landscape.

Deceit is a particular challenge to internal harmony. Political deception ranges from routine dishonesty to get out of attending a legislative debate to rare deviousness that erupts during internal power struggles. Whips across Canada recount stories about fabricated excuses. Members can complain about not feeling well as a ruse to leave the legislature, or they develop a reputation for having many dying relatives who require attention. Some of them lack the necessary self-assurance to be forthright. A former whip told of asking some bilingual members to speak to a bill using their second language. They met to run through messaging. The next morning one of them called in sick for House duty, only to reappear in the afternoon after his allotted time to speak on the bill had passed. The whip deduced that the member wanted to maintain a reputation for being agreeable even though he did not want to address the assembly in another language: "Had he told me that he was uncomfortable, I would have said 'okay, great, no problem,'" the former whip told me. "I would never pressure somebody. There's always some reason, but they don't want to tell you what it really is."[7]

Digital technology has emerged as a tool to monitor absenteeism. Another former whip recounts how reviewing social media updates can catch members who feign poor health or allege fictitious meetings:

Always check social media! Facebook, Twitter, and Instagram are your greatest friends when it comes to whipping. One individual came up to me in the legislature saying he was really sick. I told him to go home and get some rest. When he was out in the parking lot, he was already tweeting that he was on his way to a turkey dinner event. I sent him a private message saying "you might want to turn around and come back to the legislature." Another time a member of the executive was in a very important meeting, was running late, and couldn't make it back. I happened to go on the minister's Facebook, and there was a photo of the person down by the beach eating a sandwich saying "no better way to spend the day than on the beach." Social media are an incredible tool for catching out members with excuses for why they can't be in the legislature.[8]

Happenstance can catch people in a lie. A former party leader recalls that the whip authorized an MP to be away from Ottawa for five days of important meetings throughout the constituency. Later some mayors casually mentioned that they had enjoyed a week-long fishing trip with the MP. The leader phoned him to request information about the fictitious constituency meetings. The MP obliged by inventing details: "Stop that, I want to know how many fish you caught!" interrupted the leader. The member was irate and accused the party of spying on him. The leader retorted by commenting on the member's poor judgment and made the ominous threat that the incident would be remembered.[9]

Members who admit to making a fib, apologize, and learn from it can repair broken trust. Serial liars incur the leadership's wrath. As payback, their requests are denied, and opportunities are not extended. Far more sinister are duplicitous attempts to undermine the leader, such as by leaking confidential information. A former leader opens up about an ambitious backbencher who planned a coup, which began with a few colleagues whispering at group events, and escalated into spreading caucus gossip. The schemer deviously twisted words and played people off one another while feigning group loyalty. Media stories based on distortions, falsehoods, and caucus leaks undermined her leadership, but she felt unable to refute misinformation because to regain caucus confidence she needed to preserve confidentiality. She reflects on the havoc:

> It was a very, very difficult time. The hardest part was there were things that went on in our caucus that, on an ethical level, I didn't think I could say publicly. The media took what happened at face value and didn't give me the benefit of the doubt as leader. If you have somebody in the caucus looking to position herself or himself in power, they can be looking for weaknesses in other people so they can move in and get that person's support and turn people against each other while looking like they believe in the team. It is sociopathic.[10]

Alternatively, a leader can be the manipulator. Some interview participants recounted a notorious story from 1968 about Joey Smallwood, the first premier of Newfoundland (1949–72), who planned to award a sizable unsecured government loan to a businessman.[11] Two ministers said that they would leave the cabinet if the financing provisions appeared in a bill. The premier threatened them: "If you do that, I'll stop at nothing! One other fellow did that once and wasn't heard from for a long time!" Smallwood thundered.[12] He sought to divide the ministers by privately instilling doubt in Minister 1 about the motives of Minister 2. After some deliberation, the ministers went to the premier's office to announce that they were resigning. Keep in mind that one minister, let alone two, resigning from cabinet over a policy disagreement is a major political salvo: "You're not going to have a chance to resign. Here's a letter demanding your resignation," Smallwood said to Minister 2, producing a letter of termination with allegations of impropriety. According to the premier, the cabinet had decided the minister had to be fired in light of the supposed misdeeds. "These things aren't true," protested the minister, to which Smallwood retorted "I'll get affidavits stating they are true." Minister 1 also resigned. The premier spun his version of events to waiting journalists. In the House of Assembly that afternoon, the ex-ministers found their desks on the opposite side of the chamber, and Smallwood had a backbencher move a confidence motion in the government to ensure caucus solidarity. Later it became known that the first time cabinet heard of the allegations against Minister 2 was when the premier went public with them, which he had to retract when faced with legal action.

Cabinet secrecy, control of a majority of seats, and a cult of personality were considerable advantages for the premier. The confidence motion and financing bill passed; however, losing two ministers was a significant blow. It is impossible to know how common these sorts of internal standoffs are given that the details rarely become public. The SNC-Lavalin debacle that occurred half a century later is a prolific exception and has some parallels with its Newfoundland antecedent.

Uncivil Behaviour

The longer that people are immersed in party politics, the more that they become desensitized to insolence that would shock most people and oblivious to coercive control. Many talk about the need for thick skin. Politicians contend with criticism, undermining, and soft innuendo in private and public as well as insults, mocking, shaming, and cyberbullying. Ad hominem attacks are painful for their family members, especially if a child is bullied at school because the parent is publicly scorned. Sticking it out requires a personal resolve that negative energy will not stop an elected representative from achieving political objectives. Political veterans recommend that a Canadian who is afraid of disparagement should not seek elected office.

Politicians gain familiarity with the scope of human behaviour through their interactions with constituents who share stories of hardship. People disclose terrible things happening in their lives. Survivors of domestic violence can require assistance to secure emergency shelter; constituents with suicidal thoughts reach out for help. Hostile communications from citizens with mental disorders can be a serious problem, and abusive emails and irate constituents can provoke panic attacks among elected officials and their staff.[13] Some politicians are the target of misogyny or racism. One told me that for a year someone anonymously mailed letters insulting her looks; another told of a man and his son yelling racial epithets in her campaign office. Some politicians deal with personal affronts by disengaging and can cancel events because of concerns that participants will be berated and feel intimidated. One MP stopped offering town halls because "only the mad, the bad, and the sad" attend them.[14] Politicians try to ignore social media criticism in part because responding to it would escalate to include all of the politician's followers.

There is mixed evidence about whether politicians and their staff are the sources of hostilities. Many of those interviewed for this book believe that uncivil behaviour among elected officials rarely involves repetitive actions designed to break somebody down. Some report never having experienced raised voices in cabinet or caucus meetings, while others tell of colleagues who quash condescending behaviour. A former minister describes how senior parliamentarians instilled a respectful tone in the caucus environment: "On occasion, some of our veterans stood up and said 'what you just said is offensive. I don't mind you making your point, but I'm not going to tolerate that language in this room, and I expect better from you,'" he recalls. "When a senior party stalwart says that, it sets a very,

very powerful tone."[15] A premier's chief of staff describes how tolerance of old-style abrasive politicking is eroding even as the need for solidarity persists:

> In today's environment, you have to be cautious about how you interact. Things have changed in terms of how you can speak with people. You have to rewire how you do things and be more considerate. Interactions have to be respectful. You have to listen to the other person. You need to pause and really think before you speak or take a certain action. Years ago it was far more direct: if you don't like it, there's the door. But there's still someone in charge, and your supervisor should have expectations. Fairly direct conversations can be necessary. You still need discipline to make sure everyone in the same canoe is paddling in the same direction.[16]

Political tolerances are clearly evolving. Nevertheless, a caucus can portray a complainant as disruptive and invoke retribution for sounding the alarm.[17]

Workplace bullying stems, in part, from stress caused by divergent opinions, different status, job satisfaction, and whether or not people are socialized into a group.[18] Harassment is offensive behaviour that can involve discrimination, threats, and/or unwanted physical contact; bullying involves repeated unwelcome actions that cause degradation and anguish. Political workplaces are not for the faint of heart. Unleashing their exasperation and mental burdens, partisans can yell and swear, causing the target(s) to find solace in Kleenex.[19] In the heat of the moment, a pen is tossed across the room: "I've been screamed at, I've had things thrown at my face. Stuff that had me go home and cry at the end of the day," says a government whip. "People get under enormous stress, and they don't necessarily vent that stress appropriately."[20]

Party whips can be coarse when frustration boils over with an unrepentant private member who is a constant source of trouble: "More than once I had to yell and use colourful language. But mostly it's going up to people with a quiet reminder as well as praising them when there are little improvements," a former whip says.[21] Sometimes party leaders express their anger in a forceful manner. An argumentative backbencher shares that a national leader sometimes muttered profanities whenever they passed in a parliamentary hallway.[22] An upset leader might swear and throw papers or shout so much that spittle sprays on a member's face.[23] Brian Mulroney was susceptible to "towering rages" and colourful language.[24] Jean Chrétien and Justin Trudeau have used angry tones in caucus meetings with backbenchers.[25] Stephen Harper sometimes erupted in profanity-laced fits of anger, once kicking a chair across a room after a heated exchange with his press secretary.[26]

Caucus members can engage in heated verbal exchanges as well. Altercations between ministers can spill outside the cabinet room.[27] Ministers and backbenchers can quarrel in elevators and hallways; on occasion, angry exchanges carry over from a caucus meeting to the floor of the legislative chamber. Digital communication adds a new dimension. Parliamentarians and political staff bypass go-betweens by emailing and texting. The impersonal immediacy can contribute to a relationship breakdown when they vent on a digital device: "You are causing a f*ck load of trouble for me, being vocal about this ... policy. There are ways to do things but undermining your colleagues isn't one of them I assure you," a minister texted a backbencher who had freelanced on Facebook.[28]

Women are more likely to experience uncivil behaviour in political backrooms and in the legislature. Some personnel in the Canadian political arena observe a masculine work culture in which women are subject to sexualized comments.[29] To feminists, heckling embodies the masculinity embedded in adversarial politics and the standing orders.[30] In 2018, the #MeToo movement reverberated throughout Canada's legislatures, leading to accusations of impropriety in all political parties, mostly involving men accused of sexually harassing women. The explosive events created greater urgency for legislatures to update their codes of conduct and to require parliamentarians to complete anti-harassment training.[31] Among the revelations was one that some partisans worry that voicing concern about experiencing harassment could harm their party's electoral fortunes.

Brazen political staff are another category of concern. Self-important young men in executive offices are derided as boys in short pants,[32] an epithet that became "kids in short pants" to include assertive young women.[33] These types of staff cause problems of morale when they speak in sharp tones: "There are ministers' offices where the staff think they're the minister and who are just obnoxious to the Members of Parliament," reflects Kim Campbell.[34] During Question Period preparation, members of the cabinet are taken aback at the lack of respect when a young, inexperienced staffer schools an older, experienced minister about how to improve an articulate reply by injecting better lines. Prime Minister Harper's inner circle developed a particularly notorious reputation as henchmen. A Conservative campaign director allegedly "operated like a tyrant, bullying people left and right," while a deputy chief of staff "had an out-of-control temper ... and would let fly on the slightest of provocations."[35] One director of communications caused fear in the PMO and PCO, occasionally bringing people to tears in meetings.[36] A Conservative chief of staff reportedly said the following to an MP who was freelancing in the media and online: "If you want to f*ck with us, we will certainly f*ck with you. Do you want to sit as an Independent? Then we can arrange that. Count on it."[37] Some Conservatives contest such characterizations, including the validity of a story that ministers sobbed after a tongue-lashing.[38]

When a senior staffer so sternly scolds a backbencher that she cries, we can deduce that low-ranking personnel experience similar treatment or worse.[39] Young political employees' expendability and stage of career can lead to exploitation, bullying, and harassment.[40] One junior staffer provides a glimpse of such treatment. She tells of how staff are expected to work long days. Overtime and vacation time are to be used for working on an election campaign. Senior staff are coarse with nervous subordinates: "If you want a f*cking union job, go get one. You work nine hours a day; I don't want any of this overtime bullsh*t," and "we have a stack of résumés as high as my knee. You aren't here because you are brilliant, you are here because of your loyalty to the party."[41] Low-ranking staff who do not donate enough money to the party are summoned to private meetings at which they are admonished for insufficient contributions. By her account, concern about politicians who exploit their positions might overlook the power that senior staff brandish.

Party whips and others are mindful that the societal turn against power imbalances creates an opening for fabricated stories. A former MLA tells of how opponents took advantage of her political naivete about speaking with people across party lines.[42] Between elections she regularly canvassed in her electoral district, as did an aspiring candidate for another party. One day while canvassing she spotted a cluster of young supporters of the other party. She introduced herself, praised them for participating in the democratic process, and reportedly said: "These are my neighbours and friends, so have fun knocking on their doors." In the next Question Period, the premier was asked why a member of his caucus was harassing volunteers, and the official opposition filed a motion of contempt. Media questions ensued about her bullying youth. It was a teachable moment about political hyperbole and the safety of staying in a message silo.

Much remains to be worked out about uncivil behaviour in parliamentary party politics.[43] To what extent is it acceptable for a minister to swear at a backbencher who persistently lobbies for project funding? Does it constitute mobbing if a group of ministers exclude another minister from their discussions? What can be done when a voice of dissent is subject to so many lies, denials, and distortions from a powerful caucus adversary that the minority voice ends up questioning their own personal sense of reality? There can be different interpretations of legislative assembly codes of conduct, harassment-free workplace policies, labour law, and the Criminal Code. Party whips and others spend an inordinate amount of time on these sorts of internal disputes.

DISCIPLINARY ACTION

Those who rebuff group norms learn that political parties are clubs with mostly unwritten codes of conduct. New parliamentarians in particular might lack appreciation for party legacies, rituals, and the legitimate supremacy of the leader. They signed a candidate contract, but once in office they do not care about the path dependence behind institutional traditions, and it might not be clear to them that their reckless behaviour in defiance of established political rules is an affront to the group itself: "Every caucus, every community organization, every sports team, every business, has rules of conduct for its members. And being in a caucus and being in an organization requires those rules to be followed," says a premier. "Principles of behaviour have to be established. They have to be maintained."[44] A former premier echoes that view. "It is always interesting when people join a club and then don't like the rules," she observes.[45]

Many parliamentarians support, if not advocate, consequences for layabouts and troublemakers. An industrious member might demand the whip's intervention when a prominent politician shirks legislative responsibilities. Colleagues might tattle on someone who goes off-message or who is otherwise disrupting a political agenda: "In my experience, MPs are often more than happy to rat each other out," says a staffer in the Trudeau PMO. "It's everybody watching everything."[46] A former government whip describes the internal jockeying:

> A member of caucus will say to the whip "there is a member who never shows up at committee, yet is on the foreign affairs committee, one of the top-notch committees of the House. I'm on a lesser committee. I always show up for work. Why does that person get rewarded with the good job and I get the lousy one? Do your job, whip. Kick that person off the committee and put me on it." The MPs expect the whip's authority and will criticize the whip for inaction.[47]

Party leaders tread carefully with enforcement of club rules. A leader who treats an esteemed individual as expendable can spur colleagues to disapprove publicly of the sanction.[48] As well, a caucus can have sympathy for a vulnerable politician who made a valid point or an honest mistake. Greater caution might be prudent when descriptive representation is a factor. Some women interviewed for this book witnessed the formation of a coalition of women to defend a woman whom others (mostly men) believed should be disciplined for egregious behaviour. There are countless political calculations when the leadership contemplates imposing disciplinary measures on a member of caucus.

Disciplinarians

The whip and chief of staff are the main disciplinarians. Sometimes it is a deputy leader, deputy chief of staff, or deputy whip. In some caucuses, including the Trudeau Liberals, the leader's staff deal with ministers, and the whip deals with backbenchers. Communications personnel might be involved. In small legislatures, the House leader can play the heavy to free up the caucus chair to maintain friendly relations. All of these disciplinarians allow the party leader to stay out of the fray as much as possible. As the party's primary spokesperson, the leader cannot be preoccupied with human resource issues and needs to be on the good side of the caucus to encourage cohesion. Emissaries advise the leader not to worry about intraparty conflict because they will take care of it and report back as appropriate. Agents are counterweights: a sociable leader has someone else do the gruff work, whereas a hot-tempered leader needs a fair-minded associate to cool things down.

When confronted with a problem that seems to warrant corrective action, disciplinarians curate information to establish facts. They might farm out detective work to support staff, such as a social media scan. Many disciplinarians are empathetic listeners, intent on gaining the trust of their colleague as they work out ways to resolve the situation, although a small number are taskmasters who warn of the grave consequences of noncompliance. Whips are good choices for outreach so that a peer is the one who addresses an affront. When tasked with confronting a minister of the Crown who has caused trouble, a government whip needs full awareness of the situation and clearance from the chief of staff, possibly requiring a chat with the prime minister or premier.

Every disciplinarian learns on the job, as do leaders: "I don't have a rule book that's been handed down to me from Wilfrid Laurier as leader of the Liberal Party on how to handle these situations," Trudeau once said.[49] A premier's chief of staff recalls trepidation during his first disciplinary moment.[50] A minister who went off-key was summoned to the premier's office to review her responsibilities to the government. In the moment, the chief of staff was thinking about how he was supposed to sanction a minister and was self-conscious that he had never been elected to anything. As disciplinarians gain experience, they recognize that every calamity requires unpacking. For instance, if a private member threatens to defy the party line because the whip's office did not offer a briefing on a bill, institutional knowledge will get at the subtext that the person is distraught about something else. Calm reassurance and commitment to obtain information can defuse the situation.

Internal Conversations

Ryan Cleary reflects on his time in Ottawa with awe at the institution of Parliament. For someone used to life in rural communities and small towns, the capital city is a bustling place, and the architecture of the Parliament Buildings is jaw-dropping. No matter where you are from it is a humbling experience to take your seat in the House of Commons for the first time. But positive memories transition to dejection when party discipline comes up: "Having to work within the party line was stifling," Cleary declares. "I was not happy as a Member of Parliament. I spent too much time walking around with my head down, going over different problems, different challenges that I had in front of me. I didn't like being an MP. I didn't like the loss of freedom, of being corralled, of not being able to stand up for the people I represented." He goes on to explain that conformity expectations linger, especially for someone micromanaged after speaking out. It zaps morale from those who get into politics with high hopes of making a difference: "There was always the threat of discipline that keeps you in line," he says. "You don't want to be on the outs with the party, you want to do things right, and you'll get ahead. And if you don't, well, you're not going to get ahead, you're not going to get your critic portfolio, you're not going to be able to ask questions. The threat is always hanging over your head."[51]

Some of his frustrations turn on the scolding that Cleary endured from the leader's agents, upset with some of his policy commentary in media interviews. To this day, he is baffled about the exuberance of party message managers. The former MP is among a number of interview participants who explained the discipline enforcement process to me, as they experienced it. There can be no definitive account of what happens in private settings. Parties have their own cultures, with the tone set by the leader. Disciplinarians know all too well that circumstances are fluid, and pressure corresponds to the intensity of controversy. Nevertheless, summarizing what goes on behind closed doors when an off-message situation occurs can make intelligible some of the murkiest aspects of party discipline.

The leader's agents are on the lookout to identify and manage disgruntlement before it festers and builds. Whips know to reach out when they hear that a private member is unhappy with the party's position. As a backstop, leaders decree that the onus is on members of the caucus to initiate contact with the whip's office if there is a possibility of going offside. A member whose vote defies the party line rarely catches a whip off guard, but wayward remarks usually do because of the unpredictability of human behaviour and fickleness of media interest.

The stakes are high following a public outburst. The leader's office and whip's office are alerted by any number of personnel in the political system who spot an errant public remark. Social media simplify locating the alleged wrongdoing; however, language and cultural divides can delay detection, with anglophones taking days or weeks to discover remarks circulating on French-language news, Chinese social media, or ethnic community media.[52] When a problem is identified, rapid response communication protocols take over. Disciplinary measures are already under way if the whip circulates a memo asking members to refer any media enquiries about a colleague to the whip's office.[53]

Information is exchanged internally prior to contacting the person who caused a disruption. Disciplinarians assess the situation by mulling it over or talking it through: *Was the matter discussed with appropriate authorities beforehand? Was permission granted to stray from the party line in order to represent constituents? Does it appear to be an understandable error? Is the action a direct challenge to the authority of the party or leader? Can the situation be contained? What needs to happen to get things back on track? Is this the first incident, or is the culprit a repeat offender? Is there irreparable damage?* An enforcer might look the other way if a brand ambassador has deviated slightly from the party's position on a relatively minor matter, especially if it relates to constituent representation.

With a mild incident, a staffer in the leader's or whip's office reaches out to an intermediary for a conversation, such as the parliamentarian's assistant. Casual interaction keeps the peace. A disciplinarian who nonchalantly (but intentionally) bumps into a member in or around the legislative chamber conveys happenstance. The whip can wander over to sit next to the member during a lull in chamber business. Alternatively, an informal discussion might be best coming from a friend in the caucus or a respected stalwart unaffiliated with the leader's office. A major predicament requires immediate contact. A situation in the news and/or that has gone viral negates the luxury of informal, soft negotiation, and a serious public break from the party line requires an urgent conversation by telephone and/or in the whip's office, as occurred with some of the episodes recounted earlier. An inconspicuous approach is better than a closed-door meeting in the member's office or a discussion in a cafeteria, which would be grist for the political gossip mill.

A lack of information about possible motivations means that an initial conversation about mixed messaging can be soft. An inquisitive tone is used to build rapport: *How are you? What's happening here? Can we discuss this? How do you think the interview went? What did you mean when you said X? Can we walk through things so I can understand how you ended up saying what you said?* Disciplinarians know to probe deeper when politicians complain that they are not being listened to within their party. They might feel excluded, but perhaps they are not doing everything that they can to be heard. Those who say that they are ignored might mask other bitterness, such as thwarted ambition. The leader's agent wants to understand why a backbencher feels insignificant while others in the same caucus feel valued.

The conversation turns to establishing intent: *Did you mean it the way it was reported? Did you know that is not the party's position? Did you intend to differentiate yourself from the party line? Do you see why this is a problem for the party?* Accidents and naivete are common explanations, with some members proffering a valid reason. Sometimes the disciplinarian establishes that the parliamentarian stands by the unsanctioned action. Now the inquisitor is keen to understand the member's motivations in order to propose alternatives: *What are you hoping to accomplish here? How can we encourage people to listen? How can we make them understand?* The member might need to be talked down from a philosophical ledge. If mediation fails, then the conversation turns to getting the member to think through the situation: *Have you considered the consequences of what you are proposing to do? Will you get what you want? How about you play out the next day for me?* There is constant probing to see whether other issues are involved.

If the parliamentarian is adamant, then the disciplinary tone becomes more forceful. A bad cop persona emerges: *Is this something you need to do now? Do you realize some people will agree with you, some will disagree, but everyone is going to see you are offside with party policy? Have you thought about how your opponents are going to use that public stance? Do you want to go down that path?* The conversation becomes firm if the member does not back down, while exercising caution not to provoke further upset: *Is this the hill you want to die on? How about staying away for the vote? Do I need to ask the leader what punishment this involves?* The whip might ask a reliable member to take the dissident out for a drink or meal to discuss why divisiveness is a problem in Canadian party politics.

Irrespective of their fearsome job title, Canadian whips usually prefer the good cop persona, as do most other functionaries of the leader's office who try to sort out trouble: *Listen, the leader is angry, but if you do everything I say we can work this out.* A common pathway is to direct an agitator to speak with the relevant minister or critic to sort out a solution and, if applicable, obey instructions from a communications specialist. A gaffe is addressed by guiding the member how to "walk back" offending comments by making a public retraction or deleting social media posts. For a minor bumble, a parliamentarian is expected to issue a statement of clarification, retraction, and/or apology. An MP whose inflammatory tweet became newsworthy tells what happened internally:

> There was a pile on. That's when the party messaging mechanics kicked in. I had to talk with my fellow MPs. Someone from the PM's communications department called. They said the issue is too complicated for Twitter. They walked me through the technology of deleting the tweets and how to appropriately phrase the apology. They said "keep it simple, don't explain why, here's the standard apology language, and here's why you're going to use it." Then they said to take a couple of days off. They sent me home. If I had some InfoLib lines that day, I might have said "oh, yeah, I'd better steer clear of that." I wanted to be out publicly on the issue, but I wasn't focusing enough on how people would respond emotionally. Lesson learned.[54]

Rising on a point of order at the first opportunity in the legislature might be required. Depending on the circumstances, specialized training or advice from legal personnel might be warranted. Disappearing from public view is the usual practice after a gaffe, bozo eruption, or other off-brand moment, with the hope that depriving the story of new information will cause the matter to fade away. Occasionally, a public statement is not issued because doing so would require the party to declare a policy position on a wedge issue.[55]

The whip and chief of staff mull over apprising the leader when reasonable efforts have failed to persuade an unwavering member to reverse course: *What is this person about? Is this person one of us? Is this person going to be a constant problem? Will this person cause problems in the next election campaign?* Heated discussions ensue when the situation reaches a boiling point. Being castigated by the leader's agents is an emotional event, so later on it can be surprising when the leader acts as though nothing happened and never raises the matter. A backbencher might not recognize that distance from disciplinary action enables positive leader-follower relations. As well, an arm's-length process allows the leader to be an arbitrator if the accused insists on a personal hearing.

A serious predicament dictates that the leader meet with the nonconformist. Leaders can be empathetic when someone is going through a rough patch.[56] Some use a firm tone to impress that unity is non-negotiable. A former government whip outlines how a typical meeting went with Stephen Harper:

> The leader lays out the transgression and says "look, for this type of issue, here's why it's critical that we're all singing from the same song sheet and all on-message. We can't have any doubt about where we stand as a party or as a government on this issue." The leader explains why that is in order to hopefully bring the person around. Perhaps the individual hadn't considered the gravity of it. Ultimately, the leader leaves it in no uncertain terms that, if the individual is unwilling to correct this behaviour, and perhaps apologize for the specific instance, then the leader would question the member's role and place in the caucus.[57]

Party leaders operate in a rougher political world than most caucus members, whose wayward actions add to the leader's mental strain. The power imbalance means that a disciplinary tone is likely to be received more harshly than what was delivered or intended. Recall bias sets in: a disciplinarian recalls being firm but fair, whereas those on the receiving end remember harsh treatment similar to admonishment by a school principal or worse. In any event, a stern talk that carries the weight of officialdom might be interpreted as a scolding unlike any the parliamentarian has experienced in adulthood: *You've got to get along, you can't keep bucking the system! You and your ideas, you'd better shut your mouth and do what I say!* Some leaders find such interactions so distasteful that they refuse to participate in a disciplinary conversation. "Just do it!" was the pet expression of one premier who delegated the rough work to senior staff.[58]

Disciplining a parliamentarian is a delicate act of assessing whether consequences, or the lack thereof, will disrupt group harmony. There are too many variables for anything other than arbitrary exercise of power, if only because members have a higher tolerance of leader-imposed sanctions during moments that group bonds are strong and a lower tolerance when bonds are weak.[59] Most likely, there is no immediate punishment, which incites feelings of apprehension about whatever will happen next. The warning "we will remember this" might be the end of it – or foreshadow reprisal.

Hidden and Private Consequences

Whips and other enforcers can take their time picking from private and public punishments in a disciplinary toolbox. As mentioned, peer pressure can be a more potent aspect of party discipline than the leadership coercing behaviour. Parliamentarians chastise disloyalty because it undermines a culture of mutual support and team bonds.[60] Politicians who rankle the group can be shunned: political friends and acquaintances might become distant and stop talking to them, and eye contact is avoided. An experienced legislator divulges how a caucus can transform from being communitarian to casting off a colleague as undesirable:

> Peer pressure is a big factor in keeping people in line. One of the most intense forms of punishment is if you step outside the lines. How your colleagues react is sometimes worse than what the leader does to you. There's always the possibility your colleagues are going to ostracize you, not speak to you, say nasty things to you. People don't want to go near you because they don't want the leadership to know you're associating with that person. If people come into a room, most likely they won't sit by you. It's the subtle things. If there's a luncheon for somebody, you're the only one excluded.[61]

Leaders set the tone in ostracizing non-conformists. A rival who makes a forceful argument in a cabinet meeting or a non-compliant backbencher might get the silent treatment.[62] Covert passive-aggressive tactics include freezing out parliamentarians by ignoring communications or excluding them from conference calls, meetings, and social events. Those not considered team players can experience delays in obtaining approvals for routine requests. Stamps of disapproval are expressed in petty ways, such as staff moving a *persona non grata* away from the leader during group photo ops, and being left out when the leader passes around Christmas gifts at the office. Some parliamentarians feel bad about the poor treatment and reach out to support a colleague on the outs. During such moments, the whip walks a political tightrope as disciplinarian and consoler.

Escalation occurs when small rewards are rescinded – recall that guards in the Stanford University prison experiment exerted control by transforming necessities into privileges that can be withheld in exchange for compliance. For example, the whip can deny a request for time away from the legislature to convey the importance of showing up on time for committee meetings, or membership in a parliamentary association can be vetoed based on poor attendance in the House of Commons.[63] A back-bencher who is too busy with constituency casework to help the whip, but who suddenly becomes available when informed that the request involves a foreign trip, is advised that someone else will now be asked. Parliamentarians who deliver garbled messages are unaware that the leader's office works behind the scenes to stop them from giving speeches and media interviews. Pretending that there is no room on the list of speakers submitted to the Speaker's office is a standard ploy: "The whip works hand in glove with the House leader," explains a former MP who has served in both of those House officer roles. "The whip can go to the House leader and say 'you know what? Joe Blow has been out of line for a while now. I don't want him up speaking.' You prevent that individual from participating in a debate."[64] The House leader can postpone a motion on which a member intends to disobey the whip's instructions and bring it to the floor at the last moment when that person is not present. As well, a parliamentarian can be told that they have been bumped down an imaginary list of people being considered for advancement. A former Conservative recalls Prime Minister Harper admonishing him before holding out the lure of a potential appointment if the MP conformed: "I was going to offer you something, a role, something I had that is delicate, something important. But now I'm not going to do that anymore. Instead we will just see what happens, what you do, over the next few weeks," Harper reportedly said.[65] Keeping these types of transactions private eludes scrutiny of heavy-handed or inequitable treatment. Privacy also avoids setting a precedent.

Some private sanctions are more overt. A parliamentary secretary might not be permitted to answer questions on behalf of the minister for a few days, or a backbencher might lose the chance to deliver a member's statement. Members are understandably upset when the whip denies them permission to travel with a committee to their own regions or cancels plans for a foreign trip with a parliamentary delegation. The loss of prime office space is a cogent rebuke: "What you giveth, you can also taketh away," says a former whip. "Inevitably, a whip has to use a stick. But a good whip won't brandish the stick, and the stick will be subtle. The general course of pressure comes from not getting the carrots."[66] Confusion is part of control. A head of government who announces at a caucus meeting that a cabinet shuffle is possible motivates ministers and backbenchers alike, all without committing to anything. Sometimes government-side members are surprised to find no apparent consequences for voting against their party, either as individuals or as a group, including parliamentary secretaries.[67] Moving a weak performer out of a role during a general shuffle of positions avoids an explanation that would establish causality. Promoting someone who was previously punished signals that anyone who repents is eligible for promotion.

A predicament for the party leadership is that punishment can send a member on a downward spiral as a group outcast, giving rise to more disruption. As internal mistrust and animosity build, communicating with colleagues is replaced by internalizing. The member feels wronged, is dispirited by amateurism, and is angered by a herd mentality. One unhappy MP summarizes the sentiments of pariahdom:

> You never quite know what you are doing wrong. That's the sign of a toxic workplace. It's almost an abusive relationship in the sense that you can't ever figure out what is the right thing to do. You get labelled as a certain type of person, as someone who has to be managed, and there's really no way out of that no matter how well you perform in other parts of the job. Staff tell you that you'll never get another question in the House, you'll never move off the back benches. Once you're labelled as a troublemaker, that's it.[68]

A social exile might withdraw from participating in the group or become more confrontational. The increasingly isolated individual can disrupt caucus cohesion if withholding privileges merely achieves more irritation. Arguably, the most damning form of private punishment occurs when the party machine unofficially supports another nominee to represent the party in the next general election. In the meantime, the leader must somehow keep the caucus united.

Visible and Public Consequences

Disciplinary measures in the public eye that imply cause and effect are harsh because the member endures the shame of negative press. Being dropped from the cabinet is a high-profile penalty that is topical for political pundits, as is demotion in rank or losing another type of title. Abruptly relinquishing the power, status, and money associated with a frontbench seat is a degrading feeling, especially for a party stalwart with a sizable ego. One former opposition leader tells of relieving a high-profile critic of his place in the shadow cabinet as punishment for ignoring instructions to obtain prior approval from the leader's office to make policy comments.[69] Moving the media darling to a chair in the back of the assembly set a public tone that the leader wanted an orderly, disciplined group. The leader stood firm against pleas from the shunned member's district association and from another member threatening to cross the floor, among other pressures. The fortitude that leaders require to withstand blowback is an underappreciated deterrent to levying a reprimand.

An equivalent public punishment for backbenchers is for the whip, normally with the leader's blessing, to assign someone else to a parliamentary committee. In 2017, a Liberal MP voted in favour of a Conservative motion urging more consultation on the government's small business tax policy. He was removed swiftly from two committees. The backbencher went silent for several months until he was reappointed to one of them: "It's been difficult. I kept a low profile. I didn't say a lot. Of course, I continued to work on my projects in the riding," he said. "But it always bothered me that I didn't have a seat at that table."[70] That another member might welcome being relieved of the extra workload is one reason that comparable situations can have different disciplinary consequences.

It is often caucus members themselves, led by hard-bound partisans and leader devotees, who pressure the leader to expel a colleague whose behaviour splinters caucus unity.[71] Eviction from the caucus occurs when an act constitutes the breaking point after a series of problems or a controversy so egregious that ties must be severed with even the most respected of colleagues. Publicly disparaging the leader or a noxious public action that tarnishes the party's brand are examples. Less well understood in the outside world is that partisans believe that breaking the code of caucus confidentiality is impeachable conduct. A chief of staff reflects on how an MLA was dismissed following escalating internal disputes that had culminated in the public disclosure of information from a caucus meeting:

> Caucus very much self-polices itself, has its own rules, especially confidentiality. One opinionated member released confidential information. That was the last straw. The caucus didn't want him part of their group anymore. They lost the ability to trust him. They want to be able to have discussions without someone walking out the door and telling someone else. In addition, he was offside with some policies in the party platform, which is something we were working through. But going outside of the room was the final straw.[72]

When a relationship frays beyond repair, the communications reality sets in that it is normally better for a leader to push someone out before they jump. As mentioned, securing permission to run for the party again is believed to be what motivates many parliamentarians above all else.[73] Aside from caucus eviction, the ultimate weapon that a party leader wields is blocking a member from seeking re-election with the party: "The leaders use this as a sword of Damocles over MPs' heads: 'Behave and obey, or we won't sign your [nomination] papers,'" explains a two-time MP.[74] On the surface, the Reform Act, 2014, seems to have tempered that worry for MPs by rescinding the exclusivity of a federal party leader as the final authority over whom can be a party candidate. The Canada Elections Act now requires that party officers sign nomination papers instead of the leader, a change that seems to be an administrative formality given that a signatory is likely to be in lockstep agreement with the leader. Regardless, parliamentarians who worry about excommunication might not recognize how desperately the leadership wants to avoid the commotion of a public divorce. A leader is hypersensitive to the possibility of them quitting the caucus, with news of a floor-crossing event potentially putting downward pressure on party support, as with losing a by-election. To minimize disruption, leaders try to wait things out until the next general election, at which point they might shelter behind the candidate vetting process to prevent an incumbent's re-nomination. Things can become so toxic that the leader's decision to demote, suspend, or expel a member of caucus might be conveyed in a terse email or public statement, possibly resulting in the person finding out abruptly on social media or in the news.[75]

A rare case of hidden political management spilled into the public domain in Ontario in 2019. A long-time Member of Provincial Parliament (MPP) built a reputation as a disruptive force in the Progressive Conservative Party of Ontario, epitomized by his populist beliefs that the standing orders need adjustment so that private members can better represent constituents' interests.[76] The MPP caused an uproar by being rude to some parents of children with autism, so Premier Ford suspended him from the caucus, and then a letter from the party president itemizing the backbencher's alleged misconduct somehow became public. It stated that the MPP disobeyed a request that caucus members be mindful of decorum during Question Period. The official alleged poor attendance at caucus meetings and QP preparation. The MPP was said to be late for meetings and/or left them early; he did not attend a party convention or a caucus retreat; he was absent when the legislature was recalled; and he complained about the PC government to the media. Apparently, the premier's office was upset that he promoted self-interests on social media instead of highlighting government activities and that he granted an Independent member time to pose a question in the assembly. The letter concluded with advice that the suspended member should "demonstrate that he is willing to change and be part of a team."[77] In response, the MPP aired grievances on Facebook with micromanagement of the caucus by the chief of staff and a political consultant.[78] He alleged that the premier's office wanted more clapping from backbenchers to support ministers during Question Period and more sharing of government social media posts. The allegations were reminiscent of Robyn Luff's criticisms about the Alberta NDP, and voicing concerns on social media had the same outcome. The MPP's suspension from the caucus became permanent the next day.

INDEPENDENTS

For most parliamentarians who fall out with their party, joining another party is the best path to re-election. Sometimes switching while in office can prove to be a shrewd political move. For most, it can be hazardous given that voters tend to be suspect about the switcher's motives and are unlikely to change their own partisan allegiances (not to mention the social upheaval). Historically, the vote share of MPs who seek re-election with a different party is 5.5 percent lower than if they had remained, a figure that is worse for those who switch for personal gain or are banished from their original party.[79] The exception is incumbents who change parties for policy reasons; they fare about the same in an election with a different party.

The great fear for many partisans interested in continuing to serve is seeking re-election as an Independent. In a Canadian federal election, nearly 5 percent of candidates run as Independents.[80] On average, they obtain less than 2 percent of the vote, barely twice that number in by-elections.[81] The Independents who obtain the most votes often have a spurned party affiliation, or they lost a heated party nomination contest. Between 1972 – the first federal election featuring party labels on the ballot – and 2019, there were 15 federal and 128 provincial general elections, comprising thousands of races in electoral districts. During that time frame, political parties' candidates won 99.8 percent of constituency campaigns, and five provinces did not elect even one Independent candidate (Table 10.1). Just three people elected as an Independent were elected a second time as an Independent.[82] If all of the candidates elected in nearly half a century of elections could be assembled in a midsize hockey arena, the ones wearing the jersey of a political party would fill the stands, the incumbents re-elected as Independents would fit on the team bench, and the non-incumbents elected as Independents could not ice a starting lineup.

Evidently, Independents face significant barriers to election.[83] Election rules favour parties: federally, a party can transfer money to a candidate's campaign, whereas Independents can begin raising funds and issuing tax receipts only when the official campaign begins. There is little motivation for voters to pay attention to Independents or support them, and a

TABLE 10.1
Partisans and Independents elected in Canada (general elections, 1972–2019)

General Elections (n)	Partisans elected	Non-incumbents elected as Independents	Incumbents re-elected as Independents	Seats won by partisans (%)
Canada (15)	4,463	3	8	99.8
British Columbia (12)	856	1	1	99.8
Alberta (13)	1,071	0	3	99.7
Saskatchewan (11)	667	0	0	100
Manitoba (13)	740	0	0	100
Ontario (13)	1,540	0	1	99.9
Quebec (13)	1,589	0	0	100
New Brunswick (12)	663	0	0	100
Nova Scotia (13)	666	0	2	99.7
Prince Edward Island (14)	413	0	0	100
Newfoundland and Labrador (14)	670	1	2	99.6
Total (143)	13,338	5	17	99.8

Notes: Tabulates individual contests, so eight-time MP Carolyn Bennett appears eight times. Treats Independents with a party affiliation as partisan (e.g., Independent Social Credit). Three Independents re-elected as Independents appear in the table twice.
Sources: Federal and provincial electoral offices, election reports, and legislative libraries.

smaller donor pool inhibits their fundraising. Social media are accessible and increase Independents' ability to be noticed, which might explain the recent increase in the number of people seeking election without party affiliation. However, the same communications technology is available to other candidates, including those running with small political parties.

In the legislature, resources and privileges are withheld from members who belong to a parliamentary group too small to constitute official party status. The standing orders limit the ability of Independents to address the assembly.[84] Independents struggle to obtain unanimous consent, to present motions, or to pose a question in Question Period. They might be ineligible to participate in parliamentary committees or interparliamentary groups. The dilemma of styles of representation, combined with limited staff supports, means that it takes considerable time to figure out how to vote on bills and motions, let alone to propose policy. Amendments and trap votes can be especially taxing.[85] Without central monitoring, there is less pressure on Independents to engage with constituents, and there is no whip to help with human resource issues. An Independent told me that the entire experience can be synthesized in one word: *lonely.*

Independent private members do of course enjoy advantages of being free from party discipline. There are no whipped votes, they are free to express themselves, and they can form relationships across party lines. They use social media to raise different points of view, attract a loyal following, and generate media attention. They can develop a reputation for specialized topic expertise and for putting the government on the hot seat. If they get comfortable with the standing orders, they can harangue legislative proceedings by raising points of order and denying unanimous consent on proposed motions, which they can leverage to negotiate privileges with other parliamentary parties. Finally, going home to their families when the House is sitting late into the night is a sense of normalcy that a partisan does not enjoy.[86]

SUMMARY

Party leaders must find an optimal point between loose configuration and strict order. Heated discussions among members of the caucus rarely turn into bullying or harassment, at least by the standards of the political world, though whips do contend with human resource management issues, and some politicians are manipulative in ways that would not be tolerated in other workplaces. Disciplinarians encourage consensus, talk through problems, and explore resolutions. The leader is briefed when necessary and must authorize any significant corrective action. Punishments are dispensed after careful consideration, with a preference for keeping things private, unless there is a pointed need to go public. The final recourse is to sever the relationship. Sitting as an Independent offers refuge, but the prospects of re-election are slim. Occasionally, internal disruption becomes a media extravaganza, as occurred with the SNC-Lavalin affair, discussed next.

11

The SNC-Lavalin Affair

In this chapter, I chronicle the spectacular chain reaction of events known as the SNC-Lavalin affair, which is one of the most significant cases of a Canadian prime minister who expelled MPs from the caucus. The story was headline news for many weeks in 2019. The main public actors were

- SNC-Lavalin Group, a Montreal-based international engineering and construction company
- Prime Minister Justin Trudeau, a Montreal Liberal MP
- Minister Jody Wilson-Raybould, a Vancouver Liberal MP
- Minister Jane Philpott, an Ontario Liberal MP
- Celina Caesar-Chavannes, an Ontario Liberal MP
- Gerald Butts, the prime minister's principal secretary in the PMO
- Michael Wernick, the clerk of the Privy Council.

The story involves SNC-Lavalin's lobbying of government of Canada officials to negotiate an alternative to criminal charges against the company. Some members of the Trudeau government differed about how to respond to the company's request. As internal disagreement played out in the public arena, the news media, particularly the *Globe and Mail,* demonstrated that watchdog journalism can challenge the messaging that results from government lobbying.[1] When a subsidiary of SNC-Lavalin pleaded guilty to a single charge of fraud that December – four years after its lobbying of government personnel began and ten months after conflict within the executive branch was exposed – Prime Minister Trudeau reflected that

FIGURE 11.1 MP Jody Wilson-Raybould testifying to Standing Committee on Justice | Canadian Press/Adrian Wyld (February 27, 2019).

"there are things we could have, should have, would have done differently had we known ... But you don't get do-overs in politics."[2]

What follows is a chronology of events, with emphasis on party discipline and political communications. Original insights from some Members of Parliament and PMO staff supplement a review of public information.[3] The affair's most enduring symbol is MP Jody Wilson-Raybould testifying to a House of Commons committee (see Figure 11.1). The former attorney general exposed the internal politicking by senior members of the Trudeau government who had carefully attempted to persuade her to authorize an alternative for SNC-Lavalin. Wilson-Raybould's defiance resulted in the Canadian Press proclaiming her its 2019 newsmaker of the year. As we shall see, she and others endured significant political repercussions when their private disagreements became public.

PROLOGUE

To grasp the party discipline side of the SNC-Lavalin saga, which transpired from February to April 2019, we need an understanding of what led to those public events. The backstory reveals the many interconnected layers of public policy in a global society. Some of these layers were hidden in plain sight. Readers uninterested in the policy minutiae might wish to skip to the section "Internal Disagreement Becomes Public" on page 292.

Events Prior to the Trudeau Liberals Forming the Government

In Canada, an attorney general is simultaneously the minister of justice. The latter is partisan and political; the former ought not to be. An attorney general is "the person responsible for defending the rule of law" and "the chief law officer of the Crown" who puts the public interest first.[4] A minister of justice participates in developing public policy and provides legal advice to the cabinet. By convention, at the federal level the positions are jointly held by a minister with legal training.[5] The minister of justice and attorney general of Canada (MoJAG) is therefore an officeholder whose two roles sometimes conflict.

The role conflict is embodied in the interpretation of a constitutional convention that originated with a statement in the United Kingdom's House of Lords in 1951. Attorney General for England and Wales Hartley Shawcross stated that, when deciding whether or not to proceed with a criminal prosecution, it is up to an attorney general to weigh available information, including the broad public policy implications, and to be the one to make a final decision:

> The responsibility for the eventual decision rests with the Attorney General, and he is not to be put, and is not put, under pressure by his colleagues in the matter ... If political considerations which in the broad sense that I have indicated affect government in the abstract arise it is the Attorney General, applying his judicial mind, who has to be the sole judge of those considerations.[6]

This became known as the Shawcross doctrine, which shields an attorney general from "pressure" from colleagues who advocate for special treatment in criminal prosecutions. It accords deference to the rule of law over politics yet acknowledges the need to acknowledge "political considerations." Historically, a Canadian attorney general who opted to interfere with a decision to prosecute could evade public scrutiny. To reconcile that at the national level, the Harper Conservative government introduced the Director of Public Prosecutions Act (2006), which created the Public Prosecution Service of Canada. The Act assigns prosecutorial decisions to the director of public prosecutions (a public servant), unless the attorney general (a politician) overrules the director. If so, then the government must formally announce the minister's decision. Section 15(1) of the Act states that "the Attorney General may only assume conduct of a prosecution after first consulting the Director. The Attorney General must then give to the Director a notice of intent to assume conduct of the prosecution and publish it in the *Canada Gazette* without delay."[7] That an attorney general must contemplate the political aspects of criminal prosecution without others trying to exert political pressure constitutes a unique form of policy process.

A further contextual element in the SNC-Lavalin affair is Canada's membership in the Organisation for Economic Co-operation and Development (OECD). The OECD promotes global policy norms. In the 1990s, the intergovernmental organization discussed ways to address foreign bribery by corporations.[8] It sought to resolve the lack of incentive for domestic prosecutors in the wealthy West to investigate an international company that benefited from corruption in the developing world. The lack of political will to pursue prosecution incurs a significant cost to developing economies. In 1999, an OECD convention took effect for member nation-states, including Canada, to combat the bribery of foreign public officials in international business transactions. The Chrétien Liberal government passed the Corruption of Foreign Public Officials Act in response to these concerns. Enforcement has been limited.[9]

Enter SNC-Lavalin. Founded in 1911 in Montreal, it grew to become Canada's largest engineering and construction company. One of its largest shareholders is the Caisse de dépôt et placement du Québec, which manages the Quebec Pension Plan. Worldwide, SNC-Lavalin employed approximately 50,000 people in 2019, of whom 9,000 were in Canada, including 3,400 in Quebec, 3,000 in Ontario, and 1,000 in British Columbia.[10] The company occupies a prominent place in the Quebec economic landscape, but it has a shifty legal history. Its executives have paid bribes to public officials to win a McGill University Health Centre contract and to build a bridge in Bangladesh as well as circumvented laws prohibiting corporate donations to Canadian political parties.[11]

From 2001 to 2011, SNC-Lavalin Construction placed $127 million in two shell companies operated by a senior executive in the company. Approximately $47 million was given to the son of Libyan dictator Muammar Gaddafi on top of paying for an assortment of luxury personal expenses.[12] In return, the Libyan government awarded the company dozens of contracts for designing and building public infrastructure, including an irrigation project, an airport, and a jail. In February 2015, under the Corruption of Foreign Public Officials Act, the RCMP laid criminal charges of fraud and corruption against SNC-Lavalin Group, SNC-Lavalin International, and SNC-Lavalin Construction. If convicted, the company and its subsidiaries would be subject to a multi-million-dollar fine and be ineligible to bid on government of Canada contracts for up to a decade.[13] Furthermore, conviction would disqualify the company from obtaining Quebec government contracts as per that province's Integrity in Public Contracts Act. A criminal conviction would also be a major stain on its global brand. SNC-Lavalin's public relations stance was that the company no longer employed the executives involved with the alleged crimes. As early as 2014, its chief executive officer (CEO) was warning that business would shrink if the company was charged. A foreign multinational might acquire it and relocate the Montreal headquarters outside Canada. The CEO was concerned that "some lower-level person" would pursue charges without regard for the economic implications: "We operate on image," he added.[14] This constituted the company's position: legal proceedings would lead to job losses because of the international damage to its reputation and its ineligibility to bid on government contracts. It warned that thousands of jobs would be lost in Montreal.

The Conservative government led by Stephen Harper was unlikely to intervene. The party's constitution refers to a belief that members of the government should conduct themselves in an ethical manner.[15] Law and order were part of the Harper government's brand, and one of its priorities had been to pass the Federal Accountability Act to toughen conflict of interest rules in the wake of the Liberal sponsorship scandal that besmirched the Chrétien and Martin governments.[16] That omnibus bill amended the Lobbyists Registration Act (2006) to toughen the regulation of lobbying, introduced tougher ethical standards through the Conflict of Interest Act (2006), and created the aforementioned Public Prosecution

Service of Canada. In 2015, it was the Conservatives who adopted an integrity regime for procurement, including the policy that suppliers of goods and services convicted of an offence be suspended from doing business with the federal government. A further element is that the Conservative power base is in western Canada. The party's support is low in Montreal, which is a Liberal stronghold.

Justin Trudeau Heads a Liberal Government

In October 2015, the Liberal Party of Canada vaulted from thirty-four seats in the previous general election to 184 seats. The Liberals had forty seats in Quebec, of which twenty-five were in the Montreal region, including one represented by Trudeau. Many MPs were relatively new to party politics, including first-timers Celina Caesar-Chavannes, Jane Philpott, and Jody Wilson-Raybould. A greater presence of women in the government and a renewed relationship with Indigenous peoples were among an assortment of ways that the Trudeau-led Liberals planned on doing politics differently. The party had pledged to make policy decisions based on facts, to promote transparent government, to stop the abuse of omnibus bills, and to strengthen standing committees.[17] As well, Liberal MPs would have more free votes.

After the swearing-in ceremony, Prime Minister Trudeau announced that "government by cabinet is back," a purposeful divergence from centralized power in the Harper PMO.[18] He unveiled what was dubbed the first gender-balanced cabinet, presiding over fifteen men and fifteen women. Wilson-Raybould was the minister of justice and attorney general of Canada, the first Indigenous person to hold those positions. Her experiences with Indigenous politics were different from party politics:

> I was an Indigenous politician before getting involved in federal politics. I was never a member of a political party. Indigenous communities don't function or operate based on partisanship. We have vigorous debates and discussions, but they're not broken down in terms of predetermined lines around parties. I was unaware of how deeply rooted the party system is or how far reaching party discipline and message discipline [are]. It's very tightly controlled. I actually believed that we were going to do politics differently. I still believe we must.[19]

Philpott was the minister of health and later served as the minister of Indigenous services. Caesar-Chavannes was a parliamentary secretary to the prime minister.

At its first meeting after the general election, the Liberal caucus did not follow new provisions to hold four votes about curtailing the leader's authority, brought about by the Reform Act, 2014. There was some mild confusion about how to administer and register a vote; as a result, Trudeau would continue to make the final decision about an MP sitting in the Liberal caucus. He informed the caucus that the government whip would have a delicate touch. Rather than being a disciplinarian, the whip would be an interlocutor between the cabinet and backbenchers when a bill or motion progressed.[20] The whip would encourage private members to raise concerns at the earliest opportunity and urge ministers to consider the suggestions.

Lobbying Leads to a Criminal Code Amendment

The formation of a Liberal government was a political opportunity for SNC-Lavalin to negotiate pausing the charges. In December 2015, the self-described "experts at mastering complexity" company was approved to continue bidding on federal government contracts while facing the criminal charges.[21] In early 2016, a sustained lobbying campaign got under way as representatives met with the prime minister, ministers, and political staff, during which the CEO informed Trudeau of the company's interest in a negotiated agreement.[22] The PM asked a senior adviser to look into the matter and monitor developments. Company representatives did not meet with Wilson-Raybould, presumably because of the Shawcross doctrine.[23]

Political staff and public servants across a swath of central agencies and departments were now discussing remediation agreements (defined below), used in the United States and United Kingdom, and a decision was made to hold public consultations. In late 2017, the government released a discussion paper on the possibility that Canada would introduce rules to permit deferred prosecution agreements (DPAs). The consultation document explained the negotiated agreements this way:

> A DPA is a voluntary agreement negotiated between an accused and the responsible prosecution authority. Under a DPA, the criminal prosecution

is suspended for a set period of time. During that time, the accused must comply with the terms of the agreement. If the accused complies, the charges are withdrawn when the DPA expires and no criminal conviction results. If the accused does not comply, charges may be revived at any point during the term of the DPA and a prosecution may be pursued and a conviction sought.[24]

SNC-Lavalin used a more succinct definition in its filings with the federal registry of lobbyists: "DPAs are sentencing agreements negotiated between a prosecution authority and a corporation charged with an offence, usually in the context of white collar crime."[25] The low-key public consultations found that a majority of participants were in favour of the idea.[26] The cabinet discussed it on several occasions,[27] and the Department of Justice developed a memorandum to the cabinet about amending the Criminal Code, which required Minister Wilson-Raybould's approval.

As the bill was being prepared for introduction in the House of Commons, an incident arose in February 2018 signalling that the prime minister and MoJAG were open to politicizing the rule of law. In a controversial criminal case, a Saskatchewan jury found a white man not guilty of murder for fatally shooting a young Indigenous man who was part of a group causing mischief on the farmer's property. The acquittal led to public protests by Indigenous peoples amid allegations of a discriminatory legal system. Trudeau, Wilson-Raybould, and Philpott all tweeted empathy for the victim's family. Their calls to "do better" (Trudeau and Wilson-Raybould) and to "improve justice and fairness" (Philpott), retweeted by some Liberal MPs, alarmed some members of the legal community who voiced concern about politicians compromising the independence of the criminal justice system.[28]

The next month Minister of Finance Bill Morneau (a Toronto MP) presented Bill C-74, Budget Implementation Act, 2018, No. 1. Budget implementation bills are omnibus bills because of their scope. They often contain proposals that the government does not want to receive scrutiny, a practice that the Liberal platform had deemed "undemocratic."[29] The 582-page omnibus bill was organized into six parts, the last of which included twenty divisions to amend a variety of other acts. The final division was summarized as follows:

> Division 20 of Part 6 amends the Criminal Code to establish a remediation
> agreement regime. Under this regime, the prosecutor may negotiate a
> remediation agreement with an organization that is alleged to have com-
> mitted an offence of an economic character referred to in the schedule
> to Part XXII.1 of that Act and the proceedings related to that offence are
> stayed if the organization complies with the terms of the agreement.[30]

The proposed amendments to the Criminal Code outlined the scope of a remediation agreement, including a provision that such an agreement could be negotiated if an alleged offence occurred before the Act was granted royal assent. The amendments were buried in the Budget Implementation Act for reasons of expediency and because Minister Wilson-Raybould was unwilling to be their public spokesperson.[31] The Speaker did not use his authority to split up an omnibus bill that contains unrelated topics.

SNC-Lavalin lawyers had already reached out to the Public Prosecution Service of Canada when MPs scrutinized Bill C-74 in May 2018.[32] At the Standing Committee on Finance, members put questions to a public servant with the Department of Justice. Some Liberals and Conservatives were perplexed about the need for, and the appropriateness of, the DPA idea.[33] Partisan posturing replaced scrutiny in the bigger forum of budget estimate debates by a Committee of the Whole – a meeting of the House presided over by the deputy Speaker – where Liberal backbenchers gushed about the government's accomplishments. The Criminal Code amendment was the subject of a single question from a Conservative MP, and the finance minister responded by saying that the change would help the economy.[34]

A week later the company's CEO briefed Conservative leader Andrew Scheer.[35] Company representatives also met with some senators, including the government representative in the Senate.[36] Among the first public signs of tension occurred when a Senate committee reviewing the omnibus bill was informed that Wilson-Raybould was unavailable to appear to address its questions about amendments to the Criminal Code.[37] The budget passed third reading on June 6; she was among those voting in favour of it. It was now a foregone conclusion that remediation agreements would soon be a legal tool available to the government.

A tangential matter occurred in August 2018. Celina Caesar-Chavannes's social media activism had contributed to an abrasive relationship with PMO message managers (see pp. 69–70). By this time, Caesar-Chavannes was parliamentary secretary to the minister of international development. That month she decided against continuing as a parliamentary secretary, citing the negative toll of her online skirmishes.[38] As a backbench MP, she was not privy to information about the SNC-Lavalin issue. Nevertheless, the stories would end up intersecting.

Deadlock over Deferred Prosecution Agreement

In early September 2018, the director of public prosecutions (Kathleen Roussel) notified the Office of the Attorney General that she would not authorize a DPA for SNC-Lavalin. She arrived at that decision because of "the severity and breadth of the offence," coupled with the company's legal history.[39] A ministerial staffer informed the PMO and the finance minister's office.[40] Wilson-Raybould researched the matter, decided not to intervene, and apprised the PMO that she would let the director's decision stand.

The stance befuddled the prime minister, the finance minister, and their staff. Many conversations were held that month. SNC-Lavalin representatives presented a slide show to the Department of Finance showing that a criminal conviction would split up the company and result in its headquarters being moved to another country.[41] In a mid-September meeting, the prime minister and the clerk (Michael Wernick, the nonpartisan head of the public service) warned Wilson-Raybould of potential economic impacts. In another encounter, Morneau did the same after she requested that the finance minister's staff cease pursuing the matter with her staff. In a phone call with her, Wernick delved into partisan politics by pointing out that the Quebec election campaign was under way and that Trudeau is a Quebec MP.[42] Squabbling erupted among staff, including between the finance minister's office and the MoJAG's office, and a "communication breakdown" occurred as information was withheld from or not received by the PMO and PCO.[43] Later the controversy turned on different interpretations of these exchanges, particularly whether the prime minister and his agents were directing the attorney general about what to do.

In October, SNC-Lavalin disclosed that the government had denied its request to negotiate an agreement, prompting the company's share price to drop. The PMO asked the director of communications in the justice department to contact news media with the following clarification: "The director of public prosecutions made the decision. It is independent of the government of Canada."[44] SNC-Lavalin's representatives lobbied ministers, at least one of whom discussed the issue with Wilson-Raybould.[45] The PMO decided to seek external legal advice about the authority of the attorney general so that she could better equip herself to consider the public interest. The company stepped up its efforts. It applied for a judicial review of the director of public prosecutions' decision based on the economic implications of a criminal prosecution. Its representatives provided government personnel with a legal opinion from a former Supreme Court justice declaring that "a deliberate decision from the centre" would be required.[46] That opinion circulated among senior PMO staff and numerous ministers but not the attorney general. The CEO wrote a letter to the prime minister seeking a meeting. The Privy Council Office recommended that Trudeau refer the request to the MoJAG, which he did.

That November, the PMO worked out a number of strategies to achieve its objective of authorizing a deferred prosecution agreement, including bringing in a former chief justice of the Supreme Court as a mediator. According to Trudeau, his chief of staff (Katie Telford) did not tell him about this idea.[47] Early that December his principal secretary (Gerald Butts) met with Wilson-Raybould to discuss the file.[48] A week later the president of the Treasury Board (Scott Brison) informed Butts that he would retire from politics in the New Year. That unexpected news coincided with Wilson-Raybould's sending a letter to the prime minister emphasizing that the Public Prosecution Service of Canada "is solely responsible" for decisions on deferred prosecution agreements and that it "operates at arms-length and is independent."[49] Telford and Butts urgently summoned the MoJAG's chief of staff. Exasperated, the government's two pre-eminent political staffers urged a resolution in order to save jobs.[50] The next day, December 19, the clerk spoke with the attorney general by telephone to convey that the prime minister wanted to negotiate an agreement and was "quite determined ... to get it done one way or another" in order to preserve nine thousand jobs with "a signature Canadian firm."[51] Wilson-Raybould repeated that she would not support political interference in prosecutorial independence. They were at an impasse.

Cabinet Shuffle

On January 7, 2019, Justin Trudeau phoned Jody Wilson-Raybould to inform her that she was being reassigned. It was the first time since mid-September that they had directly spoken; other communication about SNC-Lavalin had occurred through intermediaries.[52] It later emerged that Wilson-Raybould turned down redeployment as minister of Indigenous services because of her opposition to the Indian Act.[53]

A cabinet shuffle on January 14 was spun as predicated by the need to fill an unexpected vacancy. Wilson-Raybould was moved to veterans' affairs, and Jane Philpott was shuffled from Indigenous services to oversee the Treasury Board. A parliamentary secretary (David Lametti, a Montreal MP) was promoted to MoJAG. The redeployment of Wilson-Raybould to a lower-profile role struck some as unusual, especially given that she tweeted a letter of reflection about her service in the vacated portfolio, which included the following passage:

> It is a pillar of our democracy that our system of justice be free from even the perception of political interference and uphold the highest levels of public confidence. As such, it has always been my view that the Attorney General of Canada must be non-partisan, more transparent in the principles that are the basis of decisions, and, in this respect, always willing to speak truth to power.[54]

A parliamentary convention is that ministers do not speak about their former portfolios without authorization.[55] Therefore, the remarks signalled that something was amiss but lacked context for the outside world. Similarly, reasons were not apparent why her chief of staff was transferred to veterans' affairs instead of the normal practice of providing continuity by remaining in justice.[56]

Trouble was brewing. Privately, Philpott had warned the prime minister that Wilson-Raybould might link the redeployment to the deadlock.[57] On February 5, the latter informed Butts that the *Globe and Mail*'s Ottawa bureau chief (Robert Fife) was preparing a story on SNC-Lavalin.

Wilson-Raybould relayed that she "did not say anything" in her conversation with Fife: "He seemed to know a great deal. Not sure how this could be," she wrote to Butts.[58] A well-honed image of government unity shattered when the story broke two days later, setting in motion a cascading series of events.

INTERNAL DISAGREEMENT BECOMES PUBLIC

In early February 2019, the *Globe and Mail* reported that, as attorney general, Minister Wilson-Raybould had refused to give in to pressure from the PMO to authorize negotiating a deferred prosecution agreement for SNC-Lavalin. The allegations from unnamed sources prompted two months of public debate about ministerial independence, political interference, the rule of law, and the political system itself. Party discipline and political communications are the focus of the following pages.

A News Bombshell

Prime Minister Trudeau was at a train station north of Toronto on February 7, 2019, to drum up publicity about government support for regional transit. The headline in that morning's *Globe and Mail* had brought the policy stalemate into the open: "PMO Pressed Justice Minister to Abandon Prosecution of SNC-Lavalin."[59] In the story, a spokesperson stated that the "Prime Minister's Office did not direct the attorney-general to draw any conclusions on this matter."[60] Trudeau repeated that line when the media asked him to comment: "The allegations reported in the story are false. At no time did I or my office direct the current or previous attorney-general to make any particular decision in this matter ... As I've said, at no time did we direct the attorney-general, current or previous, to make any decision whatsoever in this matter."[61] It was the moment that many private members became aware of the topic. The Liberal Research Bureau sent urgent messaging to Liberal MPs and their Parliament Hill assistants (see Figure 11.2), by which time the caucus was already taking its cue from the prime minister's remarks. Observers noticed the legalistic emphasis on the word *direct*.[62] In Question Period, the Conservatives parroted message lines as they denounced Trudeau for sticking to a script.[63] As media attention intensified, it was pointless for backbenchers to ask ministers for information because of cabinet confidentiality, providing fertile ground for

FIGURE 11.2
Urgent messaging about SNC-Lavalin story, Liberal Research Bureau

From: Liberal Research Bureau
Sent: February 7, 2019 12:25pm
To: Liberal MPs, Hill assistants
Subject: Urgent: Lines re: SNC-Lavalin

Hello,

Media may ask Members on the way into QP or the House about the SNC Lavalin and the Globe and Mail story.

Below are suggested lines. If you are pressed for more, simply say that you have nothing to add to the story.

EN
- The allegations in this story are false.
- Neither the current or previous AG has been directed by the PMO to make any decision on this matter.

FR
- Les allégations contenues dans cet article sont fausses.
- Ni la procureure générale antérieure, ou le procureur général actuel, n'ont reçu de directives en ce qui a trait à la prise de décision dans ce dossier.

Thank you,

Source: Interview participant.

gossip on the Hill. Internal messages would attempt to reassure the caucus that everything was under control. Many Liberals would have reasons to doubt those reassurances whenever public events showed otherwise.

Unnamed sources were the foundations of successive news reports. On February 9, the Canadian Press quoted anonymous government personnel who criticized Wilson-Raybould. According to them, "she had become a thorn in the side of the cabinet, someone insiders say was difficult to get along with, known to berate fellow cabinet ministers openly at the table, and who others felt they had trouble trusting."[64] The news agency later acknowledged that reporting from nameless sources who cast aspersions did not meet its journalistic standards.

The crisis percolated as details trickled out and the opposition agitated. On February 10, the new MoJAG confirmed that the government might pursue a deferred prosecution agreement – which signalled to Wilson-Raybould that her resistance to a negotiated agreement was the reason that she was shuffled.[65] She met with the prime minister to discuss the situation. On February 11, the New Democrats revealed that the conflict of interest and ethics commissioner had initiated an investigation. Trudeau held a press conference in Vancouver to make an announcement about affordable housing; instead, journalists peppered him with questions about the dispute. The PMO and Wilson-Raybould's staff negotiated the messaging that he had informed the then attorney general in September that "any decisions on matters involving the director of public prosecutions were hers alone."[66] Trudeau added that as a member of the cabinet Wilson-Raybould evidently supported the government. Hours later her resignation would catapult the story into the dramatized personal conflict that transcends politics.

Executive Resignations

Jody Wilson-Raybould stepped down from the cabinet on February 12.[67] In a letter of resignation posted to Twitter, she acknowledged media interest in recent events and stated that a former Supreme Court justice would counsel her about speaking publicly. Below her signature was her Kwak'wala name, Puglaas.

Among those who voiced personal support on social media were Minister Philpott and MP Caesar-Chavannes.[68] The hashtag #StandWithJody began trending. The prime minister, who was in Winnipeg to make an announcement about transit infrastructure, held an emergency conference call with the cabinet, followed by a one-way call with the Liberal caucus to assure them that discussions on SNC-Lavalin were above board.[69] Caesar-Chavannes informed Trudeau by telephone that she would not seek re-election. They agreed to delay a public announcement in order to avoid "the optics of having two women of colour leaving."[70] That he used an angry tone would emerge later.

On February 13, the House of Commons Standing Committee on Justice and Human Rights held an emergency closed-door meeting to explore whether to investigate the allegations. Michael Wernick was one of the public servants whom they heard from in camera. There were no obvious recriminations when Wayne Long – the MP previously punished for voting in favour of an opposition motion seeking more consultation about small business tax changes – posted letters on Twitter calling for a transparent investigation of the SNC-Lavalin matter (February 11) and proclaiming that the justice committee should expand its witness list (February 13).[71] On February 14, the committee chair, a Montreal Liberal MP, gave media interviews in which he suggested that Wilson-Raybould was shuffled because she does not speak French.[72] He apologized on Twitter. The speculation exposed a party marred by the trials of a bilingual federation: punditry in Quebec favoured negotiating with SNC-Lavalin, whereas political commentators in the rest of Canada favoured prosecution.[73]

The story catapulted into executive turmoil when the prime minister's principal secretary resigned on February 18. The announcement shocked Ottawa circles because Gerald Butts wielded considerable power and is close friends with Trudeau. In his resignation letter on Twitter, Butts denied that anyone in the PMO pressured the former attorney general and explained that he was resigning so as not to be a distraction. The next day the cabinet spent two hours deliberating a request from Wilson-Raybould to address them before agreeing to let her in. Patty Hajdu, the minister of labour, who previously served as the minister of the status of women, was among those urging that their former ministerial colleague be permitted to speak.[74] The ex-minister was unapologetic at the cabinet meeting. Afterward, she took her regular spot on the government front benches in the House of Commons.[75]

The national caucus meeting on February 20 was almost entirely devoted to the need for unity. The chief of staff began a hiatus from attending the meetings; no other PMO personnel were present.[76] It was the first caucus meeting for Wilson-Raybould since the dispute had become public. Trudeau apologized for not defending her against what many, including the Union of BC Indian Chiefs, were condemning as racist and sexist media portrayals. Afterward, the prime minister broke caucus confidentiality by informing reporters that he had apologized, and the caucus chair – another Montreal MP – spun a message of cohesion: "We had a fantastic meeting today. There's complete solidarity and the mood was great," the chair said.[77] The House went on to debate an NDP motion urging the prime minister to waive solicitor-client privilege to permit Wilson-Raybould to reveal what had transpired and calling for a public inquiry.[78] Liberal backbenchers could vote freely because the motion did not concern the platform, confidence matters, or the Charter of Rights and Freedoms. The cabinet, including Minister Philpott, and all but two Liberals voted to defeat it. Nathaniel Erskine-Smith – the Toronto MP who rebuffed the party line the most often in the 42nd Parliament – and Long were the two Liberal dissenters. All NDP, Conservative, and Bloc Québécois MPs present voted in favour of the motion, as did all Independents and the lone MPs with the Green Party and People's Party. Caesar-Chavannes and Wilson-Raybould did not vote. The former MoJAG informed the House that she needed the prime minister to waive solicitor-client privilege and cabinet confidentiality in order "to speak my truth."[79]

Committee Testimony

The justice committee began hearing public testimony on February 21. The strange preamble from Wernick that he worried about the possibility of an assassination in the upcoming federal election campaign overshadowed the rest of his testimony. On February 25, Trudeau authorized an Order-in-Council to extend a limited waiver of cabinet confidence so that Wilson-Raybould and others could testify to the committee, a rare occurrence that affirmed the gravity of the situation for the government. Canadian news outlets were now treating developments as breaking news, briefly elevating the political crisis into a focusing event. The implication was that Trudeau's political future was at stake.

On February 27, with the national news networks cutting away for live coverage, Wilson-Raybould met with the justice committee for approximately four hours (see Figure 11.1). She testified about experiencing sustained pressure from eleven people in central agencies: the PM and, in the PMO, his principal secretary, the chief of staff, the director of policy, two senior advisers and a policy adviser; the finance minister and his chief of staff; the clerk of the Privy Council; and the deputy minister of justice. Wilson-Raybould alleged that meetings, phone calls, emails, and texts included "express statements regarding the necessity of interference in the SNC-Lavalin matter, the potential of consequences and veiled threats if a DPA was not made available to SNC."[80] Trudeau was among those who had urged a solution. During the fourth round of questioning, the former attorney general made her position clear:

> I was protecting a fundamental constitutional principle of prosecutorial independence, and the independence of our judiciary ... As long as I was the attorney general, I was going to ensure that the independence of the director of public prosecutions in the exercise of their discretion was not interfered with ... There was a concerted and sustained effort to attempt to politically interfere with my role as the attorney general. As the attorney general, I did not let that happen ... It is incumbent upon all of us to uphold our institutions and to uphold the rule of law. That's why I'm here.[81]

The testimony hinted at the PMO's communications management thinking: the chief of staff had apparently offered reassurances that, if the then attorney general was nervous about overruling the director of public prosecutions, the PMO would "line up all kinds of people to write op-eds saying that what she is doing is proper."[82] For their part, the Conservatives had switched some higher-profile MPs onto the committee for rhetorical advantage. One Conservative's questioning led Wilson-Raybould to urge an examination of whether or not the jointly held roles of minister of justice and attorney general should be bifurcated, as occurs in the United Kingdom.[83] The Conservatives also remarked on the long-standing professional relationships between two vice-presidents at SNC-Lavalin and two PMO staff involved with the file. After the gripping testimony, Scheer asserted that Trudeau had lost the moral authority to govern, and called on the prime minister to resign. NDP leader Jagmeet Singh repeated the party's calls for a public inquiry. Trudeau ignored them.

The executive instability was punctuated by more cabinet changes. On March 1, a cabinet shuffle filled the vacancy created by Wilson-Raybould's departure. By this point, Jane Philpott had advised the prime minister, some ministers, and some senior political staff that the issue was so disconcerting that she too might resign. On March 4, she did. In a letter of resignation that she posted on Twitter, Philpott declared an inability to uphold cabinet solidarity over the government's handling of the criminal case:

> In Canada, the constitutional convention of cabinet solidarity means, among other things, that ministers are expected to defend all cabinet decisions. A minister must always be prepared to defend other ministers publicly, and must speak in support of the government and its policies. Given this convention and the current circumstances, it is untenable for me to continue to serve as a cabinet minister ... Sadly, I have lost confidence in how the government has dealt with this matter and in how it has responded to the issues raised.[84]

Philpott was troubled by messaging that the allegations were false when she believed them to be true ("I draw the line at lying," she would later say).[85] Despite her public declaration of a lack of confidence, she stayed in the caucus, and for the remainder of the 42nd Parliament both she and Wilson-Raybould remained in the parliamentary offices assigned to them as ministers. Adding to the bedlam, the NDP ethics critic sent an open letter to the prime minister calling for the resignation of the clerk.

The next day, March 5, the prime minister intended to be in Regina to talk at a Canadian Tire store about climate change rebates and to attend a party fundraiser.[86] At this point, events were paralyzing the government, and it could no longer take caucus support for granted. Erskine-Smith remarked that he would "lose some confidence" if it were determined "that the intervention was made for naked partisan gain and electoral gain."[87] Although rare, such comments exposed the serious concerns in the Liberal caucus, causing the PMO to worry about the possibility of more resignations. It cancelled the Regina events so that Trudeau could participate in undisclosed private meetings in Ottawa.

The prime minister's former principal secretary injected a measure of calm by testifying on March 6 with a competing interpretation of events. Butts's primary message to the justice committee was that private executive-level conversations are a normal political function. He asserted the need for an agreement because nine thousand Canadians could lose their jobs otherwise.[88] If Wilson-Raybould was gravely concerned, he said, she had not made that abundantly clear to him. The testimony underscored the central coordination role of the PMO. An extrinsic detail was that text messaging on smartphones is a preferred method of communication.

Butts exposed a senior staffer's power over elected officials. He reflected on his experience advising heads of government about the suitability of backbenchers to appoint to the cabinet and which portfolios to assign. Earlier that year, identifying a new minister involved weighing whether MPs passed over for promotion would consequently not seek re-election. Butts declared that Wilson-Raybould's redeployment to veterans' affairs was a routine reassignment. Wary of her refusal to move to Indigenous services, he advised the prime minister that, "if you allow a minister to veto a cabinet shuffle by refusing to move, you soon will not be able to manage cabinet."[89] The Liberals would go on to use their majority of committee votes to end the investigation.

On March 7, Prime Minister Trudeau assumed the responsibility to be aware when there is a breakdown in trust between the PMO and ministers. He conceded that there was room for improvement in how he and his staff interact with the caucus, but he telegraphed that if anyone had trepidations the onus was on that person to inform him: "I've always tried to foster an environment in which people can come and share with me their concerns, large or small, whether they be cabinet ministers or caucus members," he said.[90] Celina Caesar-Chavannes contradicted those claims in a provocative tweet that led to a news story in the *Globe and Mail* on March 8 revealing that Trudeau had yelled on the phone when she had informed him that she would not seek re-election. The coverage on International Women's Day was the antithesis of the type of headlines the PMO tries to corral for its feminist prime minister and was more evidence that improved internal routing was necessary in the PMO: "I'm rethinking some of the processes of how we support cabinet and caucus members, how we function as an office," Trudeau reflected.[91] Some Liberal stalwarts from past governments were asked for advice about how to manage internal disagreement.

The next day a number of deleted Liberal MPs gushed on social media about Trudeau's willingness to listen to women. Two of them were caught posting verbatim heartfelt messages. Confronted with the blatant mimicry, they denied coordination or plagiarism, and the PMO added that "MPs speak for themselves."[92] The consequences for another backbencher who refused to participate in the messaging brigade would emerge months later. A former deputy PM to Jean Chrétien injected a dose of controversy when she advocated against mischaracterizing the dispute as an attempt to silence women. She urged the ex-ministers to leave the caucus.[93]

On March 13, the Liberals used their majority on the justice committee to deny the opposition's request to call Wilson-Raybould to testify again. Another cabinet shuffle – the third in as many months – occurred on March 18. Trudeau announced that a former Liberal MoJAG (Anne McLellan) would provide advice about whether to separate the justice and attorney general portfolios. As well, Wernick declared that he would be retiring. It was a response to pressure from the opposition about the top civil servant's impartiality, notwithstanding that the ethics commissioner would later clear him of conflict of interest allegations.[94] The next day was budget day. In an election year, there should be sustained media coverage of budget goodies. That did not happen given the swirling controversy.

The Last Straw

The presence of dissenters in the Liberal caucus shook its team ethos. On March 20, prior to the national caucus meeting, the Liberals' BC and Ontario caucuses were under strict instructions to keep their discussions private. Nevertheless, it emerged that BC MPs accused Wilson-Raybould of leaking information to the media and harming the government.[95] MPs interrupted when she defended herself. She took notes, denied that she had leaked information, and affirmed her support for the party. At the Ontario meeting, MPs chastised Caesar-Chavannes and especially Philpott for undermining the leader. Some attendees told Philpott that they liked her, that they had stood by her on controversial issues, but that her public stand put Liberal jobs on the line. They asked her to stop taking notes. Her colleagues demanded that she make information available when she cautioned that more details had yet to come out; she did not disclose that *Maclean's* had interviewed her the day before.[96] The confrontation was so upsetting that Philpott did not go to the ensuing national caucus meeting at which the creation of a PMO caucus relations office was announced.[97] Caucus engagement had become a sudden priority to Trudeau, who up to that point could be difficult to reach. The conversations at the regional caucus meetings were not raised at the national meeting. Afterward,

Caesar-Chavannes informed the PMO that she would sit as an Independent, resulting in media headlines that a Liberal MP had quit the caucus and Conservative messaging that the prime minister was a "fake feminist."[98]

It proved to be a long day for other reasons. March 20 was an opposition day, when the official opposition controls the House of Commons agenda. A thirty-hour filibuster ensued as the Conservatives prompted voting on 257 motions related to budget estimates. The confidence convention applied, which meant that Liberal MPs had to be present to avoid losing a vote in the middle of the night, lest the government fall. The Conservatives pledged to withdraw the motions in exchange for the full release of cabinet confidence so that Wilson-Raybould could testify again.

On March 21, *Maclean's* published the first interview with Philpott since her departure from the cabinet. She stated her unwavering belief that, if pursued, overruling the director of public prosecutions would compromise the independence of the justice system. Philpott discussed the internal conflict of whether to stay silent so as not to harm colleagues' electoral fortunes or to stand up against perceived wrongdoing. She affirmed her support for the Liberal Party – "I'm not trying to damage our party or our government" – but that message was lost amid headlines that Trudeau was hiding damaging information and trying "to shut down the story."[99] On that weekend's political talk shows, several women Liberal MPs, including a minister (Montreal MP Mélanie Joly), challenged their two rogue colleagues to come clean. A veteran Ontario MP was blunt on CBC Radio's *The House,* taking issue with "innuendo" and calling on them to "put up or shut up" because "it affects all of us when one of our members of the team decides to go out and speak against the rest of us, or unnerve the rest of us."[100] The pointed remarks hinted at the exasperation felt by many Liberals, including the prime minister, and the rising acrimony in the caucus.

A tipping point came on March 29 when the justice committee released additional written testimony from Wilson-Raybould, including an audio file. In December she had recorded a seventeen-minute telephone call with the clerk. Political discussion turned on the ethics of recording someone without consent. At this point, a battery of Liberal ministers and backbenchers went public with their diverse opinions, and their comments exposed a divided caucus whose collective patience had worn thin. Some voiced outrage and wanted the ex-ministers out of the caucus, a smaller number felt they should remain, and others said that it was an internal matter. The discord added to the absence of message cohesion while showing why Trudeau had been resisting calls to remove the two MPs from caucus; however, an opinion was crystallizing that enough was enough. An air of finality was evident in the remarks of Patty Hajdu, the minister who had encouraged the cabinet to allow the former attorney general to address them: "I think it's unethical. It's deceptive," she said. "I personally don't feel comfortable ... with a colleague who may be recording me without my knowledge."[101] Wilson-Raybould countered that recording her conversation with the clerk "was a reasonable and rational thing to do in an unreasonable and irrational situation."[102]

Seizing the opportunity, Trudeau contacted regional caucus chairs to establish consensus about expelling the two MPs. Meanwhile, the Conservatives availed themselves of a procedural manoeuvre that the first opposition MP to speak on the budget debate has no time constraints during government orders and is interrupted only for essential items such as Question Period. A Conservative spoke for nearly fifteen hours spread over four days, often to a nearly empty chamber.[103] As Liberals mobilized to close ranks, Philpott prepared notes to address the regular Wednesday national caucus meeting. She would not get the opportunity to do so.

Caucus Expulsion

On April 2, nearly two months after the *Globe and Mail* exposed disagreement within the Trudeau government, the Liberals' Ontario regional caucus met to discuss the former ministers. Philpott left after ten minutes. Wilson-Raybould tweeted a letter that she wrote to the national caucus via the chair. The letter declared her commitment to the party and a desire to "break old and cynical patterns of centralizing power in the hands of a few unelected staffers, the marginalization of hundreds of Members of Parliament with expertise and insights to offer, and the practice of governing in the shadows, out of sight of Canadians."[104] Liberals were unmoved: a significant consensus existed that a breakdown of trust had occurred. Trudeau summoned the caucus chair to join him in a final meeting with each former minister to relay the news.

At an emergency national caucus meeting that Tuesday evening, with national media present, Trudeau announced that the two ex-ministers were no longer welcome in the Liberal team. He explained the process:

> In the course of the day, regional caucuses got together to discuss the situation. I then met with the chairs of the different caucuses who talked about their discussions, before having a discussion with the chair of the national caucus, the whip, and the assistant whip. It was following those discussions, during which I was told that the caucus had an opinion, that I made the decision to expel Jody Wilson-Raybould and Jane Philpott from our caucus. I met with Ms. Wilson-Raybould and Dr. Philpott to inform them of my decision. I just met with national caucus, and now I am addressing media and Canadians.[105]

The prime minister referred to broken trust and the damage of a civil war. He singled out Wilson-Raybould for making an audio recording without consent, which he described as "wrong" and "unconscionable."[106] Trudeau also cited Philpott's public expressions of a lack of confidence. She too had broken the cardinal rule that Canadian *parliamentarians must exercise extreme caution about going off-message in public.*

Afterward, the prime minister recalled withstanding demands from "older-style political operatives" to remove the MPs from caucus immediately.[107] He said that considerable effort was exerted to reconcile political differences, which reportedly included a rookie MP in Vancouver acting as an intermediary between the PMO and the former ministers.[108] On resigning from the cabinet, Philpott says that she had no further interaction with Trudeau until he told her that she was out of the caucus. The only direct outreach was a phone call from the chief of staff approximately a week before that: "There are so many ways that we could have come together to find a collective solution. It was a missed opportunity," Philpott says. "It saddens me that the narrative is out there that there were efforts made to resolve the circumstances, when they weren't. I was basically presented with a final decision that had already been made."[109] For her part, Wilson-Raybould declared her belief in loyalty, solidarity, and teamwork while conveying a willingness to challenge political allegiances if circumstances warrant.[110]

The story lost momentum after the decoupling. On April 7, the Conservatives revealed that Trudeau's lawyer had sent a letter threatening legal action over Scheer's comments.[111] The intended chill had an opposite effect because the Conservative leader repeated the remarks, and his party cheekily solicited donations for a legal defence fund. On April 11, the Speaker ruled that the Liberal caucus's violation of the Parliament of Canada Act years earlier – that is, not holding an internal vote on caucus membership as per the Reform Act, 2014 – was outside his authority. The controversy periodically reappeared, including a news flurry in July that Butts would be a strategic adviser for the Liberal re-election campaign. Among those critical of his return was an anonymous Liberal MP who complained about rule by triumvirate: "The whole government's run by Trudeau, Butts, and Telford. That's the sum total."[112] The party's election machinery was ramping up when the prime minister was thrust into the SNC-Lavalin spotlight again.

Ethics Commissioner Report

The hazy days of summer are usually bereft of political news, even when an election is on the horizon. In August 2019, the conflict of interest and ethics commissioner (Mario Dion) released his report on Justin Trudeau's actions. The independent officer of the House of Commons determined that PMO staff were repeatedly informing SNC-Lavalin representatives that the door to an agreement was open while the attorney general was saying that it was closed. The report answered questions that some Liberal MPs held privately, such as whether the Shawcross doctrine applied (it did) and whether the Department of Finance had independently examined the economic impacts of a criminal conviction (it had not).[113] The commissioner ruled that the prime minister had contravened Section 9 of the Conflict of Interest Act, which states that "no public office holder shall use his or her position as a public office holder to seek to influence a decision of another person so as to further the public office holder's private interests or those of the public office holder's relatives or friends or to improperly further another person's private interests."[114] Dion concluded that "the evidence abundantly shows that Mr. Trudeau knowingly sought to influence Ms. Wilson-Raybould both directly and through the actions of his agents."[115] The Act does not provide for significant penalties.

The key message from the prime minister, repeated by his ministers, was that he accepted responsibility but disagreed with the commissioner's conclusion and could not apologize for defending Canadian jobs. Trudeau committed to implementing the recommendations of the former MoJAG tasked with examining whether or not to separate the intertwined positions. Anne McLellan recommended maintaining a joint position in part because an attorney general cannot be divorced from political considerations. She also found "a strong consensus" among legal experts "that exempt political staff should not be involved in the substance" of prosecutorial consultations.[116] Among her recommendations was the need for a protocol to clarify the consultation process within the government.

The Conservatives, supported by the NDP, called for the commissioner to testify at the Standing Committee on Access to Information, Privacy and Ethics. MP Erskine-Smith declared that he wanted to identify legal flaws in the commissioner's finding against Trudeau. He voted with the opposition, immaterial to the outcome because six of nine committee members were Liberal MPs. The motion failed. The Liberals turned the morality tables with a destabilizer: a minister tweeted an old video of Scheer opposing same-sex marriage. The Conservatives retrenched; their leader vanished from public view. Liberal support recovered somewhat in public opinion surveys, and the 42nd Parliament was dissolved on September 11. The election campaign was under way.

FEDERAL ELECTION AND PLEA DEAL

Normally, when a prime minister announces that the governor general has agreed to a general election, the communications strategy is to present a rhetorical frame that influences what the media ought to focus on. Instead, Justin Trudeau had to contend with yet another *Globe and Mail* scoop.

"Ottawa Blocks RCMP on SNC Inquiry," proclaimed the headline that morning.[117] The newspaper reported that the prime minister's refusal to withdraw cabinet confidentiality was stymying the national police force's investigation of possible obstruction of justice. The Liberals responded with another destabilizer: Carolyn Bennett, the minister of Crown-Indigenous relations, tweeted an archived video of a Conservative candidate talking about wanting abortion laws. The Conservative leader, once again in the media's crosshairs as he contended with wedge politics, accused the

Liberals of being "desperate to change the channel on their scandals and corruption."[118]

During the campaign, a Montreal-area Liberal MP alleged that she had been red-lighted during the candidate vetting process as payback for not defending Trudeau when his commitment to feminism was questioned. Eva Nassif had refused to post Facebook and Twitter messages after the *Globe and Mail* story about the prime minister's yelling at Caesar-Chavannes. As well, she revealed that Minister Joly had texted and phoned her to shore up support: "I was punished for failing to hail Justin Trudeau as a great feminist in the wake of SNC-Lavalin when I didn't post anything," Nassif said. "I was called by [a] minister to ask why I wasn't going to support the prime minister. And I said that I didn't feel I would be authentic to come and post that he is a feminist after what he had done."[119] The MP had also hugged the former ministers in the West Block. Trudeau would only say that he could not disclose the reasons for rejecting her candidacy.

Otherwise, the SNC-Lavalin controversy lacked drama on the campaign trail. The Conservatives pledged to hold a public inquiry and to allow the RCMP to apply to the Supreme Court of Canada to obtain information shielded by cabinet confidentiality. At the leaders' debates, Trudeau repeated the line of standing up for Canadian jobs and that the decision is up to the attorney general.[120] The topic arose tangentially whenever the national media checked in on the Independent campaigns of Wilson-Raybould and Philpott. More salient issues dominated, such as climate change.

Election Day was October 21, 2019. The Liberals held on to power with a minority of seats (157 seats on 33.1 percent of the vote). Their incumbents named in this chapter who sought re-election were returned to office. Liberals won in the ridings represented by Caesar-Chavannes and Nassif, as well as the riding of Philpott, who placed third.[121] However, the Conservatives won the popular vote (121 seats on 34.4 percent), the Liberals were shut out in Alberta and Saskatchewan, and regional frustrations translated into major gains for the Bloc Québécois. In Vancouver, Wilson-Raybould became the first federal Independent candidate elected since 2008 and the first woman to do so since party labels appeared on federal ballots in 1972: "This win means that it's okay to stand up for what you believe in, to speak your truth, to act with integrity," she said to a cheering crowd.[122] The next day SNC-Lavalin shares jumped on the prospect of a plea deal. The stock had dropped to multi-year lows many times since February.

The issue came to an unexpected conclusion within a month of the new cabinet being sworn in. As per a recommendation in the McLellan report, Attorney General David Lametti took a revised oath to "uphold the Constitution, the rule of law and the independence of the judiciary and the prosecutorial function."[123] That wording also appeared in his ministerial mandate letter in which Trudeau directed him to act on the report's recommendations. The letter did not mention deferred prosecution agreements. As 2019 drew to a close, a former vice-president of SNC-Lavalin was found guilty of fraud and corruption for coordinating millions of dollars in kickbacks to the Gaddafi regime, including a $25 million yacht for Colonel Gaddafi's son. The company capitulated a few days later.

A plea deal between the director of public prosecutions and SNC-Lavalin Construction was announced on December 18. The construction subsidiary pleaded guilty in the Court of Quebec to a single count of fraud over $5,000. It was assessed $280 million in fines, put on probation for three years, and became subject to periodic reviews by an independent monitor. All charges against SNC-Lavalin Group and SNC-Lavalin International were stayed. Because fraud had been committed against a foreign country, and not against Canadian governments, the company was deemed eligible to bid on government contracts in Canada. In a statement, the company indicated that it did "not anticipate that the plea will have any long-term material adverse impact on the company's overall business."[124] Its stock price jumped again. Trudeau and Lametti emphasized that the plea deal was an independent decision; they omitted that it was a political decision not to intervene. Independent MP Wilson-Raybould turned the page: "The justice system did its work. It is time to move forward and for the company to look to its future," she tweeted.[125]

Relatedly, a change in the executive branch hinted at improved oversight of political exempt staff. In the new cabinet, Chrystia Freeland was appointed deputy prime minister, a position that had ceased to exist. Her ministerial mandate letter directed her to work closely with Prime Minister Trudeau and the Privy Council Office.[126] Her ministerial office was situated in the Office of the Prime Minister and Privy Council building, intended to operate in a "highly integrated and collaborative" manner with the PMO and PCO, and her chief of staff was cross-appointed senior adviser to the prime minister.[127] Early media coverage suggested that the new triumvirate (Trudeau, Freeland, and Telford) was an improvement over the old one.

INSIGHTS AND ANALYSIS

The SNC-Lavalin affair was only the fourth time in Canadian history, and the first involving women, that multiple ministers resigned from the federal cabinet over a policy dispute.[128] In considering any interpretation of pressure or political interference, it is important to recall that executive-level staff are often unaware of the extent to which others perceive their authority and that even a minor remark by a staffer can be interpreted with severity.[129] In hindsight, the Trudeau government could have called the company's bluff that Canadian jobs were at risk. Looking ahead, extraparliamentary members of the Liberal Party of Canada would be smart to amend the party constitution to establish values of upholding the rule of law and high ethical standards, which in turn would become part of the party's candidate contracts.

My objective is to examine the party discipline side of the story. The communications arena, the dynamics of partisan teams and parliamentary caucuses, and the involvement of political staff were prominent variables.

The Communications Arena

A spat involving a head of government is always newsworthy. Unlike previous episodes on this scale, letters of resignation were posted on social media, and members of the cabinet, caucus, and staff had digital megaphones to amplify messages. The story had intrigue because Jody Wilson-Raybould was more credible than Justin Trudeau, whose incongruent messaging contrasted with her consistency as a defender of the rule of law. Problems were evident from the moment that Trudeau repeated a denial – "the allegations reported in the story are false" – without proper explanation. He exhibited a confusing moral compass of being publicly virtuous about repelling old (male) ways of dispensing discipline while being cagey about his government's antiquated (Liberal) style of backroom politicking as (female) spokespersons were deployed to defend him. Credibility shifted when discussion turned on Wilson-Raybould's making an unauthorized recording, which pierced her ethical armour. At that point, Trudeau claimed the moral high ground to justify removing her from caucus – though, given the eventual finding that he had contravened the Conflict of Interest Act, admonishing her ethics was hypocritical.

The affair threw the government's corporate communications calendar into disarray. A fast-changing political landscape flustered strategic agenda planning because government personnel were reacting to events instead of controlling them. Announcements did not get traction; others were re-scheduled. Regional caucus meetings were preoccupied with instability instead of discussing how to allocate infrastructure spending. The decision-making bottleneck intensified as the PMO tried to contain the political firestorm. A political staffer relays how impromptu the government's messaging development was:

> If you're announcing pollution pricing or a plastics ban, you get your messaging lined up, and you can map things out day by day in terms of what you want to say and how you want to say it. Something like this is more like a bomb going off. You're responding to it. You're not necessarily testing lines because everything is moving so quickly and unexpectedly. It is more rapid response in terms of getting lines to people and trying to keep people united.[130]

The spiral of silence among most members of the Liberal caucus was palpable, which implied a lack of enthusiasm for the prime minister. Back-benchers lacked message lines and, in any event, recognized it was better not to fuel the story. Some Liberal MPs comment on the media logic:

> Most issues are reasonable disagreements, not grievances. The Liberal Party is better for reasonable disagreement. Usually, we are more suc-cessful as a team when grievances are not aired in public. The SNC dispute was framed as a matter of personal integrity, which moved it beyond a policy debate. The way a disagreement is portrayed matters a great deal in terms of not jeopardizing the overall objectives of the party.[131]

> The media tends to exaggerate conflict. They made the SNC story into more of an issue than it is. What was different is the role of identity

politics and the time frame involved. It shows what kinds of minefields exist when things get out of control. It's why there is always a strong effort by the centre of every party to control the message. But messages designed in the Ottawa bubble don't necessarily work in a small community in Saskatchewan or Prince Edward Island.[132]

The clash between identity politics and party politics was a crucial dynamic. The involvement of three outspoken women – one Indigenous, one white, one Black – caused the story to grow organically because feminism, Indigenous reconciliation, and diversity are among the Trudeau government's core brand promises. The prime minister wanted to be portrayed as an ally; the conflict framed him as an adversary. He calculated that jointly expelling Philpott and Wilson-Raybould would dampen outcries of colonialism, discrimination, and racism that would have arisen from singling out one over the other. Consulting the regional caucuses about expelling the former ministers circumvented sowing internal division by engaging the women's or Indigenous caucus. The inconsistency of male backbenchers who avoided public sanction for vocalizing divergent opinions and a female MP who would not be renominated as a Liberal candidate added to confusion about the application of discipline. As Philpott sees it, "there are lots of men that have been able to say contrary things. Women are expected to follow."[133] Yet some Liberals, including women, believe that the ex-ministers were afforded more leeway because of identity politics and believe that white men would have been abruptly shown the door. The absence of standardized caucus rules gives rise to such conjecture. To what extent gender, race, and Indigeneity played a role is subject to interpretation.[134]

Partisan Teams and the Parliamentary Caucus

The dispute was a trying time for Liberals. Many hard-core partisans were infuriated that newcomers were callous about damaging the party brand and the leader's image. They were beside themselves that one of their own had inflicted a political maelstrom and that another remained a Liberal after declaring a loss of confidence in the government. Privately, they were incredulous as the prime minister eschewed swift punishment and as the PMO struggled with communications management. Others were more empathetic. Weighing their options, backbenchers thought that the best one was to stand by their leader. Some Liberal MPs reflect that

it was a very frustrating time. Many members of the caucus and the party at large disagreed with Jody Wilson-Raybould. They felt the team was let down and there was a fundamental breach in solidarity. The caucus stayed remarkably disciplined even though there was frustration with the seeming patience for dissent. In public, the clash of personalities turned into a proxy war. Political parties put their fights to control the agenda through the protagonists of the story. All sorts of political cleavages emerged.[135]

When it comes to caucus politics and governing the country, you have to have a team that trusts each other and it was obvious ... that that trust had been eroded and you need trust in order to have a well functioning caucus ... I'd hoped that there was a way forward, because I've just had such a productive relationship with both of them, and I've learned so much from both of them, and I know that on 99 per cent of issues, our vision and values are the same ... but the prime minister made the right decision.[136]

When there's a new Parliament, with a lot of new MPs, there needs to be a clearer understanding of what caucus solidarity means. People who are loyal to the party were absolutely furious and hurt that some new Liberals jeopardized what we worked so hard for. It is an honour to be appointed a minister ... Betraying the trust of a leader and a party that obtained a mandate to govern made a lot of us really angry.[137]

Some of them did not give Wilson-Raybould the benefit of the doubt because of thorny interactions with her as MoJAG. At times, she had been non-responsive to their concerns about substantive topics, including Bill C-14, Medical Assistance in Dying, and Bill S-201, Genetic Non-Discrimination Act. Some thought that she could be too cavalier about their interest in private members' business. Examining ways to amend the Criminal Code is a popular choice because a private member's bill cannot propose to spend money unless the government supports it. A minister of justice has a special responsibility to have a strong working relationship with backbenchers; otherwise, complaints mount. Yet those who wanted to speak with Wilson-Raybould sometimes found that only her parliamentary secretary was made available. Executive-level challenges arose too. She sometimes rebuffed the desire of the PMO for "political expediency."[138] She was the most interconnected minister as measured by cabinet committee membership, yet some perceived her to be a colleague who could be mistrustful and disruptive.[139] The interpersonal friction surely contributed to the prime minister's decision to shuffle her to a lower-profile role.[140] Those exasperated with an unconventional teammate held a view different from that of Canadians enamoured with a principled individual with a backbone willing to speak truth to power. Wilson-Raybould reflects that

> I was doing my job on SNC and what I knew to be right. It makes me wonder how many people over the course of history did the wrong thing, or did what the party or the PMO told them to, and for what reasons, and nobody knows about it. I wonder how common it has been. We cannot just rely on a single individual's ethics or principles to do what is right. We must have strong institutional controls, particularly in the PMO. Thankfully, our democratic institutions have checks and balances to ensure the independence of particular officials of the Crown and of the judiciary.[141]

In comparison, after a bumpy start, Jane Philpott exemplified conventional standards of a team player. Some backbenchers thought that she did not value their concerns when, as minister of health, she promoted the passage of Bill C-14. They stood by her while the ethics commissioner investigated allegations that a campaign worker had provided the minister with expensive car travel; Philpott was cleared but endured negative headlines. Later, as the minister of Indigenous services, she reached out to private members to assist them with their advocacy work. She met one on one with MPs and created caucus working groups on policy files. Interested backbenchers could become informed about the government's general direction and – as one put it – participate in a "deep dive" into legislation.[142] An initial information debriefing led to smaller breakouts at tables chaired by ministerial staff acting as facilitators. MPs could provide feedback to government personnel who paid close attention. Actively involved backbenchers were proclaimed "caucus champions" on topics such as First Nations water issues. The caucus champion label instilled such a sense of pride that some MPs mentioned it in their online biographies and on social media. Respect for Philpott gave many Liberals reason to doubt what the PMO was telling them.

Those relationships were strained the moment that the ministers tweeted their resignation letters. Many Liberals passive-aggressively censured them and Caesar-Chavannes while they were still part of the caucus. Colleagues stopped calling. People whispered in parliamentary hallways and avoided eye contact. Some ministers passing through the West Block turned around on spotting them: "With the flick of a switch, the mentality of people who I thought were colleagues, if not friends, completely changed," says Wilson-Raybould.[143] It became clear that friendships in partisan politics are conditional on supporting the team. Philpott reflects on how Liberals treated her after she resigned from the cabinet:

> Perhaps most painful of all was the political staff with whom I worked on projects that were deeply important to me, such as the Indigenous child welfare bill. I wasn't doing it so that Liberals would succeed or so that we would get re-elected or for any reason apart from the fact that we have been tearing families apart for generations, and we had a chance to make a difference. After everything happened, several staff from that minister's office stopped looking at me in the eye. They wouldn't speak to me. The relationship was destroyed. It is confusing because I thought I was working with those people because the issue is really important to us, something that has nothing to do with partisanship or trying to prove that Liberals are great. It was about trying to serve people and make the country better. I still fail to understand why my relationship with those staff members is so broken.[144]

Liberals who reached out did so at the risk of recrimination. A small number of ministers and MPs were compassionate and supportive. Their willingness to offer kind words and a hug in the parliamentary precinct demonstrates that some personal relationships can endure political strife. As Independents, the MPs were able to forge new relationships with MPs in other parties. But most of their former teammates angrily dismissed them as traitors. Some fast friends no longer speak to them.

A point made throughout this book is that backbenchers bear responsibility for scrutinizing government decisions. Some Liberal MPs – particularly those with experience in party politics – thought that they had a good read on the situation. Others were confused. Neophytes were unable to differentiate between traditional processes and new ones. Even though they did not always trust messaging, they lacked the knowledge, confidence, support, and/or incentive to investigate the spin. Operating in an information vacuum created a taxing environment. Consequently, many reasoned that silence was better than proving their ignorance. One first-time MP rationalizes remaining quiet:

> It is a lesson learned too easily, and perhaps too often, that if you don't know what you're talking about it is better not to say anything. I didn't know what happened and suspect most MPs didn't know what happened. We certainly weren't experts on things like the Shawcross doctrine or DPAs, and it was a hard task to get up to speed on the basics. Even from the supposed inside, it was a classic he said, she said situation, except that it was difficult to figure out what precisely was being alleged. My perception was that any MP's decision to speak or not about the affair was their own – irrespective of whether or not we were directed not to speak. What benefit was there to speak? Backbenchers like me didn't have inside knowledge of the story. Nobody knew what was going on. It was better to stay in your lane and wait for it all to blow over and listen to the committee testimony with everyone else. As the adage goes, it is better to be silent and thought a fool than to open your mouth and remove all doubt.[145]

Backbenchers did not want to impose stress by asking for a debriefing, as they sometimes do at a regional caucus meeting. They could not ask the Liberal Research Bureau to research the matter because doing so would have signalled a lack of trust in the prime minister and PMO. Self-preservation and resource structures discouraged independent investigation.

The stakes were high in an election year. Taking a public stand would more than harm a Liberal's career: it would compromise the entire team's electoral prospects, potentially resulting in a Conservative government. The Liberals were the most popular party from September 2018 through January 2019.[146] Beginning in late February 2019, the Conservatives moved into first place in public opinion polls, and party fundraising reports filed with Elections Canada every quarter show that the number of donors and total donations plummeted for the Liberals during the first three months of 2019.[147] The party was still behind in opinion polls on May 27 when Philpott and Wilson-Raybould announced that they would run as Independents. A dearth of Liberals willing to agitate shows how the bonds of cohesion harden with proximity to an election.

The stakes were especially high for Justin Trudeau. It would be simplistic to suggest that he ought to have immediately suspended the former ministers from caucus. Trudeau, who is highly attuned to image management, reasoned that it was best to practise a patient disciplinary style of building consensus that expulsions were necessary. The justice committee was granted more leeway to investigate than other prime ministers might have permitted. The authorization of a limited waiver of cabinet confidence and of solicitor-client privilege, combined with divulging information to the ethics commissioner, meant that there was a public airing buttressed by a trove of tabled documents. Supporters assert that Trudeau is a quicker study than people realize. He thinks things through, he is decisive when he needs to be, and he is purposely less autocratic than many of his contemporaries. He moved on caucus evictions when he felt that it was appropriate to do so. After the election, Liberal MPs affirmed that they wanted him to continue to make decisions about caucus membership.[148]

Political Staff and Caucus Relations

The SNC-Lavalin affair demonstrates that problems arise when a leader is carefree with delegating authority to senior staff. An unprecedented number attended Liberal caucus meetings, and Trudeau advertised from the outset that Telford and Butts were his lieutenants. He leans on staff to work out business matters so that he can focus on building relationships in meetings: "It's not who do you know in the PMO, it's do you know Katie and Gerald?" lamented one Liberal MP in 2018.[149] The self-described "co-CEOs" boosted their power with an active social media presence,[150] and Butts had forged such a reputation for aggressively calling out the government's critics that his tweets were a Question Period topic.[151] Their empowerment resulted in the classic principal-agent problem of delegated authority whereby agents apply their own interpretations as instructions filter down the organizational hierarchy.[152] Once staff had a sense of the position of the prime minister, they managed the file, assumed that they were acting on his behalf, and did not always keep him abreast of pertinent developments.[153] Similarly, the clerk of the Privy Council sometimes conveyed messages to ministers different from how the prime minister intended them. As his lawyers tell it, Trudeau is not responsible when his staff do not follow his directions.[154] The integration of a deputy prime minister into the PMO's operations might induce greater accountability.

Delegation of authority was compounded by an alarming number of backbenchers who felt that Trudeau was accessible only at caucus meetings. He claimed to foster a welcoming environment, but many Liberals interviewed for this book echoed the *Globe and Mail*'s portrayal of a prime minister sheltered by a royal guard:

> At odds with the way he has been sold to Canadians – as someone who is open and empathetic – the prime minister has not been as accessible as many members of his caucus wanted. Even members of his cabinet have struggled to get past his top staff to meet directly with him, especially without Ms. Telford or Mr. Butts in the room, and many would have appreciated having him informally reach out to them on occasion ... Mr. Trudeau may have suffered, relatedly, for the extent to which he delegated his dealings with cabinet ministers to his staff and to Mr. Wernick, the Privy Council clerk.[155]

During the height of the crisis, the Prime Minister's Office took interest in two-way internal communication. Personnel contacted Liberal MPs out of concern that some might speak against the prime minister or cross the floor. Trudeau, his chief of staff, and select ministers initiated conversations with them. As mentioned in Chapter 3, Trudeau became more available, and he designated caucus liaison officers. A PMO staffer reflects on the multipronged efforts to hold the caucus together:

> There were many lengthy phone calls with caucus from the chief of staff, by people in caucus relations, and by cabinet ministers who could be counted on. A lot of caucus outreach in terms of touching base with people, calling them to ask about their thoughts on next steps about what to do, and to see how they were feeling. It was genuinely listening to the caucus and making sure they felt that they were being responded to. Steps were taken to keep those connection points a bit more live by appointing two caucus liaisons and a policy where the prime minister will call MPs back more quickly. There was a sense in the lead-up to this that there wasn't as much of that direct caucus connection as caucus would have liked there to have been.[156]

The internal outreach found that a segment of the caucus, particularly veteran MPs, viewed Wilson-Raybould and Philpott as turncoats. These partisans wanted speedy punishment. Others, especially rookies, were sympathetic. They wanted to find a way to reconcile with the former ministers. This dichotomy is to be expected, given that experienced hands have been socialized into party discipline whereas it can be a recurring source of cognitive dissonance for newcomers. Consensus to expel the ex-ministers reflected a collective will to ensure that a caucus is a sanctum, aptly summarized by a Vancouver MP in office since 1993: "We don't feel comfortable sitting in the same room with someone who we think will break the confidentiality of this room."[157]

SUMMARY

The events described in this chapter show that a government without message discipline is compromised. The many components of this high-profile policy disagreement – regional pressures, identity politics, rule of law, economic implications, electoral repercussions, caucus unity, information management, role of staff – meant that there was no clear pathway to exit the political maze. The elasticity of party discipline was tested as Prime Minister Trudeau extended more leeway to off-message MPs than is the Canadian norm; nevertheless, the ultimate penalty of caucus eviction still prevailed. It is unlikely that we will learn further details any time soon: the protection of cabinet confidences means that some information will be a state secret until at least 2038, if not forever. Ways that parliamentarians can make a difference while members of a political party are the subject of the final chapter.

12

Advice for a New Parliamentarian

Party interests and individualism can be irreconcilable in Canadian parliamentary politics. Rigorous private discussion goes unseen, fuelling a perception of backbenchers as party lackeys. How can parliamentarians adequately express their views or represent constituents if being offside with the leader stirs controversy and triggers a disciplinary process? How can they have a satisfying parliamentary career if toeing the party line causes mental anguish? In this chapter, I present ways to be a strong advocate within the confines of party discipline and message conformity. I revisit the research objectives presented in Chapter 1. I conclude by outlining some pragmatic reform measures and identifying areas for further research.

NAVIGATING THE CONFINES OF PARTY DISCIPLINE

Dilemmas of representation have emerged throughout this book, placing a premium on party loyalty. Party discipline has many benefits, including that it forces difficult decisions. But it is a serious problem for democracy when its advocates are overexuberant, causing despondency among citizens about the quality of representation and disillusionment with political institutions. Individualism is withering away as extraparliamentary parties reject potential disrupters from standing for election and persuade nominated candidates about the need for message unity. Legislators who vote as regimented partisan blocs are so normal in Canadian politics that it can shock the political system when one of them does otherwise, and concern about following the party whip's voting instructions on bills and motions has moved on to concern about legislators who repeat messaging: "Enough with the mechanistic politics," says one political commentator. "Talking point, after talking point, targeting different segments of voters. Political marketing is killing originality and neutering personality. Make it stop."[1]

Many Canadians want their representatives to be free of party shackles.[2] Canadians get confused by parliamentarians' rhetoric, are suspicious of their motives, doubt that their promises will be kept, and believe that private members are powerless because of party lines.[3] They perceive a systematic problem when an elected representative publicly supports a counterintuitive policy or stays silent during a groundswell of public anger. For those who get involved in politics, the experience of running for office and serving in the legislature exposes them to a sordid side of democracy, and they quickly realize that partisanship inhibits the blunt candour that excites democratic romanticists. In 2017, Arnold Chan, a terminally ill Liberal MP, delivered a final speech in the House of Commons. He called on members to resist scripting: "We can disagree strongly, and in fact we should. That is what democracy is about. However, we should not just use the formulaic talking points. It does not elevate this place. It does not give Canadians confidence in what democracy truly means," he stated.[4] Chan's remarks resonated because the soft underbelly of party discipline is that it makes citizens believe that their elected representatives mindlessly prioritize the interests of political parties.

Power pyramids are proving to be resilient in major political parties even as digital technologies flatten elite political structures. Canadians appear to crave representatives with the resolve to have unimpeded conversations, yet they can distrust those who switch political parties, they rarely elect Independents, and they perceive weakness when a leader presides over a group that expresses divergent views. Party leaders know that a campaign promise to change the standing orders that govern parliamentary procedure is not a vote winner. In opposition, leaders complain about problems with the system; in government, they exploit the rules to their advantage. On both sides of the aisle, there is little room for refreshing honesty if it is interpreted as a challenge to the leader's supremacy, and members of a parliamentary caucus are under substantial pressure to support the team.

Research by the Samara Centre for Democracy offers some indication of how to be a strong parliamentarian within these constraints. A survey of MPs in the 42nd Parliament found that standing committees are where private members feel most empowered to influence government policy and legislation as well as through direct interactions with ministers and at caucus meetings.[5] Previously, the Toronto think tank found that MPs from

---

FIGURE 12.1
Advice for a new Member of Parliament

Advocacy
- Agree wholeheartedly when you agree; disagree intelligently when you disagree.
- Do things outside of your comfort zone.
- Have a clear sense of what you want to accomplish. Focus.
- In caucus, when you raise a concern follow up with advice to resolve the problem.
- Make good use of parliamentary committees and private members' business.
- Recognize that private members have limited individual power or influence.
- Seize opportunities to affect change. Find a niche issue.
- Stay true to your convictions. Be consistent. Be authentic. Be committed.

Communications
- Be courteous. Be humble. Check your ego.
- Customize your speeches.
- Get media training. Practice fielding journalists' questions.

Constituency Matters
- Guard your time. Be selective about attending events in the capital city.
- Pay attention to your constituents and your electoral district.

Research
- Ask people with specialized expertise or experience for advice and help.
- Avail of library resources and supports.
- Learn parliamentary rules and procedures.
- Surround yourself with people who are smarter, more experienced and/or better connected.
- Thrash out ideas with a small group of people who you trust.
- Try to understand a topic thoroughly before advancing it.

Teamwork
- Assist your colleagues with managing their House duty assignments.
- Be respectful of members with a portfolio. Consult with them before raising a topic.
- Build trustworthy relationships. Seek out like-minded people in all parties.
- Listen and observe more than you talk. Look for compromise.
- Talk with as many members of caucus as possible about an issue that you want to change.

Source: Samara Centre for Democracy transcripts of exit interviews with former MPs.

minority Parliaments were cynical about parliamentary committees, when policy success is achieved by developing expertise and building coalitions within the caucus.[6] In their exit interviews, Samara representatives asked recently retired MPs what advice they would give a new Member of Parliament. In Figure 12.1, I summarize that guidance as it relates to navigating the confines of party discipline. Much of what the former MPs suggest has to do with team play, such as building relationships. A theme of taking initiative is evident. Parliamentarians should equip themselves with knowledge, avail themselves of support networks, and be strategic with their choices. Other common advice (not shown) is to take steps to minimize the personal toll of a political career on health, family, and friends. The people interviewed for this book reiterate that counsel.

ADVOCACY WITHIN PARTY DISCIPLINE

How can members of Canadian legislatures channel their ingenuity within a system of strict party discipline? How does one parliamentarian make a difference? *Globe and Mail* interviews with former MPs found that they placed responsibility on current MPs to have the courage to exert sovereignty.[7] It is not enough to call on parliamentarians to be courageous; they need support. Equipping them with knowledge can help, provided here as a description of stereotyped roles, followed by what I was told an industrious private member can do within the constraints of a partisan team.

Party Robots, Team Players, Mavericks, and Troublemakers

We have seen that jargon is used to stereotype members of parliamentary assemblies, who are divided into frontbenchers and backbenchers, and that role confusion arises from the use of the word *government*. In Britain, MPs have written about mantra chanters, procedural buffs, serial rebels, and party diehards.[8] In Chapter 2, I described legislators, constituency caseworkers, and brand ambassadors. The media calls them cheerleaders and bobbleheads; academics and think tanks refer to sheep and clones; and politicians worry about being potted palms, parrots, or nobodies. In Canada, the most common trope is surely that of a trained seal, an outdated pejorative because it refers to behaviour on the floor of the legislative chamber without regard for message repetition fifty yards away, particularly on social media.

TABLE 12.1
Stereotypes of Canadian parliamentarians

	Party robot	Team player	Maverick	Troublemaker
Communications	Scripted	Amplified	Populist	Outbursts
Cooperation	Deferential	Solve problems	Strategic alliances	Disruptive
Flexibility	Malleable	Responsive	Selective	Rebellious
Messaging	Verbatim	Reworded	Authentic	Rejected
Participation	Passive	Active	Choosy	Disengaged
Party values	Programmed	Personified	Push boundaries	Indiscriminate
Reliability	Compliant	Loyal	Circumstantial	Undependable
Socializing	Tepid	Partisan	Cross-party	Ostracized

Table 12.1 identifies some stereotypes used in Canada today, which I shall describe in turn. Unpacking the characteristics of each will help us recognize what it means when someone chides a politician for being a robot, why a team player is so revered by the party leadership, why a maverick instills fear in caucus officers, and why a troublemaker puts partisans on edge. These social categorizations are loaded with meaning and layered overtop a parliamentarian's multifaceted roles in the legislature, in local communities, and online (and, increasingly, their role as a data collector). As with any overgeneralization, in reality each parliamentarian exhibits an array of traits from multiple stereotypes, which might be specific to the situation at hand or reflect the personalities of the people involved. Many of the attitudes and behaviours have existed for decades, if not longer.[9]

One extreme of this conformity spectrum is robotic. This is less disparaging than suggesting that elected officials are low functioning animals thumping on their desks in unison, barking, and standing up to vote when their masters tell them to. A programmable machine is capable of carrying out a variety of repetitive and sophisticated tasks. Party robots dutifully follow the leadership's instructions, including demands from political staff. Their mechanical behaviour includes reading scripted speeches and posting supplied messaging on social media, sometimes without rewording. Their performance is unremarkable, keeping them out of trouble, and they are reluctant to challenge people in authority. The leadership views them as party salespersons who are replaceable. All party-affiliated elected officials behave as robots, by necessity, on some files because they cannot be subject matter experts or engage in critical thinking on every topic. They understandably recoil at the portrayal as automatons despite habitually voting the party line.

At the other extreme is a politician with a pattern of disruptive behaviour. A bozo eruption and repenting is one thing; playing havoc with caucus collegiality to the point of sedition is quite another. Troublemakers can be non-conforming newbies who defy the system, or alienated veterans whose outbursts go too far, and are unconcerned that the party existed before their arrival or that it will outlast their departure. They can go months without talking to the party leader as they gradually withdraw from group activities. The disrupter's acerbity can escalate to a tirade against a system perceived to lobotomize the people's elected representatives. When parliamentarians behave as troublemakers, they challenge group norms in ways that cause serious problems for the leadership and colleagues, possibly undermining the stability of parliamentary institutions. People who bring the caucus, leader, or party into disrepute are punished or pushed out, or else they leave of their own accord.

Nestled between the two extremes is respectful agitation. Team players are loyal partisans, which means a predisposition to expressing public support for the leader even in the absence of a personal connection. Advocacy occurs in private because publicly challenging people who wear the same party colours goes against their belief system. Team players want to make the party look good when they go on a political panel or use social media. They are comfortable with the leader's staff attending caucus meetings because they see them as an integral part of the team decision-making process, but where they differ from party robots is that they contribute more to the group and get more out of the group. Provided that normal consultation processes were followed, they usually have no qualms about following the whip's instructions because they believe in group success. Their engagement in the party hones a deep appreciation for the immeasurable work and resources that go into developing party infrastructure, ranging from a constitution and leadership contest to fundraising and platform development. Their prospects for promotion are good.[10]

In Canada, political mavericks have healthy skepticism about party politics, which can frustrate team players. Their affiliation is opportunistic rather than engrained; righteousness guides their world views, but they recognize that the benefits of party affiliation outweigh being an Independent. Mavericks chafe under the social constructs to which their colleagues might be oblivious. They pick their battles as they figure out how to play the political game, within which the leader's staff are both facilitators and obstacles. A team player bottles up anger when the group decides to move in a different direction, whereas a maverick might feel obliged to take a stand. When a maverick is boxed into a dilemma, an anti-establishment streak can erupt against the constraints of party unity; after some introspection, a maverick might do nothing, or might speak out publicly on principle but is calculated when doing so and willing to incur punishments. The timing of an off-message remark, often carefully selected, can augment the disruption. Leaders are wary of promoting mavericks because of a lack of complicity, especially if the parliamentarian has a reputation for putting self-interest ahead of team interests and for engaging in disputes on social media.

Advice for Private Members

Although it can be grating, most Canadian politicians come to appreciate that discipline is essential for the House of Commons and provincial assemblies to operate, an opinion uniformly shared by political staff. Intrinsic attraction to the party means that all parliamentarians share an interest in its success. Recognizing its necessity does not mean that politicians believe that party discipline as it functions today is good for democracy. A former party leader adds her voice: "We don't get good government by recruiting talented, smart people to run for office, and then they have to read questions and members' statements written by the leader's staffers, and if they express a strongly held view they face punishment," she says.[11] If that is true, then where can a parliamentarian turn for advice on how to be a strong representative within a stifling political system? Colleagues are the natural go-to resource, except that they are prone to indoctrination by partisanship, social conditioning, and institutionalism. Fresh thinking requires access to a wide variety of perspectives that crosses party lines and traverses stereotypes.

In the following pages, I synthesize the advice offered by the federal and provincial parliamentarians whom I interviewed, buttressed by insights obtained from autobiographies and other secondary sources. Understand that the collective wisdom concerns working within the existing system as opposed to changing it. To Canadian parliamentarians, nobody is above the team. The overall portrait is of a hard-working private member who embodies Hanna Pitkin's substantive representation in American politics: no matter what the issue, and regardless of socio-demographic traits, the representative takes deliberative action. A vital difference is that a Canadian parliamentarian must somehow negotiate strict party discipline.

Be Aware Frontbenchers Think Backbenchers Can Speak Up

Experienced frontbenchers are adamant that, though Canada's political system is flawed, it works. They accept that political parties are entrenched, and they reject the notion that there is no room for individualism in a caucus: "A member can bring forward a perspective that has not been considered by the government. It doesn't mean dissent," says Paul Martin, who had a twenty-year parliamentary career. "Similarly, an MP may champion an issue that the government hasn't championed. On newer issues, or those that are not nationally known but are locally known, those are absolutely things that MPs should speak up about, and the good MPs do."[12] Across all parties, federal and provincial, people who have served in the executive branch echo these sentiments. Some go so far as to propose that party discipline is an exaggerated myth. As one former minister puts it,

> the idea that you cannot be an individual as part of a team is bunk. You can be. Does it mean speaking your mind? If you cannot, is that a reflection of you or of the leadership? Do you not have confidence in yourself? Are you aspiring to be more than a backbencher? You make up your own mind where you stand.[13]

A former premier concurs that the onus is on parliamentarians to be spirited. Acting as a local face of the government is reasonable as long as there is a quid pro quo that backbenchers believe the executive listens to what they have to say. When circumstances warrant, they should be able to pressure the cabinet and push back against being its ciphers. He adds that they need to show conviction without throwing the caucus into disarray:

Backbenchers spend their time trying to figure out how to get in cabinet. That tempers debate. It can be mistaken ambition. If you want to get into cabinet, you have to show the leader and others that you have some independent view that brings perspective to the table. I would hope most leaders do not want sheep inside their caucus who automatically support the government on everything. They want honest opinion, as long as it is not belligerent or obstructionist.[14]

Resolve and determination are essential. Two former ministers acknowledge the need to show initiative, whether as a member of cabinet trying to convince the prime minister about a course of action, or as a rookie backbencher trying to raise a competing point of view amid ingrained thinking in the caucus room:

If you're confident in your idea, you need to not allow yourself to be put in a position where you lose. There are definitely issues that I differed with the prime minister on. When I won the day, it was because I could make a thoughtful, logical path that he understood. You have to fight for what you want. You have to put in effort. I worked through my mandate letter, then started doing other things. Not once did Stephen Harper shut down any of the new ideas I had. Not once. People have to be bold and not listen to the media rhetoric. But don't get me wrong, at the end of the day the prime minister is the boss, just like any CEO of a company.[15]

My advice to a new parliamentarian is to take your space, with your voice, immediately. Don't go into the caucus room and let your voice be taken from you. Some senior politicians might counsel you that if you start advocating loudly you will be isolated and ostracized. Recognize that's counterintuitive to how caucus should operate. It's the place where people should be heard and should communicate their opinions respectfully. Creatively disruptive conversations in caucus are important. Dialogue should be robust. Otherwise, you end up with narrow pathways of power that do not provide sufficient public sector oversight and are not necessarily informed enough.[16]

Others with cabinet experience affirm that an individual parliamentarian can make a difference. Some of them have never known life on the back benches; others have clawed their way up through the ranks. All of them contend that influence comes down to confidence, a variation on the courage urged in the aforementioned *Globe and Mail* study. This point of view tends to overlook that the will to push partisan boundaries can be connected to job security and experience. For example, a prolific member confident of re-election and financially independent is in a better position to be assertive with the party hierarchy than a new member in a marginal seat who depends on a parliamentary paycheque.[17] A party stalwart holds particular sway in a caucus. Conversely, it takes a while for rookies to learn how the system works, to develop profiles, and to form alliances. The relative amateurism of the membership in Canadian legislative assemblies has long been considered a significant factor in members' subservience to parliamentary parties.[18] Another dynamic is the socio-demographic makeup of the caucus, what Pitkin calls descriptive representation. People with a minority opinion must overcome additional barriers to self-assurance when they are already in the minority due to their gender, skin colour, ethnicity, or other characteristics. Some frontbenchers might not always be sensitive to the varied reasons for the spiral of silence.

Recognize the Trade-Offs of Party Affiliation and Pick Your Battles

Common advice from experienced parliamentarians is that you need to get along to go along, put some water in your wine, and pick your battles. Successful advocates accept that political parties are aggregators. They recognize that you give up something as part of any group, and they are sensitive to the party custom of supporting the party platform: "In this business, you have to be true to your convictions but also open to compromise," says Yvonne Jones, the Labrador MP who is one of the handful of politicians since 1972 whose parliamentary career began as an Independent: "My job is to influence the change that best represents my constituency. How do I ensure that my constituents are going to be looked after? That they're going to benefit? That they are going to be protected? You have to be strong in your arguments, and persistent, and work hard to try to get out of it what you want. But you always have to be open to compromise in politics."[19]

By running as a party candidate, legislators are indebted to the hard work of countless people who built the party brand and mounted a strong campaign. A parliamentary caucus is expected to be devoted to the cause, and loyalty includes following established practices for internal advocacy. Bernard Lord, the former New Brunswick premier, observes that parliamentarians are obliged to cooperate with the caucus and its leader:

> You want to recruit strong-minded, independent thinkers. But they are not independent political activists once they choose to belong to a political party. The quid pro quo is the party helps individuals get elected and to participate in moving policies and ideas forward. In exchange a certain loyalty and team spirit are expected. These individuals need to cooperate within the political party.[20]

Advancing a policy idea should not cause anyone to question a member's commitment to the party. A parliamentarian should bring colleagues along on a policy journey as opposed to forcing a policy idea on them. Greater success is possible when there is a clear connection between a proposed action and the party's values, as expressed in its constitution. Lord continues that

> there has to be buy-in for the agenda of the political party and what we are trying to do as an organization. That doesn't mean that everybody always agrees on how to translate those values into concrete policies that are actionable. It would be unhealthy to be in a caucus where everybody agrees on everything. It would mean nobody is thinking. There should be consensus on the core values and principles of the party.[21]

New parliamentarians can be unaware of the limited role of backbenchers in public policy decisions or fully appreciate that they have joined an established club. The system engages them in government business long after considerable work has already gone into preparing a bill or policy announcement (see Figure 2.2). Industrious private members can look for opportunities to contribute at an earlier stage of the process, ideally before they seek election. They can provide input through the extraparliamentary party during the policy development phase or mobilize support for a motion at a policy convention. They can volunteer for an election platform committee or perhaps participate in a leadership race. Their involvement comes with the recognition that the leader has the final say on which policy to advance. A parliamentarian determined to be the one who makes policy decisions should contemplate contesting the leadership and try to lead the party to victory in an election campaign.

Astute politicians know that party leaders are aware that sometimes policies are made without sufficient consultation or knowledge of local circumstances. Things are missed.[22] A parliamentarian's efforts to improve a policy, to point out a nuance, or to save the leadership from embarrassment adds value. Jones, who also has experience as a provincial party leader and minister, remarks on the merits of providing input to decision makers:

> Lots of times you're educating your own. You can't assume that every minister knows everything there is to know about every region and every issue. It's up to you to make sure that they are informed, that they're educated, that they understand the issue, and that they know who the players are. It's very time consuming, but it's a rewarding part of the job. You often find that by educating others they generate new ideas and interesting ways to address the problems that you're bringing forward. It works.[23]

Impatient reformers need to take the time to learn how much work is required to effect change, especially for a backbencher. As an opposition MP says, "it's very slow. It's possible to change the government, ideas, or to influence, but it takes a lot of effort."[24] Clever parliamentarians spot a viable opportunity when a topic is not in the campaign platform. They can make a well-reasoned case that is supported by other members of the caucus. Being nimble and attuned to how colleagues will react is crucial, because the caucus is unlikely to be supportive if members foresee being cornered into supporting a proposal that might prompt backlash from constituents. Less evident is that some members recoil when they think a colleague is trying to build a profile. Politicians can detect raw ambition. It is strategic utility maximizer thinking in a competitive political environment: why should private members help a colleague get ahead if doing so harms their own interests? A party whip discloses that the caucus assesses a proposal on a personal level rather than solely on its merits:

> Perhaps the greatest binding element is whether members think what you are doing is self-serving or is a matter of genuine conscience. If somebody is promoting a vote who is not particularly passionate about the issue, it's just that they think it will play well for them personally, that ends up being very upsetting to other members who then have to face the consequences if they vote in a different direction. There isn't a lot of sympathy if people think you're just doing it for your own aggrandizement. There's a lot of social pressure not to do that to fellow members. But if it's known that someone has a very heartfelt view, and that they have worked for a long time on a particular issue, then there is a lot of leniency.[25]

Thus, a proposition that hugs party values can be rebuffed by the caucus when the person promoting it is perceived to be bringing it forward for selfish reasons. Anything viewed as blatantly egoistic has implications for that individual's reputation. A private member must consider that colleagues are more likely to support a policy and the individual if they perceive genuine conviction, as will the party leader, especially if the proposal rights a wrong and will help constituents in need.

Research, Consult, and Build an Internal Coalition

Michael Chong is the Conservative MP who initiated the Reform Act, 2014, as a private member's bill. He is the minister who resigned on principle from the cabinet over Stephen Harper's handling of the Bloc Québécois motion to declare Quebec a nation. Chong was among the most independent-minded MPs in the 42nd Parliament, siding with his party on 98 percent of recorded votes (dissenting 13 of 793 times). His advice on how to be a strong parliamentarian mirrors what many of his peers, past and present, recommend: "Do your homework. Ensure you know what you're talking about. Work with your caucus colleagues, including the leadership, and pick the battles you want to fight," Chong says.[26] The hard work, research, persuasion, and preparation that can carry a private member through the ranks are valued skill sets when appointments are distributed – as long as that person is viewed as a devotee of the cardinal rule about being vigilant in public forums.

Chong and others recognize that frontbenchers and senior political staff are keen to hear from backbenchers mindful of brand values who bring forward well-researched perspectives. Frontbenchers tend to be partial to those who learn by doing and do not repeat errors, including gaffes made by colleagues. They admire those who sound out ideas in a courteous manner. Heads of government find that vocal backbenchers can be more influential than weak ministers, and, as long as opinions are voiced appropriately, those individuals are noticed for promotion. The key is to be well prepared when engaging with senior officeholders. When planning to speak in a caucus meeting, a parliamentarian should reflect: *Who is my audience? How many people are with me on this? How urgent and/or important is the issue? Who should care about it? Has the leader pronounced on the issue? Who is the decision maker? Can I change people's minds?* The member should research a file and articulate the concern succinctly.[27] Those who make an argument in the caucus or assembly without thorough familiarity with the file can be eviscerated in front of others, setting their careers back.[28]

Activist parliamentarians read. They request details. Their research causes them to spot opportunities to make a difference and to develop subject expertise on an otherwise overlooked policy issue. They build procedural skill sets to champion a topic that is a low priority for the government. They might pen intelligent, respectful policy memos to the leader, thereby demonstrating interest in serving in a competent manner. A discreet backbencher can meet with ministers to make progress on files without stirring up opposition within the caucus.[29] A former government whip recommends researching a topic thoroughly and lobbying internally to achieve peer support:

> There are so many policy vacuums that need to be filled. Pick something that matters to you. Do your homework. That's how you get caucus members onside, the minister onside, and the prime minister onside. Making a big noise in the media about something is not what works. Hard work works! Simply toeing the party line is not always the way to solve problems.

If you really think something's important, you do the work to find the solutions that everybody else can agree with.[30]

Other times it falls to a backbencher to be the canary in the coalmine. It can take self-assurance to express a counteropinion when everyone else is nodding: "If you put forward a logical argument, more often than not you can win the day," says a former minister. "I encourage people to be bold. If you work hard, you can get ahead. You have the potential to lead great things. But if you're too afraid to do anything, how do you stand out?"[31] Another former minister lays out how to take a professional approach to expressing counterviews within the caucus:

> You have to do extra work. You need to present your case with empirical evidence, knock on doors, be persuasive, and alert people that there may be unintended consequences about the path they are going down. Before speaking up at caucus, you can seek a one-on-one meeting with the leader, which shows a degree of courage and commitment to your team. You don't want to needlessly humiliate anyone. You get a fair hearing, you present your case, and sometimes you are able to influence and carry the day. Other times that is not the case. It's not dismissing you. We take it seriously, but you may not have a representative sample, you may not have all the information, you may not have done a complete analysis. People will respect the endeavour as long as it is done with a degree of professionalism.[32]

In his experience, representatives are more persuasive when they substantiate their arguments with quantified constituency data: "If you walk into caucus and you say 'listen, on the weekend I knocked on 200 doors, and this issue came up fifteen times,' then you have more credibility to say it is something we need to pay attention to," the former minister explains. "You quickly begin to see the convergence of data intelligence coming out of caucus and out of door-knocking with what is coming out of polling and focus groups. If people want their views to be considered in caucus, then that level of local effort and rigour lends legitimacy."[33] As we have seen, there is an increasing expectation that party representatives add information to the party database, which creates competitive pressure to present a well-researched case when advocating a course of action.

Determined parliamentarians leverage support through collegial consultation. They recognize the mutual value of exchanging information by phoning colleagues, meeting with people, and holding public forums. They stop by offices for a chat. They strike up a conversation with a fellow private member or a minister while someone is delivering a long speech in the chamber or during House duty when people are milling around: "I find conversations about the evolution of policy to be fundamentally the most important part of the job," says an MP. "I often call people up, especially ones who have taken positions that I may disagree with, to ask 'what are you thinking? What are we trying to do? How do we create consensus around this? The position you have taken has caught my interest.' As the prime minister says, better is always possible."[34] Hard work is necessary: a private member's mobilization efforts are constrained by colleagues who do not want to incur the label of a maverick or troublemaker, worries about the potential for schemes being leaked, and by shifting loyalties.[35] Members lobby within the enigma that politics requires considerable trust to function, yet its existence engenders suspicion.

Political acumen is necessary to figure out when the party leadership is obscuring disapproval of a policy idea. Instead of saying "no" to a pitch from a backbencher, which would result in disgruntlement, a leader can send the member on a fool's errand of trying to mobilize the caucus.[36] After pitching a policy idea to the prime minister (or premier), a government-side backbencher might be encouraged to get the applicable minister, parliamentary secretary, parliamentary committee chair, and caucus chair onside. For some policies, consultation can span multiple portfolios and actors. After a lot of effort, the member informs the leader that most colleagues are indeed supportive. The leader realizes that the social desirability of being agreeable is not a true measure of support and, in any event, weighs other factors, including the reaction of the media, the extraparliamentary party, and public opinion. The member is advised that the next step is full caucus support. The member dutifully carries on with internal lobbying. But time is passing, and an election is approaching. Turnover in personnel means that a new chief of staff, new minister, and/or a new committee chair need to be persuaded. The new minister avoids taking a position by saying that the issue is now with the people preparing the election platform. Finally, the leader requires the member to consult with the party's election campaign chair. The chair flatly shuts down the member's policy idea by saying that it is not a good strategic fit for the party or the voters that it is targeting. There is no recourse; the parliamentarian must recalibrate. As this runaround suggests, leaders are keen to listen when a sizable contingent of the caucus supports a policy idea, particularly if there is enthusiasm among members assigned to the applicable portfolio(s) and the suggestion is consistent with brand values. Otherwise, the leadership has little interest in a policy suggestion from a backbencher, especially a topic that might divide the caucus or the party's electoral base. As with discipline, the leader devises ways for others to deliver bad news.

Many parliamentarians are mindful of the no surprises rule. Before raising an issue in a forum, they follow the timeless advice to "never mousetrap a colleague," to "always raise the issue first in private," and to "make sure your allies are on side before the meeting even starts."[37] The wisdom of an MP from the 1970s that infiltration through caucus networking is more productive than spontaneously going up to the microphone remains astute today:

> Whoever wanted to make a point, MPs and senators alike, just went to the mic, giving one's opinion, frustration, criticism, suggestion, then simply went back to one's seat. I concluded that if some of us wanted to push a particular point or oppose a project, it was better to do it not through a succession of speakers, which were too clearly identifiable and immediately reduced to a specific bloc, but through loose networks of different colleagues sharing common values, one here, one there, from various regions of the country, thus infiltrating the environment more subtly.[38]

Sometimes animated members praise the leadership's initiatives, other weeks they offer thoughtful criticism in a constructive manner, and at some meetings they say nothing so that others can do so. When they rise to make compelling arguments, they build on the support that they have cultivated in order to convert a critical mass of colleagues. There is safety in numbers: when several private members speak out, it is harder for the party leadership to rein them in. A caucus vehemently opposed to a proposed action tends to get its way.

Members on both sides of the aisle can avail themselves of their privileged access to senior officeholders outside a caucus setting. Some ministers instruct staff to prioritize issues raised by parliamentarians irrespective of party affiliation, possibly according greater urgency to opposition members. Some ministers welcome the opportunity to offer input on the drafting of a private member's bill. Equally, a minister might phone a backbencher who voiced policy differences at a caucus meeting or parliamentary committee in order to hear that member out as well as to convey disappointment that the concerns were not raised in advance. A frank conversation can generate a solution before the issue advances to the next stage in the policy process or magnifies into a bigger issue.

Advocate without Embarrassing the Leader

It should be axiomatic to backbenchers as brand ambassadors that diverging from core party messaging is a serious political problem. They can express an opposing view as long as they do so "in a way that is conscious of the fact that you're part of the team," says an MP. "Part of how you get elected is on the party brand and you're always working to try and make sure you're not doing anything to damage that."[39] Backbenchers can avoid discipline for speaking out of turn when they voice concern about a local issue. It is fine to commit publicly to fight hard for something of obvious importance to constituents or call for more resources in the riding. A government-side backbencher can grant a media interview that telegraphs action to political staff in a non-threatening manner, for example by publicly pledging to raise a concern with officials. Skilfully generating media interest can put a topic on the government's agenda: "It is probably okay to talk about a specific local issue locally. Now, if what's said contradicts a broader message, it would be a problem," declares a member of the Trudeau PMO. "You're not going to get lines or materials on an issue if it's not getting wider traction. It's not worth people's time to put that together."[40] Public advocacy that does not contradict the party leadership demonstrates strong representation without causing problems.

It can be good retail politics for a backbencher to pick a moment to take a disruptive public stand. Doing so involves a calculated decision to build on the generic promise to fight hard by entering the risqué terrain of open criticism. A government-side backbencher emboldened by public outrage trending online can reject messaging on the basis that no public consultation appears to have occurred. One MP in such a circumstance messaged the following to a minister's office moments before a live interview about a local policy issue:

> I am not using those lines on CBC in 20 minutes. Two questions:
> 1. Who consulted the public on this?
> 2. When?[41]

A private member who tries to contain constituent unrest can seek authorization from the whip, the chief of staff, or even the full caucus to go public with an expression of disappointment with a policy.[42] The public stance comes with constraints. When expressing divergence, a member needs to respect the imaginary line between core and non-core party messaging. A news story about a governing party backbencher who vows to lobby the minister is acceptable, but headlines about that member's criticism of the government or demand for the reversal of a recent policy announcement triggers disciplinary measures.

Considerable internal work is required when preparing to defy the whip on a significant issue. It will be recalled that Conservative MP Scott J. Reid threatened to withhold unanimous consent to swiftly pass the COVID-19 Emergency Response Act when he protested the abuse of parliamentary process. The long-time MP, first elected as a member of the Canadian Alliance Party in 2000, voted with his party 99 percent of the time in the 42nd Parliament (11 dissents of 1,082 recorded divisions). Despite this intense partisanship, he cultivates a populist base of loyal supporters because he periodically challenges the establishment, and his constituents see that he cares what they think. Occasionally, Reid's office organizes constituency consultations on hot-button policy issues to guide how he should vote on them. It takes roughly six weeks to design a referendum ballot, print it, mail it to all residences, and receive the completed ballots.[43] A low number of responses still requires him to interpret public sentiment. Then the real work of internal negotiation begins, because a member who collects constituency feedback at cross-purposes with the party line is in a predicament. Reid recalls what happened when he determined that constituents wanted him to support Bill C-45, the Cannabis Act, in spite of leader Andrew Scheer's opposition to it:

> I voted in favour of Bill C-45 to legalize marijuana, whereas my party's caucus voted against it. There were all kinds of questions to consider if I voted against my colleagues: about how I would vote, what my messaging would be, whether I would issue a press release, what it would say. The upside for the party is it shows they don't boss our members around; they're not just trained seals. But an enormous amount of effort goes into coordinating a message that it's not a proxy on supporting the leader. As well, when the public is divided and many do not agree with a party's position, the fact you are going to go offside creates a problem for some members of the caucus because you're making the heat on them worse.[44]

His Bill C-45 experience has layers all too familiar to backbenchers. The Conservative caucus discussed the issue, and the leadership took a position without vote or explanation. As Reid tells it, Scheer dismissed the constituency consultations as "worthless" and advised the MP that voting in favour of the bill would require forfeiting the position of critic of democratic institutions.[45] Reid was given a letter of resignation to sign. It stated the bill was flawed and that a member of the shadow cabinet who listens to constituents must nevertheless vote with the leader. Reid refused to sign the letter. Two months later, without notice, the leader's office issued a news release relieving him of the critic position. When a journalist sought an explanation, Reid did not want to disrupt caucus unity, so he fibbed that the demotion was because of other commitments. That partisans might see nothing wrong with lying to protect an image of party unity "is a sign of just how craven our political culture has become," Reid believes.[46] It is significant that he felt liberated to recount the tale on his website only after Scheer announced that he was stepping down as leader. Unsurprisingly, the veteran MP was left off House of Commons committees at the start of the 43rd Parliament, a trade-off that was probably necessary for him to resolve cognitive dissonance.[47] As Jane Philpott tweeted when she resigned from the cabinet, "there can be a cost to acting on one's principles, but there is a bigger cost to abandoning them."[48]

However they choose to go about it, private members ought to provide constituents with tangible evidence that their members are working hard on their behalf, not on behalf of the party or the government. Those who push the party line without crossing it cause headaches and might endure personal sacrifice. Privately, leaders confide that such individuals are begrudgingly respected, especially those who have the ability to rally the caucus or have a bedrock of regional support.

Consider Partisans' Ideal Type of Parliamentarian

Revered characteristics emerge when speaking with politicians and political staff who sketch a portrait of an elusive ideal type of parliamentarian who is highly effective within a system of strict party discipline. Members of a caucus should consider the existence of these mythical creatures.

As partisans tell it, a politician who combines the best forms of representation should possess uncanny shrewdness that elevates their collective ability to accomplish objectives. There ought to be sensitivity to helping the group, such that an individual accomplishment elevates the group's standing. There is a sense of fair play: a parliamentarian should call out executives who circumvent appropriate consultation processes, and hold firm with latecomers who skipped opportunities for input. Work ethic should reflect an infectious passion to improve society or to assist a constituent, causing the representative to fixate on achieving a policy objective or stopping another party from doing so. Their public profile and their drive to get ahead are means to an end and not ends in themselves. The widely admired politician is mindful that a parliamentary career can be short, which spurs a sense of urgency to make a mark.

Model parliamentarians know that raising a concern for the first time at a caucus meeting can be poorly received. They lay the groundwork for being critical, recognizing that it can take months or years of effort to advance an idea. They might work on multiple files simultaneously, choosing to prioritize topics that align with the government's agenda that have better chances of progressing, irrespective of being on the opposition benches. They talk with the person responsible for the file or with the applicable staffer; in small caucuses, they discuss their positions with the leader directly. They might attend a multitude of caucus committees to ask for support and be forceful about the consequences of inaction. They can persuade a colleague to switch slots in the queue to present a private member's bill. If their party is in government, then they know to work with the minister and then lobby other members of the cabinet, particularly those on the applicable cabinet committee that will end up scrutinizing a proposal, because their ability to convince a minister about a course of action increases if another minister agrees. If their party is in opposition, then they keep its critic informed as they cautiously cross party lines to build a coalition. They obtain validation from stakeholder groups and opinion leaders who help to build external support. As they gain momentum, they arrange to debrief the leader, whose interest perks up if evidence of public support is produced and a critical mass of caucus is onside.

The pertinent people might receive notice when a quintessential party parliamentarian is intent on voicing an opinion in the caucus. As a former MP puts it, when "people understand that you are trying to solve a problem at the local level with the least disruption possible, it is amazing how much co-operation you will get."[49] Instead of grandstanding or causing tension, the parliamentarian makes a reasoned argument; instead of seeking accolades, that person conveys the humility of caring less about getting credit for their work than about advancing the issue. These types of parliamentarians are proud when they manage to convince their colleagues how to vote, but they are also comfortable backing off when someone proposes a better way forward, and while they are disappointed when their efforts at persuasion fail they recognize that it is not possible to win all arguments. They show respect by expressing disappointment instead of making accusations or hurling insults, because conceding that a colleague is correct keeps the focus on policy rather than on personality. In return, they find more latitude when the next issue comes along.

Of course, it is unlikely that any MP, MLA, MPP, MNA, or MHA can or should exhibit all of these traits. For one thing, the above is an "inside the bubble" perspective with little regard for what constituents want or need, and does not take into account the representative's job security, caucus dynamics, or political resolve. But equipping backbenchers with knowledge is possibly the most crucial step toward empowering them in a system that produces trained seals and party robots.

CONCLUSION AND RECOMMENDATIONS

Understanding how discipline both enhances and corrodes democracy is essential for identifying how private members can exert political influence. The research presented in this book means that we can now better describe hidden components of party discipline in Canadian politics. Social conditioning, institutional structures, leader-centric systems, personal ambition, and communications are some of the many factors that contribute to its intensification. The biggest unknown is how to relax its iron grip.

I have looked at the evolution of representation from the late twentieth century through to today's political terrain of permanent campaigning, marketing, and digital communication. Information collected from current and former elected officials and political staff shows that strict party discipline is no longer a characteristic that should be associated mainly with activity in legislative chambers. The revelations about strategic thinking and internal practices add to our awareness of the strains among Burkean thinkers, constituency advocates, team players, and other representative styles. We can grasp why Canadian partisans, particularly government-side backbenchers, are acclimatized to avoid saying anything publicly that hints at caucus division. Whether the occupants of a legislative assembly have more collective strength than the political institutions that condition their behaviour seems to point to the negative.[50] The vast majority of parliamentarians recognize the considerable advantages of strong parties given that their actions and inactions endorse party superiority.

The overall contribution of this book is a fresh account of how parliamentary politics operates in Canada. The work of private members has expanded from law-making and casework to embodying the party brand. Specifically, we now have a better understanding that party discipline has spread, like a social contagion, to become message discipline in all public forums. But the question remains: why do Canadian parliamentarians so rarely stray from party boundaries? Politicians have their own minds; they aren't programmable. Surely, only demagogues can demand that parliamentarians behave as yes-men and yes-women. Reality is more unsettling: across Canada, party leaders and their agents leverage the psychology of groups within team structures to motivate cohesion. They point to media alarmism as evidence of what happens when someone goes rogue. A human predisposition to conformity is helped along by requiring applicants interested in being election candidates to sign a values contract, reinforced by group pressure, rewards, and punishments. The ontology of discipline spans many escalating steps of internal conversations, and there is inconsistency of consequence. It can take years for members to learn how to mobilize within these structural constraints, by which time they are firmly entrenched within them – provided they are re-elected.

Message discipline is both a curse and a blessing. The integration of branding into party politics helps political groups to achieve their objectives. Staying on-message provides citizens with clear options, including in the information swamp of social media, in which parliamentarians benefit from knowing the party line on innumerable issues. The pressure to post new content online, the grind of examining draft legislation, and the esotericism of standing orders mean that private members, including those stereotyped as team players, mavericks, and troublemakers, behave as party robots more often than they care to admit. Acting as a party representative generates a public impression of substandard representation. That can create an opening for blunt populists to provide a refreshing alternative to plastic politicians.

Several case studies shed light on the practicalities of parliamentary politics in Canada. The dogged determination of Brian Mulroney to form personal relationships with his caucus is a master class in fostering party cohesion; the havoc during the SNC-Lavalin affair is a seminal example of the consequences of internal disputes playing out in public. Other stories bring to the fore how backbenchers are absorbed into the government, at the potential cost of relinquishing their responsibility to keep it accountable. Documentary films show despondent MPs in Ottawa in the early 1970s and downcast MLAs in BC forty years later. Amateur video of MP David Wilks lays bare the perils of having honest conversations with constituents, and the open letter from MLA Robyn Luff about the intricacies of party discipline incurred inevitable career consequences. Vignettes pull back the curtain. How Carolyn Bennett coped with a trap vote, the digital brand experiences of Celina Caesar-Chavannes, the disillusionment of Ryan Cleary, the resolve of Kathleen Wynne, the constituent surveys organized by Scott J. Reid, and the caucus evictions of Jane Philpott and Jody Wilson-Raybould are indicative of the varied ways that parliamentarians struggle with the domination of parliamentary parties. Individual agency is further suppressed during focusing events when cross-party solidarity shelves partisan sniping, as occurred in the coronavirus pandemic. Other incidents and anecdotes spanning more than half a century show that party discipline is embedded in Canadian parliamentary politics. It bears repeating that in 1962 a Canadian MP said that the "party system simply does not tolerate MPs who disagree publicly with their party."[51] Message discipline is not new; it is stricter, it is more organized, and it is omnipresent. As Harold Innis might observe, digital tools to monitor compliance are contributing to cohesive messaging and, in turn, to the subjugation of election candidates and backbenchers.

At a more granular level, we can see the hidden side of parliamentary politics. It is clearer why party discipline shields the cabinet from backbench colleagues who might take them to task. We now have a much better idea of the work of party whips, the dynamics of caucus meetings, and the communication functions of caucus research bureaus. We can see why partisans push topics that contrast their united caucus with the disarray of an opponent that frantically tries to temper internal disagreement while contending with the news value of dissent. A culture of secrecy and an abhorrence of surprises align with a political marketing philosophy of controlling communications, which includes urging parliamentarians to amplify digital messages as part of an authentic story. The vanguard of party discipline is the use of databases that augment the sales role of individual backbenchers. The sum of these institutional structures makes representatives replaceable. Yet parliamentarians have more leeway than they think because the disruption wrought by a public divorce means that leaders desperately want to avoid banishing a rogue agent who has broken the party franchising covenant.

What can be done to achieve a better equilibrium between the circle of power around a party leader and the repressed agency of individual politicians? I see little point in replicating a wish list of changes that are exceedingly difficult to implement, of supporting democratic reforms with a side effect of tighter party messaging, or daydreaming about flights of fancy such as expecting the media to behave differently. It is possible that change will erupt from the experiments with virtual sittings of legislatures required during the pandemic and, at each electoral cycle, from digital natives who instill new norms of behaviour on partisans whose formative political learning occurred before social media. In the meantime, we can contemplate ways that parliamentarians can augment their roles within existing constraints as part of a political family.

The Samara Centre has suggestions.[52] Parliamentarians can organize into coalitions that make it hard for the leader to ignore. Backbenchers can insist on having a say in committee chair appointments and membership, and cross-party interactions can reduce political polarization. They can mingle with opponents in informal spaces within the parliamentary precinct, by travelling with committees, and by participating in all-party caucuses and parliamentary friendship groups. As well, a caucus can require the leader to answer to backbench committees. In Ottawa, MPs can elect to opt in to the provisions of the Reform Act, 2014, a model that parliamentarians in provincial legislatures might consider emulating.

A close reading of this book can generate other ideas. Advocates of electoral reform ought to examine how any proposed change would affect the power of political parties over legislators. Backbenchers could work to convince the extraparliamentary party to define the limits of party discipline in the party constitution, which in turn would lay the groundwork for providing election candidates and private members with greater clarity about their freedoms and obligations, and for revising the legislature's standing orders. Organizations such as the Samara Centre could deliver civic education training to the general public, including aspiring candidates, possibly by engaging a network of former parliamentarians. Another possibility is to create a parliamentarian bill of rights or a caucus code of conduct, including a statement outlining roles and responsibilities, in order to provide some transparency around discipline. In Ottawa, the Reform Act could be expanded; for example, the caucus could vote on whether the caucus research bureau ought to report to the caucus chair and to require the party to release constituent data to a parliamentarian who leaves the caucus. Across Canada, parliamentarians can insist on regular opportunities to engage with a leader without staff present, including a dedicated in camera segment of caucus meetings requiring staff to exit the room and turn over notetaking to the caucus chair.

A new wave of research on discipline in party politics would help us to comprehend what, if any, rule changes are warranted. Some aspects of internal party affairs that attracted attention from the 1960s to the 1980s remain intriguing today, including parliamentarians' job satisfaction. A recent spurt of research on political staff is promising.[53] Newer research methodologies such as computerized counting of keywords could ascertain coordinated message repetition versus genuine two-way interactions with citizens. Thinking about where parliamentarians fit within a partisan "team" is more holistic than analyzing their voting records. Because so much is walled off to outside observers, parliamentary scholars might wish to consider interdisciplinary research, for example exploring the pathology of rigid team discipline in other sectors of society.

Three areas of internal party affairs stand out for study. First, candidate vetting. On balance, party politics is more ethical, inclusive, transparent, and accountable than ever. However, the pre-nomination process of candidate selection is largely unregulated and can curtail the political careers of people who have learned from their mistakes. Non-conformists are unlikely to make it through, thus depriving Canadians of a contingent of potential representatives willing to take on power brokers for the betterment of society. Put another way, screening out people most likely to speak truth to power means that legislative assemblies are increasingly likely to be filled with representatives unwilling to mount a healthy challenge to party discipline. Any research in this murky area must bear in mind that state regulation of political parties is a prickly topic.[54]

Second, caucus research bureaus. Private members require research assistance to conduct informed scrutiny of the government and investigate policy ideas. However, in Ottawa the research bureaus have become partisan communications departments for leaders' offices, and the governing party's bureau is a messaging service for the PMO and ministers' offices. We lack information to assess whether these political staff improve or hinder a backbencher's role in the public policy process, and to what extent the lines between parliamentary and extraparliamentary operations are blurred. To date, there has not been a study of caucus services in the provinces, which would help us further comprehend "executive creep" and party discipline.[55] Greater scrutiny of the public finance arrangements could help ensure that government-side backbenchers can hold the political executive to account and receive timely research support for their own initiatives that is arms-length from the leader's office.

Third, party databases. Who controls the collection, storage, and usage of data on individual Canadians has repercussions for representation. The little that we know about these digital platforms is unsettling, given that they can be used to ramp up political divisions in society and communicate deceptive information, and privacy commissioners are sounding the alarm about the ethics of data harvesting and database marketing.[56] An unstudied angle is the erosion of parliamentarian sovereignty when party operatives control the digital infrastructure vital to public outreach, fundraising, and getting out the vote.

These are some of the unseen institutional systems that combine with social forces to pressure Canadian politicians to toe the party line. This book has explained that team thinking, party values, and brand conformity narrate political representation in Canada, especially for backbenchers on the government side of the House. It argues that party discipline is a problematic necessity whose advocates demand consistent messaging from all public figures affiliated with the party. It clarifies that the party whip, whose image is indelibly tied to the harsher side of party discipline, is more aptly described as a human resources manager than a disciplinarian. It also demonstrates why so many parliamentarians lose their voice despite the availability of social media platforms without gatekeepers. Ultimately, it shows that people elected to the House of Commons and provincial legislatures must overcome considerable obstacles to develop a style of representation that their constituents believe is more inquisitive than compliant.

Appendix 1

INTERVIEW PARTICIPANTS

The following individuals were formally interviewed for this book. Position titles refer to the highest level of political office that they held or had held at the time of the interview. Tables showing distribution by position title, party, province, and gender appear in Appendix 2.

Supplementary conversations were held by telephone, email, and/or in person with some participants. Informal conversations were also held with approximately a dozen people not listed here who were asked for details about a specific event or topic related to their expertise, some of whom are identified in the chapter notes.

Alward, David. Thirty-second premier of New Brunswick and former PC MLA for Woodstock. November 14, 2018.

Andrews, Scott. Former Independent MP for Avalon. July 10, 2018.

Barbot, Vivian. Former Bloc Québécois MP for Papineau and former interim party leader. October 29, 2018.

Bennett, Carolyn. Minister in PM Justin Trudeau's government and Liberal MP for Toronto–St. Paul's. August 9, 2018.

Bennett, Cathy. Liberal MHA for Virginia Waters and former minister in NL Premier Ball's government. August 2, 2018.

Bernier, Maxime. People's Party of Canada leader, MP for Beauce, and former minister in PM Harper's government. November 6, 2018.

Blady, Sharon. Former minister in Manitoba Premier Selinger's government and former NDP MLA for Kirkfield Park. July 25, 2018.

Boessenkool, Ken. Former chief of staff to BC Premier Christy Clark and senior adviser to PM Harper. July 18, 2018.

Boudria, Don. Former minister and chief whip in PM Chrétien's government and former Liberal MP for Glengarry-Prescott-Russell. October 26, 2018.

Caesar-Chavannes, Celina. Independent MP for Whitby. July 19, 2019.

Campbell, Kim. Nineteenth prime minister of Canada and former PC MP for Vancouver Centre. May 1, 2018.

Carter, Stephen. Former chief of staff to Alberta Premier Redford. July 25, 2018.

Catterall, Marlene. Former chief whip in PM Chrétien's government and former Liberal MP for Ottawa West–Nepean. November 26, 2018.

Charest, Jean. Twenty-ninth premier of Quebec, former PC Party of Canada leader and federal minister, and former PC MP and Liberal MNA for Sherbrooke. August 6, 2018.

Chong, Michael. Conservative MP for Wellington–Halton Hills and former minister in PM Harper's government. November 1, 2018.

Churley, Marilyn. Former minister in Ontario Premier Rae's government and former NDP MPP for Toronto-Danforth. November 6, 2018.

Clark, Glen. Thirty-first premier of British Columbia and former NDP MLA for Vancouver-Kingsway. September 25, 2018.

Clark, Joe. Sixteenth prime minister of Canada and former PC MP for Yellowhead and Calgary Centre. January 24, 2019.

Cleary, Ryan. Former NDP MP for St. John's South–Mount Pearl. March 29, 2018.

Clement, Tony. Conservative MP for Parry Sound–Muskoka and former minister in PM Harper's government. July 3, 2018.

Cooper, Michael. Conservative MP for St. Albert–Edmonton. November 15, 2018.

Cotton, Melissa. Managing director of the Liberal Research Bureau. June 21, 2018.

Davis, Paul. Twelfth premier of Newfoundland and Labrador and PC MHA for Topsail-Paradise. May 8, 2018.

Day, Stockwell. Former Canadian Alliance Party leader, former minister in PM Harper's government, and former Conservative MP for Okanagan-Coquihalla. July 27, 2018.

Delacourt, John. Former director of communications in the Liberal Research Bureau. July 13, 2018.

Donolo, Peter. Former director of communications in Jean Chrétien's PMO and former chief of staff to Liberal leader Michael Ignatieff. May 4, 2018.

Doyle, Teresa. Green candidate in Cadigan in the 2015 federal election. November 23, 2018.

Dubé, Matthew. NDP MP for Beloeil-Chambly and caucus chair. May 3, 2018.

Duceppe, Gilles. Former Bloc Québécois leader and former MP for Laurier–Sainte-Marie. October 30, 2018.

Dufour, Valérie. Former deputy director of communications to NDP leader Tom Mulcair. August 23, 2018.

Dunderdale, Kathy. Tenth premier of Newfoundland and Labrador and former PC MHA for Virginia Waters. May 17, 2018.

Easter, Wayne. Liberal MP for Malpeque and former minister in PM Chrétien's government. July 27, 2018.

Edwards, Jim. Former minister and chief whip in PM Campbell's government and former PC MP for Edmonton Southwest. November 16, 2018.

Erskine-Smith, Nathaniel. Liberal MP for Beaches–East York. August 2, 2018.

Finn, John. Liberal MHA for Stephenville–Port au Port and party whip in NL Premier Ball's government. July 10, 2018.

Fletcher, Steven. Independent MLA for Assiniboia, former minister of state in PM Harper's government, and former Conservative MP for Charleswood–St. James–Assiniboia. August 3, 2018.

Fournier, Jean-Marc. Minister in Quebec Liberal Premier Couillard's government, former leader of the official opposition, and Liberal MNA for Saint-Laurent. October 15, 2018.

Fox, Bill. Former director of communications in Brian Mulroney's PMO. June 4, 2020.

Gallant, Suzanne. Digital video producer in the 2017 BC and 2018 Ontario NDP election campaigns. June 29, 2018.

Graham, Kate. Liberal candidate in London North Centre in the 2018 Ontario election. June 20, 2018.

Grimes, Roger. Eighth premier of Newfoundland and Labrador and former Liberal MHA for Exploits. June 15, 2018.

Groguhé, Sadia. Former NDP MP for Saint-Lambert and deputy whip. October 22, 2018.

Harder, Peter. Government representative in the Senate for PM Justin Trudeau. March 26, 2019.

Harquail, Maureen. Conservative candidate in Willowdale in the 2008 federal by-election, St. Paul's 2011 federal election candidate, and Don Valley East 2015 federal election candidate. November 29, 2018.

Hill, Jay. Former government House leader and chief whip in PM Harper's government and former Conservative MP for Prince George–Peace River. August 22, 2018.

Holland, Mark. Liberal MP for Ajax and chief whip in PM Justin Trudeau's government. July 27, 2019.

Houde, Philip. Chief of staff to Manitoba Premier Pallister. July 18, 2018.

Ignatieff, Michael. Former Liberal Party of Canada leader and former MP for Etobicoke-Lakeshore. August 6, 2018.

Jones, Yvonne. Liberal MP for Labrador, former minister in NL Premier Grimes's government, and former MHA for Cartright. July 23, 2018.

Krawetz, Ken. Special adviser to Saskatchewan Premier Moe, former minister in Saskatchewan Premier Wall's government, and former Saskatchewan Party MLA for Canora-Pelly. November 22, 2018.

Kusie, Stephanie. Conservative MP for Calgary Midnapore. August 2, 2018.

Lalonde, Marie-France. Liberal MPP for Orléans, former government whip, and former minister in Ontario Premier Wynne's government. November 6, 2018.

Leffler, Sandra. Former special adviser to a minister in PM Chrétien's government and former assistant to a Liberal MP. August 14, 2018.

Leichnitz, Jordan. Former deputy chief of staff to NDP leader Tom Mulcair. July 31, 2018.

Leitch, Kellie. Conservative MP for Simcoe-Grey and former minister in PM Harper's government. December 16, 2018.

Leslie, Andrew. Liberal MP for Orléans and former chief whip in PM Justin Trudeau's government. July 5, 2018.

Leslie, Megan. Former NDP deputy leader and former MP for Halifax. July 27, 2018.

Lord, Bernard. Thirtieth premier of New Brunswick and former PC MLA for Moncton East. December 10, 2018.

Luff, Robyn. Independent MLA for Calgary East. November 15, 2018.

MacKay, Peter. Former PC Party of Canada leader, former minister in PM Harper's government, and former Conservative MP for Central Nova. October 30, 2018.

MacKinnon, Steven. Liberal MP for Gatineau. August 14, 2018.

MacLauchlan, Wade. Thirty-second premier of Prince Edward Island and Liberal MLA for York–Oyster Bed. June 28, 2018.

Maguire, Brendan. Liberal MLA for Halifax Atlantic and former government whip in Nova Scotia Premier McNeil's government. October 16, 2018.

Marshall, Elizabeth. Conservative senator, former Senate whip for PM Harper's government, minister in NL Premier Williams's government, and former PC MHA for Topsail. April 27, 2018.

Marshall, Hamish. Manager of Andrew Scheer's Conservative leadership campaign and former manager of strategic planning in Stephen Harper's PMO. July 4, 2018.

Martin, Paul. Twenty-first prime minister of Canada and former Liberal MP for LaSalle-Émard. July 26, 2018.

May, Elizabeth. Federal Green Party leader and MP for Saanich–Gulf Islands. October 24, 2018.

Mayer, Colleen. Minister in Manitoba Premier Pallister's government, former government whip, and PC MLA for St. Vital. November 16, 2018.

McDonald, Ken. Liberal MP for Avalon. June 26, 2018.

McGrath, Anne. Former chief of staff to NDP leader Jack Layton and chair of the 2015 NDP federal campaign. April 24, 2018.

McGuinty, Dalton. Twenty-fourth premier of Ontario and former Liberal MPP for Ottawa South. August 16, 2018.

McLellan, Anne. Former minister in PM Chrétien's government and PM Martin's government and former Liberal MP for Edmonton Centre. April 18, 2018.

Ménard, Nicole. Opposition whip, former chief whip in Quebec Premier Couillard's government, and Liberal MNA for Laporte. December 11, 2018.

Mendès, Alexandra. Liberal MP for Brossard-Saint-Lambert. July 27, 2018.

Menezes, Jacqueline. Former ministerial staffer in Ontario Premier McGuinty's government and Liberal candidate in Oshawa in 2011 Ontario election. August 7, 2018.

Michael, Lorraine. Former provincial party leader and NDP MHA for St. John's East–Quidi Vidi. November 27, 2018.

Mitchell, Grant. Independent Senators Group senator, former provincial leader, and former Liberal MLA for Edmonton Meadowlark. June 11, 2018.

Morton, Ted. Former minister in Alberta Premier Stelmach's government and Premier Redford's government and former PC MLA for Foothills–Rocky View. July 21, 2018.

Mulroney, Brian. Eighteenth prime minister of Canada and former PC MP for Charlevoix. December 17, 2018.

Muttart, Patrick. Former deputy chief of staff in Stephen Harper's PMO. June 4, 2018.

Name withheld. Coalition Avenir Québec MNA. January 14, 2019.

Name withheld. Director of communications, minister's office in PM Justin Trudeau's government. July 12, 2018.

Name withheld. Employee in Conservative opposition whip's office. March 6, 2019.

Name withheld. Employee in Justin Trudeau's PMO. July 13, 2018.

Name withheld. Employee in Liberal Research Bureau. October 29, 2018.

Name withheld. Former minister in PM Justin Trudeau's government. September 24, 2018.

Name withheld. Former PC MHA in Newfoundland and Labrador. November 13, 2018.

Name withheld. Former political assistant in Manitoba Premier Pallister's government. October 11, 2018.

Name withheld. Liberal candidate in Ontario in the 2015 federal election. August 8, 2018.

Name withheld. Minister in PM Justin Trudeau's government. November 30, 2018.

Name withheld. Parliamentary assistant to a Nova Scotia Liberal MP. August 21, 2018.

Name withheld. Parliamentary assistant to an Alberta Conservative MP. April 6, 2018.

Norris, Rob. Former minister in Saskatchewan Premier Wall's government and former Saskatchewan Party MLA for Saskatoon Greystone. November 16, 2018.

O'Brien, Jordan. Former chief of staff to New Brunswick Premier Gallant and director of communications to Premier Graham. November 26, 2018.

Obhrai, Deepak. Conservative MP for Calgary Forest Lawn. June 12, 2018.

Oliphant, Rob. Liberal MP for Don Valley West. July 23, 2018.

Ouellette, Robert-Falcon. Liberal MP for Winnipeg Centre. October 2, 2018.

Paradis, Melanie. Candidate support communications in the 2018 Ontario PC election campaign. August 9, 2018.

Philpott, Jane. Former minister in PM Justin Trudeau's government and Independent MP for Markham-Stouffville. June 19, 2019.

Purchase, Kate. Executive director of communications and planning in Justin Trudeau's PMO. October 12, 2018.

Rae, Bob. Twenty-first premier of Ontario, former interim Liberal Party of Canada leader, former Liberal MP for Toronto Centre, and former NDP MPP for York South. August 15, 2018.

Raitt, Lisa. Conservative MP for Milton and former minister in PM Harper's government. January 10, 2019.

Redman, Karen. Former chief whip in PM Martin's government and former Liberal MP for Kitchener Centre. October 26, 2018.

Reid, Ross. Former minister in PM Campbell's government, former PC MP for St. John's East, and manager of NL Premier Williams and Premier Dunderdale election campaigns. October 17, 2018.

Reid, Scott. Former director of communications in Paul Martin's PMO. July 17, 2018.

Reid, Scott J. Conservative MP for Lanark-Frontenac-Kingston. September 19, 2018.

Roberts, Edward. Former minister in NL Premier Smallwood's government and Premier Wells's government, former provincial party leader, and former Liberal MHA for White Bay North. April 12, 2018.

Robinson, Svend. Former NDP MP for Burnaby. August 16, 2018.

Rogers, Chad. War room staff in the 2006 Conservative federal election campaign and secretary in the 2011 PC Ontario election campaign. February 28, 2019.

Rutkowski, Jim. Principal secretary to Alberta Premier Notley. June 12, 2018.

Semansky, Paris. Former ministerial chief of staff in Ontario Premier Wynne's government and minister's director of communications in Premier McGuinty's government. August 15, 2018.

Settee, Priscilla. NDP candidate in Saskatoon-Wanuskewin in the 2004 federal election. January 11, 2019.

Simard, Amanda. Independent MPP for Glengarry-Prescott-Russell. February 20, 2019.

Simms, Scott. Liberal MP for Coast of Bays–Central–Notre Dame. July 4, 2018.

Smith, Danielle. Former Wildrose Party leader in Alberta and former PC MLA for Highwood. July 20, 2018.

Steele, Graham. Former minister in Nova Scotia Premier Dexter's government and former NDP MLA for Halifax Fairview. November 16, 2018.

Stewart, Kennedy. NDP MP for Burnaby South. July 13, 2018.

Stubbs, Shannon. Conservative MP for Lakeland. December 21, 2018.

Therrien, Carole. Former executive assistant for appointments in Jean Chrétien's PMO. June 14, 2018.

Thompson, Allan. Liberal candidate in Huron-Bruce in the 2015 federal election. June 8, 2018.

Turp, Daniel. Former Bloc Québécois MP for Beauharnois-Salaberry and former Parti Québécois MNA for Mercier. October 24, 2018.

Vaughan, Adam. Liberal MP for Spadina–Fort York. July 31, 2018.

Weir, Elizabeth. Former party leader in New Brunswick and former NDP MLA for Saint John Harbour. November 1, 2018.

Weir, Erin. Independent MP for Regina-Lewvan. July 20, 2018.

Weiss, Julie. Constituency director for an Ontario Independent MP. June 25, 2019.

Weissenberger, John. Former manager of Jason Kenney's United Conservative leadership campaign and minister's chief of staff in PM Harper's government. August 10, 2018.

Wells, Clyde. Fifth premier of Newfoundland and Labrador and former Liberal MHA for Bay of Islands. May 24, 2018.

Whalen, Nick. Liberal MP for St. John's East. May 11, 2018.

Wilks, David. Former Conservative MP for Kootenay–Columbia. April 17, 2019.

Wilson-Raybould, Jody. Former minister in PM Justin Trudeau's government and Independent MP for Vancouver Granville. July 21, 2019.

Wynne, Kathleen. Twenty-fifth premier of Ontario and Liberal MPP for Don Valley West. December 7, 2018.

Appendix 2

INTERVIEW SAMPLING
AND RECRUITMENT

In the 1990s, only two MPs turned down David Docherty's interview requests for *Mr. Smith Goes to Ottawa,* and Donald Savoie was denied just once for *Governing from the Centre.*[1] Such high participation rates are unheard of in a digital world. Details about the interview recruitment process used in this book can help researchers to customize their own attempts.

SAMPLING AND RECRUITMENT

Identifying potential interview respondents was guided by maximum variation sampling. To collect information from the widest range of perspectives, I used my judgment to identify a diverse pool of potential participants to make generalizations. During the research, I tracked the distribution of types of occupational role, province, gender, race, and party affiliation of participants. When I noticed that participation in a category was underrepresented, and when information saturation occurred from other forms of sampling, I recruited people in specific categories to reach a minimum number in a participant group. I used three specific sampling methods to develop a robust sample.

1 *Purposeful sampling* (recruiting people who meet specific criteria). In April 2018, letters of introduction were mailed to all premiers, Prime Minister Trudeau's chief of staff, federal party whips and deputy whips, federal caucus chairs, and whips in the Senate. Letters to former prime ministers, former leaders of the opposition, and former federal

party whips were mailed through the Canadian Association of Former Parliamentarians. I phoned and/or emailed a number of provincial party whips, a random sample of MPs with an oversample of governing party backbenchers, federal and provincial private members who were recently featured in news stories about party discipline, and MPs who contributed to the book *Turning Parliament Inside Out.* A research assistant searched LinkedIn profiles to identify recent staff in the Liberal Research Bureau. When forty interviews were completed, follow-up reminders with white male MPs were paused, and efforts were redoubled to connect with women, Indigenous peoples, visible minorities, and representatives in select provinces.

2 *Convenience sampling* (recruiting participants because of their ease of access). I requested interviews with some people whom I know personally, have met at events, and/or previously interviewed. Newfoundland and Labrador was oversampled to benefit from my ability to obtain candid information and as a counterbalance to larger polities. I mailed letters of introduction to all seven MPs in Newfoundland and Labrador, and I reached out to many of the province's former premiers. Later I contacted approximately a dozen people for information about specific events or issues, such as the SNC-Lavalin affair.

3 *Snowball sampling* (obtaining referrals from participants). I asked some colleagues and a small number of participants for referrals within specific cohort criteria. Staff who replied to my letters to sitting premiers sometimes referred the requests to another participant. When approximately eighty interviews were completed, in July 2018 journalist Susan Delacourt posted a Facebook message inviting women interested in participating in the study to contact her.

Generally, women were more likely than men to exhibit one or more of the following behaviours: to require persistent contact, including post-interview; to ignore requests instead of declining them; to withdraw after agreeing; to volunteer a resumé; to mention that infants required their attention; to ask who else had participated; to check with a senior political staffer about participating; to require anonymity; to deny permission to be audio recorded; to request the audio recording and/or transcript; or to return a transcript or quotation with edits. Regardless of gender, the greatest caution was exhibited by sitting members of cabinet, current caucus officers, and active political staff.

All told, I attempted to connect with nearly two hundred people by telephone, email, and/or mail over many weeks until I was informed of a decision or abandoned the request. Approximately two-thirds of requests became interviews listed in Appendix 1 ($n = 131$), and roughly one-third refused ($n = 31$) or did not acknowledge the communication ($n = 36$). Refusals were often couched in soft tones that the person was unavailable, travelling, or busy. The nicest refusal was from former Prime Minister John Turner, whose phone call to turn me down became a pleasant conversation. Tables A1 and A2 present a distribution of participation.

Interviews were administered by telephone, except for some in-person conversations in St. John's. Two interviews were in French, and a few used both official languages. Notes were typed during the conversations, and students were hired to prepare transcripts of some audio recordings. Some quotations were lightly edited for clarity before presenting them to participants for approval.

INTERVIEW DISCUSSION GUIDE

As part of interview recruitment, participants were provided with a researcher biography, project information, a consent form, and a discussion

TABLE A1
Distribution of interview participants by position and party

Highest position	Liberal	Tories[1]	NDP	Other	Independent[2]	Total
PMs and premiers	7	7	2	–	–	16
Ministers	12	12	3	3	3	33
Opposition leaders	2	–	2	4	–	8
MPs and MLAs	16	7	6	2	5	36
Election candidates	3	1	1	1	–	6
Staff, executive	10	8	1	–	–	19
Staff, non-executive	5	3	4	–	1	13
Total	55	38	19	10	9	131

Notes:
1 Conservative, Progressive Conservative, and United Conservative.
2 Members or their staff no longer affiliated with a political party at the time of the interview.

TABLE A2
Distribution of interview participants by province and gender

Province	Men	Women	Total
Ottawa[1]	9	8	17
British Columbia	6	4	10
Alberta	10	6	16
Saskatchewan	3	1	4
Manitoba	3	3	6
Ontario	15	18	33
Quebec	9	6	15
New Brunswick	3	1	4
Nova Scotia	4	1	5
Prince Edward Island	2	1	3
Newfoundland and Labrador	11	7	18
Total	75	56	131

Note:
1 Ottawa-based political staff.

guide. Most interviews were semi-structured, guided by the questions listed below. After forty interviews were completed, "party discipline" was replaced with "party cohesion" to reduce the emphasis on the punitive nature of party politics. After seventy interviews were completed, conversations became open ended and began by asking "what do you think should appear in a book about party discipline?" After one hundred interviews were completed, the remaining ones transitioned to specific topics and/or experiences.

1 In your experience, what does party discipline/cohesion involve? Why is party discipline/cohesion necessary? What happens without it? When is party discipline/cohesion excessive?
2 Thinking about communications, to what extent is staying on-message an appropriate mindset? Can you tell me about times that you witnessed political parties try to coordinate their messages?
3 Drawing on your own experiences, can you offer examples of people promoting consistent messaging?
4 Please describe forums where candidates and parliamentarians are free to speak their minds – where they can question the party line, raise new ideas, disagree with leadership, challenge messaging, et cetera.

5 In your experience, what are the implications for a party if someone goes off-message? For the individual?

6 Can you help me to understand what is involved with the screening/vetting of election candidates and political staff?

7 To what extent, if any, do party discipline/cohesion and message co-ordination constitute harassment? Bullying?

8 It would be helpful to understand ways that I could access internal political party files related to party discipline/cohesion and message coordination. Do you have any suggestions?

9 Should anything else appear in a book about party discipline/cohesion and message coordination in Canada?

Unstructured follow-ups were conducted with some participants to collect information on specific topics, such as asking a former party whip for details about how things work or sharing a draft chapter with select practitioners to prompt a focused conversation.

Notes

CHAPTER 1: PARTY DISCIPLINE IN CANADA

1 Kohut (2015); MacLeod (2018).
2 Helliwell, Layard, and Sachs (2019).
3 Some of the top sources of pride in Canada, according to a public opinion survey (Jedwab 2019).
4 Applicable sources for this paragraph include Aucoin (2012); Katz and Mair (2018); Patten (2017).
5 Moore (2001), 8–9. See also Cullen (2011), 10.
6 In Manitoba, "upperbencher" is sometimes used.
7 Strøm and Müeller (1999), 1.
8 Galloway (2013); Ibbitson (2013). But see Chartash et al. (2020); Kam (2009), 8.
9 Carty and Young (2012), 105; Thomas (1985a), 80. See also Strøm and Müeller (1999), 2–3.
10 Clarke et al. (2019), Chapter 2.
11 Stanbury (2003), 17. See also Environics (2013); Godbout (2020), 228.
12 Martin (2002).
13 Docherty (1997), 136–70; Franks (1987), 99–115; Jackson (1968), 6–7.
14 Chong (2017), 81. See also Godbout (2020); Malloy (2006), 117–18.
15 For example, Wilson (2016a). Most adopted motions become non-binding resolutions that express an opinion. Occasionally, they are a binding order.
16 For warnings about leaders' power, see Carrigan (1968), 206, 210, 225; Kornberg and Campbell (1978), 556. For the growth of political staff, see Craft (2016), 45–70; Esselment and Wilson (2017), 225–26. For a history of political staff, see Benoit (2006); D'Aquino (1973).
17 For example, Franks (1987); Martin (2010); Simpson (2001); Stewart (1971); Turner (2009); Wilson (2016a), 27–28.
18 Stewart (1971), 159.
19 Boyer (2003), 248.

20 Gibson (1978), 51.
21 Rathgeber (2014), 119.
22 Kornberg and Campbell (1978), 558, 564. See also Johnston (1986), 263.
23 Thomas (1978), 155.
24 For example, Morden, Hilderman, and Anderson (2018a).
25 Martin (2013).
26 Simpson (2001), 51.
27 Wells (2018).
28 Godbout (2020), 5–7.
29 Clark (2006); Ditchburn (2016); Loat and MacMillan (2014); Martin (2010).
30 Curry and Thompson (2013).
31 Voting data calculations courtesy of Jean-François Godbout. Note that some MPs do not serve the entire Parliament, and none participated in all 1,379 votes.
32 The willingness of Nathaniel Erskine-Smith, Liberal MP for Beaches–East York, to challenge the party line is mentioned in Chapter 10.
33 Heard (2014), 130; Steele (2014), 34; Stewart (1989), 26–27.
34 Massicotte (1989), 509.
35 Holman (2013).
36 Thomas and White (2015), 371. See also Docherty (2005), 120; Franks (2007).
37 For example, Bill S-201 in the 42nd Parliament, which sought to prevent genetic discrimination (Canadian Press 2017a).
38 D'Aquino, Doern, and Blair (1983), 31.
39 Docherty (1997). See also Atkinson and Docherty (1992); Franks (1987); Kerby and Blidook (2011); Kerby and Snagovsky (2019).
40 "You never vote against the government on third reading," a senior minister warned a backbencher in the 1970s (Johnston 1986, 57).
41 Franks (1987), 115.
42 Ibid., 5.
43 Smith (1999), 417.
44 Smith (2007), 77.
45 Thomas (1978), 155.
46 For example, D'Aquino, Doern, and Blair (1983), 31.
47 Atkinson and Docherty (1992); Kerby and Blidook (2011).
48 Walsh (2017), 43. See also Matheson (1976), 1–5; Pitkin (1967), 3.
49 Baker, Gamble, and Ludlam (1993), 152.
50 For example, Ball (1987).
51 Westmacott (1983), 14.
52 Gash (1982), 145.
53 For an interesting take on this era of political history, see Trudeau (1958).
54 Franks (1987), 21; Thomas (1985a), 81; Underhill (1935), 369. See also Godbout (2020).
55 Ward (1966), 34. See also Godbout (2020), 104–5; Trudeau (1958), 301.
56 Carty and Young (2012), 105.
57 Godbout and Høyland (2017).

58 *Ottawa Citizen* (1926).

59 Godbout and Høyland (2013).

60 Morton (1950), 5.

61 Courtney (1978), 33–34.

62 Godbout (2020), 188–91; Godbout and Høyland (2017), 559; Guay (1988), 42–43; Kornberg and Mishler (1976), 22; McGrath (1985a), 11.

63 Brodie (2018), 96. For House of Commons definitions of government orders and government business, see Marleau and Montpetit (2000).

64 McGrath (1985a), 13.

65 House of Commons (2019).

66 Baker (2003), 79. See also Reid (2020).

67 Scheer (2013). See also Young (1969).

68 Standing Committee on Procedure and House Affairs (2016). See also Morden, Hilderman, and Anderson (2018a), 17.

69 Lincoln et al. (2001), 14. The confidence convention can be exploited when standing orders are silent. For more about the confidence convention, see Docherty (1997), 142–43; Heard (2014), 113–22; Kam (2009), 52–54; McGrath (1985a), 5–9.

70 Carty and Young (2012), 106.

71 *Globe and Mail* (1972); Lithwick and Spano (2015). Some sources confuse the first federal election to use party labels as 1970 when the Canada Elections Act was amended for the next election or 1974 when the Election Expenses Act came into effect to regulate party finance.

72 *Globe and Mail* (1965).

73 Prior to 1972, unsuccessful nomination contestants caused disruption if they continued to publicize their party affiliation when seeking election as an Independent (Barbeau 1966, 40; Thomas 1955). See also Courtney (1978), 51–52; Trudeau (1993), 118.

74 For more on how parties nominate candidates, see Thomas and Morden (2019).

75 Hazan (2014), 218–19.

76 For example, Gerson (2018).

77 Brodie (2018), 143–49; Geisler (2015). See also Cross (2016); Godbout (2020), 244; Marland (2016), 50–51; Samara Centre (2020).

78 Aiello (2019d). In 2019 the Bloc caucus voted on regaining official party status (Samara Centre 2020).

79 Clark (2019); Ditchburn (2015); Samara Centre (2020). The Liberal caucus did not vote in 2015, and the NDP did so in 2016. Both caucuses held the required votes in 2019.

80 MacGuigan (1978), 680.

81 Docherty (1997), 170.

82 Jones (2016), 25–46.

83 For a summary of political values as heuristics, see Montpetit, Lachapelle, and Kiss (2017). See also Chaiken (1980); Clarke, Kornberg, and Scotto (2009); Tolley (2015), 43–44.

84 Wesley and Nauta (2020).

85 Section 43 in Liberal Party of Canada (2016). See also de Clercy (2018).

86 Liberal Party of Canada (2015).

87 Liberal Party of Canada (2019), 54.

88 For example, Docherty (1997), 167.

89 Franks (1987), 21.

90 Axworthy (2008), 54; Cullen (2011), 51–52; Loat and MacMillan (2014), 173; Martin (2002), 11; Reid (2019).

91 Heard (2007).

92 Franks (1987), 105; Commissioner for Legislative Standards (2018b), 14.

93 Conservative Party of Canada (2018b).

94 See Article XIV in New Democratic Party of Canada (2013).

95 McGrane (2019), 119–20.

96 New Democratic Party of Canada (2013, 2018).

97 Bouchard (1994), 259.

98 For example, Venne (2003).

99 Green Party of Canada (2016).

100 Elizabeth May, quoted in Green Party of Canada (2013).

101 Blais et al. (2003); Stevens et al. (2019). See also Axworthy (2008), 21; Loat and MacMillan (2014), 172.

102 Stevens et al. (2019).

103 American Political Science Association (1950).

104 Morton (1950), 117.

105 Ibid., 150.

106 Ibid., 176–77. See also Godbout (2020).

107 Morton (1950), 159.

108 Morton (2006).

109 Some information about the new Senate configurations was obtained from Peter Harder (March 26, 2019); Elizabeth Marshall (April 27, 2018); Grant Mitchell (June 11, 2018).

110 *R. v Duffy* (2016).

111 Wright Allen (2019a). See also Godbout (2020), Chapter 9.

112 On stonewalling, see Tasker (2017); on sparring, see Wright Allen (2019b).

113 White (2005), 58–62.

114 Hwang (2018).

115 For example, see Alcantara, Spicer, and Leone (2012).

116 Information in this paragraph is drawn from Breux and Couture (2018).

117 Kornberg (1966), 84.

118 Matheson (1976), 187–88.

119 Benno Friesen, Progressive Conservative MP for Surrey–White Rock–North Delta, quoted in McGrath (1985a), 5.

120 Parliament of Canada (1991).

121 Venne (2003), 2.

122 Malloy (2006), 128; Smith (2007), 133.

123 Kam (2009). See also Kam (2006); Thomas and Lewis (2019), 367.

124 Godbout (2020), 246. See also Godbout and Høyland (2013, 2017).

125 Godbout (2020), 123; Krehbiel (1993), 238; Owens (2006), 15–17.

126 For example, Delacourt (2016a, 2016b); Esselment (2012, 2014); Flanagan (2014); Lalancette and Tourigny-Koné (2017); Marland (2012, 2014, 2016, 2017); Marland and Wagner (2020); McLean (2012); Patten (2017); Small (2014).

127 McGrane (2019), Chapter 3. See also Campion-Smith (2018); Delacourt (2016a), Chapter 10; McGrane (2017). Opposition parties often undergo internal reorganization when a new leader decides that caucus message cohesion is necessary. For example, after some communications mishaps as leader of the official opposition Jean Chrétien required ministerial critics to obtain approval from a caucus committee for policy positions prior to making public pronouncements, and an executive committee established a weekly message line (Howard 1991; see also Jeffrey 2010).

128 McGrane (2019), 121.

129 Malloy (2006), 121.

130 Noelle-Neumann (1993), 36.

131 B. Mason (2018).

132 Thomas (1985a), 122. See also Cullen (2011), 61; Franks (1987), 102; Thomas (1985b), 54.

133 de Clercy (2018), 162–63. Note that sub-caucuses and interparty caucuses can have written agendas.

134 Canada (2018a).

135 Brodie (2018), 134.

136 Dempson (1968), 157; Brodie (2018), 134.

137 McGrane (2019), 20–21.

138 Telephone conversation with Office of Pablo Rodriguez, Liberal MP for Honoré-Mercier, June 15, 2018.

139 Wright Allen (2018a).

140 Email exchange, Office of Anita Vandenbeld, Liberal MP for Ottawa West–Nepean, June 18, 2018.

141 Owens (2006), 15.

142 Jones (2016).

143 Evans and Hayden (2018). See also Godbout (2020), 242.

144 Loat and MacMillan (2014), 9.

145 Morden, Hilderman, and Anderson (2018a), 41.

146 Loat and MacMillan (2014).

147 Trudeau (2019a).

CHAPTER 2: REPRESENTATION

1 For a history of the bozo eruption expression, see Thomson (2018).

2 Thomas and Morden (2019), 21.

3 Emmanuel (2019).

4 Curran (1988), 4.

5   Brodie (2018), 47.
6   See, in part, Reform Party of Canada (1989), 9–11.
7   Canadian Press (1992).
8   Morton (2006), 7.
9   Marland (2016), 168–70. See also Docherty (1997), xiv.
10 Todd (1994).
11 Marland (2016), 193–94; McGrane (2019), 98; McLean (2012), 57.
12 Ala Buzreba, former Liberal candidate in Calgary–Nose Hill, quoted in Mouallem (2015).
13 Wright (2019a).
14 Zimonjic (2019a).
15 Canada (2000), c 9, s 550.
16 See Dyer (2019).
17 Clark (2004).
18 Fifteen years after Liberals lifted the question, it continued to appear in an undated British Columbia temporary articles enrolment form, as did many other sentences found in Canadian political parties' screening questionnaires. The verbatim question was also used by the PEI Progressive Conservatives in 2010; the BC Conservatives in 2013; the Wildrose Party of Alberta in 2014; the federal Conservatives in 2014 and 2016; and, in 2018, the Green Party of Ontario, the Newfoundland PC Party, and the United Conservative Party of Alberta.
19 In 2015, the federal NDP used the digital avatar Fred Checkers; see Richler (2016), 38. The Alberta United Conservatives have used the pseudonym Josh Brooks.
20 Smith (2018b).
21 Wood (2018).
22 Clancy (2018).
23 Cullen and Laskowski (2018).
24 Barrera and Deer (2019); Bascaramurty (2019).
25 I obtained Liberal candidate contracts for the 2015 Canadian federal election, the 2018 Ontario election, and the 2019 Newfoundland and Labrador election.
26 Liberal Party of Canada (2018c).
27 Quoted in Tolley (2015), 159.
28 Thomas and Morden (2019).
29 Quoted in Bell (2019).
30 Richler (2016).
31 Rana (2020a).
32 Heather McPherson, NDP MP-elect for Edmonton Strathcona, quoted in Giovannetti (2019).
33 For example, Blidook (2012), 75.
34 Chuck Strahl, former Reform MP for Fraser Valley, interviewed in 2011 by the Samara Centre.
35 Blidook (2012), 9.

36 Quoted in Axworthy (2008), 41. See also Cowley and Stuart (2009); Martin (2002), 12; Simpson (2001), 45–46.

37 Marlene Catterall (November 26, 2018).

38 Elizabeth May (October 24, 2018).

39 Axworthy (2008), 41–45; Pitkin (1967), Chapter 9. See also Smith (2017), 98–99.

40 Pitkin (1967). See also Koop, Bastedo, and Blidook (2018, 5); Snagovsky and Kerby (2019).

41 Pitkin (1967), 89.

42 White (2018).

43 Cathy Bennett (June 18, 2019).

44 CBC (2019a).

45 Bégin (2018), 326.

46 Pitkin (1967), 221.

47 Stockwell Day (July 26, 2018).

48 For more on this distinction, see Walsh (2017), 65–66.

49 Lisa Raitt (January 10, 2019).

50 Wayne Easter (July 27, 2018).

51 Stella Ambler, former Conservative MP for Mississauga South, interviewed in 2017 by the Samara Centre.

52 House of Commons (2019).

53 Rathgeber (2014), 106. See also Franks (1987), 10.

54 Akin (2017); Delacourt (2016a), 218; Marland (2016), 342. See also Docherty (1997), 181.

55 Unnamed Liberal staffer, quoted in *PressProgress* (2020). See also Hannay (2017).

56 CBC (2016).

57 Respectively, Copps (2019a); Copps (2019b).

58 For example, Aiello (2018a).

59 Bernard Lord (December 10, 2018).

60 White (2005), 125–29.

61 Blakeney and Borins (1998), 72–74. In 1969, the Trudeau Liberals approved a system of caucus committees to mirror cabinet committees, with meetings held every second Wednesday in place of the national caucus. The purpose was to review with ministers "principles involved in forthcoming legislation, bills on the order paper before they are given second reading and general policy decisions" (Goldblatt 1969). In the 1980s, Brian Mulroney's parliamentary secretary attended PMO strategy meetings to act as an intermediary with the caucus (Bill Fox, June 4, 2020).

62 Stone (2019a).

63 Rob Norris (November 16, 2018).

64 White (2005), 43–45, 105–25.

65 Thomas and Lewis (2019).

66 Rathgeber (2014), 64.

67 Koop, Bastedo, and Blidook (2018), 7–13.

68 Ibid., 52–65.

69 Ibid., 175.

70 Claudeawad (2012a, 2012b).

71 David Wilks, quoted in Claudeawad (2012a); transcribed by the author. See also CBC (2012).

72 Coyne (2012); Fitzpatrick (2012).

73 Quoted in Cooper (2012).

74 CBC (2012).

75 Harowitz (2014).

76 David Wilks (April 17, 2019). See also the 2017 Samara Centre exit interview with Wilks.

77 Marlene Catterall (June 28, 2019). See also the 2009 and 2013 Samara Centre exit interviews with Catterall. News reports indicate that youth unemployment was a caucus priority in early September 1997 and that by January 1998 the caucus was interested in restoring funds for student research grants (Bryden 1998).

78 Ted Morton (July 21, 2018).

79 Flynn (2012), 16.

80 Trudeau (1969), 11635.

81 Ibid. See also Axworthy (2008), 45; Westell (1972), 94.

82 Franks (1987), 92; Franks (2007), 35; White (2005), 129.

83 McGrath (1985b), 214.

84 Quoted in CBC (1971); transcribed by the author.

85 Grenier (2017).

86 Clarke and Price (1981).

87 Reid (2006), 3.

88 Vivian Barbot (October 29, 2018).

89 Scott Andrews (July 10, 2018). See also Bégin (2018), 98.

90 Rob Oliphant (July 23, 2018).

91 Member of Parliament 1 (name withheld). See also Thompson (1997).

92 Calis (2016); Pessian (2016).

93 Loat (2010), 28; Loat and MacMillan (2014), Chapter 4.

94 D'Aquino, Doern, and Blair (1983), 79. See also McGrath (1985a).

95 Hoffman (1972), 148.

96 Minister 1 in Justin Trudeau's cabinet; see also Curran (2016).

97 Pierre De Bané, Liberal MP for Matane, quoted in CBC (1971); transcribed by the author.

98 Unidentified Liberal MP sitting at a desk, quoted in ibid.; transcribed by the author.

99 John Roberts, Liberal MP for York-Simcoe, quoted in ibid.; transcribed by the author.

100 Philip Givens, Liberal MP for York West, quoted in ibid.; transcribed by the author. See also Young (1969).

101 Unnamed Liberal MP, quoted in Ivison (2019).

102 Docherty (1997), 187.

103 For example, Allmand (2006), 18.

104 Docherty (1997), 169.

105 Steele (2014), 44.

106 Downs (1957), 89; Franks (1987), 91; Franks (2007), 28, 89–96; Hoffman (1972), 159–60; Kornberg and Mishler (1976), 25, 222, 309; Loat and MacMillan (2014), 112.

107 McGrath (1985b), 18.

108 Docherty (1997), 37; MacGuigan (1978), 674; Nielsen (1989), 109; Trudeau (1993), 116.

109 Bégin (2018), 97; Kornberg and Mishler (1976), 4. See also Axworthy (2008), 11, 49; CBC (1971); Crane (1969); Franks (2007), 30; Goldenberg (2006), 73; Lefebvre (1987), 28; MacGuigan (1978), 672–73; McGrath (1985b), 18.

110 MacGuigan (1978), 674.

111 Thomas (1985a), 107.

112 Clarke and Price (1981); Docherty (1997), 184–85; Franks (2007), 31.

113 Whip 3 (name withheld); see also Leitch (2019). A review of staff lists found that MPs employed an average of 1.8 staffers in their Parliament Hill office and 3.3 staffers in their constituency office(s) in 2017 (Paul Wilson, personal email, May 24, 2020). Conversely, one staffer during the 42nd Parliament estimated that MPs have between 6 and 8 employees, of whom 4 are full-time (legislative assistant, parliamentary assistant, constituency manager, and constituency assistant) and four are part-time (scheduling assistant, correspondence assistant, another constituency assistant, and a constituency scheduling assistant); see Dickin (2016). The figures are higher than the 4 staff mentioned in earlier sources; see Axworthy (2008), 49; Docherty (1997), 172; Loat and MacMillan (2014), 83.

114 Peter MacKay (October 30, 2018).

115 Koop, Bastedo, and Blidook (2018), 117; Marland and Power (2020).

116 Docherty (1997), Chapter 5.

117 Loat and MacMillan (2014), 212–14.

118 Westell (1972), 101. See also Crane (1969); MacGuigan (1978), 675–76.

119 Loat and MacMillan (2014), 178–80; Samara Centre (2011), 16.

120 Carty (2002, 2004). See also Marland and Wagner (2020).

121 Hartt (2003), 273.

122 Carty (2002), 731.

123 Bruce Stanton, Conservative MP for Simcoe-North, quoted in Raj (2020); transcribed by the author.

124 Dickson (2018b). For more about brand ambassadors, see Marland (2016); Marland and Wagner (2020).

125 Jane Philpott (June 19, 2019).

126 Franks (1987), 31.

127 Pitkin (1967), Chapter 7.

128 Wayne Easter (July 27, 2018).

129 Dawson (2018). The NDP caucus unanimously voted to expel Luff because her public allegations were deemed an affront to the caucus itself (Clancy and Graney 2018).

130 Reid (2019). Philip Givens, the Liberal MP profiled in *The Noblest of Callings*, lamented fifty years before Reid did that the role of a backbencher was that of "a buck private, or a child, to be seen and not heard" (quoted in Young 1969).

131 Robyn Luff (November 15, 2018).

132 Ryan Cleary (March 21, 2019).

133 Benzie, Ferguson, and Rushowy (2018).

134 Political staff 1 (name withheld).

135 Celina Caesar-Chavannes (July 19, 2019).

136 For example, see Evelyn (2018). Relatedly, see Pessian (2016).

137 Celina Caesar-Chavannes (July 19, 2019).

138 Bryden (2019); Evelyn (2018).

139 Bellemare and Rogers (2019).

CHAPTER 3: PARTISAN TEAMS

1 Moody and White (2003), 122.

2 Jones and George (1998).

3 Asch (1951).

4 See Flanagan (2014); Michael, Garry, and Kirsch (2012).

5 Kelman (1953).

6 Milgram (1963).

7 Haney, Banks, and Zimbardo (1973); Zimbardo (2019).

8 Haney, Banks, and Zimbardo (1973), 88.

9 Weingart and Todorova (2010).

10 For example, see Festinger (1957).

11 Rob Oliphant (July 23, 2018).

12 Kellie Leitch (December 16, 2018).

13 Robert-Falcon Ouellette (October 2, 2018).

14 Johnston (1986), 57; Steele (2014), 67. But see Godbout (2020), 110–13.

15 Kathleen Wynne (December 7, 2018).

16 Heames, Harvey, and Treadway (2006); Rink and Ellemers (2008).

17 Karina Gould, Liberal MP for Burlington and minister of democratic institutions, breastfed her baby during Question Period on June 19, 2018. Women MLAs in British Columbia (sleeveless blouses and dresses) and an MNA in Quebec (hooded sweatshirt) have challenged dress codes.

18 Katzenbach and Smith (1993).

19 Flanagan (2014), 11–17.

20 Jones (2016), 25–46.

21 Ibid., 106.

22 Ibid., 158.

23 Ibid., 25–46. See also Bégin (2018), 104; Rana (2015b).

24 Jim Edwards (November 16, 2018).

25 Maureen Harquail (November 29, 2018).

26 Franks (1987), 32–33.

27 As in the federal PC caucus led by Joe Clark; see Kempling (1988), 42.

28 Thomas (1985a), 85. More broadly, see Brodie (2018), 150–52; Franks (1987), 109; Rathgeber (2014), 104–9; Reid (1993), 2–3; Stanbury (2003), 30–31; Steele (2014), 33; Thomas (1985a), 122. The word *team* arose in 100 of 131 of the interviews that the Samara Centre conducted with MPs who left Parliament between 2004 and 2015.

29 For example, Boyer (2003), 247–48. See also Luntz (2015), 41–42.

30 Ken McDonald (June 26, 2018).

31 Political staff 2 (name withheld).

32 Ken Boessenkool (July 18, 2018).

33 Pescosolido and Saavedra (2012).

34 Brown (1994), 14. See also Bégin (2018), 103; Venne (2003), 3.

35 Garner and Letki (2005), 468.

36 Nunziata (2003), 16–17.

37 David Wilks (April 17, 2019).

38 Hartt (2003), 269.

39 L. Mason (2018).

40 de Vreese (2005).

41 Jody Wilson-Raybould (July 21, 2019).

42 Celina Caesar-Chavannes (July 19, 2019).

43 Axworthy (2008), 14; Morden, Hilderman, and Anderson (2018b), 9, 15.

44 Jay Hill (August 22, 2018).

45 Shannon Stubbs (December 21, 2018). See also Lefebvre (1987), 40.

46 Esselment (2010). See also McGrane (2019), 55, 70.

47 Liberal Party of Canada (2016); New Democratic Party of Canada (2013).

48 Conservative Party of Canada (2018a).

49 Dawson (2018).

50 Member of a provincial legislature 1 (name withheld).

51 Clarke et al. (2019), Chapter 5. See also Tolley (2015), 135.

52 Gidengil and Blais (2007).

53 Kim Campbell (May 1, 2018).

54 Owens (2006), 28–29.

55 As with Jean Chrétien and Paul Martin in the early 2000s. See Delacourt (2003), 230–31; Jeffrey (2010), 361–65.

56 Edward Roberts (April 12, 2018).

57 Ken Krawetz (November 20, 2018).

58 Morden, Hilderman, and Anderson (2018a), 34.

59 Brian Mulroney (December 17, 2018).

60 Rast and Hogg (2016).

61 Malloy (2012), 50; Woolstencroft (1994), 9.

62 In the 34th Parliament, PC MPs were much more likely to state that they followed their leader and party than to say that they prioritized their constituents (Docherty 1997, 145). Nevertheless, there were pockets of discontent among PC backbenchers (Cernetig and Freeman 1990).

63 Mulroney (2007), 606. As well, each year Mulroney asked PC MPs to write with a list of their concerns and suggestions. He personally replied to each letter (Newman 2006, 377). These types of iterative processes made the caucus members feel that they had an opportunity to provide direct input and that their voice was heard (Bill Fox, June 4, 2020).

64 Mulroney (2007), 122. Additional information in the following paragraphs from Mulroney was cross-checked with Sallot (1986).

65 Fraser (1989), 18–19; Mulroney (2007), 605.

66 Fraser (1989), 30–31.

67 Carney (2000), 250; Crosbie (1997), 235. See also Newman (2006, 383).

68 Burney (2005), 89. See also Newman (2006), 230, 410.

69 Turner (2009), 22. See also Carney (2000), 279; Crosbie (1997), 239.

70 Carney (2000), 261.

71 Segal (2006), 65. See also Bouchard (1994), 107; Simpson (2001), 8.

72 Carney (2000), 250.

73 Macdonald (n.d.). Olive Diefenbaker hosted the wives of PC MPs and senators for afternoon tea at 24 Sussex (*Globe and Mail* 1962).

74 Ward (1966), 73.

75 Axworthy (2008), 27; Graham (2016), 126; Lalonde (1971), 513. Pierre Trudeau hosted the Liberal caucus at 24 Sussex after weekend caucus meetings in June 1969 (Crane 1969).

76 Chrétien (2007), 37. See also Graham (2016), 126; Rana (2019e).

77 Unnamed Liberal MP, quoted in Taber (2004). See also Graham (2016), 126.

78 Paul Martin (April 10, 2019).

79 Haws (2018).

80 For more on Trudeau's brand and celebrity, see Marland (2016), 92, 126–34.

81 Political staff 1 in Justin Trudeau's PMO (name withheld). See also Wherry (2019), 57. As well, a spouses dinner event that provided Liberal MPs an opportunity to have informal chats with Trudeau was discontinued circa 2017, ostensibly due to overlap with the much larger caucus holiday party (Member of Parliament 11, name withheld).

82 Member of Parliament 3 (name withheld).

83 Rana (2019a).

84 Rana (2019b); Ryckewaert (2019); Wherry (2019), 57. It is unclear if hosting caucus members is encumbered by Trudeau's decision to reside in Rideau Cottage instead of 24 Sussex Drive.

85 As relayed by Judy Sgro, Liberal MP for Humber River–Black Creek, in CBC (2019f).

86 As with Andrew Scheer; see Haws (2018).

87 Graham (2016), 420.

88 For example, see Blakeney and Borins (1998), 75.

89 Ken Boessenkool (July 18, 2018).

90 Political staff 1 (name withheld).

91 Ibid. Staff experienced similar challenges with Mulroney; see Gratton (1987), 191–92.

92 For example, Morden, Hilderman, and Anderson (2018a), 37–38.

93 Goldenberg (2006), 76; Ryckewaert (2016).

94 Docherty (1997), 14–15, 259–60. See also Downs (1957); Kam (2009), 13; Perlin (1980), 6.

95 Docherty (1997), 17–20, 260–62. See also Thomas (2016).

96 Strøm and Müeller (1999). See also Godbout (2020), 43; Kam (2009), 17; Snagovsky and Kerby (2018).

97 Kam (2006, 2009).

98 Hazan (2014), 213.

99 Kerby (2009), 606–7. See also Kerby (2014).

100 Owens (2006), 27.

101 Mulroney (2007), 356. See also Axworthy (2008), 24.

102 Graham (2016), 129; Kam (2009), 30.

103 Kerby and Snagovsky (2019).

104 Kathleen Wynne (December 7, 2018).

105 Thomas and Lewis (2019).

106 Megan Leslie (July 27, 2018).

107 Lefebvre (1987), 28–29. Backbenchers might ask to be moved away from someone for personality reasons, due to body odour and so forth (Member of Parliament 12, name withheld).

108 Docherty (1997), 166.

109 Smith (2011), 7.

110 Karen Redman, Liberal MP for Kitchener Centre and chief government whip, quoted in Pender (2005).

111 Brodie (2018), 46. See also Smith (2007), 133; Thomas (1985b), 62; Walker (1971), 260. For an overview of the role of the party whip, see Docherty (2005), 67–69; Franks (1987), 104–8; Heard (2014), 132–33; Jones (2016); Walker (1971).

112 King (2020).

113 Framed whips different from those in Figure 3.1 appear behind Bernard Pilon, the chief government whip who died in 1970, in CBC (1971). Relatedly, see Brodie (2018), 46; Catterall (2003), 112; Pender (2005).

114 Quoted in Geddes (2017).

115 *House of Cards* (1990).

116 Jones (2016), 43.

117 Ibid., 152. See also Flynn (2012), 117–18; Kempling (1988), 57–58.

118 Jones (2016), 147, 149.

119 Ibid., 38.

120 Ibid., 22.

121 Walker (1971), 260.

122 Lefebvre (1987), 16. In the early 1980s, the federal Liberals designated anglo-phone and francophone deputy whips to deal with English and French MPs; see Turner (1987), 48.

123 See, in part, MacGuigan (1978), 676. See also Reform Act, 2014.

124 Whip 1 (name withheld).

125 Pablo Rodriguez, Liberal MP for Honoré-Mercier and chief government whip, quoted in Aiello (2017).

126 Mark Holland, Liberal MP for Ajax and chief government whip, quoted in Stone (2018a).

127 Colleen Mayer (November 16, 2018).

128 Jay Hill (April 1, 2019).

129 Brendan Maguire (October 16, 2018).

130 Member of Parliament 1 (name withheld).

131 Member of Parliament 8 (name withheld).

132 Ryan Cleary (March 29, 2018). Initial orientation for new MPs emphasizes staff hiring, constituency casework management, work-life balance, harassment prevention training, and Library of Parliament services. Before the House opens, a second orientation session is offered to discuss the House schedule, debate procedures, and voting. Online courses are also available (House of Commons 2019b). Training of an MP's office staff encompasses technical details explained by House of Commons personnel and communications training via the party's caucus research bureau (see Dickin 2016, 11).

133 Carney (2000), 187–88; Graham (2016), 121–22,235. See also Guay (1988), 33.

134 Whip 1 (name withheld).

135 Garner and Letki (2005).

136 Kerby and Blidook (2011), 623.

137 Thomas (1985a), 122.

138 Jay Hill (August 22, 2018).

139 Brodie (2018), 47; Weekes (2012), 9. See also the transcript of Dale Johnston, former Conservative MP for Wetaskiwin and former party whip, interviewed in 2009 by the Samara Centre.

140 Don Boudria (June 1, 2019).

141 Karen Redman (October 26, 2018).

142 Bob Rae (August 15, 2018).

CHAPTER 4: THE COMMUNICATIONS ARENA

1 Party leader 1 (name withheld).

2 Hamilton (1957); Stursberg (1975), 49; Thomson (1967), 516–17. A Toronto historical website that reproduced the photographs obtained them from the City of Toronto Archives, fonds 1257, series 1057 (Bradburn 2011).

3 Landerer (2013); Marland (2016), 73–98.

4 Rollwagen et al. (2019).

5 Bastien (2018).
6 Templeton (1969).
7 As occurred with Prime Minister Louis St. Laurent; see Dempson (1968), 62.
8 Rathgeber (2014), 178.
9 Aalberg, Strömbäck, and de Vreese (2011).
10 Comber and Mayne (1986), 17–18.
11 Kellie Leitch (December 16, 2018).
12 Matthew Dubé (May 3, 2018).
13 Trudeau (2014), 221.
14 For example, Tolley (2015).
15 Many Reform MPs were mocked for their clothing; see the Samara Centre's interview transcript of Dale Johnston. See also Marland (2016), 124.
16 Francoli (2009), 224.
17 Marland and Power (2020); Small (2008).
18 Innis (1972), 7.
19 Frost (2003), 21.
20 Dubois and McKelvey (2019); McKelvey, Côté, and Raynauld (2018).
21 For example, Dhanraj (2019a).
22 Peter MacKay (October 30, 2018).
23 Political staff 3 (name withheld).
24 John Weissenberger (August 10, 2018).
25 McIntosh (2019).
26 Member of Parliament 2 (name withheld). See also Marland and Power (2020).
27 For example, Beeby (2018).
28 For example, Whitehead (2015).
29 Loury (1994).
30 Laycock (2005); Morden and Anderson (2019).
31 Cross and Young (2002), 871; Smith (2007), 56.
32 See PC and NDP campaign platforms of 1953 and 1957 in Carrigan (1968), 206, 210, 225.
33 Stursberg (1975), 38.
34 For example, Perlin (1980), 62–63.
35 A 2016 survey found that 76 percent believed political correctness had gone too far and that 67 percent thought people are too easily offended over language choices (Angus Reid Institute 2016).
36 A 2019 survey found 40 percent much more likely and 39 percent somewhat more likely to support an anti-elite candidate (SFU Morris J. Wosk Centre for Dialogue 2019).
37 Maxime Bernier (November 6, 2018).
38 Lisa MacLeod, PC MPP for Nepean-Carleton, quoted in CBC (2018b). See also Luntz (2015), 6.
39 Greenspon and Wilson-Smith (1996), 292; Heard (2014), 131.
40 Peter Donolo (May 4, 2018).
41 Joe Clark (January 24, 2019).

42 For example, Cochrane (2019).

43 For instance, Bryden (2019); *Toronto Sun* (2019).

44 Alexandra Mendès (July 27, 2018).

45 Tony Clement (July 3, 2018).

46 Nick Whalen (May 11, 2018).

47 James Maloney, Liberal MP for Etobicoke-Lakeshore, quoted in Raj (2020); transcribed by the author.

48 Scott J. Reid (September 19, 2018).

49 Graham Steele (November 16, 2018).

50 Small (2014).

51 Rocha (2019).

52 Turcotte (2015).

53 Giasson and Small (2017), 120–21. See also Elmer, Langlois, and McKelvey (2014), 251; McLean (2012), 121.

54 Political staff 4 (name withheld).

55 Political staff 5 (name withheld).

56 McKelvey and Dubois (2017); Dubois and McKelvey (2019).

57 Political staff 4 (name withheld).

58 Rocha (2019). People's Party candidates retweeted the *Post Millennial* most often.

59 Dubois et al. (2018).

60 Kellie Leitch (December 16, 2018).

61 Joe Clark (January 24, 2019).

62 Turcotte and Raynauld (2020); Wilson and Turnbull (2001).

63 Akin (2018).

64 For example, Rabson (2019a).

65 Lisa Raitt (January 10, 2019).

66 Galloway, Curry, and Dobrota (2006). See also Brodie (2018), 135–36; Graham (2016), 424–25.

67 Dickson (2019).

68 Mulroney (2007), 270. At the time, Mulroney was described as "clever" for avoiding "a trap that would leave his caucus badly divided" (Maser 1983). For more about the all-party resolution that Manitoba should constitutionally entrench access to provincial services in French, see Hébert (2004), 127–29; Newman (2006), 64–65.

69 Mulroney (2007), 271–72.

70 Wallace (1988).

71 Conservative Party of Canada (2018a).

72 Mulroney (2007), 277–81.

73 Unnamed Liberal MP, quoted in Scandiffio (1998).

74 Quoted in Pole (1998). "The first step in politics is to stand up for something that you truly believe in and everything else falls into place," Bennett had said months earlier on becoming an MP (quoted in Thompson, 1997).

75 Mark Assad, Liberal MP for Gatineau–La Lièvre, quoted in Scandiffio (1998).

76 Lewis, Lalancette, and Raynauld (2019).

77 Carolyn Bennett (August 9, 2018).

78 Member of Parliament 2 (name withheld).

79 MacKinnon (2014). Worries that a Conservative government would restrict access to abortion was a wedge issue in the 2019 Canadian federal election (Turcotte and Raynauld 2020).

80 Trudeau (2018).

81 Provided by Member of Parliament 3 (name withheld). Nothing went out from Trudeau's social media accounts. Liberal MPs were conspicuously quiet.

82 Email from a parliamentary staffer for a Member of Parliament (May 16, 2018).

83 Liberal Party of Canada (2018a, 2018b).

84 Marquis (2018).

85 Laurence (2018).

CHAPTER 5: MESSAGE DISCIPLINE

1 Member of a provincial legislature 2 (name withheld).

2 Lewis, Lalancette, and Raynauld (2019), 186–87.

3 Governor General of Canada (2019).

4 *Babcock v Canada* (2002). See also Stanbury (2003), 12–14.

5 Canada (1985b).

6 For example, Carney (2000), 269–70.

7 Axworthy (2008), 24.

8 Office of the Prime Minister (2016).

9 Canada (2003).

10 Canada (2012).

11 Canada (1985a).

12 Pugliese (2018).

13 Wright Allen (2018c).

14 Thomas (1985a), 130.

15 Paez (2020a).

16 Craft (2016), 24. See also Burney (2005), 91; McGrane (2019), 95.

17 Carolyn Parrish, Liberal MP for Mississauga-Erindale, quoted in Leblanc (2003).

18 John McCallum, minister of defence, quoted in Leblanc (2003).

19 Carolyn Parrish, personal email, March 17, 2020.

20 Panetta (2019); Rana (2016). See also Wherry (2019), 119.

21 Panetta (2017).

22 McGrane (2019), 90–91. Freelancing is not to be confused with the Samara Centre's reference to the development of topic expertise that is of little interest to the party leadership (Loat and MacMillan 2014, 85, 101).

23 Ken Boessenkool (July 18, 2018).

24 Peter Kent, Conservative MP for Thornhill, quoted in Stone (2018c).

25 Marilyn Gladu, Conservative MP for Sarnia-Lambton, quoted in ibid.

26 Matthew Dubé (May 3, 2018).

27 McGrane (2019), 103.

28 Jean Charest (August 6, 2018).

29 Megan Leslie (July 27, 2018).

30 Jordan O'Brien (November 26, 2018).

31 Jane Philpott (June 19, 2019).

32 For example, Turner (2009), 65.

33 Delacourt (2003), 212–13.

34 Kathleen Wynne (December 7, 2018).

35 Stewart (1971), 207.

36 Kempling (1988), 54.

37 Greenspon and Wilson-Smith (1996), 168.

38 Canadian Press (2019b); Fraser (1989), 18–19; Mulroney (2007), 605.

39 Delacourt (2017).

40 Brodie (2018), 122; Delacourt (2016a), 225; Elmer, Langlois, and McKelvey (2014); Esselment (2014); Flanagan (2014), Chapter 7; Marland (2016), 40–42; McLean (2012), 58. See also Burney (2005), 87.

41 Esselment (2014), 37.

42 McGrane (2017); Thomas (2013), 65–67. See also Blidook and Byrne (2013).

43 Akin (2019).

44 Political staff 6 (name withheld).

45 Wilson (2017).

46 Jay Hill (August 22, 2018).

47 Marland (2014), 55–56; Marland (2016), 36–40. See also Bertilsson and Rennstam (2018).

48 Rob Oliphant (July 23, 2018).

49 Ditchburn (2016), 68–69.

50 Bertilsson and Rennstam (2018), 269. See also Guay (2002), 8.

51 See Luntz (2015), Chapter 4.

52 Canada (2016). See also Marland (2016), 267–72.

53 Blidook (2012), 64.

54 Clarke, Kornberg, and Scotto (2009), 279.

55 Chaiken (1980). See also Luntz (2015), 82.

56 Downs (1957), Chapter 11.

57 Patrick Muttart (June 4, 2018). See also Delacourt (2016a), 182–83; Marland (2016), 144–48.

58 For more on message simplicity, see Luntz (2015), 4–8; Marland (2016), Chapter 5.

59 McGrane (2019), 61.

60 Paul Martin (July 26, 2018).

61 David Wilks (April 17, 2019).

62 In the early twentieth century, candidates received a speaker's handbook outlining party positions taken in Parliament (Ames 1911, 186). In the 1970s, they received a large speaker's manual with briefing notes on party policy (Simpson 1980, 64). In 2015, the Trudeau Liberals circulated a pre-platform electronic booklet described as an "internal reference tool intended to provide reactive

messaging to respond to questions on the ground" (CBC 2015), and NDP candidates received a "message guide" (Richler 2006, 56). In the lead-up to the 2019 campaign, Conservative candidates gained access to a password-protected website called Campaign Hub that housed banked talking points to equip candidates with reactive lines for topics raised by constituents. During the campaign, the party emailed messaging about policy announcements that it immediately stored in Campaign Hub. Political staff 15 (name withheld), personal email, June 6, 2020.

63 Jeffrey (2010), 231–34. See also Delacourt (2016a), 131–33; Docherty (1997), xv; Goldenberg (2006), 48–51; Savoie (1999), 78–79.

64 Wesley and Nauta (2020).

65 Marlene Catterall (November 26, 2018).

66 Rathgeber (2014), 110.

67 Koop, Bastedo, and Blidook (2018); Turner (1987), 26.

68 Paul Davis (May 8, 2018).

69 Quoted in Wherry (2019), 48.

70 Malloy (2006), 121.

71 Jean Charest (August 6, 2018).

72 Montpetit, Lachapelle, and Kiss (2017).

73 Cairns (1968).

74 Esselment (2012), 136.

75 Chrétien (2007), 154, 236, 258.

76 Kelly (2019).

77 Turcotte and Vodrey (2017), 156.

78 Delacourt (2016a), 202–5; Luntz (2015).

79 Bernard Lord (December 10, 2018).

80 Marland (2016), 149–55; Turcotte and Vodrey (2017).

81 Faucheux (2002), Chapter 4.

82 Delacourt (2016a); Turcotte and Vodrey (2017).

83 Graham Steele (November 16, 2018).

84 Rae (2015), 9.

85 Flanagan (2014), 19–24.

86 Quoted in Bryden (2013). See also Trudeau (2014), 222.

87 Dalton McGuinty (August 16, 2018).

88 Celina Caesar-Chavannes (July 19, 2019).

89 Unnamed Liberal MP, quoted in Ivison (2019).

90 Sharon Blady (July 25, 2018).

91 Jordan Leichnitz (July 31, 2018).

92 Ken Krawetz (November 20, 2018); Rob Norris (November 16, 2018).

93 According to one survey, 81 percent of Canadians pay attention to politics between elections. See Vigliotti (2018).

94 Pechmann and Stewart (1988). See also Campbell and Keller (2003).

95 Green and Zelizer (2017), 117.

96 Gentzkow, Shapiro, and Taddy (2017). Relatedly, see Delacourt (2016a), 101; Simpson (2001), 52.

97 Campbell and Keller (2003); Luntz (2015), 11–13; Marland (2016), 119–20, 136–37. In the 1980s, message repetition was fashionable with Canadian ministers who responded "to whatever imprecise or repetitive question is raised with the answer they have prepared" (Fraser 1988).

98 Minister 2 in Justin Trudeau's cabinet (name withheld).

99 Jane Philpott (June 19, 2019).

100 Steele (2014), 66.

101 Robyn Luff (November 15, 2018).

102 MacCharles (2018). See also McLeod (2016).

103 Hernandez (2017). See also *Toronto Star* (2017); Simpson (2019).

104 Member of Parliament 4 (name withheld).

105 Dhanraj (2019b).

106 Santoni (1995).

107 Luntz (2015), 92–94.

108 Danielle Smith (July 20, 2018).

109 For a notorious case of scripting in the House of Commons, see *Globe and Mail* (2014).

110 Megan Leslie, quoted in Paez (2020b).

111 Jane Philpott (June 19, 2019).

112 John Delacourt (July 13, 2018).

113 King and Janis (1956).

114 van Rijn (2000).

115 Marland (2014), 60. See also Marland (2012).

116 Lalancette and Tourigny-Koné (2017).

117 Quoted in Geddes (2017).

118 Quoted in Delacourt (2016b), 94.

119 Andrew-Gee (2016); Parry (2017).

120 Quoted in Andrew-Gee (2016).

121 Quoted in ibid.

122 Kate Purchase (October 12, 2018). See also Delacourt (2016a), 306.

123 Abma (2017).

124 Delacourt (2016a); Giasson and Small (2017), 117; Mazereeuw (2019a); McEvoy (2019); Munroe and Munroe (2018); Patten (2017).

125 Wylie (2018).

126 Delacourt (2016a); McEvoy (2019), 12.

127 Giasson and Small (2017), 118. See also McKelvey and Piebiak (2019).

128 Lavigne (2020). See also Delacourt (2016a), Chapter 9.

129 Bernard Pilon, chief government whip and Liberal MP for Chambly, quoted in CBC (1971); transcribed by the author. Relatedly, see Clarke and Price (1981), 376.

130 Hamish Marshall (July 4, 2018).

131 Yvonne Jones (July 23, 2018).

132 Ken Hardie, Liberal MP for Fleetwoods–Port Kells, quoted in Rana (2020d).
133 Scott Simms, Liberal MP for Coast of Bays–Central–Notre Dame, quoted in Roberts (2019).
134 As with the Conservative Party; see Rana (2020b).
135 Political staff 7 (name withheld).
136 Ibid.
137 As stated in the Liberal candidate contract for the 2015 Canadian federal election. Some information in this section is courtesy of a Liberal politician not listed in Appendix 1 who showed me how Liberalist works.
138 Wylie (2018).
139 Member of Parliament 5 (name withheld).
140 Ibid.
141 Leblanc (2019). Relatedly, see Burney (2005), 88.
142 Inky Mark, former Conservative MP for Dauphin–Swan River–Marquette, quoted in Ditchburn (2012).
143 Scott Reid (July 17, 2018).

CHAPTER 6: GOVERNMENT CENTRALIZATION

1 An excellent synopsis of the political executive in Canada is White (2005).
2 Martin (2010); Savoie (1999); Simpson (2001); Thomas (2013), 60–62; White (2005), Chapter 3.
3 Bouchard (1994), 194.
4 Wayne Easter (July 27, 2018).
5 On super ministers, see Simpson (1980), 94. On regional ministers, see White (2005), 42, 57, 163. On cabinet committees, see le (2019). See also Matheson (1976), 66–67.
6 Francoli (2002).
7 Loyola Hearn, Conservative minister of fisheries and oceans, quoted in Delacourt (2016a), 206–7.
8 Jones (2016), 82, 158.
9 Steele (2014), 83. See also Carney (2000), 263; Trudeau (1993), 108–12.
10 Chrétien (2007), 156.
11 Clark (1985), 186. See also White (2005), 53–54.
12 Heeney (1946).
13 Boyko (2010), 208.
14 Stursberg (1975), 175–80; Perlin (1980), 64. See also Malloy (2012), 48–49.
15 Clark (1985), 187.
16 Wearing (1981), 154–55. See also Lalonde (1971), 516; Westell (1972), 129. As mentioned, the Liberal caucus under Pierre Trudeau also set up caucus committees to offer input to ministers.
17 Lincoln et al. (2001), 15.
18 Templeton (1969); Wearing (1981), 207; Westell (1972), 128.
19 Johnston (1986), 61.
20 Clark (1985), 189.

21 Clark (1985).

22 Burney (2005), 91.

23 Chrétien (2007), 32; Greenspon and Wilson-Smith (1996), 8; Savoie (1999), 261.

24 Simpson (2001).

25 Goldenberg (2006), 101.

26 Paul Martin (April 10, 2019).

27 For example, Malloy (2012), 52.

28 Martin (2010), 55.

29 Marland (2016), 178–79; Rathgeber (2014), 85; Taber (2010); Wilson (2015a); Wilson (2016a), 33–34.

30 Wherry (2019), 24, 42–43, 61.

31 Political staff 2 in Justin Trudeau's PMO (name withheld).

32 Ryckewaert (2015). See also Ditchburn (2016), 67.

33 Stursberg (1975), 156–57.

34 Dempson (1968), 143–44.

35 Quoted in Ryckewaert (2015). See also Ling (2015).

36 Zeng (2016).

37 Chamandy (2019).

38 At the time, the secret exit was described as "a private escape route – known as the Sir John A. Macdonald staircase – which runs directly from his Justice ministry office to a side road on Parliament Hill" (Westell 1968).

39 Beeby (2017); Ditchburn (2016), 64; Esselment and Wilson (2017), 225–26; Lalonde (1971), 519–20; Thomas (2013), 68–69; Westell (1972), 115.

40 Martin (2010), 62.

41 Brian Mulroney (December 17, 2018).

42 Greenspon and Wilson-Smith (1996), 307; Jeffrey (2010), 370.

43 Graham (2016), 238–39.

44 Jeffrey (2010), 356. See also Carney (2000), 269; Goldenberg (2006), 84–85.

45 Martin (2002). See also Axworthy (2008), 124.

46 Paul Martin (July 26, 2018).

47 Unnamed Liberal MP, quoted in Taber (2004).

48 Among many sources, see Brodie (2018), 118; Esselment and Wilson (2017), 229; Marland (2016), 303–9; Marland (2017), 39–40; Martin (2010), 58–60.

49 Moore (2014).

50 Martin (2010), 61. See also Clark (2006); Newman (2006), 377.

51 Marland (2017), 45–46.

52 Minister 2 in Justin Trudeau's cabinet (name withheld).

53 Marland (2016), 295–303.

54 Kate Purchase (October 12, 2018). See also Marland (2016), 295–303.

55 Beeby (2018); Boutilier (2016). See also Public Policy Forum (2015), 10.

56 Harris (2015).

57 Smith (2018a).

58 Harjit Sajjan, quoted in Aiello (2018b).

59 Akin (2016).

60 Campion-Smith (2017).

61 Chase and Fife (2019).

62 Burney (2005), 85; Goldenberg (2006), 75–78.

63 Aucoin (2012); Public Policy Forum (2015). See also Hartt (2003), 275.

64 *Globe and Mail* (2019). See also Boyer (2003), 246.

65 Whip 1 (name withheld).

66 Rana (2015b).

67 Radwanski and Leblanc (2019). See also Dawson (2017, 22).

68 Brodie (2018); Goldenberg (2006), Chapter 5. See also Savoie (1999), 319; Wilson (2016a).

69 Curran (2016).

70 White (2005), 71.

71 Brodie (2018), 117–29; Esselment and Wilson (2017); Marland (2016), 214–17; Wilson (2020).

72 Ken Boessenkool (July 18, 2018).

73 Canadian Press (2019c).

74 Steele (2014), 87, 93.

75 Dhanraj (2018). See also Radwanski (2018).

76 Political staff 2 (name withheld).

77 Political staff 8 (name withheld).

78 White (2005), 49–50.

79 Wilson (2015b), 468. See also Benoit (2006), 172–74. The Harper PMO reportedly asked ministerial chiefs of staff to give money to the party and requested that they wrangle donations from other political staff in the minister's office (Laghi and Leblanc 2007).

80 Don Boudria (June 1, 2019).

81 Fife and Curry (2017).

82 Interview with political staff 9 (name withheld). See also Dickin (2016), 12; Marland (2016), 289–95.

83 Political staff 9 (name withheld).

84 Quoted in Howlett (2017).

85 Political staff 10 (name withheld).

86 Wilson (2016b). See also Craft (2016), 190; Curran (2016). Relatedly, the Chrétien PMO ran a "communications coordination group" to synchronize government messaging. Chaired by the director of communications, the group included senior PMO staff, select ministerial staff, and PCO communications personnel (Murphy 2002).

87 For a summary of deliverology in the Trudeau government, see May (2019); Wherry (2019), 278–80.

88 Telford (2018); transcribed by the author. See also Wherry (2019), 279.

89 Mendelsohn (2020).

90 Leblanc and Fife (2020).

91 Minister 3 in Justin Trudeau's cabinet (name withheld).

92 McGrath (1985b), 18–19.

93 According to Pierre Trudeau at the time, regional desks "are merely to provide an additional source of information to me as to what might be happening in various parts of the country ... MPs who want to see me, and do not have time to wait for the appointment I could give them, would be invited to see regional desk officers" (quoted in *Globe and Mail*, 1968). See also D'Aquino (1974); Lalonde (1971), 526; Wearing (1981), 156–57.

94 Regional desks were discontinued circa 1972 (D'Aquino 1974) and circa 1985 (McGrath 1985b, 80).

95 Westell (1972), 118.

96 Ryckewaert (2018a).

97 During a focusing event, politicians want to assure citizens that multiple departments and levels of government caucuses are working together. For example, coordination is necessary during mass flooding, an ice storm, or a wildfire to deploy and manage emergency response personnel, evacuation, medical supplies, temporary shelter, food, toiletries, clothing, weather forecasting, and telecommunications. Birkland (1998); Worrall (1999).

98 Mazereeuw (2020a).

99 Quoted in MacCharles (2020).

100 Mazereeuw (2020b).

101 The composition was proportionate to party standings, plus a deputy Speaker and an assistant deputy Speaker (Thomas 2020).

102 Candice Bergen, Conservative MP for Portage–Lisgar, quoted in Tumilty (2020).

103 Unnamed political staffer quoted in Delacourt (2020). Note that amid controversy in May 2016, the Liberal government had withdrawn plans to assume control over some procedural tools available to the opposition (Brodie 2018, 94).

104 Paez (2020a).

105 Reid (2020).

106 Rana (2020c). See also Leblanc and Fife (2020).

107 Moss (2020).

108 BC Green and NDP caucuses (2017).

109 Government of New Brunswick (2020); Government of Newfoundland and Labrador (2020); Government of Prince Edward Island (2020); Poitras (2020a, 2020b). I obtained additional information from some media stories and, in Newfoundland and Labrador, from three MHAs, two political staff, and a legislative librarian.

CHAPTER 7: PARLIAMENTARY CAUCUSES

1 Heard (2014), 134.

2 Reid (1993), 3; White (2005), 125–30.

3 Anne McLellan (April 18, 2018).

4 Michelle Rempel Garner, Conservative MP for Calgary Nose Hill, quoted in Rands (2017); transcribed by the author.

5 For example, Franks (1987), 103–4. See also Turner (2009), 63; Wesley and Nauta (2020), 124.

 6 For example, Hutton (2018).
 7 Nielsen (1989), 129.
 8 Martin (2010), 117.
 9 Major (2019); Boyko (2010), 211.
10 Turner (2009), 9.
11 Rands (2017). See also Cullen (2011), 64.
12 Rana (2015a).
13 Gilles Duceppe (October 30, 2018). Relatedly, in 1966 MPs were able to listen to Liberal caucus meetings via crossed wiring in a translator's booth in the PC caucus room (Hunter 1986).
14 Gerson (2018); Rana (2016).
15 Rana (2019c). See also Morden, Hilderman, and Anderson (2018b), 30–31.
16 Radwanski (2014).
17 CBC (1971); Matheson (1976), 186; Savoie (1999), 92–93. The Samara Centre's exit interview transcripts refer to sixty-second limits.
18 Chrétien (1985), 41–42; Nielsen (1989), 119; Westell (1972), 102.
19 Lisa Raitt (January 10, 2019).
20 Lambert (2018); Rathgeber (2014), 83.
21 Loat and MacMillan (2014), 152–53. See also Chrétien (2007), 35.
22 Savoie (1999), 92.
23 Hoffman (1972), 149; Thomas (1985b), 52.
24 Morton (1950), 179.
25 Boyko (2010), 211.
26 O'Sullivan with McQueen (1986), 49.
27 CBC (1971); transcribed by the author.
28 Thomas (1985b), 52–53. See also Hoffman (1972), 149.
29 Bégin (2018), 97–98, 101. As one Liberal MP remarked about Pierre Trudeau at the time: "In caucus, when he sums up an argument at the end, he is so plausible, articulate, persuasive ... [he has] the ability to reply, retaliate, put down a guy in such a way that you hardly know it's happening" (quoted in Young 1969).
30 Fraser (1989), 18–19; Mulroney (2007), 605. Additional information was obtained, in part, from Brian Mulroney (December 17, 2018), Jim Edwards (November 16, 2018), and Bill Fox (June 4, 2020).
31 Burney (2005), 89. Staff who made a presentation exited the caucus room afterward.
32 Mulroney (2007), 284–85. See also Burney (2005), 86; Fraser (1990).
33 Mulroney (2007), 375.
34 Jim Edwards (November 16, 2018).
35 Mulroney (2007), 284.
36 Ibid., 384. Pat Nowlan, PC MP for Annapolis Valley–Hants, observed about Mulroney: "The prime minister is a magician in caucus, and that may be one of the problems. He is absolutely fantastic, and it is very difficult to raise a question after his mastery of the rhetoric and the argument. And then he concludes, and that's the end of caucus" (quoted in Cernetig and Freeman, 1990).

37 Jim Edwards (November 16, 2018). According to one account at the time, "most of the MPs seem to emerge dazzled by Mr. Mulroney's cheerleading skills and partisan morale-boosting. He is apparently serious, colloquial, scornful, flattering, scathing, and defiant" (Fraser 1990). See also Fraser (1989), 19.

38 Chrétien (1985), 43.

39 Quoted in Rands (2017); transcribed by the author.

40 Cullen (2011), 24.

41 Chrétien (2007), 36. See also Graham (2016), 124–25; Greenspon and Wilson-Smith (1996), 6; Rana (2019e).

42 Don Boudria (June 1, 2019).

43 Chrétien (2007), 210.

44 Simpson (2001), 46.

45 Delacourt (2003), 220–21.

46 Scott Simms, quoted in Antle (2005).

47 Brodie (2018), 134–35; Rathgeber (2014), 108. As well, information provided by interview participants.

48 Quoted in Mas (2015). See also Rana (2015b).

49 Member of Parliament 3 (name withheld).

50 Wherry (2019), 49.

51 Minister 4 in Justin Trudeau's cabinet (name withheld).

52 Unnamed Liberal MP, quoted in Rana (2019a).

53 Bob Bratina, Liberal MP for Hamilton East–Stoney Creek, quoted in Rana (2018b).

54 Unnamed Liberal MP, quoted in Rana and Aiello (2017). Quotes in this paragraph are from three different MPs. Abbas Rana, personal email, April 14, 2020.

55 As with federal PC leader Robert Stanfield; see Kempling (1988), 14.

56 McGrane (2019), 91–93, 102.

57 Anne McGrath (April 24, 2018).

58 McGrane (2019), 92, 101, 103.

59 Ward (1966), 77.

60 de Clercy (2018).

61 Graham (2016), 128.

62 Bernard Lord (December 10, 2018).

63 Kathleen Wynne (December 7, 2018).

64 Ibid.

65 Such as the strategy session of Liberal MPs depicted in CBC (1971). See also Graham (2016), 125.

66 Megan Leslie (July 27, 2018).

67 Steven Fletcher (August 3, 2018).

68 Nunziata (2003), 17; Thomas (1985a), 122. See also Kornberg (1966), 85; Savoie (1999), 92.

69 Commissioner for Legislative Standards (2018b), 6; Copps (2019a).

70 Carney (2000), 188–89.

71 Joe Clark (January 24, 2019).

72 Wayne Easter (July 27, 2018).

73 As occurred with John Diefenbaker (Nielsen 1989, 117; Stursberg 1976, 71–78).

74 Minister 2 in Justin Trudeau's cabinet (name withheld).

75 Noelle-Neumann (1993). See also Loury (1994).

76 Michael Ignatieff, former Liberal MP for Etobicoke–Lakeshore, quoted in Ibbitson (2013).

77 Erin Weir (July 20, 2018).

78 Robyn Luff (November 15, 2018).

79 Member of Parliament 1 (name withheld).

80 Robert-Falcon Ouellette (October 2, 2018).

81 Jones (2016), 76, 161.

82 Antle (2005); Rana and Aiello (2017).

83 McGrane (2019), 95.

84 Wright Allen (2017).

85 Ibid. See also Cullen (2011), 61; Graham (2016), 124.

86 Thomas (1985a), 105.

87 Savoie (1999), 92.

88 Jim Edwards (November 16, 2018).

89 Don Rusnak, Liberal MP for Thunder Bay–Rainy River, quoted in CBC (2016).

90 Cullen (2011), 64–65.

91 Wright Allen (2017).

92 Marlene Catterall (November 26, 2018).

93 Anita Vandenbeld, quoted in Ryckewaert (2018b).

94 Thomas (2016).

95 Rana (2017).

96 Cullen (2011), 61–64.

97 Political staff 1 (name withheld).

98 Ken Boessenkool (July 18, 2018). See also Graham (2016), 128.

99 Shannon Stubbs (December 21, 2018).

100 Member of Parliament 1 (name withheld).

101 Member of Parliament 5 (name withheld).

102 As occurred in Prime Minister Mulroney's caucus (Gratton 1987, 151) and Premier Ford's caucus (Benzie 2019).

103 For example, Radwanski (2018).

104 Steven MacKinnon (August 13, 2018).

105 Kate Purchase (October 12, 2018).

106 Bill Fox (June 4, 2020). See also Lalonde (1971), 513.

107 Brodie (2018), 134; Chrétien (2007), 36; Simpson (2001), 34. See also Graham (2016), 124; Rana (2019e).

108 Paul Martin (April 10, 2019).

109 Brodie (2018), 134; Rana (2018a).

110 Canadian Press (2017b).

111 Member of Parliament 6 (name withheld).

CHAPTER 8: CAUCUS RESEARCH BUREAUS

1 Axworthy (2008), 82–85; Flynn (2012), 95–96.
2 Ryckewaert (2011).
3 Wilson (2020).
4 Ryckewaert (2017).
5 Ryckewaert (2011).
6 Ames (1911), 186.
7 Boyko (2010), 178–79.
8 Parliament of Canada (1968). See also Axworthy (2008), 46; Black (1972), 26; Courtney (1978), 54; Jeffrey (2010), 39; Lalonde (1971), 512; May (2017), 20–21; Thomas (1985a), 88, 107; Wilson (2020).
9 Kornberg and Mishler (1976), 27. See also Crane (1969).
10 Progressive Conservative Party of Canada (1985), 19; Thomas (1985a), 107.
11 Carroll (2012). One parliamentary reporter has described caucus research bureau staff as "the people who put words in politicians' mouths" by turning facts "into ammunition fired daily by MPs at their opponents" and by "selecting points of attack and defence in the battle of words" (Warren 1986).
12 An example of the accountability function of an opposition caucus research office is LRB staff calculating the accumulated expense of Prime Minister Campbell using a government jet to tour the country in the lead-up to the 1993 election (Taber 1993).
13 Robin Sears, NDP strategist, quoted in Ryckewaert (2011).
14 Greg MacEachern, Liberal strategist, quoted in ibid.
15 Elly Alboim, Liberal strategist, quoted in ibid.
16 Daniel Lauzon, LRB director of communications, quoted in ibid.
17 Allmand (2006), 19. See also Axworthy (2008), 19, 47, 117–18.
18 Liberal Research Bureau (2007), 2.
19 MPs can get caught in a circular search for assistance: bureau staff refer them to the leader's office, which sends them to the House leader's office, where they are told that the issue is the responsibility of the caucus research bureau (Taber 2007). See also Wilson (2020).
20 Political staff 11 (name withheld).
21 New Democratic Party of Canada (2016).
22 A Conservative provided me with the master file for review.
23 Ryckewaert (2016).
24 Thomas (1985a), 98. See also Thomas (1985b), 56.
25 Thomas (1985a), 107–8. As well, in 1982 the Liberal Research Bureau set up "the Good News Bureau" to compile positive stories about the Trudeau government that it circulated to the Liberal caucus (McGillivray 1987).
26 Liberal Research Bureau (2007), 18, 20; Marland (2016), 155–59; McGrane (2019), 96, 119.
27 Political staff 12 (name withheld).
28 Patrick Muttart (June 4, 2018). See also Delacourt (2016a), 182–83.
29 Marland (2016), 155–60; McGrane (2019), 96.

30 Quoted in Ryckewaert (2017).

31 Wylie (2018).

32 Carroll (2012); McLean (2012), 57; Thompson (2007).

33 Hannay (2017). Other examples of questionable partisan work include the PC caucus research office contracting private detectives (*Globe and Mail* 1977), staff coordinating MP interviews with a TV news service contracted by the party (Naumetz 1987), and researchers compiling a list of people supporting opposition party leadership contestants (Bryden 1989).

34 Brett Thalmann, LRB managing director, quoted in Ryckewaert (2016).

35 Kait LaForce, former staffer in the LRB, personal email, May 4, 2020.

36 Political staff 11 (name withheld).

37 Wayne Easter (July 27, 2018).

38 Jeffrey (2010), 42, 457, 629. Among the duties of a PMO communications planner is providing "message direction and advice" to the caucus research bureau (Office of the Prime Minister 2018).

39 Aiello (2019a).

40 The Liberal messaging about abortion in Chapter 4 is another example. During Chrétien's leadership, the LRB faxed key messages under the banner "Talking Points," and when Martin was leader it sent "infoFlash" emails (*Globe and Mail* 2004). For a Conservative example, see Figure 2.5 in Marland (2016), 52.

41 Nick Whalen (May 11, 2018).

42 Bouchard (1994), 112; Marland (2016), 220. See also Graham (2016), 238 39.

43 Political staff 11 (name withheld).

44 Nick Whalen (May 11, 2018). Relatedly, see Marland and Power (2020).

45 *Toronto Star* (2017). See also Hannay (2017); Simpson (2019).

46 Political staff 7 (name withheld).

47 Political staff 11 (name withheld).

48 Minister 2 in Justin Trudeau's cabinet (name withheld).

49 Wayne Easter (July 27, 2018).

50 Leitch (2019), 22.

CHAPTER 9: LEGISLATIVE ASSEMBLIES

1 Chong, Simms, and Stewart (2017).

2 Rob Oliphant, quoted in Raj (2016a).

3 Marleau and Montpetit (2000). See also Robertson (2002).

4 Brodie (2018), 96; Godbout and Høyland (2017), 546; Morden, Hilderman, and Anderson (2018b), 13; Underhill (1935), 385. See also Godbout (2020), 243.

5 McLeod (1988), 30–31. In the 1960s, some MPs sent their staff to liquor stores in preparation for evening sittings (Campbell 1964).

6 Bosc (1988), 24–25.

7 Nielsen (1989), 88.

8 Drew (1951), 2902. As leader of the official opposition from 1948 to 1956, Drew and other PC MPs often ridiculed Liberal backbenchers for being trained seals. Originally, the moniker referred to heckling and desk thumping. For example,

in 1948 John Diefenbaker said in the House: "These interruptions have all the spontaneity of trained seals" (Murray 1948). The expression grew to imply "that the Liberal rank and file would accept and approve unquestionably whatever their leaders did or said" (*Winnipeg Free Press* 1959). In 1966, Diefenbaker would go on to use the label to dismiss PC party members agitating for a leadership review to force him out.

9 Baker (2003), 80; Boyer (2003), 245; Nielsen (1989), 87, 112. In the 1930s, it was believed that backbench MPs were motivated to speak at length in the House so that they could mail Hansard printouts to their constituents (*Globe* 1936).

10 Dempson (1968), 157–58.

11 Franks (1987), 157; Nielsen (1989), 113. Increased security protocols in the Parliament Buildings have put distance between MPs and journalists. In the late 1980s, journalists could tap on the door of an MP's office to have an impromptu conversation about constituency issues, and prior to the 2001 US terrorism attacks they could scrum politicians exiting through the Centre Block's main doorway (Lapointe and Eloria 2020).

12 Trudeau (1976), 11234.

13 Trudeau (1958), 308. See also Godbout (2020), 37.

14 Lefebvre (1987), 9, 52–53; McGrath (1985b), 103; Turner (1987), 32. See also Fraser (1988); Soroka, Redko, and Albaugh (2015).

15 Cooper (2017), 53; McGrath (1985b), 54–55. Previously, MPs jumped up and down trying to get the Speaker's attention, which was a physical imposition for some (Young 1969).

16 Dale Kirby, Liberal MHA for Mount Scio, quoted in Commissioner for Legislative Standards (2018b), 15.

17 Campion-Smith (2018); McIntyre (2018), Steele (2014), 27.

18 Samara Centre (2016). See also Collier and Raney (2018b).

19 Brendan Maguire (October 16, 2018).

20 Jay Hill (May 31, 2019).

21 Ibid.

22 Cullen (2011), 21–22.

23 Marlene Catterall (November 26, 2018).

24 Jones (2016), 40.

25 Mazereeuw (2019b).

26 Karen Redman (October 26, 2018). See also Dawson and Woods (2005); Francoli (2005).

27 In this chapter, some information about procedural matters and their history is from Marleau and Montpetit (2000).

28 Blidook and Byrne (2013); Loat and MacMillan (2014), 118–20; Walsh (2017), 23–24.

29 Blidook (2013).

30 Scott Simms (July 4, 2018).

31 Member of Parliament 1 (name withheld).

32 Wawara (2013). See also Blidook (2013), 25; Brodie (2018), 188.
33 Long (2019).
34 Walsh (2017), 138.
35 Graham (2016), 421; Patterson (2019). See also Burney (2005), 90; Fraser (1988); Marland (2016), 217–18.
36 Unnamed Liberal MP, quoted in Campion-Smith (2018).
37 Simpson (2001), 38.
38 For example, Stone (2017). See also McGrane (2019), 97, 110.
39 For example, Cooper (2017), 53.
40 Jeffrey (2010), 33–35.
41 Information based on a QP list provided by the Office of the Clerk, House of Commons (July 22, 2019). See also Campion-Smith (2018).
42 Political staff 6 (name withheld). Giving government-side MPs more opportunities to ask questions in the House was a topic in 1969 during the aforementioned Liberal caucus deliberations about ways to empower backbenchers (Crane 1969).
43 For example, Weekes (2012), 6.
44 O'Malley and Solomon (2014). See also Walsh (2017), 137.
45 David Tilson, Conservative MP for Dufferin–Caledon, quoted in Kennedy and Oved (2018).
46 Heard (2014), 93–95; Walsh (2017), 136.
47 For example, Bouchard (1994), 203.
48 Raj (2016b). In comparison, Stephen Harper missed 36 percent of Question Periods in his first year as prime minister, which increased to 52 percent over the course of his time in the top office when he presided over a majority government (McGregor 2015). Brian Mulroney's schedulers followed a "no wheels up until after caucus" practice, meaning that on Wednesdays he was only available to depart Ottawa after the national caucus meeting concluded at 12 p.m. and might be in the air when QP began at 2:15 p.m. (Bill Fox, June 4, 2020).
49 Loop (2016).
50 McEvoy (2019), 18
51 Graham (2016), 122–23; Loat and MacMillan (2014), 128; Rathgeber (2014), 65–66.
52 Ryan Cleary (March 29, 2018).
53 Member of Parliament 7 (name withheld).
54 Marleau and Montpetit (2000). The rule of five hours per week has been in place since 1991.
55 Kornberg and Campbell (1978), 561.
56 Brodie (2018), 96–101.
57 Blidook (2012), Chapter 7; Docherty (2005), 110–14; Hillier (2013); Morden, Hilderman, and Anderson (2018a), 26–32.
58 Moore (2001), 10.
59 Raj (2019). See also Docherty (2005), 111.
60 Cullen (2020).

61 Information about the private members' business lottery was obtained from the Office of the Clerk, House of Commons (July 22, 2019). See also Lincoln et al. (2001), 12.

62 McGrane (2019), 95–96; Samara Centre (2011), 21.

63 Don Boudria (October 26, 2018).

64 David Wilks (April 17, 2019).

65 Bain (1955); McGrath (1985b), 17.

66 Lefebvre (1987), 29.

67 Matheson (1976), 199.

68 Aiello (2016); Loat and MacMillan (2014), 147; Public Policy Forum (2015), 12. Certain chairs are always members of the official opposition; see House of Commons (2019).

69 Wright Allen (2018a).

70 Aiello (2019e).

71 Calis (2016).

72 Smith (2011), 4.

73 Matheson (1976), 198. See also Graham (2016), 129–30.

74 Martin (2010), 97–98; Wilson (2016a), 29–30.

75 Curry (2018); Delacourt (2018); Joseph (2019); Vigliotti (2016).

76 Member of Parliament 8 (name withheld).

77 Chong (2017), 91.

78 Jane Philpott (June 19, 2019).

79 Jody Wilson-Raybould (July 21, 2019).

80 Minister 2 in Justin Trudeau's cabinet (name withheld).

81 Bégin (2018), 118; Lincoln et al. (2001), 16.

82 Loat and MacMillan (2014), 140; Morden, Hilderman, and Anderson (2018a), 18–25; Petit-Vouriot, Hilderman, and Morden (2018), 7–8; Public Policy Forum (2015); Smith (2011), 6.

83 Jennifer O'Connell, Liberal MP for Pickering–Uxbridge, quoted in Calis (2016).

84 Paul Martin (July 26, 2018).

85 Chrétien (2007), 64; Martin (2008), 143–46.

86 Greenspon and Wilson-Smith (1996), 168.

87 Savoie (1999), 172–87.

88 Unnamed source, quoted in Gray (2003), 126.

89 Paul Martin (July 26, 2018).

90 Boucher (2016, 2018); Wright Allen (2018b).

91 Chad Rogers (February 28, 2019).

92 John McKay, Liberal MP for Scarborough–Guildwood, quoted in Moss (2019).

93 Cullen (2011), 22.

94 Scott Fraser, NDP MLA for Mid Island–Pacific Rim, quoted in Omand (2017).

95 Guay (1988), 56; Pender (2005); Smith (2016).

 96 Lefebvre (1987), 20.
 97 As told by Bill Kempling, PC MP for Burlington and chief government whip (1988, 45–46). More broadly, see Lefebvre (1987), 35–40; Mulroney (2007), 199; Simpson (1980), 22.
 98 For example, Steele (2014), 35.
 99 Turner (1987), 45.
100 Canadian Press (2016).
101 Quoted in Aiello (2017).
102 Guay (1988), 56.
103 Cullen (2011), 19; Graham (2016), 122–23; Lefebvre (1987), 20; Samara Centre (2011), 8.
104 For example, Bégin (2018), 105–6; Cullen (2011), 23, 104; Turner (1987), 38.
105 Cullen (2011), 103.
106 Catterall (2003), 122.
107 Omand (2017). See also Weekes (2012), 7.
108 Mulroney (2007), 199.
109 Karen Redman (October 26, 2018).
110 Boudria (1995).
111 Member of Parliament 1 (name withheld); Privy Council Office (2001); Ryckewaert (2016).
112 Information provided by the Office of the Speaker (July 9, 2019). See also Rathgeber (2014), 66.
113 McKay (2014).
114 Rob Oliphant, quoted in *Hill Times* (2017).
115 Ryan Cleary (May 21, 2019).
116 Mark Holland, quoted in Stone (2018a).
117 Benoit (2006), 225.
118 Svend Robinson (August 16, 2018). See also Godbout (2020), 80; Kam (2009), 95.
119 As with Bill S-201, Genetic Non-Discrimination Act, in 2017 (Canadian Press 2017a; Rana and Aiello 2017).

CHAPTER 10: MANAGING TROUBLE

 1 Loat and MacMillan (2014), 67.
 2 Svend Robinson (August 16, 2018). See also McGrane (2019), 91.
 3 For example, see CBC (2013).
 4 Daniel Turp (October 24, 2018). See also Wiseman (2010).
 5 Member of Parliament 5 (name withheld).
 6 Guay (2002), 7; Morden, Hilderman, and Anderson (2018b), 26; Reid (1993), 2.
 7 Whip 2 (name withheld).
 8 Brendan Maguire (October 16, 2018).
 9 Gilles Duceppe (October 30, 2018).
10 Party leader 2 (name withheld).

11 Edward Roberts (April 12, 2018) and Clyde Wells (June 18, 2019). Minister 1 was Wells, and Minister 2 was John Crosbie. Roberts was the premier's parliamentary assistant. See also Crosbie (1997), 66–74; Gillan (1968).

12 Roberts and Wells reconstructed the quotations in this paragraph. Smallwood died in 1991.

13 Adams et al. (2009). See also Flynn (2012), 86–88; Jones (2016), 176.

14 Unnamed MP, quoted in Axworthy (2008), 106. See also *Pincher Creek Echo* (2019).

15 Rob Norris (November 16, 2018).

16 Philip Houde (July 18, 2018).

17 Nembhard and DeLaronde (2018).

18 Heames, Harvey, and Treadway (2006).

19 As reported with Ontario's chief of staff (Radwanski 2018).

20 Mark Holland, quoted in Stone (2018a).

21 Brendan Maguire (October 16, 2018).

22 Member of Parliament 9 (name withheld).

23 Shaw and Zussman (2018), 28; Steele (2014), 64.

24 Gratton (1987), 61. See also Carney (2000), 279–80; Newman (2006).

25 Graham (2016), 127, 136; Rana (2018a). As well, Justin Trudeau has periodically lost his temper on the floor of the House of Commons, including the "physical molestation of the member from Berthier–Maskinongé" incident in 2016 when he reached for the Conservative whip's arm and inadvertently elbowed the NDP whip.

26 Hopper (2015); Taber (2005).

27 Commissioner for Legislative Standards (2018a), 6, 25; Wherry (2016).

28 Quoted in Commissioner for Legislative Standards (2018b), 5.

29 Snagovsky and Kerby (2019).

30 Collier and Raney (2018b).

31 Aiello (2019a); Collier and Raney (2018a); Wherry (2018). See also Ryckewaert (2018b).

32 Duffy (2007) is the earliest instance of the expression that I located. See also Morden, Hilderman, and Anderson (2018a), 9; Marland (2016), 218–19; O'Malley and Solomon (2014); Rathgeber (2014), 126–27.

33 Morden, Hilderman, and Anderson (2018b), 38; O'Malley and Solomon (2014); Wilson (2015b), 457.

34 Kim Campbell (May 1, 2018). Sometimes relations between exempt staff and ministers can be rougher than what backbenchers experience. A former member of the Mulroney PMO recalls: "If a PMO staffer was highhanded with an MP, you got your ass kicked" (Bill Fox, June 4, 2020).

35 Martin (2010), 63–64.

36 Marland (2016), 205.

37 Turner (2009), 51–52.

38 Brodie (2018), 116, 136–37.

39 As reportedly occurred in the Ontario government of Doug Ford (Benzie 2019).
40 Samara Centre (2018).
41 Political staff 10 (name withheld). Relatedly, see Dickin (2016), 11.
42 Sharon Blady (July 25, 2018). See also *Winnipeg Sun* (2013).
43 Bartlett (2018); CBC (2018a).
44 Premier of Manitoba Brian Pallister, quoted in Martin and Kusch (2017).
45 Kathy Dunderdale (May 17, 2018).
46 Political staff 3 in Justin Trudeau's PMO (name withheld).
47 Don Boudria (June 1, 2019).
48 Stone (2018b).
49 Stone and Zilio (2018).
50 Political staff 13 (name withheld).
51 Ryan Cleary (March 29, 2018).
52 Blatchford (2018); Yakabuski (2019).
53 As occurred with Justin Trudeau's chief government whip (Pinkerton 2018).
54 Nick Whalen (May 11, 2018).
55 For example, Dyer (2018).
56 Blakeney and Borins (1998), 75.
57 Jay Hill (August 22, 2018).
58 Political staff 13 (name withheld).
59 Owens (2006), 13.
60 Perlin (1980), 115.
61 Member of a provincial legislature 3 (name withheld). See also Morden, Hilderman, and Anderson (2018b), 31.
62 Shaw and Zussman (2018), 50–51.
63 Turner (1987), 45, 68.
64 Jay Hill (August 22, 2018).
65 Quoted in Turner (2009), 43.
66 Whip 1 (name withheld). For a synthesis of the sticks and carrots of party discipline, see Geisler (2015), 24–29.
67 Canadian Press (2017a); MacGuigan (1978), 680.
68 Member of Parliament 9 (name withheld).
69 Party leader 3 (name withheld).
70 Wayne Long, Liberal MP for Saint John–Rothesay, quoted in Leger (2018).
71 Dickson (2018a); Jones (2016), 23.
72 Philip Houde (July 18, 2018).
73 Hazan (2014), 213.
74 Bruce Hyer, NDP MP for Thunder Bay–Superior North, quoted in MacKreal (2013).
75 For example, Dawson (2018); Martin (2002), 236; Nunziata (2003), 21.
76 Hillier (2013).
77 Patterson (2019).
78 Hillier (2019).

79 Snagovsky and Kerby (2018). See also Morton (2006).

80 Calculated from Elections Canada data for the seven federal elections held from 2000 to 2019 (679 of 14,399 candidates). I treat candidates with no affiliation as Independents.

81 Loewen and Bastien (2010), 101.

82 Nova Scotia MLA Paul MacEwan in 1981 and 1988 (in 1984 he won as leader of the Cape Breton Labour Party), Quebec MP André Arthur in 2006 and 2008, and BC MLA Vicki Huntington in 2009 and 2013.

83 Dewing (2016); Huntington (2012); Small and Philpott (2020).

84 For example, Huntington (2012), 3.

85 Cowley and Stuart (2009), 21–22.

86 Ibid., 22.

CHAPTER 11: THE SNC-LAVALIN AFFAIR

1 Four *Globe and Mail* journalists (Steven Chase, Robert Fife, Sean Fine, and Daniel Leblanc) who covered the story were subsequently awarded the National Newspaper Award for politics.

2 Quoted in Zimonjic (2019c).

3 Those who participated are not necessarily listed in Appendix 1. I did not request or receive information that would betray cabinet confidences. For a summary of events, see Bezanson (2019); Dion (2019); Wherry (2019), Chapter 12; Wilson-Raybould (2019a).

4 McLellan (2019), 6, 10. See also Bezanson (2019).

5 A joint position held by a lawyer does not always happen in the provinces. For example, in 2019 a dairy farmer was appointed to both roles in PEI. On occasion, the provincial positions have been split up, at times with only one held by a lawyer and/or by a member of the legislative assembly.

6 Quoted in Stenning (2009), 344. See also Bezanson (2019); Dion (2019), 13–14, 51–53; McLellan (2019).

7 Canada (2006a). See also Wilson-Raybould (2019a, 2019b).

8 Baum and Fine (2019). See also Dion (2019), 48–49.

9 Bezanson (2019), 772–75; Canadian Press (2019a).

10 Baum and Fine (2019).

11 CBC (2019d).

12 Friedman (2019); Perreaux, Gray, and Marotte (2015); Zimonjic (2019c).

13 Public Works and Government Services Canada (2015).

14 Robert Card, quoted in Blackwell (2014).

15 Conservative Party of Canada (2018a, 2018b).

16 Allmand (2006); Benoit (2006); Marland (2016), 231–33.

17 Liberal Party of Canada (2015).

18 Marland (2016), xvii; Radwanski and Leblanc (2019).

19 Jody Wilson-Raybould (July 21, 2019).

20 Whip 3 (name withheld).

21 Baum and Fine (2019); Dion (2019), 6. Self-description is from SNC-Lavalin (2020).
22 Dion (2019), 6.
23 Baum and Fine (2019); Dion (2019), 6; Wilson-Raybould (2019a).
24 Canada (2017).
25 Office of the Commissioner of Lobbying of Canada (2019).
26 Bezanson (2019), 775; Dion (2019), 9.
27 Wilson-Raybould (2019b), 4, 13. See also Wilson-Raybould (2019a).
28 CBC (2018). Conversely, Trudeau's messaging to China in 2020 about the legal case against a Huawei company executive was that Canada has an independent justice system.
29 Liberal Party of Canada (2015), 30.
30 Canada (2018b). See also Bezanson (2019), 776–82.
31 Baum and Fine (2019); Dion (2019), 9.
32 Blatchford (2019).
33 Baum and Fine (2019).
34 Morneau (2018).
35 Boutilier (2019).
36 Baum and Fine (2019).
37 Ibid. See also Bezanson (2019), 806.
38 Evelyn (2018).
39 Quoted in Fife (2020).
40 Dion (2019), 11.
41 Ibid., 21–22.
42 Ibid., 19–20.
43 Bezanson (2019), 802. See also Wilson-Raybould (2019b), 5–6.
44 October 10, 2018, email included as Appendix B in Wilson-Raybould (2019b).
45 Dion (2019), 23.
46 Ibid., 26.
47 Ibid., 30.
48 Butts (2019); Wilson-Raybould (2019a).
49 Wilson-Raybould (2019b), 7.
50 Ibid., 8.
51 Michael Wernick, clerk of the Privy Council, quoted in ibid., 13. See also Bezanson (2019), 803–4.
52 Wilson-Raybould (2019a).
53 Butts (2019).
54 Wilson-Raybould (2019a, 2019d).
55 For example, Kerby (2014), 269.
56 Chase, Fife, and Fine (2019).
57 Butts (2019).
58 Quoted in Wherry (2019), 294.
59 Fife, Chase, and Fine (2019a).

60 PMO press secretary, quoted in ibid.

61 Quoted in Fife and Chase (2019).

62 Ibid.

63 Conservative MPs referred three times to the "carefully scripted response" (Scheer 2019).

64 Rabson (2019b).

65 Wilson-Raybould (2019b), 19.

66 Fife, Chase, and Fine (2019b); Wherry (2019), 299.

67 Wilson-Raybould's reported conditions for staying were firing Butts, Wernick, and a PMO senior legal adviser; that Trudeau apologize to the cabinet or do so publicly; and that she receive assurances that a DPA would not be offered to SNC-Lavalin (Aiello 2019c; Bezanson 2019, 807–8; Wherry 2019, 298).

68 *Toronto Sun* (2019).

69 Rana (2019a).

70 Celina Caesar-Chavannes, quoted in Stone (2019b).

71 Rana (2019a).

72 Chase and Woo (2019).

73 Smith (2019).

74 Hall (2019).

75 MacCharles and Campion-Smith (2019).

76 Rana (2019e).

77 Francis Scarpaleggia, Liberal MP for Lac-Saint-Louis, quoted in Canadian Press (2019b).

78 Angus (2019).

79 Quoted in Canadian Press (2019b).

80 Wilson-Raybould (2019a). See also Baum, Grant, and Stueck (2019); Bezanson (2019), 783.

81 Wilson-Raybould (2019a).

82 Ibid.; Wilson-Raybould (2019b). However, see Butts (2019).

83 Wilson-Raybould (2019a). Relatedly, see McLellan (2019).

84 Philpott (2019). See also Kerby (2014).

85 Quoted in Clark (2020).

86 Eneas (2019).

87 Quoted in Forrest (2019).

88 Butts (2019).

89 Ibid. Relatedly, see Wilson-Raybould (2019b), 18–19.

90 Quoted in Aiello (2019b).

91 Quoted in Stone (2019b).

92 CBC (2019e); Simpson (2019).

93 Copps (2019a, 2019b).

94 Dion (2020).

95 Rana (2019d).

96 Major (2019); Rana (2019d); Wherry (2019), 309.

97 Aiello (2019b).

 98 For example, Bryden (2019).
 99 Jane Philpott, quoted in Wells (2019).
100 Judy Sgro, quoted in CBC (2019f). See also Major (2019).
101 Quoted in Wright (2019b). See also Ballingall and MacCharles (2019).
102 Quoted in *Maclean's* (2019).
103 Moss and Haws (2019).
104 Wilson-Raybould (2019c).
105 Quoted in CBC (2019g). Translated from French.
106 Quoted in CBC (2019g). See also Bezanson (2019), 807.
107 Trudeau added: "We can't sit back as Liberals and say diversity is a source of strength without respecting that within the same team sometimes you're going to have sharp differences of opinion ... But when it became fairly obvious there wasn't a path towards accommodation or reconciliation we had to move forward with a strongly united team." Quoted in 680News (2019); transcribed by the author.
108 Gawley (2019).
109 Jane Philpott (June 16, 2019). See also Clark (2020).
110 Geddes (2019).
111 von Scheel (2019).
112 Anonymous Liberal MP, quoted in Rana (2019f).
113 Dion (2019), 51–53, 21.
114 Canada (2006b), s. 9.
115 Dion (2019), 44.
116 McLellan (2019), 35.
117 Leblanc and Fife (2019).
118 Andrew Scheer, Conservative Party leader and MP for Regina–Qu'Appelle, quoted in CBC (2019c).
119 Eva Nassif, Liberal MP for Vimy, quoted in Fife and Leblanc (2019) and Fife, Leblanc, and Walsh (2019).
120 Zimonjic (2019b).
121 Philpott's campaign experience is described in Small and Philpott (2020).
122 Quoted in Macdonald (2019).
123 *National Post* (2019). See also McLellan (2019), 42–43.
124 SNC-Lavalin (2019). See also Fife and Chase (2019); Friedman (2019).
125 Quoted in Fife and Chase (2019).
126 Trudeau (2019b).
127 LeBlanc (2020).
128 Other resignations occurred in 1896 (Manitoba schools question), 1944 (Second World War conscription), and 1963 (nuclear armament); see Lewis (2019). See also Kerby (2014).
129 One analysis determined "the Shawcross line was not crossed" (Bezanson 2019, 793).
130 Political staff 14 (name withheld).
131 Member of Parliament 8 (name withheld).

132 Wayne Easter (July 28, 2019).
133 Quoted in Clark (2020).
134 For example, Bezanson (2019), 808–11.
135 Steven MacKinnon (July 28, 2019).
136 Terry Beech, Liberal MP for Burnaby North–Seymour, quoted in Gawley (2019).
137 Alexandra Mendès (July 29, 2019).
138 Quoted in Wherry (2019), 66.
139 Dion (2019), 18, 36–37; le (2019), 479–80; Wherry (2019), 64–66, 285–86, 292.
140 Wherry (2019), 67, 297.
141 Jody Wilson-Raybould (July 21, 2019).
142 Member of Parliament 8 (name withheld).
143 Jody Wilson-Raybould (July 21, 2019).
144 Jane Philpott (June 16, 2019).
145 Nick Whalen (July 26, 2019).
146 CBC (2019b).
147 Elections Canada (2019).
148 Clark (2019).
149 Unnamed Liberal MP, quoted in Rana and Shekar (2018). See also Dawson (2017, 22).
150 Radwanski and Leblanc (2019). See also Wherry (2019), 50.
151 Kent (2018). See also Lewis, Lalancette, and Raynauld (2019), 187.
152 For example, Katz and Mair (2018), 2–3; Stanbury (2003).
153 Dion (2019), 7, 24, 26, 29, 30, 34, 36. On Trudeau's position, see 32, 36.
154 Ibid., 37–38.
155 Radwanski and Leblanc (2019).
156 Political staff 1 in Justin Trudeau's PMO (name withheld).
157 Hedy Fry, Liberal MP for Vancouver Centre, quoted in Bernardo (2019).

CHAPTER 12: ADVICE FOR A NEW PARLIAMENTARIAN

1 Powers (2019).
2 One survey found that nearly three-quarters of Canadians would support a law restricting the power of party leaders over private members (Environics 2013).
3 Compas (2007), 27.
4 Chan (2017).
5 Petit-Vouriot, Hilderman, and Morden (2018), 7.
6 Morden, Hilderman, and Anderson (2018b).
7 Ibbitson (2013). Placing the onus on MPs to urge change appeared in the same newspaper 70 years prior: "Slowly it has been dawning on a few members that the functions of the private member are degenerating: still fewer show signs of wanting to do something about it" (*Globe and Mail* 1943).
8 Flynn (2012); Jones (2016).
9 For example, see Kornberg (1966).
10 Godbout (2020).
11 Danielle Smith (July 20, 2018).

12 Paul Martin (July 26, 2018).

13 Minister 4 in Justin Trudeau's cabinet (name withheld).

14 Glen Clark (September 25, 2018).

15 Kellie Leitch (December 16, 2018).

16 Cathy Bennett (June 18, 2019).

17 Kam (2006); Koop, Bastedo, and Blidook (2018), 190–91.

18 Atkinson and Docherty (1992); Docherty (1997); Franks (1987).

19 Yvonne Jones (July 23, 2018).

20 Bernard Lord (December 10, 2018).

21 Ibid.

22 For example, White (2020).

23 Yvonne Jones (July 23, 2018).

24 Anne Minh-Thu Quach, NDP MP for Salaberry–Suroît, quoted in MacCharles, Ballingall, and Boutilier (2019).

25 Whip 3 (name withheld).

26 Michael Chong (May 31, 2019).

27 Chrétien (1985), 41–42; Chrétien (2007), 35–36.

28 Reid (2006), 3.

29 Francis (2000), 123.

30 Marlene Catterall (November 26, 2018).

31 Kellie Leitch (December 16, 2018).

32 Rob Norris (November 16, 2018).

33 Ibid.

34 Adam Vaughan (July 31, 2018).

35 Jackson (1968), 294–99.

36 Member of Parliament 10 (name withheld).

37 Carney (2000), 251. This advice for the cabinet applies equally to the caucus.

38 Bégin (2018), 101–2.

39 Blake Richards, Conservative MP for Banff–Airdrie, quoted in Wright Allen (2018a).

40 Political staff 1 in Justin Trudeau's PMO (name withheld).

41 Nick Whalen (July 19, 2019). For context, see White (2020).

42 Benzie, Ferguson, and Rushowy (2018).

43 Reid (2018). Reid's practices are rooted in the tradition of Reform MPs consulting constituents through mail-backs, telephone polls, and phone-ins. Even the Reform whip was willing to defy the party line (Ha 1995). However, as the Conservatives' deputy House leader under Prime Minister Harper, Reid conducted just one constituent referendum in nine years and ended up voting with the Conservative frontbench (Curry 2017).

44 Scott J. Reid (September 19, 2018).

45 Reid (2019).

46 Ibid.

47 Ryckewaert (2020).

48 Philpott (2019).

49 Reid (2006), 2.
50 Docherty (1997), 259.
51 Kornberg (1966), 84.
52 Morden, Hilderman, and Anderson (2018a, 2018b).
53 For example, Esselment and Wilson (2017); Wilson (2015b, 2016b, 2020).
54 Cross (2016).
55 In the provinces, electronic information summaries are typically circulated by centralized government communications services, the premier's office, and/or the whip's office. Legislative librarians also circulate topical information.
56 McEvoy (2019); McKelvey (2019). See also Delacourt (2016a), 329–31.

APPENDIX 2: INTERVIEW SAMPLING AND RECRUITMENT

1 Docherty (1997), xi; Savoie (1999), x.

References

Aalberg, Toril, Jesper Strömbäck, and Claes de Vreese. 2011. "The framing of politics as strategy and game: A review of concepts, operationalizations and key findings." *Journalism* 13(2): 162–78.

Abma, Derek. 2017. "PCO seeks 'issues ninja,' 'master storyteller.'" *Hill Times,* March 13, 2.

Adams, Susan J., Tracey E. Hazelwood, Nancy L. Pitre, Terry E. Bedard, and Suzette D. Landry. 2009. "Harassment of Members of Parliament and the legislative assemblies in Canada by individuals believed to be mentally disordered." *Journal of Forensic Psychiatry and Psychology* 20(6): 801–14.

Aiello, Rachel. 2016. "Liberals insist not interfering in House committee chair selections, despite lack of secret ballots." *Hill Times,* February 15, 4.

–. 2017. "New government whip Pablo Rodriguez promises 'collaborative' caucus management style." *Hill Times,* January 24. https://www.hilltimes.com/2017/01/24/new-government-whip-rodriguez-promises-collaborative-caucus-management-style/93535.

–. 2018a. "Liberal MP Sahota contradicts PM, foreign minister on reason for Russians' expulsion." CTV News, April 8. https://www.ctvnews.ca/politics/liberal-mp-sahota-contradicts-pm-foreign-minister-on-reason-for-russians-expulsion-1.3875105.

–. 2018b. "Sajjan says Harper's endorsement of Trump's Iran decision 'not helpful.'" CTV News, May 11. https://www.ctvnews.ca/politics/sajjan-says-harper-s-endorsement-of-trump-s-iran-decision-not-helpful-1.3923867.

–. 2019a. "Liberal staffers' anti-harassment trainer worried about 'more silence' pre-election." CTV News, January 9. https://www.ctvnews.ca/politics/liberal-staffers-anti-harassment-trainer-worried-about-more-silence-pre-election-1.4247052.

–. 2019b. "Trudeau adds new caucus-PMO liaison." CTV News, March 22. https://www.ctvnews.ca/politics/trudeau-adds-new-caucus-pmo-liaison-1.4347960.

–. 2019c. "Wilson-Raybould set conditions, wanted PM apology over course of SNC-Lavalin affair." CTV News, April 4. https://www.ctvnews.ca/politics/wilson-

raybould-set-conditions-wanted-pm-apology-over-course-of-snc-lavalin
-affair-1.4365898.

–. 2019d. "Scheer says caucus united after Conservative MPs decide against leadership vote." CTV News, November 6. https://www.ctvnews.ca/politics/scheer-says-caucus-united-after-conservative-mps-decide-against-leadership-vote-1.4672597.

–. 2019e. "In a backtrack, Liberals move to reinstate parliamentary secretaries' power at committees." CTV News, December 11. https://www.ctvnews.ca/politics/in-a-backtrack-liberals-move-to-reinstate-parliamentary-secretaries-power-at-committees-1.4726145.

Akin, David. 2016. "Climate group allowed to speak, muzzle is off." *National Post*, October 29, A4.

–. 2017. "Liberals paper the counter with cheques; $1.25 billion; MPs hit ridings with funding largesse." *National Post*, March 7, A2.

–. 2018. "In 240 Facebook ads, the Conservatives take aim at 16 Liberal MPs." Global News, March 22. https://globalnews.ca/news/4098917/david-akin-facebook-political-ads-canada.

–. 2019. "Conservatives claim Liberals broke rules with summer spending tour handing out billions." Global News, September 3. https://globalnews.ca/news/5847862/conservatives-liberals-broke-rules-summer-spending.

Alcantara, Christopher, Zachary Spicer, and Roberto Leone. 2012. "Institutional design and the accountability paradox: A case study of three Aboriginal accountability regimes in Canada." *Canadian Public Administration* 55(1): 69–90.

Allmand, Warren. 2006. "Reflections on the Gomery report and accountability." *Canadian Parliamentary Review* 29(3): 17–19.

American Political Science Association. 1950. "Toward a more responsible two-party system: A report of the committee on political parties." *American Political Science Review* 44(3): 1–96.

Ames, Herbert B. 1911. "The organization of political parties in Canada." *Proceedings of the American Political Science Association* 8: 181–88.

Andrew-Gee, Eric. 2016. "Picture perfect: The camera loves Justin Trudeau – and he knows it." *Globe and Mail*, August 13, F1.

Angus, Charlie. 2019. "Government orders [business of supply] – Opposition motion – Transparency and accountability." In Canada, Parliament, *House of Commons Debates*, 42nd Parl, 1st Sess (February 19) at 148(382).

Angus Reid Institute. 2016. "Majority of Canadians say political correctness has 'gone too far.'" News release. August 29. http://angusreid.org/political-correctness.

Antle, Rob. 2005. "MPs meet with PM." *Telegram* [St. John's], October 6, A1.

Asch, Solomon E. 1951. "Effects of group pressure upon the modification and distortion of judgments." In *Groups, Leadership and Men: Research in Human Relations*, edited by Harold Guetzkow, 177–90. Oxford: Carnegie Press.

Atkinson, Michael M., and David C. Docherty. 1992. "Moving right along: The roots of amateurism in the Canadian House of Commons." *Canadian Journal of Political Science* 25(2): 295–318.

Aucoin, Peter. 2012. "New political governance in Westminster systems: Impartial public administration and management performance at risk." *Governance* 25(2): 177–99.

Axworthy, Thomas S. 2008. "Everything old is new again: Observations on parliamentary reform." Centre for the Study of Democracy, Queen's University.

Babcock v Canada (Attorney General). 2002. 3 SCR 3, 2002 SCC 57.

Bain, George. 1955. "Commons committee will study estimates." *Globe and Mail,* January 11, 9.

Baker, David, Andrew Gamble, and Steve Ludlam. 1993. "Whips or scorpions? The Maastricht vote and the Conservative Party." *Parliamentary Affairs* 46(2): 151–66.

Baker, George. 2003. "George Baker." In *A Call to Account,* edited by Criss Hajek, 78–84. Toronto: Breakout Educational Network.

Ball, Alan R. 1987. *British Political Parties: The Emergence of a Modern Party System.* 2nd ed. Basingstoke, UK: Macmillan Education.

Ballingall, Alex, and Tondra MacCharles. 2019. "Secret recording sparks ethics questions." *Toronto Star,* March 31, A5.

Barbeau, Alphonse. 1966. *Report of the Committee on Election Expenses.* Ottawa: Queen's Printer for Canada.

Barrera, Jorge, and Jessica Deer. 2019. "4 federal candidates accused of Indigenous identity appropriation by Halifax academic." CBC News, October 10. https://www.cbc.ca/news/indigenous/federal-candidates-claims-indigenous-identity-1.5314614.

Bartlett, Geoff. 2018. "Cathy Bennett says she was intimidated within Liberal caucus, cabinet." CBC News, May 1. https://www.cbc.ca/news/canada/newfoundland-labrador/cathy-bennett-harassment-bullying-1.4642732.

Bascaramurty, Dakshana. 2019. "Candidates find themselves at centre of debate on Métis identity." *Globe and Mail,* October 19. https://www.theglobeandmail.com/canada/article-candidates-find-themselves-at-centre-of-debate-on-metis-identity.

Bastien, Frédérick. 2018. *Breaking News? Politics, Journalism, and Infotainment on Quebec Television.* Vancouver: UBC Press.

Baum, Kathryn Blaze, and Sean Fine. 2019. "Deal denied." *Globe and Mail,* July 25, A1.

Baum, Kathryn Blaze, Tavia Grant, and Wendy Stueck. 2019. "A closer look at those named by Wilson-Raybould." *Globe and Mail,* March 1, A10.

BC Green and NDP caucuses. 2017. *Confidence and Supply Agreement between the BC Green Caucus and the BC New Democrat Caucus.* May 29.

Beeby, Dean. 2017. "Costs to run Prime Minister Trudeau's office climb higher." CBC News, November 2. http://www.cbc.ca/news/politics/prime-minister-s-office-trudeau-harper-kent-expenses-public-accounts-1.4382310.

–. 2018. "Environment minister's staff signed off on tweet praising Syria for joining Paris accord." CBC News, October 25. https://www.cbc.ca/news/politics/paris-tweet-mckenna-syria-environment-social-media-raitt-climate-change-1.4876305.

Bégin, Monique. 2018. *Ladies, Upstairs! My Life in Politics and After.* Montreal and Kingston: McGill-Queen's University Press.

Bell, Rick. 2019. "Black eye for J.T." *Edmonton Sun,* September 19, A8.

Bellemare, Andrea, and Kaleigh Rogers. 2019. "Recordings reveal details of campaign to attack Maxime Bernier, PPC as racists before election." CBC News, November 26. https://www.cbc.ca/news/politics/project-cactus-kinsella-daisy-ppc-bernier-1. 5372715.

Benoit, Liane E. 2006. "Ministerial staff: The life and times of Parliament's statutory orphans." In *Commission of Inquiry into the Sponsorship Program and Advertising Activities, Restoring Accountability: Research Studies Volume 1 – Parliament, Ministers and Deputy Ministers,* 145–252. Ottawa: Public Works and Government Services Canada.

Benzie, Robert. 2019. "Ford seeks to 'reset' government with shuffle." *Toronto Star,* June 13, A1.

Benzie, Robert, Rob Ferguson, and Kristin Rushowy. 2018. "Tories fear defections to Liberals, sources say." *Toronto Star,* November 24, A1.

Bernardo, Marcella. 2019. "Longest-serving woman in Parliament admits SNC-Lavalin controversy could hurt Liberals seeking re-election." *CityNews 1130* [Vancouver], April 3. https://www.citynews1130.com/2019/04/03/longest-serving -woman-parliament-snc-lavalin-controversy.

Bertilsson, Jon, and Jens Rennstam. 2018. "The destructive side of branding: A heuristic model for analyzing the value of branding practice." *Organization* 25(2): 260–81.

Bezanson, Kate. 2019. "Constitutional or political crisis? Prosecutorial independence, the public interest, and gender in the SNC-Lavalin affair." *UBC Law Review* 52(3): 761–815.

Birkland, Thomas A. 1998. "Focusing events, mobilization, and agenda setting." *Journal of Public Policy* 18(1): 53–74.

Black, Edwin R. 1972. "Opposition research: Some theories and practice." *Canadian Public Administration* 15(1): 24–41.

Blackwell, Richard. 2014. "SNC warns charges would close company." *Globe and Mail,* October 8, B1.

Blais, André, Elisabeth Gidengil, Agnieszka Dobrzynska, Neil Nevitte, and Richard Nadeau. 2003. "Does the local candidate matter? Candidate effects in the Canadian election of 2000." *Canadian Journal of Political Science* 36(3): 657–64.

Blakeney, Allan, and Sandford Borins. 1998. *Political Management in Canada: Conversations on Statecraft.* 2nd ed. Toronto: University of Toronto Press.

Blatchford, Andy. 2018. "Dairy farmers' anger over trade deal gets awkward for one Liberal MP." *Prince George Citizen,* November 6, A17.

–. 2019. "Lawyers hustled to get SNC deal early." *National Post,* February 21, A4.

Blidook, Kelly. 2012. *Constituency Influence in Parliament: Countering the Centre.* Vancouver: UBC Press.

–. 2013. "The changing use of Standing Order 31 statements." *Canadian Parliamentary Review* 36(4): 25–29.

Blidook, Kelly, and Matthew Byrne. 2013. "Constant campaigning and partisan discourse in the House of Commons." In *Parties, Elections, and the Future of Canadian Politics*, edited by Amanda Bittner and Royce Koop, 46–66. Vancouver: UBC Press.

Bosc, Marc, ed. 1988. *The Broadview Book of Canadian Parliamentary Anecdotes*. Peterborough, ON: Broadview Press.

–. 1989. "The Commons: Then and now." *Canadian Parliamentary Review* 12(2): 24–25.

Bouchard, Lucien. 1994. *On the Record*. Toronto: Stoddart.

Boucher, Maxime. 2016. "L'effet Westminster: Les cibles et les stratégies de lobbying dans le système parlementaire canadien." *Canadian Journal of Political Science* 48(4): 839–61.

–. 2018. "Who you know in the PMO: Lobbying the Prime Minister's Office in Canada." *Canadian Public Administration* 61(3): 317–40.

Boudria, Don. 1995. "Points of order – Gun control." In Canada, Parliament, *House of Commons Debates*, 35th Parl, 1st Sess (February 22) at 133(158).

Boutilier, Alex. 2016. "Open government requires 'cultural change.'" *Toronto Star*, February 4, A1.

–. 2019. "SNC-Lavalin boss briefed Scheer on charges in 2018." *Toronto Star*, February 11, A6.

Boyer, Patrick. 2003. "Patrick Boyer." In *A Call to Account*, edited by Criss Hajek, 241–55. Toronto: Breakout Educational Network.

Boyko, John. 2010. *Bennett: The Rebel Who Challenged and Changed a Nation*. Toronto: Key Porter Books.

Bradburn, Jamie. 2011. "Historicist: How not to run a Liberal election rally." *Torontoist*. April 30, https://torontoist.com/2011/04/historicishow_not_to_run_a_liberal_election_rally.

Breux, Sandra, and Jérôme Couture. 2018. *Accountability and Responsiveness at the Municipal Level: Views from Canada*. Montreal and Kingston: McGill-Queen's University Press.

Brodie, Ian. 2018. *At the Centre of Government: The Prime Minister and the Limits on Political Power*. Montreal and Kingston: McGill-Queen's University Press.

Brown, Bert. 1994. "Parliamentary discipline: An informal survey of opinion." *Canadian Parliamentary Review* 17(2): 14–16.

Bryden, Joan. 1989. "Public pays for Tory peek at foes." *Ottawa Citizen*, August 22, A11.

–. 1998. "PM promises debt load relief." *Calgary Herald*, January 29, A6.

–. 2013. "Trudeau says his occasional gaffe part of being unscripted leader." *Guardian* [Charlottetown], December 12, A7.

–. 2019. "MP quits Liberal caucus." *Prince George Citizen*, March 21, A3.

Burney, Derek H. 2005. *Getting It Done: A Memoir*. Montreal and Kingston: McGill-Queen's University Press.

Butts, Gerald. 2019. Statement to the Standing Committee on Justice and Human Rights, House of Commons. March 6. https://www.ctvnews.ca/politics/read-gerald-butts-full-opening-statement-1.4324615.

Cairns, Alan C. 1968. "The electoral system and the party system in Canada, 1921–1965." *Canadian Journal of Political Science* 1(1): 55–80.

Calis, Kristen. 2016. "A day in the life of Pickering-Uxbridge MP Jennifer O'Connell." *News Advertiser* [Ajax], May 4, 1.

Campbell, Margaret C., and Kevin Lane Keller. 2003. "Brand familiarity and advertising repetition effects." *Journal of Consumer Research* 30(2): 292–304.

Campbell, Norman. 1964. "Parliament." *Ottawa Citizen,* March 14, 7.

Campion-Smith, Bruce. 2017. "Prime Minister Justin Trudeau's controversial Castro tribute left bureaucrats scrambling." *Toronto Star,* March 10. https://www.thestar.com/news/canada/2017/03/10/prime-minister-justin-trudeaus-controversial-castro-tribute-left-bureaucrats-scrambling.html

–. 2018. "Preparing all day for a 45 minute circus: Each scripted question takes hours of planning and even dress rehearsals." *Toronto Star,* June 23, A10.

Canada. 1985a. *Security of Information Act.* https://laws-lois.justice.gc.ca/eng/acts/o-5/page-2.html.

–. 1985b. *Canada Evidence Act.* https://laws-lois.justice.gc.ca/eng/acts/C-5/section-39.html.

–. 2000. *Canada Elections Act.* https://laws.justice.gc.ca/eng/acts/e-2.01/index.html.

–. 2003. *Public Service Employment Act.* https://laws-lois.justice.gc.ca/eng/acts/P-33.01/FullText.html.

–. 2006a. *Director of Public Prosecutions Act.* https://laws-lois.justice.gc.ca/eng/acts/d-2.5/page-1.html.

–. 2006b. *Conflict of Interest Act.* https://laws-lois.justice.gc.ca/eng/acts/c-36.65/page-2.html.

–. 2012. Policy on government security. April 1. https://www.tbs-sct.gc.ca/pol/doc-eng.aspx?id=16578.

–. 2016. Policy on communications and federal identity. May 9. https://www.tbs-sct.gc.ca/pol/doc-eng.aspx?id=30683.

–. 2017. "Expanding Canada's toolkit to address corporate wrongdoing: Discussion paper for public consultation." https://www.tpsgc-pwgsc.gc.ca/ci-if/ar-cw/documents/aps-dpa-eng.pdf.

–. 2018a. "Guidelines on managing records in a minister's office." Library and Archives Canada. February 22. http://www.bac-lac.gc.ca/eng/services/government-information-resources/guidelines/Pages/Guidelines-managing-records-minister.aspx.

–. 2018b. *Budget Implementation Act, 2018, No. 1.* https://www.parl.ca/DocumentViewer/en/42-1/bill/C-74/royal-assent.

–. 2019. "Members' allowances and services." House of Commons. April 1. https://www.ourcommons.ca/Content/MAS/mas-e.pdf.

Canadian Press. 1992. "Candidate screening." *Globe and Mail,* March 18, A8.

–. 2016. "Near-miss on Air Canada vote scares federal Liberal whip." *Times Colonist* [Victoria], May 17, A12.

–. 2017a. "Liberals defy PM, approve genetic testing bill he calls unconstitutional." *Medicine Hat News,* March 9, 7.

–. 2017b. "Small-business backlash tops agenda for federal Liberal Kelowna retreat." *Times Colonist* [Victoria], September 6, B3.

–. 2019a. "Law in SNC-Lavalin case rarely makes it to courtrooms." *Calgary Sun*, March 15, A12.

–. 2019b. "Liberals defeat motion calling for public inquiry." *National Post*, February 21, A4.

–. 2019c. "Ability to act quickly key for energy 'war room': Kenney." *Red Deer Advocate*, June 8, A11.

Carney, Pat. 2000. *Trade Secrets: A Memoir.* Toronto: Key Porter Books.

Carrigan, D. Owen. 1968. *Canadian Party Platforms 1867–1968.* Urbana: University of Illinois Press.

Carroll, Adam. 2012. "Evidence." Standing Committee on Access to Information, Privacy and Ethics. In Canada, Parliament, *House of Commons Debates,* 41st Parl, 1st Sess (April 24) at 033.

Carty, R. Kenneth. 2002. "The politics of Tecumseh Corners: Canadian political parties as franchise organizations." *Canadian Journal of Political Science* 35(4): 723–45.

–. 2004. "Parties as franchise systems: The stratarchical organizational imperative." *Party Politics* 10(5): 5–24.

Carty, R. Kenneth, and Lisa Young. 2012. "The Lortie Commission and the place of political parties as agents of responsible government." In *From New Public Management to New Political Governance,* edited by Herman Bakvis and Mark D. Jarvis, 105–27. Montreal and Kingston: McGill-Queen's University Press.

Catterall, Marlene. 2003. "Marlene Catterall." In *A Call to Account,* edited by Criss Hajek, 121–32. Toronto: Breakout Educational Network.

CBC. 1971. *The Noblest of Callings ... the Vilest of Trades.* Potterton Film Productions. Library and Archives Canada, WO#51249.

–. 2012. "At Issue" panel. *The National.* CBC Television, May 24.

–. 2013. "Justin Trudeau expense plan good 'baby step,' says ex-MP." September 18. https://www.cbc.ca/news/politics/justin-trudeau-expense-plan-good-baby -step-says-ex-mp-1.1858162.

–. 2015. "Liberals issue talking points in confidential policy document." January 15. http://www.cbc.ca/news/politics/liberals-issue-talking-points-in-confidential -policy-document-1.2911875.

–. 2016. "9 MPs form Liberal government's Indigenous caucus." June 22. https://www. cbc.ca/news/indigenous/nine-mps-liberal-indigenous-caucus-1.3646335.

–. 2018a. "MHA details harassment, bullying by former cabinet ministers in leaked letter." May 31. https://www.cbc.ca/news/canada/newfoundland-labrador/house -of-assembly-holloway-letter-1.4686131.

–. 2018b. "No writ? No problem: Ottawa candidates kick off provincial election campaigns." May 7. http://www.cbc.ca/news/canada/ottawa/yasir-naqvi-lisa-macleod -joel-harden-election-campaign-ottawa-1.4650849.

–. 2018c. "Ministers say Canada must 'do better' after Boushie verdict." February 10. https://www.cbc.ca/news/politics/trudeau-ministers-boushie-verdict-reaction -1.4530093.

–. 2019a. "Washrooms 'neutral territory' for female MHAs to meet, support each other, says Tracey Perry." April 10. https://www.cbc.ca/news/canada/newfoundland-labrador/washroom-meetings-mha-bullying-harassment-1.5091765.

–. 2019b. "Canada votes 2019: Poll tracker." July 23. https://newsinteractives.cbc.ca/elections/poll-tracker/canada.

–. 2019c. "Scheer accuses the Liberals of fear-mongering as anti-abortion video emerges." September 12. https://www.cbc.ca/news/politics/where-the-leaders-are-day-2-1.5280534.

–. 2019d. "A closer look at SNC-Lavalin's sometimes murky past." February 8. https://www.cbc.ca/news/canada/snc-lavalin-corruption-fraud-bribery-libya-muhc-1.5010865.

–. 2019e. "Liberal women MPs supporting PM Trudeau." *The National.* CBC Television, March 10.

–. 2019f. *The House.* CBC Radio, March 23.

–. 2019g. *Power and Politics.* CBC TV, April 2.

Cernetig, Miro, and Alan Freeman. 1990. "Ousted MP lashes out at PM." *Globe and Mail,* April 12, 1.

Chaiken, Shelly. 1980. "Heuristic versus systematic information processing and the use of source versus message cues in persuasion." *Journal of Personality and Social Psychology* 39(5): 752–66.

Chamandy, Aidan. 2019. "Hill reporters push back against lack of access to MPs in West Block." *Hill Times,* February 20, 1.

Chan, Arnold. 2017. "Opposition motion – Canadian economy." In Canada, Parliament, *House of Commons Debates,* 42nd Parl, 1st Sess (June 12) at 148(192).

Chartash, David, Nicholas J. Caruana, Markus Dickinson, and Laura B. Stephenson. 2020. "When the team's jersey is what matters: Network analysis of party cohesion and structure in the Canadian House of Commons." *Party Politics* 26(5): 555–69.

Chase, Steven, and Andrea Woo. 2019. "Liberal MP suggests lack of French cost minister her justice post." *Globe and Mail,* February 15, A1.

Chase, Steven, and Robert Fife. 2019. "Second former envoy says Ottawa wants single message on China." *Globe and Mail,* July 25, A1.

Chase, Steven, Robert Fife, and Sean Fine. 2019. "Review of integrity rules opens door for SNC." *Globe and Mail,* February 25, A1.

Chong, Michael. 2017. "Rebalancing power in Ottawa: Committee reform." In *Turning Parliament Inside Out: Practical Ideas for Reforming Canada's Democracy,* edited by Michael Chong, Scott Simms, and Kennedy Stewart, 80–97. Madeira Park, BC: Douglas and McIntyre.

Chong, Michael, Scott Simms, and Kennedy Stewart. 2017. "Introduction." In *Turning Parliament Inside Out: Practical Ideas for Reforming Canada's Democracy,* edited by Michael Chong, Scott Simms, and Kennedy Stewart, 1–14. Madeira Park, BC: Douglas and McIntyre.

Chrétien, Jean. 1985. *Straight from the Heart.* Toronto: Key Porter Books.

–. 2007. *My Years as Prime Minister.* Toronto: Alfred A. Knopf.

Clancy, Clare. 2018. "UCP to consider extremist database." *Edmonton Journal,* November 7, A3.

Clancy, Clare, and Emma Graney. 2018. "Luff says she made the right choice." *Edmonton Journal,* November 7, A1.

Clark, Campbell. 2004. "Candidate-screening process riles mental-health advocates." *Globe and Mail,* January 20, A4.

–. 2006. "Harper restricts ministers' message." *Globe and Mail,* March 17, A1.

–. 2019. "MPs still seem to think they operate like a private club." *Globe and Mail,* December 12, A7.

–. 2020. "Philpott reflects on how honesty got her turfed." *Globe and Mail,* January 1, A4.

Clark, Ian D. 1985. "Recent changes in the cabinet decision-making system in Ottawa." *Canadian Public Administration* 28(2): 185–201.

Clarke, Harold D., Allan Kornberg, and Thomas J. Scotto. 2009. *Making Political Choices: Canada and the United States.* Toronto: University of Toronto Press.

Clarke, Harold D., Jane Jenson, Lawrence LeDuc, and Jon H. Pammett. 2019. *Absent Mandate: Strategies and Choices in Canadian Elections.* Toronto: University of Toronto Press.

Clarke, Harold D., and Richard G. Price. 1981. "Parliamentary experience and representational role orientations in Canada." *Legislative Studies Quarterly* 6(3): 373–90.

Claudeawad. 2012a. *Revelstoke Meets David Wilks Conservative MP on May 22nd Part 1 (Raw Footage).* May 22. https://www.youtube.com/watch?v=pnGgqEpfkCw [URL now defunct; contact the author for an archived copy].

–. 2012b. *David Wilks Meets with Revelstokians on May 22nd (Part 2).* May 22. https://www.youtube.com/watch?v=zMOWARz9dp8 [URL now defunct; contact the author for an archived copy].

Cochrane, David. 2019. "Scheer strips Tory MP of committee role after confrontation with Muslim witness." CBC News, June 1. https://www.cbc.ca/news/politics/scheer-michael-cooper-justice-committee-kicked-out-christchurch-1.5159082.

Collier, Cheryl N., and Tracey Raney. 2018a. "Canada's member-to-member code of conduct on sexual harassment in the House of Commons: Progress or regress?" *Canadian Journal of Political Science* 51(4): 795–815.

–. 2018b. "Understanding sexism and sexual harassment in politics: A comparison of Westminster Parliaments in Australia, the United Kingdom, and Canada." *Social Politics: International Studies in Gender, State and Society* 25(3): 432–55.

Comber, Mary Anne, and Robert S. Mayne. 1986. *The Newsmongers: How the Media Distort the Political News.* Toronto: McClelland and Stewart.

Commissioner for Legislative Standards. 2018a. "The Joyce report." Newfoundland and Labrador. October 18. https://www.assembly.nl.ca/business/electronic documents/JoyceReport2-2018-10-18.pdf.

–. 2018b. "The Kirby report." Newfoundland and Labrador. October 3. https://www.assembly.nl.ca/business/electronicdocuments/KirbyReport2-2018-10-03.pdf.

Compas. 2007. "Public consultations on Canada's democratic institutions and practices." Privy Council Office. February 28. https://fcpp.org/pdf/RF20En_COMPASReportToPCO_20070829.pdf.

Conservative Party of Canada. 2018a. Constitution. August 25. www.conservative.ca.

–. 2018b. Policy Declaration. August 25. www.conservative.ca.

Cooper, Alex. 2012. "Update: MP David Wilks backtracks on anti-budget bill comments." *Revelstoke Times Review,* May 23, 1.

Cooper, Michael. 2017. "How to fix Question Period: Ideas for reform." In *Turning Parliament Inside Out: Practical Ideas for Reforming Canada's Democracy,* edited by Michael Chong, Scott Simms, and Kennedy Stewart, 36–57. Madeira Park, BC: Douglas and McIntyre.

Copps, Sheila. 2019a. "Take off the kid gloves, prime minister." *Hill Times,* March 11, 9.

–. 2019b. "The big debate: Should dissident Liberals stay in caucus?" *Toronto Star,* March 26, A13.

Courtney, John C. 1978. "Recognition of Canadian political parties in Parliament and law." *Canadian Journal of Political Science* 11(1): 33–60.

Cowley, Philip, and Mark Stuart. 2009. "There was a doctor, a journalist and two Welshmen: The voting behaviour of Independent MPs in the United Kingdom House of Commons, 1997–2007." *Parliamentary Affairs* 62(1): 19–31.

Coyne, Andrew. 2012. "Sad fall of Tories' back bench." *National Post,* May 31, A4.

Craft, Jonathan. 2016. *Backrooms and Beyond: Partisan Advisers and the Politics of Policy Work in Canada.* Toronto: University of Toronto Press.

Crane, David. 1969. "Backbenchers hold weekend-long gripe-in with cabinet." *Globe and Mail,* June 21, 11.

Crosbie, John C. 1997. *No Holds Barred: My Life in Politics.* Toronto: McClelland and Stewart.

Cross, William. 2016. "Considering the appropriateness of state regulation of intra-party democracy: A comparative politics perspective." *Election Law Journal* 15(1): 20–30.

Cross, William, and Lisa Young. 2002. "Policy attitudes of party members in Canada: Evidence of ideological politics." *Canadian Journal of Political Science* 35(4): 859–80.

Cullen, Catherine. 2020. "Two MPs are challenging party messaging on abortion, drug use – and putting their leaders on the spot." CBC News, March 5. https://www.cbc.ca/news/politics/abortion-drugs-private-members-bill-1.5486892.

Cullen, Catherine, and Chelsea Laskowski. 2018. "Bernier getting riding officials in his new party to sign 'no embarrassment' pledge." CBC News, November 4. https://www.cbc.ca/news/politics/bernier-peoples-party-pledge-1.4889510.

Cullen, Roy. 2011. *Beyond Question Period: Or What Really Goes on in Ottawa.* Bloomington, Indiana: Trafford Publishing.

Curran, Peggy. 1988. "Conservatives screening candidates to root out future scandal." *Gazette* [Montreal], October 4, A4.

Curran, Rachel. 2016. "Parliament returns, policy work ramps up." *Policy Options,* September 19. https://policyoptions.irpp.org/magazines/september-2016/parliament-returns-policy-work-ramps-up.

Curry, Bill. 2017. "The populist Reformer who stood alone in supporting pot bill." *Globe and Mail,* December 27, A4.

–. 2018. "Morneau's office made 'angry' calls over bank bill, insurance group says." *Globe and Mail,* May 14, A1.

Curry, Bill, and Stuart A. Thompson. 2013. "Voting records show Tory MPs more apt to break ranks." *Globe and Mail,* February 4, A4.

D'Aquino, Thomas, G. Bruce Doern, and Cassandra Blair. 1983. *Parliamentary Democracy in Canada: Issues for Reform.* Toronto: Methuen.

D'Aquino, Thomas P. 1974. "The Prime Minister's Office: Catalyst or cabal? Aspects of the development of the office in Canada and some thoughts about its future." *Canadian Public Administration* 17(1): 55–79.

Dawson, Anne, and Allan Woods. 2005. "Liberals win showdown over budget: Minority government lives another day." *Standard-Freeholder* [Cornwall], June 24, 7.

Dawson, Mary. 2017. The Trudeau Report. Office of the Conflict of Interest and Ethics Commissioner, Parliament of Canada. December.

Dawson, Tyler. 2018. "'Culture of fear': Luff fires back after NDP ouster." *National Post,* November 7, A4.

de Clercy, Cristine. 2018. "Communications as the workhorse of governmental politics: The Liberal Party leader and the Liberal caucus." In *Political Elites in Canada: Power and Influence in Instantaneous Times,* edited by Alex Marland, Thierry Giasson, and Andrea Lawlor, 151–67. Vancouver: UBC Press.

de Vreese, Claes H. 2005. "The spiral of cynicism reconsidered." *European Journal of Communication* 20(3): 283–301.

Delacourt, Susan. 2003. *Juggernaut: Paul Martin's Campaign for Chrétien's Crown.* Toronto: McClelland and Stewart.

–. 2016a. *Shopping for Votes: How Politicians Choose Us and We Choose Them.* 2nd ed. Madeira Park, BC: Douglas and McIntyre.

–. 2016b. "Permanent marketing and the conduct of politics." In *The Harper Factor: Assessing a Prime Minister's Policy Legacy,* edited by Jennifer Ditchburn and Graham Fox, 80–94. Montreal and Kingston: McGill-Queen's University Press.

–. 2017. "Leave the cabinet alone, Trudeau." *iPolitics,* June 20. https://ipolitics.ca/2017/06/20/leave-the-cabinet-alone-trudeau-youve-got-other-problems.

–. 2018. "The government says it's listening. If so, not to Parliament." *Toronto Star,* March 3, IN4.

–. 2020. "Peace in Parliament didn't last long." *Toronto Star,* March 25, A5.

Dempson, Peter. 1968. *Assignment Ottawa: Seventeen Years in the Press Gallery.* Toronto: General Publishing.

Dewing, Michael. 2016. "Changes in a parliamentarian's party affiliation." Library of Parliament, publication 2016-101-E, October 20. https://lop.parl.ca/sites/Public Website/default/en_CA/ResearchPublications/2016101E.

Dhanraj, Travis. 2018. "Management style of Premier Doug Ford's chief of staff called into question." Global News, November 21. https://globalnews.ca/news/4685695/dean-french-doug-ford-chief-of-staff-management-style.

–. 2019a. "'He's full of crap': Mom speaks out after recorded call with Doug Ford over autism program changes." Global News, April 6. https://globalnews.ca/news/5129241/doug-ford-ontario-autism-program-call.

–. 2019b. "Ontario PC MPPs sent to neighbourhood fridges with tweet templates in hand, leaked e-mail reveals." Global News, June 4. https://globalnews.ca/news/5349674/ontario-mpps-coordinated-social-media-campaign-alcohol-leaked-emails.

Dickin, Daniel. 2016. "Organizing the halls of power: Federal parliamentary staffers and members of Parliament's offices." *Canadian Parliamentary Review* 39(2): 8-16.

Dickson, Janice. 2018a. "Scheer refused call to oust Bernier." *Calgary Herald*, July 5, NP8.

–. 2018b. "Conservatives denounce Okanagan Tory website's racist comment." *Hamilton Spectator*, November 17, A10.

–. 2019. "MPs apologize to Norman for impact of failed prosecution." *Globe and Mail*, May 15, A1.

Dion, Mario. 2019. Trudeau II Report. Office of the Conflict of Interest and Ethics Commissioner, Parliament of Canada. August.

–. 2020. Wernick Report. Office of the Conflict of Interest and Ethics Commissioner, Parliament of Canada. March.

Ditchburn, Jennifer. 2012. "Former MP says he had misgivings with voter ID system." *Kamloops Daily News*, March 16, B7.

–. 2015. "Cold feet on new powers?" *Sarnia Observer*, November 3, B2.

–. 2016. "Government news management and Canadian journalism." In *The Harper Factor: Assessing a Prime Minister's Policy Legacy*, edited by Jennifer Ditchburn and Graham Fox, 62–79. Montreal and Kingston: McGill-Queen's University Press.

Docherty, David C. 1997. *Mr. Smith Goes to Ottawa: Life in the House of Commons.* Vancouver: UBC Press.

–. 2005. *Legislatures.* Vancouver: UBC Press.

Downs, Anthony. 1957. *An Economic Theory of Democracy.* New York: Harper and Row.

Drew, George. 1951. "Supply – National Defence." In Canada, Parliament, *House of Commons Debates*, 21st Parl, 4th Sess (May 10) at 2902.

Dubois, Elizabeth, Anatoliy Gruzd, Philip Maj, and Jenna Jacobson. 2018. "Social media and political engagement in Canada." Ryerson University Social Media Lab. https://doi.org/10.5683/SP2/9MCJJH.

Dubois, Elizabeth, and Fenwick McKelvey. 2019. "Political bots: Disrupting Canada's democracy." *Canadian Journal of Communication* 44(2): 27–33.

Duffy, Mike. 2007. *Countdown with Mike Duffy* [CTV program]. November 27.

Dyer, Evan. 2018. "Liberal MP Majid Jowhari's Iran tweets roil his heavily Iranian riding." *CBC News*, January 4. http://www.cbc.ca/news/politics/majid-jowhari -iran-tweet-1.4473817.

–. 2019. "MP Michael Cooper disparaged 'goat herder cultures' in 2008 law class discussion, lawyers claim." *CBC News*, June 18. https://www.cbc.ca/news/politics/ michael-cooper-goat-herder-cultures-1.5179039.

Elections Canada. 2019. Registered Party Quarterly Financial Returns. Liberal Party of Canada, December 2015–September 2019. www.elections.ca.

Elmer, Greg, Ganaele Langlois, and Fenwick McKelvey. 2014. "The permanent campaign online: Platforms, actors and issue-objects." In *Publicity and the Canadian State: Critical Communications Perspectives,* edited by Kirsten Kozolanka, 240–61. Toronto: University of Toronto Press.

Emmanuel, Rachel. 2019. "People's Party draws disenchanted Tories." *Globe and Mail,* August 10, A8.

Eneas, Bryan. 2019. "The speech that never was: Documents reveal what Trudeau planned to say at cancelled Regina event." *CBC News*, December 14. https://www. cbc.ca/news/canada/saskatchewan/the-speech-that-never-was-1.5396856.

Environics. 2013. "Your Canada, your Constitution." Omnibus survey, May 9–12. https://democracywatch.ca/wp-content/uploads/May2013survey.pdf.

Esselment, Anna Lennox. 2010. "Fighting elections: Cross-level political party integration in Ontario." *Canadian Journal of Political Science* 43(4): 871–92.

. 2012. "Market orientation in a minority government: The challenges of product delivery." In *Political Marketing in Canada,* edited by Alex Marland, Thierry Giasson, and Jennifer Lees-Marshment, 123–38. Vancouver: UBC Press.

–. 2014. "The governing party and the permanent campaign." In *Political Communication in Canada: Meet the Press and Tweet the Rest,* edited by Alex Marland, Thierry Giasson, and Tamara A. Small, 24–38. Vancouver: UBC Press.

Esselment, Anna Lennox, and Paul Wilson. 2017. "Campaigning from the centre." In *Permanent Campaigning in Canada,* edited by Alex Marland, Thierry Giasson, and Anna Lennox Esselment, 222–40. Vancouver: UBC Press.

Evans, Jocelyn, and Jessica M. Hayden. 2018. *Congressional Communication in the Digital Age.* New York: Routledge.

Evelyn, Charelle. 2018. "Stepping back to look ahead: Why this outspoken parliamentary secretary volunteered to be demoted." *Hill Times,* September 12, 1.

Faucheux, Ronald A. 2002. *Running for Office: The Strategies, Techniques and Messages Modern Political Candidates Need to Win Elections.* New York: M. Evans and Company.

Festinger, Leon. 1957. *A Theory of Cognitive Dissonance.* Stanford: Stanford University Press.

Fife, Robert. 2020. "No deal offered to SNC due to severity of charges: Prosecutor." *Globe and Mail,* February 28, A1.

Fife, Robert, and Bill Curry. 2017. "Trudeau economic adviser takes over key Finance role: Justin Trudeau to head budget-making team amid turmoil over tax changes." *Globe and Mail,* September 16, A9.

Fife, Robert, and Daniel Leblanc. 2019. "MP says Liberals forced her out for not lauding Trudeau." *Globe and Mail,* September 25, A1.

Fife, Robert, Daniel Leblanc, and Marieke Walsh. 2019. "Trudeau denies Liberal MP was pushed out." *Globe and Mail,* September 26, A3.

Fife, Robert, and Steven Chase. 2019. "Trudeau says he didn't direct justice minister on SNC case." *Globe and Mail,* February 8, A1.

Fife, Robert, Steven Chase, and Sean Fine. 2019a. "PMO pressed justice minister to abandon prosecution of SNC-Lavalin." *Globe and Mail,* February 7, A1.

–. 2019b. "Trudeau says he discussed SNC case with Wilson-Raybould." *Globe and Mail,* February 12, A9.

Fitzpatrick, Meagan. 2012. "BC Tory MP backs off budget bill criticism." CBC News, May 23. https://www.cbc.ca/news/politics/b-c-tory-mp-backs-off-budget-bill-criticism-1.1227344.

Flanagan, Tom. 2014. *Winning Power: Canadian Campaigning in the 21st Century.* Montreal and Kingston: McGill-Queen's University Press.

Flynn, Paul. 2012. *How to Be an MP.* London: Biteback.

Forrest, Maura. 2019. "Can the Liberals just turf Justin Trudeau?" *National Post,* March 6, A4.

Francis, Lloyd. 2000. *Ottawa Boy: An Autobiography.* Burnstown, ON: General Store.

Francoli, Mary. 2009. "The digital MP or how I learned to stop worrying and love MP [Garth Turner]." *Journal of Media Practice* 10(2–3): 215–25.

Francoli, Paco. 2002. "PMO vetted pro-Martin staffers." *Hill Times,* June 24.

–. 2005. "Grit MPs reluctantly return to the Hill." *Hill Times,* June 27, 13.

Franks, C.E.S. 1987. *The Parliament of Canada.* Toronto: University of Toronto Press.

–. 2007. "Members and constituency roles in the Canadian federal system." *Regional and Federal Studies* 17(1): 23–45.

Fraser, Graham. 1988. "Commons floor a TV studio where MPs play to camera." *Globe and Mail,* April 4, A1.

–. 1989. *Playing for Keeps: The Making of the Prime Minister, 1988.* Toronto: McClelland and Stewart.

–. 1990. "PM makes rare display of fabled caucus humour." *Globe and Mail,* October 20, A6.

Friedman, Gabriel. 2019. "SNC admitted funding condo décor, yacht and parties for Gadhafi's son." *Vancouver Sun,* December 20, C1.

Frost, Catherine. 2003. "How Prometheus is bound: Applying the Innis method of communications analysis to the internet." *Canadian Journal of Communication* 28(1): 9–24.

Galloway, Gloria. 2013. "Is Canada's party discipline the strictest in the world? Experts say yes." *Globe and Mail,* February 7. https://www.theglobeandmail.com/news/politics/is-canadas-party-discipline-the-strictest-in-the-world-experts-say-yes/article8313261.

Galloway, Gloria, Bill Curry, and Alex Dobrota. 2006. "'Nation' plan costs Harper." *Globe and Mail,* November 28, A1.

Garner, Christopher, and Natalia Letki. 2005. "Party structure and backbench dissent in the Canadian and British Parliaments." *Canadian Journal of Political Science* 38(2): 463–82.

Gash, Norman. 1982. "The organization of the Conservative Party, 1832–1846." *Parliamentary History* 1(1): 137–59.

Gawley, Kelvin. 2019. "Burnaby MP tried unsuccessfully to play peacemaker between Liberals." *Burnaby Now,* April 2. https://www.burnabynow.com/news/burnaby-mp-tried-unsuccessfully-to-play-peacemaker-between-liberals-1.23778608.

Geddes, John. 2017. "What Trudeau learned from watching 'The West Wing.'" *Maclean's,* July 26. https://www.macleans.ca/politics/ottawa/what-trudeau-learned-from-watching-the-west-wing.

–. 2019. "'The Liberal Party is not something I understand anymore.'" *Maclean's,* May 1, 27.

Geisler, Paul. 2015. "Will the Reform Act, 2014, alter the Canadian phenomenon of party discipline?" *Manitoba Law Journal* 38(2): 17–43.

Gentzkow, Matthew, Jesse M. Shapiro, and Matt Taddy. 2017. "Measuring polarization in high-dimensional data: Method and application to congressional speech." NBER working paper series, May. http://www.nber.org/papers/w22423.

Gerson, Jen. 2018. "'You must resign.'" *Maclean's,* April 1, 43–47.

Giasson, Thierry, and Tamara A. Small. 2017. "Online, all the time: The strategic objectives of Canadian opposition parties." In *Permanent Campaigning in Canada,* edited by Alex Marland, Thierry Giasson, and Anna Lennox Esselment, 109–26. Vancouver: UBC Press.

Gibson, Gordon F. 1978. "Comments." In *The Legislative Process in Canada: The Need for Reform,* edited by William A.W. Neilson and James C. MacPherson, 51–59. Toronto: Butterworth.

Gidengil, Elisabeth, and André Blais. 2007. "Are party leaders becoming more important to vote choice in Canada?" In *Political Leadership and Representation in Canada: Essays in Honour of John C. Courtney,* edited by Hans J. Michelmann, Donald C. Storey, and Jeffrey S. Steeves, 39–59. Toronto: University of Toronto Press.

Gillan, Michael. 1968. "Are the grey political mists creeping in on Joey?" *Globe and Mail,* May 23, 7.

Giovannetti, Justin. 2019. "Between a party and a pipeline." *Globe and Mail,* November 9, A16.

Globe. 1936. "Reform for the Commons." *Globe* [Toronto], April 17, 4.

Globe and Mail. 1943. "Yes, Parliament needs reform." *Globe and Mail,* April 1, 6.

–. 1962. "Political touch to parties." *Globe and Mail,* April 14, 18.

–. 1965. "Voter criticizes use of PM designation on ballot by Pearson." *Globe and Mail,* November 9, 8.

–. 1968. "Trudeau defends the plan: PM's regional desks to supplement MPs." *Globe and Mail,* November 23, 11.

–. 1972. "Record 1,116 seek seats in Commons." *Globe and Mail,* October 11, 9.

–. 1977. "MP gives deputy ministers fright." *Globe and Mail,* March 7, 8.

–. 2004. "The consequences of fame – a dry throat." *Globe and Mail,* February 21, A8.

–. 2014. "Democratic respect? Resistance is futile." *Globe and Mail,* September 26, A10.

–. 2019. "The perils of an imperial prime minister." *Globe and Mail,* February 16, O10.

Godbout, Jean-François. 2020. *Lost on Division: Party Unity in the Canadian Parliament.* Toronto: University of Toronto Press.

Godbout, Jean-François, and Bjørn Høyland. 2013. "The emergence of parties in the Canadian House of Commons." *Canadian Journal of Political Science* 46(4): 773–97.

–. 2017. "Unity in diversity? The development of political parties in the Parliament of Canada, 1867–2011." *British Journal of Political Science* 47(3): 545–69.

Goldblatt, Murray. 1969. "Caucus sets up plan to consult cabinet." *Globe and Mail,* November 27, 11.

Goldenberg, Eddie. 2006. *The Way It Works: Inside Ottawa.* Toronto: McClelland and Stewart.

Government of New Brunswick. 2020. "New cabinet committee on novel coronavirus appointed." News release, March 12. https://www2.gnb.ca/content/gnb/en/news/news_release.2020.03.0113.html.

Government of Newfoundland and Labrador. 2020. "Premier and opposition leaders meet, agree to course of action to respond to COVID-19." News release, March 16. https://www.gov.nl.ca/releases/2020/exec/0316n02.

Government of Prince Edward Island. 2020. "Premier King announces all-party initiatives in response to COVID-19." News release, March 19. https://www.princeedwardisland.ca/en/news/premier-king-announces-all-party-initiatives-response-covid-19.

Governor General of Canada. 2019. "Official oaths." http://www.gg.ca/en/official-oaths.

Graham, Bill. 2016. *The Call of the World: A Political Memoir.* Vancouver: On Point Press.

Gratton, Michel. 1987. *"So, What Are the Boys Saying?" An Inside Look at Brian Mulroney in Power.* Toronto: McGraw-Hill Ryerson.

Gray, John. 2003. *Paul Martin: The Power of Ambition.* Toronto: Key Porter Books.

Green, Donald P., and Adam Zelizer. 2017. "How much GOTV mail is too much? Results from a large-scale field experiment." *Journal of Experimental Political Science* 4(2): 107–18.

Green Party of Canada. 2013. "Elizabeth May tables bill targeting excessive party discipline." News release, May 2. https://www.greenparty.ca/en/media-release/2013-05-02/elizabeth-may-tables-bill-targeting-excessive-party-discipline.

–. 2016. Constitution of the Green Party of Canada. https://www.greenparty.ca/en/party/documents/constitution.

Greenspon, Edward, and Anthony Wilson-Smith. 1996. *Double Vision: The Inside Story of the Liberals in Power.* Toronto: Doubleday Canada.

Grenier, Éric. 2017. "Bill who? Canadians might not know the finance minister's name, but they know what they think of him." CBC News, November 23. https://www.cbc.ca/news/politics/grenier-ministers-polls-1.4410596.

Guay, Joseph. 1988. "Senator Joseph Guay in an interview with Tom Earle." May 3. Library of Parliament, Accession number 1988-0291.

Guay, Monique. 2002. "Party discipline, representation of voters and personal beliefs." *Canadian Parliamentary Review* 25(1): 7–9.

Ha, Tu Thanh. 1995. "Reform MPs split over gun reform." *Globe and Mail,* June 13, A3.

Hall, Chris. 2019. "Wilson-Raybould waited more than 2 hours for permission to attend Tuesday's cabinet meeting: Sources." CBC News, February 20. https://www.cbc.ca/news/politics/wilson-raybould-snc-lavalin-trudeau-1.5026225.

Hamilton, Grey. 1957. "Teen-age heckler at PM's rally taken to hospital after clash." *Globe and Mail,* June 8, 1.

Haney, Craig, Curtis Banks, and Philip Zimbardo. 1973. "Interpersonal dynamics in a simulated prison." *International Journal of Criminology and Penology* 1(1): 69–97.

Hannay, Chris. 2017. "Liberal MPs tweet non-partisan government job ads with party logo." *Globe and Mail,* January 12. https://www.theglobeandmail.com/news/politics/liberal-mps-tweet-non-partisan-government-job-ads-with-party-logo/article33595838.

Harowitz, Sara. 2014. "BC Tory MP's Facebook post reveals personal pressures of political life." *Huffington Post BC,* August 26. https://www.huffingtonpost.ca/2014/08/26/david-wilks-facebook_n_5717499.html.

Harris, Kathleen. 2015. "Justin Trudeau to push middle-class message in debut on world stage." CBC News, November 16. http://www.cbc.ca/m/touch/politics/story/1.3319141.

Hartt, Stanley. 2003. "Stanley Hartt." In *A Call to Account,* edited by Criss Hajek, 265–79. Toronto: Breakout Educational Network.

Haws, Emily. 2018. "Inside Andrew Scheer's weekly morale-boosting lunches with Tory MPs." *Hill Times,* May 30, 1.

Hazan, Reuven Y. 2014. "Candidate selection: Implications and challenges for legislative behaviour." In *The Oxford Handbook of Legislative Studies,* edited by Shane Martin, Thomas Saalfeld, and Kaare W. Strøm, 213–30. Oxford: Oxford University Press.

Heames, Joyce Thompson, Michael G. Harvey, and Darren Treadway. 2006. "Status inconsistency: An antecedent to bullying behaviour in groups." *International Journal of Human Resource Management* 17(2): 348–61.

Heard, Andrew. 2007. "Just what is a vote of confidence? The curious case of May 10, 2005." *Canadian Journal of Political Science* 40(2): 395–416.

–. 2014. *Canadian Constitutional Conventions: The Marriage of Law and Politics.* 2nd ed. Don Mills, ON: Oxford University Press.

Hébert, Raymond M. 2004. *Manitoba's French-Language Crisis: A Cautionary Tale.* Montreal and Kingston: McGill-Queen's University Press.

Heeney, A.D.P. 1946. "Cabinet government in Canada: Some recent developments in the machinery of the central executive." *Canadian Journal of Economics and Political Science* 12(3): 282–301.

Helliwell, John F., Richard Layard, and Jeffrey D. Sachs. 2019. *World Happiness Report 2019.* New York: Sustainable Development Solutions Network. https://world happiness.report.

Hernandez, Jon. 2017. "'The stakes are high': Political shills in full force online during election debate." CBC News, April 27. https://www.cbc.ca/news/canada/british -columbia/the-stakes-are-high-political-shills-in-full-force-online-during-election -debate-1.4089346.

Hill Times. 2017. "Liberal MPs exert their independence, and that's a good thing." Editorial. *Hill Times,* March 15, 8.

Hillier, Randy. 2013. "Empowering Ontario legislators." *Canadian Parliamentary Review* 36(3): 4–8.

–. 2019. Facebook post. March 13. https://www.facebook.com/randy.hillier/posts/ 2478060922204229.

Hoffman, David. 1972. "Liaison officers and ombudsmen: Canadian MPs and their relations with the federal bureaucracy and executive." In *Apex of Power,* edited by T.A. Hockin, 146–62. Scarborough, ON: Prentice-Hall.

Holman, Sean. 2013. *Whipped: The Secret World of Party Discipline* [documentary film]. Public Eye Mediaworks. https://vimeo.com/69710023.

Hopper, Tristin. 2015. "He made bland a winning brand." *National Post,* August 15, A12.

House of Cards. 1990. BBC. Episode 1.

House of Commons. 2019a. *Standing Orders of the House of Commons.* December 11. https://www.ourcommons.ca/about/standingorders/SOPDF.pdf.

–. 2019b. "Members' orientation program." Fact sheet, October. https://www. ourcommons.ca/Content/Newsroom/Articles/FactSheet-2019-10-22-e.pdf.

Howard, Ross. 1991. "Liberal caucus getting its act together." *Globe and Mail,* February 25, A5.

Howlett, Karen. 2017. "A glimpse into backrooms of power." *Globe and Mail,* August 10, A4.

Hunter, Iain. 1986. "Opposition out over eavesdropping." *Ottawa Citizen,* January 31, A1.

Huntington, Vicki. 2012. "Defining the role of an Independent member." *Canadian Parliamentary Review* 35(1): 1–5.

Hutton, Fred. 2018. "Cabinet minister seeks out Liberal leakers with email to MHAs." CBC News, April 25. https://www.cbc.ca/news/canada/newfoundland-labrador/ dale-kirby-paul-davis-liberal-harassment-bullying-1.4634290.

Hwang, Priscilla. 2018. "'I want to apologize to the people of Nunavut': Ex-premier Paul Quassa on his ousting, and public reaction." CBC News, June 15. http://www.

cbc.ca/news/canada/north/paul-quassa-oust-public-reaction-nunavut-premier-1. 4709178.

Ibbitson, John. 2013. "Reinventing Parliament: How to make it relevant again." *Globe and Mail,* February 9, A12.

Innis, Harold A. 1972. *Empire and Communications.* Toronto: University of Toronto Press.

Ivison, John. 2019. "Being a bobblehead MP is just not worth it." *National Post,* August 10, A4.

Jackson, Robert J. 1968. *Rebels and Whips: Dissension, Discipline and Cohesion in British Political Parties since 1945.* London: Macmillan.

Jedwab, Jack. 2019. "Sources of personal or collective pride in Canada." Association for Canadian Studies. July 1. https://acs-aec.ca/wp-content/uploads/2019/06/ ACS-Sources-of-personal-or-collective-pride-in-Canada-EN.pdf.

Jeffrey, Brooke. 2010. *Divided Loyalties: The Liberal Party of Canada, 1984–2008.* Toronto: University of Toronto Press.

Johnston, Donald. 1986. *Up the Hill.* Montreal: Optimum.

Jones, Gareth R., and Jennifer M. George. 1998. "The experience and evolution of trust: Implications for cooperation and teamwork." *Academy of Management Review* 23(3): 531–46.

Jones, Helen. 2016. *How to Be a Government Whip.* London: Biteback.

Joseph, Rebecca. 2019. "Opposition MPs briefly storm out of committee meeting as Liberals end SNC-Lavalin investigation." Global News, March 19. https://global news.ca/news/5071191/opposition-mps-leave-justice-committee-meeting-snc -lavalin.

Kam, Christopher J. 2006. "Demotion and dissent in the Canadian Liberal Party." *British Journal of Political Science* 36(3): 561–74.

–. 2009. *Party Discipline and Parliamentary Politics.* New York: Cambridge University Press.

Katz, Richard S., and Peter Mair. 2018. *Democracy and the Cartelization of Political Parties.* Oxford: Oxford University Press.

Katzenbach, Jon R., and Douglas K. Smith. 1993. "The discipline of teams." *Harvard Business Review* 71(2): 111–21.

Kelman, Herbert C. 1953. "Attitude change as a function of response restriction." *Human Relations* 6(3): 185–214.

Kelly, Cathal. 2019. "An everyman looks to move from Stornoway to Sussex Drive." *Globe and Mail,* September 24, A1.

Kempling, Bill. 1988. "The honourable Bill Kempling in an interview with Tom Earle." September 29. Library of Parliament, Accession number 1988-0291.

Kennedy, Brendan, and Marco Chown Oved. 2018. "'Why play that silly game?': The *Star* spoke to the MPs who say the least during Question Period." *Toronto Star,* June 22, A10.

Kent, Peter. 2018. "Oral questions." In Canada, Parliament, *House of Commons Debates,* 42nd Parl, 1st Sess (February 12) at 262.

Kerby, Matthew. 2009. "Worth the wait: Determinants of ministerial appointment in Canada, 1935–2008." *Canadian Journal of Political Science* 42(3): 593–611.

–. 2014. "Canada: Ministerial careers." In *The Selection of Ministers Around the World,* edited by Keith Dowding and Patrick Dumont, 264–82. Abingdon: Routledge.

Kerby, Matthew, and Feodor Snagovsky. 2019. "Not all experience is created equal: MP career typologies and ministerial appointments in the Canadian House of Commons, 1968–2015." *Government and Opposition,* November 6.

Kerby, Matthew, and Kelly Blidook. 2011. "It's not you, it's me: Determinants of voluntary legislative turnover in Canada." *Legislative Studies Quarterly* 36(4): 621–43.

King, Bert T., and Irving L. Janis. 1956. "Comparison of the effectiveness of improvised versus non-improvised role-playing in producing opinion changes." *Human Relations* 9(2): 177–86.

King, Nancy. 2020. "Cape Breton MLA takes aim at party whips in private member's bill." *Cape Breton Post,* February 27. https://www.capebretonpost.com/news/local/ cape-breton-mla-takes-aim-at-party-whips-in-private-members-bill-416790.

Kohut, Tania. 2015. "Canada 9th best country to live in: UN human development index." Global News, December 16. https://globalnews.ca/news/2405032/ canada-9th-best-country-to-live-in-un-human-development-index.

Koop, Royce, Heather Bastedo, and Kelly Blidook. 2018. *Representation in Action: Canadian MPs in the Constituencies.* Vancouver: UBC Press.

Kornberg, Allan. 1966. "Caucus and cohesion in Canadian parliamentary parties." *American Political Science Review* 60(1): 83–92.

Kornberg, Allan, and Colin Campbell. 1978. "Parliament in Canada: A decade of published research." *Legislative Studies Quarterly* 3(4): 555–80.

Kornberg, Allan, and William Mishler. 1976. *Influence in Parliament: Canada.* Durham, NC: Duke University Press.

Krehbiel, Keith. 1993. "Where's the party?" *British Journal of Political Science* 23(2): 235–66.

Laghi, Brian, and Daniel LeBlanc. 2007. "Tories facing $1,000 conflict." *Globe and Mail,* July 25, A1.

Lalancette, Mireille, and Sofia Tourigny-Koné. 2017. "*24 Seven* videostyle: Blurring the lines and building strong leadership." In *Permanent Campaigning in Canada,* edited by Alex Marland, Thierry Giasson, and Anna Lennox Esselment, 259–77. Vancouver: UBC Press.

Lalonde, Marc. 1971. "The changing role of the Prime Minister's Office." *Canadian Public Administration* 14(4): 509–37.

Lambert, Steve. 2018. "Pallister felt like a 'prop.'" *Winnipeg Sun,* October 9, A4.

Landerer, Nino. 2013. "Rethinking the logics: A conceptual framework for the mediatization of politics." *Communication Theory* 23(3): 239–58.

Lapointe, Mike, and Cherlene Eloria. 2020. "After nearly three decades on the Hill, 'fearless' CBC reporter Julie Van Dusen takes a step back." *Hill Times,* June 8, 37.

Laurence, Lianne. 2018. "Trudeau slams Conservative politician for truthfully shouting abortion 'is not a right.'" LifeSiteNews, May 11. https://www.lifesitenews.

com/news/trudeau-slams-conservative-politician-for-truthfully-shouting -abortion-is-n.

Lavigne, Mathieu. 2020. "Strengthening ties: The influence of microtargeting on partisan attitudes and the vote." *Party Politics,* April 23.

Laycock, David. 2005. "Populism and the new right in English Canada." In *Populism and the Mirror of Democracy,* edited by Francisco Panizza, 172–201. New York: Verso.

le, Kenny William. 2019. "Cabinet committees as strategies of prime ministerial leadership in Canada, 2003–2019." *Commonwealth & Comparative Politics* 57(4): 466–86.

Leblanc, Daniel. 2003. "Parrish says she regrets remark made 'in the heat of the moment.'" *Globe and Mail,* February 27, A1.

–. 2019. "Prime Minister's Office confirms it uses partisan database to vet prospective senators." *Globe and Mail,* May 3, A3.

–. 2020. "Freeland to work out of same building as PMO." *Globe and Mail,* January 16, A9.

Leblanc, Daniel, and Robert Fife. 2019. "Ottawa blocks RCMP on SNC inquiry." *Globe and Mail,* September 11, A1.

–. 2020. "How Ottawa's coronavirus relief plan came together so quickly." *Globe and Mail,* April 28, A1.

Lefebvre, Tom. 1987. "The Honourable Tom Lefebvre Senator: Interview conducted by Tom Earle." January and February. Library of Parliament, Accession number 1987-0091.

Leitch, K. Kellie. 2019. "Instead of increasing seats, provide more resources to Members of Parliament." *Canadian Parliamentary Review* 42(3): 21–23.

Leger, Mark. 2018. "Trudeau government ends punishment, restores Wayne Long to federal committee." *Huddle* [New Brunswick], January 30. https://huddle.today/ trudeau-government-ends-punishment-restores-wayne-long-federal-committee.

Lewis, J.P. 2019. "Justin Trudeau resignations a rarity in Canadian history." *Conversation,* March 12. https://theconversation.com/justin-trudeau-cabinet-resignations -a-rarity-in-canadian-history-113096.

Lewis, J.P., Mireille Lalancette, and Vincent Raynauld. 2019. "Cabinet solidarity in an age of social media: A case study of Twitter use by MP Carolyn Bennett." In *What's Trending in Canadian Politics? Understanding Transformations in Power, Media, and the Public Sphere,* edited by Mireille Lalancette, Vincent Raynauld, and Erin Crandall, 170–93. Vancouver: UBC Press.

Liberal Party of Canada. 2015. *Real Change: A Fair and Open Government.* https:// www.liberal.ca/wp-content/uploads/2015/06/a-fair-and-open-government.pdf.

–. 2016. Constitution. May 28. https://www.liberal.ca/wp-content/uploads/2016/ 07/constitution-en.pdf.

–. 2018a. "Women's rights are human rights." Listserv email. May 10.

–. 2018b. "Stand for choice." Listserv email. May 15.

–. 2018c. "National rules for the selection of candidates." https://www.liberal.ca/wp -content/uploads/2018/01/LPC_National-Rules-for-Candidate-Selection.pdf.

–. 2018d. "Our message is clear." Twitter post. May 10. https://twitter.com/liberal_party/status/994626893109481475.

–. 2019. *Forward: A Real Plan for the Middle Class.* https://www2.liberal.ca/our-platform.

Liberal Research Bureau. 2007. "Communications manual." Internal document.

Lincoln, Clifford, Rob Merrifield, Stéphane Bergeron, Lorne Nystrom, and Bill Casey. 2001. "Round table: Members look at parliamentary reform." *Canadian Parliamentary Review* 24(2): 11–17.

Ling, Justin. 2015. "Inside the first standoff between media and the Trudeau government." *Vice,* November 24. https://www.vice.com/en_ca/article/4wbmyw/inside-the-first-standoff-between-media-and-the-trudeau-government.

Lithwick, Dana, and Sebastian Spano. 2015. "The Canadian electoral system." Library of Parliament, publication 2013-81-E, October 22. https://lop.parl.ca/staticfiles/PublicWebsite/Home/ResearchPublications/BackgroundPapers/PDF/2013-81-e.pdf.

Loat, Alison. 2010. "Member of Parliament: A job with no description." *Canadian Parliamentary Review* 34(1): 23–29.

Loat, Alison, and Michael MacMillan. 2014. *Tragedy in the Commons: Former Members of Parliament Speak Out about Canada's Failing Democracy.* Toronto: Random House.

Loewen, Peter John, and Frédérick Bastien. 2010. "(In)significant elections? Federal by-elections in Canada, 1963–2008." *Canadian Journal of Political Science* 43(1): 87–105.

Long, Wayne. 2019. @WayneLongSJ. Tweet, February 21. https://twitter.com/WayneLongSJ/status/1098725863233863680.

Loop, Emma. 2016. "Here's where Trudeau was during an emergency debate on Indigenous suicide." *BuzzFeed Canada,* April 13. https://www.buzzfeed.com/emmaloop/trudeau-was-at-a-liberal-book-launch-during-the-indigenous-s.

Loury, Glenn. 1994. "Self-censorship in public discourse: A theory of 'political correctness' and related phenomena." *Rationality and Society* 6(4): 428–61.

Luff, Robyn. 2018. "Robyn Luff MLA statement." November 5. https://www.scribd.com/document/392445987/Robyn-Luff-MLA-Statement.

Luntz, Frank I. 2015. *Words that Work: It's Not What You Say, It's What People Hear.* New York: Hachette Books.

MacCharles, Tondra. 2018. "Truth, lies, and videotape: We review Question Period from the cheap seats." *Toronto Star,* June 20, A1.

–. 2020. "Doug Ford joins premiers calling on Ottawa to do more in the fight against COVID-19." *Toronto Star,* April 2. https://www.thestar.com/politics/federal/2020/04/02/doug-ford-joins-premiers-calling-on-ottawa-to-do-more-in-the-fight-against-covid-19.html.

MacCharles, Tondra, Alex Ballingall, and Alex Boutilier. 2019. "They're over the Hill (or are they?) – Retiring MPs talk candidly about what they will and won't miss." *Toronto Star,* June 23, A9.

MacCharles, Tondra, and Bruce Campion-Smith. 2019. "Wilson-Raybould allowed to testify." *Toronto Star,* February 20, A1.

Macdonald, Nancy. 2019. "Touting win as moral victory, Wilson-Raybould says she's likely to vote with Grits." *Globe and Mail,* October 23, A9.

Macdonald, Susan Agnes. n.d. Diary of Lady Susan Agnes Macdonald, 1867–69. Library and Archives Canada. http://central.bac-lac.gc.ca/.item?id=e008468893-t&app=fonandcol&op=pdf.

MacGuigan, Mark. 1978. "Parliamentary reform: Impediments to an enlarged role for the backbencher." *Legislative Studies Quarterly* 3(4): 671–82.

MacKinnon, Leslie. 2014. "Justin Trudeau's abortion stance leaves Liberal ranks in confusion." CBC News, May 21. http://www.cbc.ca/news/politics/justin-trudeau-s-abortion-stance-leaves-liberal-ranks-in-confusion-1.2648752.

MacKreal, Kim. 2013. "'Behave and obey': How party discipline hurts politics." *Globe and Mail,* February 5. https://www.theglobeandmail.com/news/politics/behave-and-obey-how-party-discipline-hurts-politics/article8235842.

Maclean's. 2019. "Are Wilson-Raybould and Philpott about to Liberexit from caucus?" *Maclean's,* April 2. https://www.macleans.ca/politics/ottawa/are-wilson-raybould-and-philpott-about-to-liberexit-from-caucus.

MacLeod, Meredith. 2018. "Canada ranks no. 6, U.S. 21 on global democracy index." CTV News, February 1. https://www.ctvnews.ca/canada/canada-ranks-no-6-u-s-21-on-global-democracy-index-1.3785320.

Major, Darren. 2019. "'Put up or shut up': Liberal MP challenges Philpott and Wilson-Raybould over SNC-Lavalin." CBC News, March 23. https://www.cbc.ca/news/politics/judy-sgro-wilson-raybould-philpott-1.5068509.

Malloy, Jonathan. 2006. "High discipline, low cohesion? The uncertain patterns of Canadian parliamentary party groups." In *Cohesion and Discipline in Legislatures,* edited by Reuven Y. Hazan, 116–29. London: Routledge.

–. 2012. "Not necessarily leadership but leadership if necessary: Canadian prime ministers and the management of expectations." In *Poor Leadership and Bad Governance: Reassessing Presidents and Prime Ministers in North America, Europe and Japan,* edited by Ludger Helms, 43–63. London: Edward Elgar.

Marland, Alex. 2012. "Political photography, journalism, and framing in the digital age: The management of visual media by the prime minister of Canada." *International Journal of Press/Politics* 17(2): 214–33.

–. 2014. "The branding of a prime minister: Digital information subsidies and the image management of Stephen Harper." In *Political Communication in Canada: Meet the Press and Tweet the Rest,* edited by Alex Marland, Thierry Giasson, and Tamara A. Small, 55–73. Vancouver: UBC Press.

–. 2016. *Brand Command: Canadian Politics and Democracy in the Age of Message Control.* Vancouver: UBC Press.

–. 2017. "Above and below the line: Strategic communications and media management in Canadian governments." *Canadian Public Administration* 60(3): 417–37.

Marland, Alex, and Angelina Wagner. 2020. "Scripted messengers: How party discipline and branding turn election candidates and legislators into brand ambassadors." *Journal of Political Marketing* 19(1–2): 54–73.

Marland, Alex, and Stephen Power. 2020. "Digital representation: The normalization of social media in political offices." In *Digital Politics in Canada: Promises and Realities,* edited by Tamara A. Small and Harold J. Jansen, 23–45. Toronto: University of Toronto Press.

Marleau, Robert, and Camille Montpetit. 2000. *House of Commons Procedure and Practice.* http://www.ourcommons.ca/marleaumontpetit/DocumentViewer.aspx.

Marquis, Melanie. 2018. "Tory leader says he spoke to MP about abortion comment." *Lethbridge Herald,* May 14, 1.

Martin, Lawrence. 2010. *Harperland: The Politics of Control.* Toronto: Penguin Group.

–. 2013. "A rare show of courage from Tory bobbleheads." *iPolitics,* March 27. https://ipolitics.ca/2013/03/27/a-rare-show-of-courage-from-tory-bobbleheads.

Martin, Nick, and Larry Kusch. 2017. "Outspoken PC MLA Steven Fletcher booted from caucus." *Winnipeg Free Press,* June 30. https://www.winnipegfreepress.com/local/pc-caucus-to-expel-steven-fletcher-431772503.html.

Martin, Paul. 2002. "The democratic deficit." *Policy Options,* December, 10–12.

–. 2008. *Hell or High Water: My Life in and out of Politics.* Toronto: McClelland and Stewart.

Mas, Susana. 2015. "Justin Trudeau tells Liberal MPs to be a 'strong voice' for constituents." CBC News, November 5. http://www.cbc.ca/news/politics/justin-trudeau-first-caucus-meeting-1.3305756.

Maser, Peter. 1983. "Mulroney avoids split over French rights resolution." *Ottawa Citizen,* October 6, 1.

Mason, Brian. 2018. "Oral Question Period." In Alberta, *Legislative Assembly of Alberta Debates and Proceedings (Hansard),* 29th Leg, 4th Sess (November 5) at 1772.

Mason, Lilliana. 2018. "Ideologues without issues: The polarizing consequences of ideological identities." *Public Opinion Quarterly* 82(S1): 866–87.

Massicotte, Louis. 1989. "Cohésion et dissidence à l'Assemblée nationale du Québec depuis 1867." *Canadian Journal of Political Science* 22(3): 505–21.

Matheson, W.A. 1976. *The Prime Minister and the Cabinet.* Toronto: Methuen.

May, Elizabeth. 2017. "Westminster parliamentary democracy: Where some MPs are more equal than others." In *Turning Parliament Inside Out: Practical Ideas for Reforming Canada's Democracy,* edited by Michael Chong, Scott Simms, and Kennedy Stewart, 15–35. Madeira Park, BC: Douglas and McIntyre.

May, Kathryn. 2019. "What ever happened to deliverology?" *Policy Options,* May 15. https://policyoptions.irpp.org/magazines/may-2019/what-ever-happened-deliverology.

Mazereeuw, Peter. 2019a. "'Sign up' and 'chip in': How the federal parties use Facebook ads to get your money." *Hill Times,* March 4, 1.

–. 2019b. "House leaders keep each other in the dark as last push on legislation begins." *Hill Times,* May 27, 1.

–. 2020a. "'It's incredibly dire here': Alberta MPs navigating COVID-19 and oil crises." *Hill Times,* March 23, 1.

–. 2020b. "'Decisive action was required': How MPs and senators hammered out deal to close Parliament late into the night." *Hill Times,* March 18, 1.

McEvoy, Michael. 2019. "Full disclosure: Political parties, campaign data, and voter consent." Information and Privacy Commissioner for British Columbia, Investigation Report P19-01. February 6. https://www.oipc.bc.ca/investigation-reports/2278.

McGillivray, Don. 1987. "Tories look more like Grits each day." *Gazette* [Montreal], January 31, B3.

McGrane, David. 2017. "Election preparation in the federal NDP: The next campaign starts the day after the last one ends." In *Permanent Campaigning in Canada,* edited by Alex Marland, Thierry Giasson, and Anna Lennox Esselment, 145–64. Vancouver: UBC Press.

–. 2019. *The New NDP: Moderation, Modernization, and Political Marketing.* Vancouver: UBC Press.

McGrath, James A. 1985a. *Report of the Special Committee on Reform of the House of Commons.* Ottawa: Queen's Printer for Canada.

–. 1985b. "The honourable James McGrath in an interview with Tom Earle." February 10. Library of Parliament, Accession number 1986-0270.

McGregor, Glen. 2015. "Harper's attendance at Question Period the lowest since 2006, Parliament stats show." *Vancouver Province,* May 19, A12.

McIntosh, Emma. 2019. "Lisa Raitt explains that tweet about climate change." *National Observer,* June 14. https://www.nationalobserver.com/2019/06/14/news/lisa-raitt-explains-tweet-about-climate-change.

McIntyre, Catherine. 2018. "Don't text and govern." *Maclean's,* February 1, 26–27.

McKay, John. 2014. "Standing committee on finance – Evidence." In Canada, Parliament, *House of Commons Debates,* 41st Parl, 2nd Sess (May 29) at 39.

McKelvey, Fenwick. 2019. "Cranks, clickbait and cons: On the acceptable use of political engagement platforms." *Internet Policy Review* 8(4): 1–27.

McKelvey, Fenwick, and Elizabeth Dubois. 2017. "Toward the responsible use of bots in politics." *Policy Options,* November 23. http://policyoptions.irpp.org/magazines/november-2017/toward-the-responsible-use-of-bots-in-politics.

McKelvey, Fenwick, and Jill Piebiak. 2019. "Does the difference compute? Data-driven campaigning in Canada." In *What's Trending in Canadian Politics? Understanding Transformations in Power, Media, and the Public Sphere,* edited by Mireille Lalancette, Vincent Raynauld, and Erin Crandall, 194–215. Vancouver: UBC Press.

McKelvey, Fenwick, Marianne Côté, and Vincent Raynauld. 2018. "Scandals and screenshots: Social media elites in Canadian politics." In *Political Elites in Canada: Power and Influence in Instantaneous Times,* edited by Alex Marland, Thierry Giasson, and Andrea Lawlor, 204–22. Vancouver: UBC Press.

McLean, James S. 2012. *Inside the NDP War Room.* Montreal and Kingston: McGill-Queen's University Press.

McLellan, A. Anne. 2019. "Review of the roles of the Minister of Justice and Attorney General of Canada." August 14. https://pm.gc.ca/en/news/backgrounders/2019/08/14/review-roles-minister-justice-and-attorney-general-canada.

McLeod, Jack, ed. 1988. *The Oxford Book of Canadian Political Anecdotes.* Toronto: Oxford University Press.

McLeod, Paul. 2016. "Conservatives denied using repetition to delay a bill." *BuzzFeed,* May 10. https://www.buzzfeed.com/paulmcleod/the-conservatives-say-they -didnt-use-talking-points-to-delay.

Mendelsohn, Matthew. 2020. @MattMendel. Tweet, March 4. https://twitter.com/ MattMendel/status/1235271327881342977.

Michael, Robert B., Maryanne Garry, and Irving Kirsch. 2012. "Suggestion, cognition, and behavior." *Current Directions in Psychological Science* 21(3): 151–56.

Milgram, Stanley. 1963. "Behavioral study of obedience." *Journal of Abnormal and Social Psychology* 67(4): 371–78.

Montpetit, Éric, Erick Lachapelle, and Simon Kiss. 2017. "Does Canadian federalism amplify policy disagreements? Values, regions and policy preferences." IRPP Study 65. September. http://irpp.org/research-studies/study-no65.

Moody, James, and Douglas R. White. 2003. "Structural cohesion and embeddedness: A hierarchical concept of social groups." *American Sociological Review* 68(1): 103–27.

Moore, Dene. 2014. "'Rock Snot' article gets sticky for agency." *National Post,* September 8, A5.

Moore, Terry. 2001. "An introduction to procedure in the House of Commons." *Canadian Parliamentary Review* 24(1): 8–11.

Morden, Michael, Jane Hilderman, and Kendall Anderson. 2018a. "Flip the script: Reclaiming the legislature to reinvigorate representative democracy." Samara Centre for Democracy. www.samaracanada.com.

–. 2018b. "The real House lives: Strengthening the role of MPs in an age of partisanship." Samara Centre for Democracy. www.samaracanada.com.

Morden, Michael, and Kendall Anderson. 2019. "Don't blame 'the people': The rise of elite-led populism in Canada." Samara Centre for Democracy. www.samara canada.com.

Morneau, Bill. 2018. "Government orders [business of supply] – Department of Finance – Main estimates, 2018–19." In Canada, Parliament, *House of Commons Debates,* 42nd Parl, 1st Sess (May 22) at 148(298).

Morton, Desmond. 2006. "A note on party switchers." *Canadian Parliamentary Review* 29(2): 4–8.

Morton, W.L. 1950. *The Progressive Party in Canada.* Toronto: University of Toronto Press.

Moss, Neil. 2019. "House committees to have renewed importance in minority Parliament." *Hill Times,* October 28, 6.

–. 2020. "Presence of backbench MPs, cross-Canada representation restricted during in-person House sittings amidst physical distancing." *Hill Times,* April 22, 1.

Moss, Neil, and Emily Haws. 2019. "'I spoke almost 100,000 words over four days': Poilievre sets a record for longest speech in the House." *Hill Times,* April 8, 2.

Mouallem, Omar. 2015. "When tweets defeat candidates." *Metro* [Ottawa], September 3, 10.

Mulroney, Brian. 2007. *Brian Mulroney: Memoirs 1939–1993.* Toronto: McClelland and Stewart.

Munroe, Kaija Belfry, and H.D. Munroe. 2018. "Constituency campaigning in the age of data." *Canadian Journal of Political Science* 51(1): 135–54.

Murphy, Jonathan. 2002. "Your candle's flickering, Jean." *Globe and Mail,* May 17, A15.

Murray, Victor Vereker. 1948. "Tribune trumps." *Winnipeg Tribune,* March 11, 8.

National Post. 2019. "Oath." *National Post,* November 21, A5.

Naumetz, Tim. 1987. "Tories deny public paying for TV service." *Ottawa Citizen,* September 17, A4.

Nembhard, Kemlin, and Sandra DeLaronde. 2018. *NDP Commission to Establish a Safe and Respectful Political Environment: Interim Report.* Winnipeg: Manitoba New Democratic Party. https://media.winnipegfreepress.com/documents/NDP+Safe+Polical+environment.pdf.

New Democratic Party of Canada. 2013. Constitution. http://xfer.ndp.ca/2013/constitution/2013_CONSTITUTION_E.pdf.

–. 2016. "Communications officer (social media)." NDP Research Office, job advertisement, July 21. https://www.ndp.ca/job/communications-officer-social-media-permanent-full-time-position-1.

–. 2018. Policy of the New Democratic Party of Canada. February. https://xfer.ndp.ca/2018/Documents/2018-POLICY.pdf.

Newman, Peter C. 2006. *The Secret Mulroney Tapes: Unguarded Confessions of a Prime Minister.* Toronto: Vintage Canada.

Nielsen, Erik. 1989. *The House Is Not a Home.* Toronto: Macmillan.

Noelle-Neumann, Elisabeth. 1993. *The Spiral of Silence: Public Opinion – Our Social Skin.* 2nd ed. Chicago: University of Chicago Press.

Nunziata, John. 2003. "John Nunziata." In *A Call to Account,* edited by Criss Hajek, 15–21. Toronto: Breakout Educational Network.

Office of the Commissioner of Lobbying of Canada. 2019. "Advanced registry search results." https://lobbycanada.gc.ca.

Office of the Prime Minister. 2016. "Guide for parliamentary secretaries." January 5. https://pm.gc.ca/eng/news/2016/01/06/guide-parliamentary-secretaries.

–. 2018. "Communications planner." Job advertisement, March 26. https://twitter.com/jrdndeagle/status/978297873044406272.

O'Malley, Kady, and Evan Solomon. 2014. "Paul Calandra apologizes for non-answers as sources pin blame on PMO." CBC News, September 26. https://www.cbc.ca/news/politics/paul-calandra-apologizes-for-non-answers-as-sources-pin-blame-on-pmo-1.2779046.

Omand, Geordon. 2017. "Whip key to survival of minority government." *Gazette* [Montreal], June 12, N4.

O'Sullivan, Sean, with Rod McQueen. 1986. *Both My Houses: From Politics to Priesthood.* Toronto: Key Porter Books.

Ottawa Citizen. 1926. "Party politics." *Ottawa Citizen,* April 15, 1.

Owens, John E. 2006. "Explaining party cohesion and discipline in democratic legislatures: Purposiveness and contexts." In *Cohesion and Discipline in Legislatures,* edited by Reuven Y. Hazan, 12–40. London: Routledge.

Paez, Beatrice. 2020a. "Pandemic crisis tests durability of MPs' parliamentary privileges, say MPs, experts." *Hill Times,* April 15, 1.

–. 2020b. "Rookie MPs get crash course on life in 'Ottawa bubble.'" *Hill Times,* January 27, 6.

Panetta, Alexander. 2017. "PMO's Trump unit." *Calgary Sun,* August 21, A13.

–. 2019. "Trudeau's reelection bid faces the Trump test." *Politico,* May 2. https://www. politico.com/story/2019/05/02/trump-justin-trudeau-canada-handshake -1400635.

Parliament of Canada. 1968. Speech from the throne to open the first session, 28th Parliament of Canada. https://lop.parl.ca/staticfiles/ParlInfo/Documents/ ThroneSpeech/En/28-01-e.pdf.

–. 1991. Speech from the throne to open the third session, 34th Parliament of Canada. https://lop.parl.ca/sites/ParlInfo/default/en_CA/Parliament/procedure/ throneSpeech/speech343.

Parry, Tom. 2017. "Military emails reveal turmoil after Harper's team released 2015 images from battlefield." CBC News, December 27. http://www.cbc.ca/news/ politics/harper-iraq-images-bettlefield-1.4454794.

Patten, Steve. 2017. "Databases, microtargeting, and the permanent campaign: A threat to democracy?" In *Permanent Campaigning in Canada,* edited by Alex Marland, Thierry Giasson, and Anna Lennox Esselment, 47–64. Vancouver: UBC Press.

Patterson, Brian. 2019. Letter to the president of Lanark-Frontenac-Kingston Constituency Association, PC Party of Ontario. March 10. https://ottawacitizen. com/news/local-news/ontario-pc-party-president-says-hilliers-comment-in -legislature-was-the-final-straw.

Pechmann, Cornelia, and David W. Stewart. 1988. "Advertising repetition: A critical review of wearin and wearout." *Current Issues and Research in Advertising* 11(1–2): 285–329.

Pender, Terry. 2005. "Cool whip." *Record* [Kitchener], June 16, A1.

Perlin, George C. 1980. *The Tory Syndrome: Leadership Politics in the Progressive Conservative Party.* Montreal and Kingston: McGill-Queen's University Press.

Perreaux, Les, Jeff Gray, and Bertrand Marotte. 2015. "SNC-Lavalin charged with fraud, bribery after settlement talks fail." *Globe and Mail,* February 20, A1.

Pescosolido, Anthony T., and Richard Saavedra. 2012. "Cohesion and sports teams: A review." *Small Group Research* 43(6): 744–58.

Pessian, Parvaneh. 2016. "A day in the life of Whitby MP Celina Caesar-Chavannes." *This Week* [Whitby], May 4, 1.

Petit-Vouriot, Adelina, Jane Hilderman, and Michael Morden. 2018. "The 2018 Member of Parliament Survey: Evaluating the House of Commons and Options for Reform." Samara Centre for Democracy. www.samaracanada.com.

Philpott, Jane. 2019. @janephilpott. Tweet, March 4. https://twitter.com/janephilpott/status/1102660614307172352.

Pincher Creek Echo. 2019. "Minister cites 'bullying' in cancelling public meetings on Alberta parks plan." *Pincher Creek Echo,* January 9, A5.

Pinkerton, Charlie. 2018. "MP Raj Grewal resigned due to gambling addiction, PMO reveals." *iPolitics,* November 23. https://ipolitics.ca/2018/11/23/mps-told-not-to-talk-publicly-about-raj-grewal-resignation.

Pitkin, Hanna Fenichel. 1967. *The Concept of Representation.* Berkeley: University of California Press.

Poitras, Jacques. 2020a. "'The cause of our lifetime': Inside New Brunswick's COVID-19 war room." CBC News, April 15. https://www.cbc.ca/news/canada/new-brunswick/covid-19-pandemic-public-health-officials-coronavirus-1.5531463.

–. 2020b. "Opposing during COVID: How New Brunswick's 3 opposition parties are holding government to account." CBC News, March 25. https://www.cbc.ca/news/canada/new-brunswick/opposing-covid-nb-government-1.5508568.

Pole, Ken. 1998. "Bumpy week for hepatitis C victims as governments quarrel: Ontario full compensation offer reopens deal." *Medical Post* 34(18): 6.

Powers, Tim. 2019. "Don't write off the NDP, ditch the talking points." *Hill Times,* October 23, 19.

PressProgress. 2020. "Liberal MPs' offices stand by 'partisan' COVID-19 ad that misleadingly uses official government of Canada logo." *PressProgress,* April 9. https://pressprogress.ca/liberal-mps-offices-stand-by-partisan-covid19-ad-that-misleadingly-uses-official-government-of-canada-logo.

Privy Council Office. 2001. *Guide to Making Federal Acts and Regulations.* 2nd ed. https://www.canada.ca/content/dam/pco-bcp/documents/pdfs/fed-acts-eng.pdf.

Progressive Conservative Party of Canada. 1985. "Constituents first: A guide for Members of Parliament." National Headquarters, PC Party of Canada, Ottawa.

Public Policy Forum. 2015. *Time for a Reboot: Nine Ways to Restore Trust in Canada's Public Institutions.* October. https://ppforum.ca/wp-content/uploads/2018/03/PPF_TimeForAReboot_ENG_v6.pdf.

Public Works and Government Services Canada. 2015. "Archived – Ineligibility and Suspension Policy." July 3. https://www.tpsgc-pwgsc.gc.ca/ci-if/politique-policy-2015-07-03-eng.html.

Pugliese, David. 2018. "Ottawa cloaks purchase of jets in secrecy." *National Post,* March 5, A3.

R. v Duffy. 2016. ONCJ 220 (CanLII). http://canlii.ca/t/gplvk.

Rabson, Mia. 2019a. "Liberals, NDP pushing climate change motions." *Prince George Citizen,* May 15, A5.

–. 2019b. "Wilson-Raybould entered federal politics hoping to be a bridge builder." CTV News, February 9 [updated March 6]. https://www.ctvnews.ca/politics/wilson-raybould-entered-federal-politics-hoping-to-be-a-bridge-builder-1.4289856.

Radwanski, Adam. 2014. "Tory right-to-work debate turns ugly." *Globe and Mail,* January 22, A4.

–. 2018. "The omnipresent force in Doug Ford's government." *Globe and Mail*, November 17, A16.

Radwanski, Adam, and Daniel Leblanc. 2019. "System breakdown." *Globe and Mail*, April 20, A10.

Rae, Bob. 2015. *What's Happened to Politics?* Toronto: Simon and Schuster.

Raj, Althia. 2016a. "Trudeau's pledge of freer votes embraced by independent-minded Liberals." *Huffington Post Canada*, July 28. http://www.huffingtonpost.ca/2016/07/28/nathaniel-erskine-smith-trudeau-freer-votes_n_11239876.html.

–. 2016b. "Trudeau skipped more Question Periods than he attended in first year as PM." *Huffington Post Canada*, June 12. https://www.huffingtonpost.ca/2016/12/06/trudeau-question-period_n_13454956.html.

–. 2019. "Is there a point to heritage days and months? Some MPs aren't sure." *Huffington Post Canada*, February 2. https://www.huffingtonpost.ca/2019/02/02/is-there-a-point-to-heritage-days-and-months-some-mps-arent-sure_a_23659573.

–. 2020. "Parliament's top rebel explains why it's healthy to dissent." *Follow-Up with Althia Raj*, March 6. https://soundcloud.com/huffpost-follow-up/52-parliaments-top-rebel-explains-why-its-healthy-to-dissent.

Rana, Abbas. 2015a. "Cellphones barred from Liberal caucus meetings, Goodale says Grits don't want any distractions." *Hill Times*, December 14, 1.

–. 2015b. "PM instructs cabinet to attend all caucus meetings." *Hill Times*, December 7, 1.

–. 2016. "Trudeau tells nervous Grits not to criticize Trump, cabinet also talks about U.S. president-elect." *Hill Times*, November 28, 1.

–. 2017. "Liberals' black caucus members visit Casey's Nova Scotia riding after his constituency staffer faces racism." *Hill Times*, May 29, 4.

–. 2018a. "Upcoming gun bill 'scaring the hell out of the Liberal caucus,' and Trudeau's response to Harvey's concerns have put a chill on backbenchers: Liberal MPs." *Hill Times*, March 12, 1.

–. 2018b. "Rookie Liberal MP Bratina speaks out against controversial attestation in summer job program, says caucus should be consulted more." *Hill Times*, April 9, 1.

–. 2019a. "SNC-Lavalin and Wilson-Raybould's resignation 'serious concern' for Liberal MPs, Hill staffers, and Liberal insiders." *Hill Times*, February 18, 1.

–. 2019b. "'We're really getting important now': In midst of ongoing SNC-Lavalin saga, Trudeau reaches out to caucus, sets up caucus relations office." *Hill Times*, March 25, 1.

–. 2019c. "Liberals now focusing 'completely' on election readiness in regional, national caucus meetings." *Hill Times*, May 20, 6.

–. 2019d. "Wilson-Raybould and Philpott expected to be kicked out of Liberal caucus in the coming days: Liberals." *Hill Times*, April 1, 1.

–. 2019e. "PM Trudeau should 'reset the tone' by being accessible and having a 'two-way,' meaningful communication with his 179 MPs." *Hill Times*, March 18, 1.

–. 2019f. "Some Liberal MPs 'happy' with Butts' return, others concerned he could be a liability for Grits' re-election campaign." *Hill Times*, August 12, 1.

–. 2020a. "Conservative riding presidents, candidates, MPs rebelling against party's decision to claw back half of election rebates." *Hill Times,* March 9, 1.

–. 2020b. "Conservatives considering 2019 Liberal nomination model to protect incumbent MPs from nomination challenges." *Hill Times,* March 2, 1.

–. 2020c. "In the time of the pandemic, Liberals holding national caucus meetings seven days a week." *Hill Times,* April 13, 1.

–. 2020d. "Liberals consulting MPs, party base on nomination rules for the next election." *Hill Times,* May 11, 4.

Rana, Abbas, and Rachel Aiello. 2017. "Liberals to meet for two-day caucus, some Grit MPs dissatisfied with level of consultation." *Hill Times,* March 20, 1.

Rana, Abbas, and Shruti Shekar. 2018. "Newly-created, rebranded cabinet posts expected to be key policy planks in 2019 Liberal election platform, say political insiders." *Hill Times,* July 23, 1.

Rands, Chris. 2017. *How Parliament Works.* Video, CBC News, August 31. http://www.cbc.ca/news/politics/parliament-behind-the-scenes-videos-1.4229648.

Rast, David E., and Michael A. Hogg. 2016. "Who trusts charismatic leaders who champion change? The role of group identification, membership centrality, and self-uncertainty." *Group Dynamics: Theory, Research, and Practice* 20(4): 259–75.

Rathgeber, Brent. 2014. *Irresponsible Government: The Decline of Parliamentary Democracy in Canada.* Toronto: Dundurn.

Reform Party of Canada. 1989. Platform and Statement of Principles. Internal document.

Reid, John. 1993. "The case for party discipline." *Canadian Parliamentary Review* 16(3): 2–4.

–. 2006. "Democracy in the 21st century: Advice for newly elected Members of Parliament." *Canadian Parliamentary Review* 29(1): 2–3.

Reid, Scott J. 2018. "Scott Reid's annual report to constituents." MP newsletter, August 1.

–. 2019. "Conservatives should be leading on democracy issues." Blog, December 30. https://scottreid.ca/conservatives-should-be-leading-on-democracy-issues.

–. 2020. "Why I am in the House today." Blog, March 24. https://scottreid.ca/why-i-am-in-the-house-today.

Richler, Noah. 2016. *The Candidate: Fear and Loathing on the Campaign Trail.* Toronto: Doubleday Canada.

Rink, Floor, and Naomi Ellemers. 2008. "Diversity, newcomers, and team innovation: The importance of a common identity." In *Diversity and Groups,* edited by Katherine W. Phillips, 221–43. Bingley, UK: Emerald Group.

Roberts, Terry. 2019. "Here's why rebel MP Scott Simms is the only N.L. Liberal without a nomination." CBC News, March 8. https://www.cbc.ca/news/canada/newfoundland-labrador/scott-simms-nomination-1.5048343.

Robertson, James R. 2002. "House of Commons procedure: Its reform." Research Branch, Library of Parliament. http://publications.gc.ca/collections/Collection-R/LoPBdP/CIR/8215-e.htm.

Rocha, Roberto. 2019. "How candidates use Twitter says a lot about how parties communicate in Canada." CBC News, October 26. https://www.cbc.ca/news/politics/twitter-candidates-retweets-1.5335220.

Rollwagen, Heather, Ivor Shapiro, Geneviève Bonin-Labelle, Lindsay Fitzgerald, and Lauriane Tremblay. 2019. "Just who do Canadian journalists think they are? Political role conceptions in global and historical perspective." *Canadian Journal of Political Science* 52(3): 461–77.

Ryckewaert, Laura. 2011. "NDP Caucus Services set to expand from 46 to more than 100 staffers in Ottawa." *Hill Times,* August 8, 6.

–. 2015. "Hill media, Liberals settle on cabinet 'outs.'" *Hill Times,* December 14, 19.

–. 2016. "Liberals $2.4-million research bureau headed by Thalmann, Bosch." *Hill Times,* February 22, 1.

–. 2017. "NDP continues court challenge against BOIE." *Hill Times,* November 6. https://www.hilltimes.com/2017/11/06/ndps-court-challenge-boie-decision-continues-current-former-mps-repaying-money-cleary-says-left-bad-taste/124607.

–. 2018a. "PMO scoops up ex-national manager for ministers' regional offices." *Hill Times,* January 10, 17.

–. 2018b. "May wants to see all-party women's caucus tackle issues of sexual harassment, misconduct on the Hill." *Hill Times,* January 22. https://www.hilltimes.com/2018/01/22/gpc-leader-may-wants-see-party-womens-caucus-tackle-issue-harassment-misconduct-hill/131460.

–. 2019. "Veterans minister MacAulay Mann's up." *Hill Times,* April 1, 31.

–. 2020. "No committee or caucus roles, longtime Tory MP Scott Reid still sidelined after breaking rank." *Hill Times,* March 11, 1.

Sallot, Jeff. 1986. "Phone dominates PM's 16-hour working day." Globe and Mail, September 2, A5.

Samara Centre. 2011. "'It's my party': Parliamentary dysfunction reconsidered." www.samaracanada.com.

–. 2016. "Cheering or jeering? Members of Parliament open up about civility in the House of Commons." www.samaracanada.com.

–. 2018. "Elephant on the Hill." www.samaracanada.com.

–. 2020. "Is the Reform Act still a thing? The Samara Centre investigates." Blog, January 17. www.samaracanada.com.

Santoni, Ronald E. 1995. *Bad Faith, Good Faith, and Authenticity in Sartre's Early Philosophy.* Philadelphia: Temple University Press.

Savoie, Donald. 1999. *Governing from the Centre: The Concentration of Power in Canadian Politics.* Toronto: University of Toronto Press.

Scandiffio, Mike. 1998. "Was Trudeau right? MPs nobodies 50 feet off the Hill: Confidence vote for hepatitis C package." *Hill Times,* May 4.

Scheer, Andrew. 2013. "Privilege – S.O. 31 – Speaker's ruling." In Canada, Parliament, *House of Commons Debates,* 41st Parl, 1st Sess (April 23) at 238.

–. 2019. "Oral questions." In Canada, Parliament, *House of Commons Debates,* 42nd Parl, 1st Sess (February 7) at 380.

Segal, Hugh. 2006. *The Long Road Back: The Conservative Journey, 1993–2006.* Toronto: HarperCollins.

SFU Morris J. Wosk Centre for Dialogue. 2019. "Canadians' views on democracy – Report 1: State of democracy and appeal of populism." August. https://www.democracydialogue.ca.

Shaw, Rob, and Richard Zussman. 2018. *A Matter of Confidence: The Inside Story of the Political Battle for BC.* Victoria: Heritage House.

Simpson, Jeffrey. 1980. *Discipline of Power: The Conservative Interlude and the Liberal Restoration.* Toronto: Personal Library Publishers.

–. 2001. *The Friendly Dictatorship.* Toronto: McClelland and Stewart.

Simpson, Katie. 2019. "Liberal MP denies coordinated support for Trudeau, despite nearly identical online messages." CBC News, March 11. https://www.cbc.ca/news/politics/liberal-mp-denies-coordinated-support-for-trudeau-1.5051773.

680News. 2019. "Trudeau on Wilson-Raybould and Philpott's departure from Liberal Party." Video. 680News [Toronto], June 18. https://www.680news.com/video/2019/06/18/trudeau-on-wilson-raybould-and-philpotts-departure-from-liberal-party.

Small, Tamara A. 2008. "Equal access, unequal success – Major and minor Canadian parties on the net." *Party Politics* 14(1): 51–70.

–. 2014. "The not-so social network: The use of Twitter by Canada's party leaders." In *Political Communication in Canada: Meet the Press and Tweet the Rest,* edited by Alex Marland, Thierry Giasson, and Tamara A. Small, 92–108. Vancouver: UBC Press.

Small, Tamara A., and Jane Philpott. 2020. "The independent candidate." In *Inside the Campaign: Managing Elections in Canada,* edited by Alex Marland and Thierry Giasson, 197–206. Vancouver: UBC Press.

Smith, Alison. 2011. "The standing committee system and how Members of Parliament view its work." Institute on Governance. https://iog.ca/docs/2011_January_The-Standing-Committee-System.pdf.

Smith, David E. 2007. *The People's House of Commons: Theories of Democracy in Contention.* Toronto: University of Toronto Press.

–. 2017. *The Constitution in a Hall of Mirrors: Canada at 150.* Toronto: University of Toronto Press.

Smith, Jennifer. 1999. "Democracy and the Canadian House of Commons at the millennium." *Canadian Public Administration* 42(4): 398–421.

Smith, Jennifer. 2016. "Minister's fast return expensive for Liberals." *Ottawa Citizen,* August 11, N4.

–. 2018a. "Ottawa wanted all of Canada speaking with one voice on NAFTA: Emails." *Owen Sound Sun Times,* May 5, A7.

–. 2018b. "Tories to question candidates about sex misconduct." *National Post,* February 6, A4.

Smith, Marie-Danielle. 2019. "Quebec's views on SNC-Lavalin starkly different." *National Post,* February 14, A5.

Snagovsky, Feodor, and Matthew Kerby. 2018. "The electoral consequences of party switching in Canada: 1945–2011." *Canadian Journal of Political Science* 51(2): 425–45.

–. 2019. "Political staff and the gendered division of political labour in Canada." *Parliamentary Affairs* 72(3): 616–37.

SNC-Lavalin. 2019. "SNC-Lavalin Group settles federal charges." News release, December 18. https://www.newswire.ca/news-releases/snc-lavalin-group-settles-federal-charges-803132956.html.

–. 2020. "About us." https://www.snclavalin.com/en/about.

Soroka, Stuart N., Olga Redko, and Quinn Albaugh. 2015. "Television in the legislature: Cameras in the House of Commons." *Parliamentary Affairs* 68(1): 203–17.

Stanbury, W.T. 2003. "Accountability to citizens in the Westminster model of government: More myth than reality." Fraser Institute, February. https://www.fraserinstitute.org/sites/default/files/WestminsterModelofGovernment.pdf.

Standing Committee on Procedure and House Affairs. 2016. "Interim report on moving toward a modern, efficient, inclusive and family-friendly Parliament." House of Commons, 42nd Parl, 1st Sess, June 15.

Statistics Canada. 2020. "Population estimates, quarterly." Statistics Canada, Table 17-10-0009-01. https://doi.org/10.25318/1710000901-eng.

Steele, Graham. 2014. *What I Learned about Politics: Inside the Rise – and Collapse – of Nova Scotia's NDP Government.* Halifax: Nimbus.

Stenning, Philip C. 2009. "Discretion, politics and the public interest in 'high-profile' criminal investigations and prosecutions." *Canadian Journal of Law and Society* 24(3): 337–66.

Stevens, Benjamin Allen, et al. 2019. "Local candidate effects in Canadian elections." *Canadian Journal of Political Science* 52(1): 83–96.

Stewart, Ian. 1989. "Prince Edward Island: A damned queer parliament." In *Provincial and Territorial Legislatures in Canada,* edited by Gary Levy and Graham White, 13–28. Toronto: University of Toronto Press.

Stewart, Kennedy. 2017. "Empowering the backbench: The story of electronic petitions." In *Turning Parliament Inside Out: Practical Ideas for Reforming Canada's Democracy,* edited by Michael Chong, Scott Simms, and Kennedy Stewart, 58–79. Madeira Park, BC: Douglas and McIntyre.

Stewart, Walter. 1971. *Trudeau in Power.* New York: Outerbridge and Dienstfrey.

Stone, Laura. 2017. "Conservative pit bull zeroes in on Morneau." *Globe and Mail,* November 18, A10.

–. 2018a. "'A good whip pulls people together': Mark Holland discusses new role on Parliament Hill." *Globe and Mail,* September 10, A5.

–. 2018b. "Singh backs down from punishing MP." *Globe and Mail,* March 28, A3.

–. 2018c. "Conservative MPs express disappointment in Bernier." *Globe and Mail,* April 11, A4.

–. 2019a. "Ford faces resistance from PC caucus, sources say." *Globe and Mail,* June 15, A10.

–. 2019b. "MP describes 'hostility, anger' in private talks with the PM." *Globe and Mail,* March 9, A4.

Stone, Laura, and Michelle Zilio. 2018. "PM dealing with sexual misconduct claims 'case-by-case.'" *Globe and Mail,* January 31, A4.

Strøm, Kaare, and Wolfgang C. Müeller. 1999. "Political parties and hard choices." In *Policy, Office, or Votes? How Political Parties in Western Europe Make Hard Decisions,* edited by Wolfgang C. Müeller and Kaare Strøm, 1–35. New York: Cambridge University Press.

Stursberg, Peter. 1975. *Diefenbaker: Leadership Gained, 1956–62.* Toronto: University of Toronto Press.

–. 1976. *Diefenbaker: Leadership Lost, 1962–67.* Toronto: University of Toronto Press.

Taber, Jane. 1993. "Liberal pencils prod at Tories' timetable." *Ottawa Citizen,* August 30, A2.

–. 2004. "Martin faces backlash over PMO powers." *Globe and Mail,* August 25, A9.

–. 2005. "As witnesses tell it, the poor chair didn't stand a chance." *Globe and Mail,* March 21. https://www.theglobeandmail.com/opinion/as-witnesses-tell-it-the -poor-chair-didnt-stand-a-chance/article735272.

–. 2007. "Dion's the leader, but who's in charge?" *Globe and Mail,* April 23, A4.

–. 2010. "Harper Tories to vet potential political land mines." *Globe and Mail,* September 11, A7.

Tasker, John Paul. 2017. "Don Meridith faces ethics hearing as Senate blocks media access." CBC News, April 4. https://www.cbc.ca/news/politics/don-meredith -committee-media-access-1.4054791.

Telford, Katie. 2018. "Replay: Katie Telford in conversation with Paul Wells." Video. *Maclean's,* April 25. http://www.macleans.ca/politics/ottawa/trudeaus-chief-of -staff-katie-telford-on-life-inside-the-pmo.

Templeton, Charles. 1969. "'My first year as prime minister' – Pierre Trudeau." *Maclean's,* June 1, 26–28.

Thomas, Paul E.J. 2016. "Across enemy lines: A study of the all-party groups in the Parliaments of Canada, Ontario, Scotland and the United Kingdom." PhD diss., University of Toronto.

–. 2020. "Parliament under pressure: Evaluating Parliament's performance in response to COVID-19." Samara Centre for Democracy. Blog, April 2. https://www. samaracanada.com/democracy-monitor/parliament-under-pressure.

Thomas, Paul E.J., and Graham White. 2015. "Evaluating provincial and territorial legislatures." In *Provinces: Canadian Provincial Politics,* 3rd ed., edited by Christopher Dunn, 363–97. Toronto: University of Toronto Press.

Thomas, Paul E.J., and J.P. Lewis. 2019. "Executive creep in Canadian provincial legislatures." *Canadian Journal of Political Science* 52(2): 363–83.

Thomas, Paul E.J., and Michael Morden. 2019. "Party favours: How federal election candidates are chosen." Samara Centre for Democracy. www.samaracanada.com.

Thomas, Paul G. 1978. "Comments." In *The Legislative Process in Canada: The Need for Reform,* edited by William A.W. Neilson and James C. MacPherson, 154–63. Toronto: Butterworth.

–. 1985a. "The role of national party caucuses." In *Party Government and Regional Representation in Canada,* edited by Peter Aucoin, 69–136. Toronto: University of Toronto Press.

–. 1985b. "Parliamentary reform through political parties." In *The Canadian House of Commons: Essays in Honour of Norman Ward,* edited by John C. Courtney, 43–68. Calgary: University of Calgary Press.

–. 2013. "Communications and prime ministerial power." In *Essays in Honour of Donald J. Savoie,* edited by James Bickerton and B. Guy Peters, 53–84. Montreal and Kingston: McGill-Queen's University Press.

Thomas, Ray. 1955. "Private Bills – Canada Elections Act." In Canada, Parliament, *House of Commons Debates,* 22nd Parl, 2nd Sess (March 11) at 1955.

Thompson, Allan. 1997. "Just what the doctor ordered." *Toronto Star,* September 17, A35.

Thompson, Beth. 2007. "'Tory spy' outed online." *Gazette* [Montreal], March 18, A1.

Thomson, Dale C. 1967. *Louis St. Laurent: Canadian.* Toronto: Macmillan.

Thomson, Stuart. 2018. "A people's history of 'bozo eruptions' in Canada." *National Post,* December 27, A3.

Todd, Rosemary. 1994. "Dissension still rocks Reform Party." *Hamilton Spectator,* March 17, C4.

Tolley, Erin. 2015. *Framed: Media and the Coverage of Race in Canadian Politics.* Vancouver: UBC Press.

Toronto Star. 2017. "Insincerity exposed." *Toronto Star,* May 29, A10.

Toronto Sun. 2019. "Liberals in turmoil? MPs break ranks." *Toronto Sun,* February 14, A7.

Trudeau, Justin. 2014. *Common Ground.* Toronto: HarperCollins.

–. 2018. "Oral questions." In Canada, Parliament, *House of Commons Debates,* 42nd Parl, 1st Sess (May 9) at 295.

–. 2019a. "Leader of the government in the House of Commons mandate letter." December 13. https://pm.gc.ca/en/mandate-letters/2019/12/13/leader-government -house-commons-mandate-letter.

–. 2019b. "Deputy prime minister and minister of intergovernmental affairs mandate letter." December 13. https://pm.gc.ca/en/mandate-letters/2019/12/13/deputy -prime-minister-and-minister-intergovernmental-affairs-mandate.

Trudeau, Pierre. 1958. "Some obstacles to democracy in Quebec." *Canadian Journal of Economics and Political Science* 24(3): 297–311.

–. 1969. "Motion to adjourn House." In Canada, Parliament, *House of Commons Debates,* 28th Parl, 1st Sess (July 25) at 11635.

–. 1976. "Tributes to new leader of the opposition." In Canada, Parliament, *House of Commons Debates,* 30th Parl, 1st Sess (February 25) at 11234.

–. 1993. *Memoirs.* Toronto: McClelland and Stewart.

Tumilty, Ryan. 2020. "Inside the battle for $52B COVID-19 package." *National Post,* March 26, A1.

Turcotte, André, and Simon Vodrey. 2017. "Permanent polling and governance." In *Permanent Campaigning in Canada,* edited by Alex Marland, Thierry Giasson, and Anna Lennox Esselment, 127–44. Vancouver: UBC Press.

Turcotte, André, and Vincent Raynauld. 2020. "Divide et impera: Wedge politics in the 2019 Canadian federal election." In *Political Marketing in the 2019 Canadian Federal Election,* edited by Jamie Gillies, Vincent Raynauld and André Turcotte. New York: Palgrave Pivot.

Turcotte, Martin. 2015. "Civic engagement and political participation in Canada." Statistics Canada, Catalogue 89-652-X2015006. https://www150.statcan.gc.ca/n1/en/pub/89-652-x/89-652-x2015006-eng.pdf.

Turner, Charles. 1987. "Senator Charles Turner in an interview with Tom Earle." February 10. Library of Parliament, Accession number 1987-0109.

Turner, Garth. 2009. *Sheeple: Caucus Confidentiality in Stephen Harper's Ottawa.* Toronto: Key Porter Books.

Underhill, Frank. 1935. "The development of national political parties in Canada." *Canadian Historical Review* 16(4): 367–87.

van Rijn, Nicolaas. 2000. "Snapping at the heels of the PM." *Toronto Star,* June 5, A6.

Venne, Pierrette. 2003. "Parliament and democracy in the 21st century: The role of MPs." *Canadian Parliamentary Review* 26(1): 2–3.

Vigliotti, Marco. 2016. "Liberal committee meddling breaks campaign promise, say Conservatives." *Hill Times,* September 28, 1.

–. 2018. "Almost 60 per cent of Canadians don't trust promises made by politicians before an election: Poll." *Hill Times,* February 2. https://www.hilltimes.com/2018/02/02/almost-60-per-cent-canadians-dont-trust-promises-made-politicians-election-poll/133157.

von Scheel, Elise. 2019. "Trudeau threatens Scheer with lawsuit over SNC-Lavalin comments." CBC News, April 7. https://www.cbc.ca/news/politics/trudeau-threatens-scheer-with-lawsuit-over-snc-lavalin-comments-1.5088175.

Walker, James E. 1971. "The functions of the whip in Canada." *Parliamentarian* 52(4): 260–63.

Wallace, Bruce. 1988. "Mulroney takes charge." *Maclean's,* July 18, 20.

Walsh, Rob. 2017. *On the House: An Inside Look at the House of Commons.* Montreal and Kingston: McGill-Queen's University Press.

Ward, Norman, ed. 1966. *A Party Politician: The Memoirs of Chubby Power.* Toronto: Macmillan.

Warren, John. 1986. "Backroom wizards make backbenchers sound good in House." *Ottawa Citizen,* March 31, A4.

Wawara, Mark. 2013. "Privilege." In Canada, Parliament, *House of Commons Debates,* 41st Parl, 1st Sess (March 26) at 146(229).

Wearing, Joseph. 1981. *The L-Shaped Party: The Liberal Party of Canada 1958–1980.* Toronto: McGraw-Hill Ryerson.

Weekes, Randy. 2012. "The role of the whip in the Westminster parliamentary system." *Canadian Parliamentary Review* 35(1): 6–9.

Weingart, Laurie R., and Gergana Todorova. 2010. "Jury tensions: Applying communication theories and methods to study group dynamics." *Small Group Research* 41(4): 495–502.

Wells, Paul. 2018. "Maxime Bernier and the lessons of political loyalty." *Maclean's*, April 18. http://www.macleans.ca/politics/ottawa/maxime-bernier-and-the -lessons-of-political-loyalty.

–. 2019. "Jane Philpott: 'There's much more to the story that needs to be told.'" *Maclean's*, March 21. https://www.macleans.ca/politics/ottawa/jane-philpott -theres-much-more-to-the-story-that-needs-to-be-told.

Wesley, Jared, and Renze Nauta. 2020. "Party platform builders." In *Inside the Campaign: Managing Elections in Canada*, edited by Alex Marland and Thierry Giasson, 123–34. Vancouver: UBC Press.

Westell, Anthony. 1968. "Four-day suspense ends with uproar." *Globe and Mail*, April 24, 1.

–. 1972. *Paradox: Trudeau as Prime Minister*. Scarborough, ON: Prentice-Hall.

Westmacott, Martin. 1983. "Whips and party cohesion." *Canadian Parliamentary Review* 6(3): 14–19.

Wherry, Aaron. 2016. "Internal Liberal housing debate spills onto Commons floor." CBC News, March 28. http://www.cbc.ca/news/politics/morneau-adam-vaughan -housing-debate-1.3508677.

–. 2018. "What happens when #MeToo comes to Parliament Hill." CBC News, January 25. https://www.cbc.ca/news/politics/brown-hehr-me-too-analysis-wherry-1. 4503839.

–. 2019. *Promise and Peril: Justin Trudeau in Power*. Toronto: HarperCollins.

White, Graham. 2005. *Cabinets and First Ministers*. Vancouver: UBC Press.

White, Jen. 2018. "Fear and anxiety at Stephenville High: Alleged sexual assaults cause uproar." CBC News, February 5. https://www.cbc.ca/news/canada/ newfoundland-labrador/stephenville-high-alleged-sexual-assaults-1.4520474.

–. 2020. "'This will be a gong show': Behind the $65K fiasco that was the Signal Hill fence." CBC News, February 6. https://www.cbc.ca/news/canada/ newfoundland-labrador/signal-hill-fence-documents-1.5452818.

Whitehead, John W. 2015. "The emergence of Orwellian Newspeak and the death of free speech." *Amass* 20(1): 10–15.

Wilson, R. Paul. 2015a. "Minister's caucus advisory committees under the Harper government." *Canadian Public Administration* 58(2): 227–48.

–. 2015b. "A profile of ministerial policy staff in the government of Canada." *Canadian Journal of Political Science* 48(2): 455–71.

–. 2016a. "Harper and the House of Commons: An evidence-based assessment." In *The Harper Factor: Assessing a Prime Minister's Policy Legacy*, edited by Jennifer Ditchburn and Graham Fox, 27–43. Montreal and Kingston: McGill-Queen's University Press.

–. 2016b. "The inter-executive activity of ministerial policy advisors in the government of Canada." In *How Ottawa Spends 2016–2017: The Trudeau Liberals in Power,* edited by G. Bruce Doern and Christopher Stoney, 191–215. Ottawa: Carleton University.

–. 2020. "The work of Canadian political staffers in parliamentary caucus research offices." *Canadian Public Administration* 63(3).

Wilson, Shaun, and Nick Turnbull. 2001. "Wedge politics and welfare reform in Australia." *Australian Journal of Politics and History* 47(3): 384–402.

Wilson-Raybould, Jody. 2019a. "Standing Committee on Justice and Human Rights – Evidence." In Canada, Parliament, *House of Commons Debates,* 42nd Parl, 1st Sess (February 27), at 135.

–. 2019b. Submission to the House of Commons Standing Committee on Justice and Human Rights. March 26.

–. 2019c. Letter to the national Liberal caucus. April 2. https://www.cbc.ca/news/politics/liberals-wilson-raybould-philpott-caucus-1.5080880.

–. 2019d. "Statement." January 14. https://medac.qc.ca/documentspdf/articles/2019-01-14_JWilsonRaybouldStatement.pdf.

Winnipeg Free Press. 1959. "2,100 trained seals." *Winnipeg Free Press,* December 4, 29.

Winnipeg Sun. 2013. "Tories employ rare motion in PST battle." *Winnipeg Sun,* June 11, 11.

Wiseman, Nelson. 2010. "The quest for a Quebec constitution." *American Review of Canadian Studies* 40(1): 56–70.

Wood, James. 2018. "UCP vetting process includes questions about online dating." *Edmonton Journal,* April 28, A3.

Woolstencroft, Peter. 1994. "'Doing politics differently': The Conservative Party and the campaign of 1993." In *The Canadian General Election of 1993,* edited by Alan Frizzell, Jon H. Pammett, and Anthony Westell, 9–26. Ottawa: Carleton University Press.

Worrall, John L. 1999. "Focusing event characteristics and issue accompaniment: The case of domestic terrorism." *Criminal Justice Policy Review* 10(3): 319–42.

Wright, Teresa. 2019a. "Trudeau won't remove candidate for old posts." *National Post,* October 7, A3.

–. 2019b. "Wilson-Raybould criticized for recording phone call." *Prince George Citizen,* April 2, A5.

Wright Allen, Samantha. 2017. "Liberal and all-party caucuses." *Hill Times,* September 6, 5.

–. 2018a. "'Something has to give': MPs push to reform Parliament, loosen party control." *Hill Times,* June 13, 1.

–. 2018b. "Backbench MP lobbied more than most ministers." *Hill Times,* January 31, 5.

–. 2018c. "Watchdog nominee aims to tackle government culture that suppresses information, creates delays." *Hill Times,* February 28, 7.

–. 2019a. "Say yes to the feds: Voting patterns show group understands 'legislative responsibility,' says ISG." *Hill Times,* August 28, 1.

–. 2019b. "'Embarrassing,' 'bullying' social media posts prompt some senators to push for new policies governing how senators, staff use the platforms." *Hill Times,* June 19, 1.

Wylie, Christopher. 2018. "Evidence." Standing Committee on Access to Information, Privacy and Ethics. In Canada, Parliament, *House of Commons Debates,* 42nd Parl, 1st Sess (May 29) at 109.

Yakabuski, Konrad. 2019. "Ethnic politics actually are the Canadian way." *Globe and Mail,* January 19, O11.

Young, Scott. 1969. "The system and Givens' struggle for a place in the parliamentary sun." *Globe and Mail,* June 9, 7.

Zeng, Anda. 2016. "Shrinking press galleries leave little time for journalists to dig deep." *JSource,* July 8. http://j-source.ca/article/shrinking-press-galleries-leave-little-time-for-journalists-to-dig-deep.

Zimbardo, Philip G. 2019. *The Stanford Prison Experiment: A Simulation Study on the Psychology of Imprisonment.* www.prisonexp.org.

Zimonjic, Peter. 2019a. "Trudeau says he never told candidate-vetting committee about blackface because he was embarrassed." CBC News, September 20. https://www.cbc.ca/news/politics/trudeau-blackface-candidate-vetting-1.5290728.

–. 2019b. "Party leaders debate climate, deficits, Indigenous services, assisted dying, SNC-Lavalin." CBC News, October 10. https://www.cbc.ca/news/politics/french-language-commission-debate-main-1.5317209.

–. 2019c. "After year of political turmoil, SNC-Lavalin gets most of what it wanted in plea deal." CBC News, December 18. https://www.cbc.ca/news/politics/trudeau-wilson-raybould-snc-lavalin-1.5401353.

Index

In memory of Christopher Dunn,

editor of *Provinces: Canadian Provincial Politics*,
a Professor of Political Science at Memorial University
of Newfoundland who awarded an "A" as though
it were a Victoria Cross.

Chris Dunn at the Moonlight Inn restaurant, Victoria Beach,
near his hometown of Winnipeg, August 2016.

Communication, Strategy, and Politics

Thierry Giasson and Alex Marland, Series Editors

Communication, Strategy, and Politics is a groundbreaking series from
UBC Press that examines elite decision making and political communication
in today's hyper-mediated and highly competitive environment. Publications
in this series look at the intricate relations among marketing strategy, the
media, and political actors and explain how they affect Canadian democracy.
They also investigate interconnected themes such as strategic communication, mediatization, opinion research, electioneering, political management,
public policy, and e-politics in a Canadian context and in comparison to
other countries. Designed as a coherent and consolidated space for diffusion
of research about Canadian political communication, the series promotes
an interdisciplinary, multi-method, and theoretically pluralistic approach.

Other volumes in the series are

Political Marketing in Canada, edited by Alex Marland, Thierry Giasson,
and Jennifer Lees-Marshment

Political Communication in Canada: Meet the Press and Tweet the Rest,
edited by Alex Marland, Thierry Giasson, and Tamara A. Small

Framed: Media and the Coverage of Race in Canadian Politics, by Erin Tolley

*Brand Command: Canadian Politics and Democracy in the Age of Message
Control,* by Alex Marland

Permanent Campaigning in Canada, edited by Alex Marland, Thierry
Giasson, and Anna Lennox Esselment

Breaking News? Politics, Journalism, and Infotainment on Quebec Television,
by Frédérick Bastien

Political Elites in Canada: Power and Influence in Instantaneous Times,
edited by Alex Marland, Thierry Giasson, and Andrea Lawlor

*Opening the Government of Canada: The Federal Bureaucracy in the
Digital Age,* by Amanda Clarke

The New NDP: Moderation, Modernization, and Political Marketing,
by David McGrane

Gendered Mediation: Identity and Image Making in Canadian Politics,
edited by Angela Wagner and Joanna Everitt

*What's Trending in Canadian Politics? Understanding Transformations
in Power, Media, and the Public Sphere,* edited by Mireille Lalancette,
Vincent Raynauld, and Erin Crandall

Inside the Campaign: Managing Elections in Canada, edited by Alex
Marland and Thierry Giasson

See also

Canadian Election Analysis 2015: Communication, Strategy, and Democracy,
edited by Alex Marland and Thierry Giasson. Open access compilation
available at http://www.ubcpress.ca/canadianelectionanalysis2015.